NWhite
Nottingham 2003

HUMAN RIGHTS FUNCTIONS OF
UNITED NATIONS PEACEKEEPING OPERATIONS

International Studies in Human Rights

VOLUME 73

The titles published in this series are listed at the end of this volume.

Human Rights Functions
of United Nations Peacekeeping
Operations

by

MARI KATAYANAGI
*Embassy of Japan,
Sarajevo, Bosnia and Herzegovina*

MARTINUS NIJHOFF PUBLISHERS
THE HAGUE / LONDON / NEW YORK

A C.I.P. Catalogue record for this book is available from the Library of Congress.

ISBN 90-411-1910-8

Published by Kluwer Law International,
P.O. Box 85889, 2508 CN The Hague, The Netherlands

Sold and distributed in North, Central and South America
by Kluwer Law International,
101 Philip Drive, Norwell, MA 02061, U.S.A.
kluwerlaw@wkap.com

In all other countries, sold and distributed
by Kluwer Law International, Distribution Centre
P.O. Box 322, 3300 AH Dordrecht, The Netherlands

Printed in the Netherlands.

To people who fight for and work for the realisation of
human rights through peaceful means...

Table of Contents

Acknowledgements

I am immensely indebted to Mr Graham Day, Mr Henri Marinx and Mr Saijin Zhang for their constant support for my research. My gratitude also goes to many interviewees including ex-colleagues who gave me their time and insightful views on human rights monitoring and peacekeeping operations.

This book could not have been completed without the precise comments, vigorous supervision and encouragement of Professor Istvan Pogany of the University of Warwick, UK.

I am grateful to the Overseas Research Students Awards Scheme of the United Kingdom for its funding of this research over the two years of my studies in England.

I owe my family a debt of gratitude for their understanding and encouragement whilst I was conducting this long research. Also thanks to many friends for continual encouragement and provision of information from the field.

Last but not least, my sincere appreciation goes to Mr Manish Narayan, Ms Laura Mazzoli-Smith and Mr Peter Longbottom for their editing support.

Abstract

The United Nations' peacekeeping has evolved as a practical measure for preserving international peace and security, particularly *vis-à-vis* the polarisation of East-West during the Cold War. The evolution of peacekeeping since the end of the Cold War has two important features: the use of force which arguably exceeds self-defence on the one hand, and multifunctional operations on the other. The Security Council has started considering a wide range of factors including serious human rights violation as threats to international peace and security. The concept of state sovereignty is undergoing changes with regard to international peace and security. It is no longer sufficient for the states committing human rights violations to claim sovereign immunity with regard to action taken by the international community. Peacekeeping missions are often deployed to supervise the implementation of a peace agreement signed among conflicting parties within a state. Recognising the UN's principle to seek peaceful settlement which underlies the legality of peacekeeping, this research focuses on human rights functions of multifunctional peacekeeping operations. Such functions have immense potential for enhancing conflict resolution through peaceful means. In order to illustrate these issues and the diverse practices of UN peacekeeping, the author of this thesis has dealt with four detailed case studies on El Salvador, Cambodia, Rwanda and the former Yugoslavia. The achievements, problems, and defects experienced by different operations are analysed using the insights of the author's own experience in a peacekeeping operation. Further, it is argued in this book that for human rights functions to be effective in a peacekeeping operation, the mandate should be explicitly provided for in legal documents, and the functions need to cover not only the investigation and monitoring of human rights violations but also institution-building. For instance, public education on human rights is an integral part of this process. Through comprehensive human rights functions linked with the maintenance of security by presence of a military component, peacekeepers may be able to contribute to the peace-building of states that is founded on the rule of law.

List of Abbreviations

AFS	Avocats sans Frontières
AJIL	American Journal of International Law
ANSP	Academia Nacional de Seguridad Publica (National Academy of Public Security)
AOR	Area of Responsibility
BYIL	British Year Book of International Law
CGDK	Coalition Government of Democratic Kampuchea
CIVPOL	Civilian Police
CPAF	Cambodian People's Armed Forces
CVIS	International Verification and Follow-up Commission
DPKO	Department of Peace-keeping Operations
ECMM	European Community Monitoring Mission
ECOMOG	ECOWAS Ceasefire Monitoring Group
ECOSOC	Economic and Social Council
ECOWAS	Economic Community of West African States
EJIL	European Journal of International Law
FCU	Field Co-ordination Unit
FMLN	Frente Farabundo Martí para la Liberación Nacional
FRY	Federal Republic of Yugoslavia
FUNCINPEC	Front uni national pour un Cambodge Indépendent, neutre, pacifique et coopératif (United National Front for an Independent, Neutral, Peaceful and Cooperative Cambodia)
HRFOR	United Nations Human Rights Field Operation in Rwanda
HRFOs	Human Rights Field Officers
HRPOs	Human Rights Provincial Officers
ICLQ	International and Comparative Law Quarterly
ICRC	International Committee of the Red Cross
ICTR	International Criminal Tribunal for Rwanda
ICTY	International Tribunal for the Former Yugoslavia
IDPs	Internally Displaced Persons
IFOR	Implementation Force
IPTF	International Police Task Force
KPNLF	Khmer People's National Liberation Front
MINUSAL	United Nations Mission in El Salvador
MRND	Mouvement révolutionnaire national pour le développement

NADK	National Army of Democratic Kmpuchea
NATO	North Atlantic Treaty Organisation
OAS	Organisation of American States
OAU	Organisation of African Unity
OIC	Officer in Charge
ONUC	United Nations Operation in the Congo
ONUCA	United Nations Observer Group in Central America
ONUSAL	United Nations Observation Mission in El Salvador
ONUV	United Nations Office of Verification in El Salvador
ONUVEN	United Nations Observer Mission to Verify the Electoral Process in Nicaragua
OSCE	Organisation for Security and Cooperation in Europe
OSGAP	Office of the Secretary-General in Afghanistan and Pakistan
PDK	Party of Democratic Kmpuchea (Khmer Rouge)
PNC	Policia Nacional Civil (National Civil Police)
PRK	People's Republic of Kmpuchea
RAF	Rwandan Armed Forces
RPF	Rwandese Patriotic Front
SFRY	Socialist Federal Republic of Yugoslavia
SNC	Supreme National Council
SOC	State of Cambodia
SRSG	Special Representative of the Secretary-General
TPF	Transitional Police Force
UNAMIC	United Nations Advance Mission in Cambodia
UNAMIR	United Nations Assistance Mission for Rwanda
UNCRO	United Nations Confidence Restoration Operation in Croatia
UNDOF	United Nations Disengagement Observer Force
UNDP	United Nations Development Programme
UNDRO	United Nations Disaster Relief Coordinator
UNEF	United Nations Emergency Force
UNESCO	United Nations Education, Science and Cultural Organisation
UNFICYP	United Nations Force in Cyprus
UNGOMAP	United Nations Good Offices Mission in Afghanistan and Pakistan
UNHCHR	United Nations High Commissioner for Human Rights
UNHCR	United Nations High Commissioner for Refugees
UNIFIL	United Nations Interim Force in the Lebanon
UNIKOM	United Nations Iraq-Kuwait Observation Mission

UNIMOG	United Nations Iran-Iraq Military Observer Group
UNIPOM	United Nations India-Pakistan Observer Mission
UNITAF	United Task Force
UNMIBH	United Nations Mission for Bosnia and Herzegovina
UNMIK	United Nations Interim Administration Mission in Kosovo
UNMOGIP	United Nations Military Observer Group in India and Pakistan
UNOGIL	United Nations Observation Group in Lebanon
UNOMIL	United Nations Observer Mission to Liberia
UNOMUR	United Nations Observer Mission Uganda-Rwanda
UNOSOM	United Nations Operation in Somalia
UNPAs	United Nations Protected Areas
UNPF	United Nations Peace Forces
UNPREDEP	United Nations Preventive Deployment Force
UNPROFOR	United Nations Protection Force
UNSCOB	United Nations Special Committee on the Balkans
UNSF	United Nations Security Force in West New Guinea
UNSG	United Nations Security Guards
UNTAC	United Nations Transitional Authority in Cambodia
UNTAES	United Nations Transitional Administration in Eastern Slavonia, Baranja and Western Sirmium
UNTAET	United Nations Transitional Administration for East Timor
UNTEA	United Nations Temporary Executive Authority
UNTSO	United Nations Truce Supervision Organisation
UNYOM	United Nations Yemen Observation Mission

Introduction

After the end of the Cold War, United Nations peacekeeping operations evolved in two ways. The first, an increasing willingness to use armed force, as in the case of the United Nations Protection Force (UNPROFOR) in the former Yugoslavia and the United Nations Operation in Somalia II (UNOSOM II).[1] Secondly, the assumption grew that peacekeepers could carry out multiple functions, as in the case of the United Nations Transitional Administration in Cambodia (UNTAC).[2] A single operation may have both of these characteristics, but this is not always the case. For instance, although UNOSOM II became notorious for its military clash with a local faction, the operation was involved in humanitarian assistance as well as the re-organisation of the police and judicial systems, which is an example of two new features of peacekeeping.[3] UNTAC, in contrast, was a multifunctional operation which kept the principles of traditional peacekeeping and the Special Representative affirmed that the operation fell under Chapter VI of the United Nations Charter.[4]

The higher level of use of force in peacekeeping operations has caused the problem of making indistinct the difference between peacekeeping and enforcement action. Peacekeeping *per se* is not explicitly provided for in the United Nations Charter, and it has sometimes been called Chapter VI ½ operations to distinguish it from Chapter VII operations. The provisions of Article 42 explicitly allow the Security Council to take enforcement action by air, sea or land forces to maintain or restore international peace and

---

[1] UNPROFOR was established by Security Council resolution 743 of 21 February 1992 concerning the situation in Croatia. Later UNPROFOR's mandate was expanded to cover Bosnia and Herzegovina as well as Macedonia. For details of UNPROFOR, see Chapter 6. UNOSOM II was established under Security Council resolution 814 of 26 March, 1993. See '2.3 Third Generation Peace-Keeping' of Chapter 2.

[2] Security Council authorised establishment of UNTAC by Resolution 745 of 28 February 1992. For details of UNTAC, see Chapter 4.

[3] For instance, see the mandate set forth in Security Council resolution 897, 4 February 1994, SCOR, 3334th mtg., UN Doc. S/RES/897(1994).

[4] The major principles of traditional peacekeeping are the minimum use of force, neutrality and consent of the host State. See 2. 'Definitions and Principles of Peace-keeping', Chapter 2, especially FN36 & 37 and accompanying text. Regarding Special Representative Akashi's view, Sakai, 'Cambodia no shihou, hougaku kyouiku no genjou – kirihirakitai houchikokka he no michi (The current situation of Cambodian judicial system and legal education – a desired way toward a state with rule of law)', *Hou to minshushugi (Law and Democracy)* No.278, June 1996: 22-30, p.27.

security. From the point of legality and the manner in which it has developed in practice, peacekeeping is quite distinct from enforcement action.[5] The assumption of diverse functions of peacekeeping operations, on the contrary, depends more on civilian aspects including, but not limited to, civil administration, election and human rights work. This type of peacekeeping sometimes takes the form of transitional or interim administration.

Both the new features of peacekeeping operations raise the issue of sovereignty and interference in essentially domestic issues of the host State. While traditional peacekeeping operated with the consent of the host State, recent operations occasionally assumed a more coercive nature during the course of those operations. Also when a peacekeeping force is deployed in response to an internal conflict, the operation tends to be involved in issues which traditionally had been understood as essentially domestic in nature. However it is still recognised that the consent of the host State or of the conflicting parties in the host State must be secured before the deployment of a peacekeeping force. Therefore deployment of the peacekeeping force itself does not infringe on the sovereignty of that State, however the continuance of such consent during the course of the operation is becoming a more sensitive and complex issue owing to the plurality of parties representing the State and the diverse activities of peacekeeping.

The purpose of this book is to analyse UN peacekeeping operations focusing particularly on human rights functions, and to seek to develop a better design for such functions in future operations.[*] The book starts by reviewing the UN mechanism for international peace and security in Chapter 1. The role of the Security Council and the General Assembly in the mechanism will be discussed, and the origins of United Nations peacekeeping will be studied by means of four case-studies of observation missions and peacekeeping missions. Also, an examination will be made in Chapter 1 of the constitutional basis of United Nations peacekeeping operations, as well as the competence of the Security Council and of the General Assembly to create peacekeeping forces, and of the role of the Secretary-General in the area of international peace and security. The last

---

[5]   This point will be discussed in detail in Chapter 2.

[*]   This is a thesis which was prepared in order to fulfill the requirements for the degree of Ph.D. in Law at the University of Warwick, U.K., and submitted in July 2000. Therefore the research had been conducted mainly from January 1998 to July 2000. A further limited up-date was made for the purpose of publishing the same. However, the author's current position with the Ministry of Foreign Affairs, Japan, restricts additional amendments to reflect new developments in the field of research.

section of Chapter 1 will deal with peacekeeping operations by regional arrangements or agencies in the context of Chapter VIII of the UN Charter.

Chapter 2 commences with a historical overview of the United Nations peacekeeping operations. An extensive review of varied definitions and theories of peacekeeping will follow which illustrates the evolution of United Nations peacekeeping operations. The review demonstrates that two features can be found in peacekeeping operations after the end of the Cold War, as described above. To clarify the concept of peacekeeping, the legal distinction between peacekeeping and enforcement action will be discussed. Chapter 2 concludes with a focus on non-military functions of peacekeeping, which in practice contains peacemaking and peace-building functions. Human rights are essential elements of such functions. The first two chapters thus explain how the Organisation reached the point of being largely involved in human rights work within the framework of peacekeeping.

The four chapters thereafter are devoted to case-studies. These chapters contain a detailed examination of the actual human rights activities performed in four different areas of the world by UN peacekeeping missions or a UN human rights field operation. The areas being examined are El Salvador, Cambodia, Rwanda and the former Yugoslavia. The operations in each area approached and challenged the human rights problems differently, which shows that there has been a consistent lack of effort by the Organisation to study and make use of the skills and experience gained in preceding operations.[6] Several points of analysis will be set up for examination in each case-study for the purpose of enabling a comparison of similar functions in different operations. One important factor for future peacekeeping operations when they undertake human rights functions will inevitably be institution-building, such as the reform of the judicial system or the restructuring and training of police forces. Peacekeeping, as a temporary measure to create the environment for sustainable peace, needs to assist in the establishment of domestic structures and mechanisms which

---

[6] Karen Kenny, Director of the International Human Rights Trust, Ireland, states:

> ...like the origins of peacekeeping itself, HROs [human rights operations] thus far been a series of *ad hoc* arrangements rather than the consistent application of a considered policy which operationalizes and prioritizes the link between human rights violations and deadly conflict. Such an *ad hoc* approach to HROs has serious implications in terms of the failure to learn lessons and the lack of institutional memory. There is no mechanism within the United Nations, or elsewhere, by which experience accumulated in HROs may be pooled in order to learn for the future.

Karen Kenny, 'Introducing the Sustainability Principle to Human Rights Operations', *International Peacekeeping* 4(4), Winter 1997: 61-78, p.63.

protect and promote human rights. As is manifest in the case of the United Nations Mission in Bosnia and Herzegovina (UNMIBH), institution-building is becoming an integral part of peacekeeping.[7]

Chapter 7 considers the possibility of the use of force in protecting human rights. Given that the presence of UN peacekeepers did not succeed in protecting civilian lives either in Rwanda or Srebrenica (Bosnia-Herzegovina), we will examine the recent practice of the Security Council of contracting out enforcement operations to volunteering states. We will also consider the "humanitarian intervention", unilateral or multilateral intervention by one or more states without any authorisation from the UN Security Council. The problem represents a deviation from collective security as envisaged in the UN Charter. Seeking the possibility that peacekeeping forces can contribute in protecting human rights through non-military means, the potential role of peacekeepers as a "protecting power" will be studied. The potential of peacekeepers to carry out human rights functions will also be discussed.

METHODOLOGY

This research is based mainly on an analysis of primary and secondary texts. The documents used are UN documents, such as Security Council resolutions, General Assembly resolutions, reports of the Secretary-General, and reports of Special Rapporteurs on human rights. Secondly, various research projects by scholars on peacekeeping, legal studies of related issues, and the history of the areas concerned were broadly referred to and consulted. Thirdly, reports of non-governmental organisations (NGOs) that were involved with human rights and written work by people who actually worked in the field were studied carefully in order to revisit what had been represented by UN official documents and to reconstruct the view on each operation. Fourthly, some journalistic reports were used to obtain additional information. However, the use of journalistic reports was deliberately restricted, since any presentation of a situation cannot be immune from an individual's own interpretation and value judgment. This also applies to academic studies, and to any other written work, but the nature of journalism and the structure and environment where journalism functions appear to intensify this tendency. Different articles on a supposedly unique event sometimes create the impression that there were different "facts".

---

[7]   See 2.2.2 'United Nations Mission in Bosnia and Herzegovina (UNMIBH)', Chapter 6.

To supplement the documentary research, some empirical studies were conducted by means of structured interviews and a questionnaire. Such research was aimed at obtaining both grass roots information as well as the views of people who had actually worked or are working in the UN peace-keeping operations. The interviews and the questionnaire contained a few open-ended questions. It was often these questions which elicited the most vivid views of the respondents expressing what they felt strongly in their field-work. Although this book does not include all the results of such research, the views of respondents certainly gave this author valuable insights in approaching the topic of the human rights functions of UN peace-keeping operations. Efforts were made to obtain a number of interviewees for each case-study so that the analysis would not be entirely dependent on documentary research. When interviews were not possible, articles written by people who had worked in peacekeeping operations were very helpful in reconstructing the actual work in the field. Since UN documents on peace-keeping operations are summaries of diverse functions, their descriptions of human rights work need to be taken as a rough sketch of the actual work. For example, these documents may provide us with the numbers and categories of cases handled by a human rights component of a UN peacekeeping operation, or the number of victims in alleged human rights violations. However, they usually do not present the details of the interaction between human rights officers/peacekeepers and the local population, or the effects such interaction might have in the local community. Nonetheless, the part that is not described in the UN reports may have a significant influence in building the human rights concept in a society severely damaged by an armed conflict. Furthermore, UN documents do not usually make much reference to the failures of UN peacekeeping operations, in other words, UN documents tend to emphasise the positive aspects of its operations.[8] Therefore if we do not shed light on the negative aspects of UN operations we may not understand the actual situation or the effects of UN operations.

This author worked in the Civil Affairs component of the United Nations Transitional Administration in Eastern Slavonia, Balanja and Western Sirmium (UNTAES) from August 1996 to December 1997, and that experi-ence provided the perspectives of an internal observation. In addition, her membership of the Joint International Observer Group as an observer of the Cambodian election in July 1998, as well as her participation in election supervision in Bosnia-Herzegovina organised by the Organisation for the

---

[8] The remarkable exceptions are the two recent reports on UN peacekeeping operations in Srebrenica and Rwanda. See *infra* note 19.

Security and Cooperation of Europe in September 1998 gave her opportunities to observe the post-conflict situation in the two countries.

The limitation of this research is that the information that could be accessed and gathered varied from one case-study to another. It does not, however, seriously affect the purpose of this study, since the study tries to extrapolate features of different approaches to human rights work within peacekeeping operations, rather than to present a complete picture of such work in the four case-studies examined here.

UN HUMAN RIGHTS MECHANISMS

This book makes little reference to United Nations human rights mechanisms.[9] This is because there has been little interaction between such mechanisms and peacekeeping operations. The United Nations has been developing diverse mechanisms for the promotion and protection of human rights. For instance, the UN Commission on Human Rights and its Sub-Commission on Prevention of Discrimination and Protection of Minorities are authorised under resolution 1235(XLII) of the Economic and Social Council (ECOSOC) to "examine information relevant to gross violations of human rights and fundamental freedoms".[10] Under resolution 1235(XLII) the Human Rights Commission has appointed a number of Special Rapporteurs, Special Representatives, Experts, and Independent Experts for investigations. The UN Commission on Human Rights also considers "situations which appear to reveal consistent pattern of gross and reliably attested

---

[9]   On UN human rights mechanisms, see, in general, Paul Sieghart, *The International Law of Human Rights*, Clarendon Press, 1983; Hurst Hannum, ed., *Guide to International Human Rights Practice*, 2nd ed., University of Pennsylvania Press, 1992; Ellen L. Lutz, Hurst Hannum, and Kathryn J. Burke, eds., *New Directions in Human Rights*, University of Pennsylvania Press, 1989; Malcolm N. Shaw, *International Law*, 4th ed., Cambridge University Press, 1997: 225-254; Virgil Wiebe, 'The Prevention of Civil War through the Use of the Human Rights System', *New York University Journal of International Law and Politics*, Winter 1995: 409-468; Caroline Dommen, 'The UN Human Rights Regime: Is it Effective?', *American Society of International Law Proceedings*, 1997: 460-484; and Allison L. Jernow, 'Ad Hoc and Extra-Conventional Means for Human Rights Monitoring', *New York University Journal of International Law and Politics*, 1996: 785-836.

[10]   Resolution 1235 (XLII). For the procedure, see Nigel S. Rodley, 'United Nations Non-Treaty Procedures for Dealing with Human Rights Violations', in Hannum, ed., *supra* note 9: 60-85, pp. 61-62; Joan Fitzpatrick, *Human Rights in Crisis: The International System for Protecting Rights During States of Emergency*, University of Pennsylvania Press, 1994, pp.126-151; Theo Van Boven, 'Creative and Dynamic Strategies for Using United Nations Institutions and Procedures: The Frank Newman File', in Lutz *et al.* eds., *supra* note 9: 215-230, pp.222-226.

violations of human rights" in accordance with resolution 1503(XLVIII) adopted by the Economic and Social Council in 1970.[11] This procedure is, however, generally considered to be weak because of a high degree of politicisation and confidentiality. There are also thematic mechanisms that can deal with individual cases, such as the Working Group on Enforced or Involuntary Disappearances, the Special Rapporteur on Summary or Arbitrary Executions, and the Special Rapporteur on Torture.[12]

Various treaties such as the International Covenant on Civil and Political Rights, the International Convention on the Elimination of All Forms of Racial Discrimination and the Convention against Torture and other Forms of Cruel, Inhuman or Degrading Treatment, contain individual complaints procedures as well as periodic state-reporting procedures.[13] One commentator remarks with regard to these treaty procedures:

> The absence of any power of enforcement of decisions remains a principal lacuna of the UN human rights protection system. For treaty bodies, the only effective weapon remains the publicity that surrounds decisions, which are published in the treaty bodies' annual reports to the UN General Assembly. Moreover, most decisions are now available on the World Wide Web.[14]

Although treaty organs and thematic procedures have their own value in enhancing human rights, their manifest disadvantages are their limited resources and long procedures. For instance, it is said that 60 per cent of state parties are overdue in reporting in the case of each human rights treaty.[15] A commentator calculates that if all the overdue reports were actually submitted it would take the treaty bodies an average of six-and-a-half years to expunge the current backlog.[16] The human rights functions of peacekeeping operations, in a sense, supplement what such mechanisms are not able to provide, through their presence on the spot, spontaneous action, and wide sphere of activities.

---

[11]   Resolution 1503 (XLVIII). For 1503 procedure, see, Fitzpatrick, *supra* note 10, pp.116-126; Rodley *supra* note 10, pp.64-70; and Boven, supra note 10, pp.217-226.

[12]   Fitzpatrick, *supra* note 10, pp.152-166; Rodley, *supra* note 10, pp. 70-76.

[13]   Fitzpatrick, *supra* note 10, pp. 82-114, Siân Lewis-Anthony, 'Treaty-based Procedures for Making Human Rights Complaints Within the UN System', in Hannum, ed., *supra* note 9: 41-59.

[14]   Markus G. Schmidt, 'Does the United Nations Human Rights Program Make a Difference?', in Dommen, *supra* note 9: 461-466, p.464.

[15]   Remarks by Anne F. Bayefsky in Dommen, *supra* note 9: 466-472, p.466.

[16]   *Ibid.*

ONGOING DEVELOPMENT

During the course of this research, many new developments relevant to this topic have taken place. The work of two *ad hoc* international tribunals is progressing, and the jurisprudence of international humanitarian law and criminal law has been expanding remarkably.[17] New UN peacekeeping operations as an interim/transitional administration were established in Kosovo and East Timor.[18] The Secretary-General has issued two important reports reviewing the past failure of peacekeeping in Rwanda and the former Yugoslavia.[19] A panel studied peacekeeping at the request of the Secretary-General and their report was issued in August 2000.[20] Announcing the

---

[17]   Regarding the ICTR, see Jaana Karhilo, 'The Establishment of the International Tribunal for Rwanda', *Nordic Journal of International Law* 64, 1995: 683-713; Todd Howland and William Calathes, 'The U.N.'s International Criminal Tribunal, Is it Justice or Jingoism for Rwanda? A Call for Transformation', *Virginia Journal of International Law*, Fall 1998: 135-167; and Diane Marie Amann, 'Prosecutor v. Akayesu', *AJIL* 93, January 1999: 195-199. Also see 3.4 'International Criminal Tribunal for Rwanda (ICTR)' and 4.2.1 'Genocide', both in Chapter 5. For the ICTY, see Humanitarian Law in the Former Yugoslavia', *AJIL* 87, 1993: 639-659; Daphna Shraga and Ralph Zacklin, 'The International Criminal Tribunal for the Former Yugoslavia', 5 *EJIL*, 1994: 360-380; Theodor Meron, 'War Crimes in Yugoslavia and the Development of International Law', *AJIL* 88, 1994: 78-87; T. Meron, 'International Criminalization of Internal Atrocities'; *AJIL* 89, 1995: 554-577; Colin Warbrick and Peter Rowe, 'The International Criminal Tribunal for Yugoslavia: The Decision of the Appeals Chamber on the Interlocutory Appeal on Jurisdiction in the Tadić Case', *ICLQ* 45, 1996: 691-701; Christopher Greenwood, 'International Humanitarian Law and the *Tadic Case*', 7 *EJIL*, 1996: 265-283; Danesh Sarooshi, 'The Powers of the United Nations International Criminal Tribunals', *Max Planck Yearbook of United Nations Law,* 2, 1998: 141-167; David Turns, 'The International Criminal Tribunal for the Former Yugoslavia: The Erdemović Case', *ICLQ* 47, 1998: 461-474; Faiza Patel King and Anne-Marie La Rosa, *International Criminal Tribunal for the Former Yugoslavia,* 9 *EJIL*, 1998: 757-760; and Sean Murphy, 'Progress and Jurisprudence of the International Criminal Tribunal for the Former Yugoslavia', *AJIL* 93, 1999: 57-97. Also see 3.4 'International Criminal Tribunal for the Former Yugoslavia (ICTY)' and 4.2.1 'Ethnic Cleansing', both in Chapter 6.

[18]   United Nations Interim Administration in Kosovo (UNMIK) was established by Security Council resolution 1244 of 10 June 1999. SCOR, 4011th mtg., UN Doc. S/RES/1244 (1999). For more about UNMIK, see Chapter 7. United Nations Transitional Administration in East Timor (UNTAET) was established by Security Council resolution 1272 of 25 October 1999. SCOR, 4057th mtg., UN Doc. S/RES/1272(1999).

[19]   *Report of the Independent Inquiry into the actions of the United Nations during the 1994 genocide in Rwanda,* 15 December 1999. For details, see Chapter 5. *Report of the Secretary-General pursuant to General Assembly resolution 53/35: The Fall of Srebrenica,* UN Doc. A/54/549, 15 November 1999. See Chapter 6.

[20]   *Report of Panel on United Nations Peace Operations,* A/55/305-S/2000/809, 17 August 2000. Text available at: www.un.org/peace/reports/peace-operations/.

establishment of this panel, the Secretary-General explained the purpose of the panel as follows:[21]

> It is partly a question of being clear about what we are trying to do, what kind of forces we need to do it, what are the conditions in which different kinds of mission are appropriate and what you do when circumstances change and you need to move from one kind of operation to another. What do you do, for instance, if the peace you are trying to keep breaks down and large numbers of civilians are in danger of being massacred?

Some of these questions are discussed in this book, while the others are left for further study.

BRIDGING THE FIELD-WORK AND ACADEMIC STUDIES

People who work for human rights protection in the field often become frustrated by the enormous gap between the hopeless reality on the ground and the noble words of international law which do not seem to reduce the suffering of people in areas of conflict at all. However, one who suffers from human rights abuses may be encouraged simply in the knowledge that what he/she is seeking is the implementation of his/her right. Those who taught me the value of international human rights law were the people who told me about their experience of human rights violations. Even though a UN peace-keeping operation usually cannot offer immediate remedy to those victims, by reaching a common understanding that what they suffered was against their human rights, they may gain the energy to continue their claim for justice. Of course there are situations where people are deprived of any force to resist - or even of their lives. Peacekeepers are then not able to communicate with those people, but can only witness the atrocities. What is required of the international community is the prevention of such situations by every means possible, including the development of international law and political negotiation. This author believes that in such prevention, deterrence and institution-building peacekeeping operations can contribute much towards establishing a society that respects human rights to a greater extent.

One of the ambitious intents of this study is to bridge the gap between field-work and academia in human rights discourse. It is disappointing when discussion on human rights amongst academics makes light of the reality on

---

[21] *Press Release*, UN Doc. SG/SM/7324, 7 March 2000.

the ground. For instance, some commentators are content with a conditionality of human rights protection on accepting a state to the European Community without verifying whether such conditionality has actually has any effect.[22] The question is not as to what is written on paper or a promise contained in empty words, but rather to the reality. While a Western scholar is happily arguing the nominal development of human rights promotion in a political or legal sphere, people continue to suffer daily harassment and discrimination based on their ethnic affiliation in the very state in which they live. A premature recognition of the independence of a state can also gravely affect the situation of human rights on the ground.[23] Yet politicians who forget that their own decisions might possibly have resulted in the deaths of thousands of people, roundly condemn another occurrence of human rights abuse. It is lamentable if academics are not able to critically assess such politicians' arguments. Premature recognition has, politically and legally, immense effects, while human rights conditionality upon recognition of a state, without strong enforcement mechanism, has extremely weak effects. A scholar can only be happy with nominal development of human rights protection when he/she does not witness the pain of the victims of human rights abuses. Needless to say it would be impossible to change overnight a currently prevalent system that each day allows countless cases of human rights abuse to occur in the world. However, in discussing the development of international humanitarian law, human rights law or a system of human rights protection, it is a basic requirement for a scholar to remember that the issue involves people's lives.

Human rights workers in the field can contribute to development of international human rights law by reporting the reality on the ground and giving feedback on problems they face either in interpreting international human rights law or in trying to apply international human rights law. On the other hand, the flow of information from academia to the field on the legal

---

[22] One commentator stated: "It is remarkable to note ... that Croatia showed its willingness for an efficient protection of human rights and, especially, minority rights so promptly on the international level". Saskia Hille, 'Mutual Recognition of Croatia and Serbia (+Montenegro)', 6 *EJIL*, 1995: 598-611, p. 606. Another commentator also emphasises the EC's conditionality as a new development with little reference to actual implementation of that conditionality by the State in question. Stephen Tierney, 'In a State of Flux: Self-Determination and the Collapse of Yugoslavia', *International Journal on Minority and Group Rights* 6(1/2), 1999: 197-233, p.214. For the problems faced by a minority group in Croatia, see, for instance, *infra* 4.3.3 'Operation Flash and Operation Storm', Chapter 6.

[23] On premature recognition, see *infra* FN3 of Chapter 6.

discussion will support those workers who are often isolated in the middle of an insecure environment and who struggle to work for justice.

It is now time for the United Nations to study systematically the human rights functions of United Nations peacekeeping operations so that previously acquired experience and skills will be used for any operations that follow. For a UN peacekeeping operation to engage effectively in human rights activities, it must be designed from the outset to have an appropriate mandate and to ensure the consent of the host State for such work.

Chapter 1

United Nations Mechanism for International Peace and Security

The United Nations Organisation ('Organisation') was established after the cumulative experience of two World Wars in order to save succeeding generations from the scourge of war.[1] The Organisation's primary purpose is "to maintain international peace and security",[2] and an essential factor for that purpose is the strict limitation of the use of force by Member States. Article 2(4) of the United Nations Charter ('UN Charter') explicitly limits the use of force by Member States as follows:

> All Members shall refrain in their international relations from the threat or use of force against the territorial integrity or political independence of any state, or in any other manner inconsistent with the Purposes of the United Nations.

The UN Charter however recognises certain conditions under which the limitation under Article 2 (4) shall not be applicable to the Member States. The recognised exceptions are as follows: (1) the inherent right of individual or collective self-defence under Article 51 of the UN Charter, and (2) Chapter VII enforcement actions authorised by the Security Council.[3]

---

[1] Preamble of the United Nations Charter.

[2] Article 1(1), the UN Charter.

[3] Regarding the disputable scope of these exceptions, see, in general, Hans Kelsen, 'Collective Security and Collective Self-Defense under the Charter of the United Nations', *AJIL* 42, 1948: 783-796; Bowett, 'Collective Self-Defence Under the Charter of the United Nations', *BYIL* 32, 1955-56: 130-161; Oscar Schachter, 'Self-Defense and the Rule of Law', *AJIL* 83, 1989: 259-277; D.W. Greig, 'Self-Defence and the Security Council: What Does Article 51 Require?', *ICLQ* 40, 1991: 366-402; Rosalyn Higgins, 'The Legal Limits to the Use of Force by Sovereign States: United Nations Practice', *BYIL* 37, 1961:269-319; Frank and Patel, 'UN Police Action in Lieu of War', *AJIL* 85, 1991; Thomas M. Franck, 'Who Killed Article 2(4)?', *AJIL* 64, 1970: 809-837; Patrick Daillier and Alain Pellet, *Droit International Public*, Paris: Librairie Générale de Droit et de Jurisprudence, 6th ed., 1999, pp.899-902; and Shigejiro Tabata, *Kokusaihoukougi (International Law Lectures)* , Vol.2, Yushindo, 1984, pp.180-203. Two more exceptions are in the letters of the Charter. One is joint action on behalf of the Organisation under Article 106 and the other is action against an enemy state during the Second World War in

Therefore the duty of and mechanism for maintaining international peace and security is primarily vested in the Organisation, with individual Member States retaining the right to self-defence. Despite the collective security mechanism envisaged in the UN Charter, the Organisation was severely hampered from fulfilling its role because of the polarisation between the West and the East during the Cold War. The Organisation therefore evolved and developed another mechanism for preserving international peace and security, which was peacekeeping. However, it should be noted that peace-keeping was not designed to replace the system of collective security; instead it provided the Organisation with an alternative approach and method to fulfil its responsibilities.

This chapter will illustrate and analyse the Organisation's mechanisms for maintaining peace and security. Firstly, we will look at the roles of the two principal UN organs, namely the Security Council and the General Assembly, in maintaining international peace and security. Secondly, four illustrative case studies of peacekeeping operations in the early days of the Organisation will be reviewed, to examine the way peacekeeping originated and evolved. This chapter will also critically analyse the constitutional basis of peacekeeping operations and the competence and validity of the Security Council and the General Assembly to create and implement peacekeeping operations. Lastly, the role of the Secretary-General as well as regional arrangement or agents in peacekeeping will be reviewed in brief.

---

accordance with Articles 107 and 53. Anthony Clark Arend and Robert J. Beck, *International Law and the Use of Force: Beyond the UN Charter Paradigm*, London and New York: Routledge, 1993: pp.30-33. Article 106 provides for a provisional measure to be taken by the initiative of the permanent members of the Security Council pending the implementation of Article 43, which anticipated the establishment of the UN force. Even after over fifty years since the establishment of the Organisation, such a permanent UN force does not appear to be near to realisation. However, it is unlikely that permanent members will invoke Article 106 instead of acting through the Security Council. Provisions of Articles 107 and 53 virtually lost their meaning as the "enemy States" are already members of the Organisation and it is unrealistic to foresee that they would act against the Organisation with use of force. The general view has been that these provisions could not be invoked against Member States as they are characterised as peace-loving pursuant to Article 4 of the Charter upon admission to the Organisation. In addition, "it would be incompatible with the fundamental principle of the sovereign equality of all members (Article 2(1))". See, Bruno Simma, ed., *The Charter of the United Nations: A Commentary*, Oxford University Press, 1995: p.119.

1.   THE SECURITY COUNCIL

The Security Council consists of fifteen Members of the United Nations pursuant to Article 23 of the UN Charter: five permanent members (China, France, Russia,[4] the United Kingdom and the United States of America), and ten non-permanent members. Non-permanent members are elected for a term of two years. The Charter confers "primary responsibility for the maintenance of international peace and security" on this organ.[5] The Security Council is the only organ of the Organisation that has the power to take decisions which, in accordance with Article 25, all member states must accept and carry out.[6]

Chapter VI of the UN Charter sets forth measures for the peaceful settlement of disputes, that is, "negotiation, enquiry, mediation, conciliation, arbitration, judicial settlement, resort to regional agencies or arrangements, or other peaceful means of their choice".[7] The parties to disputes are, in the first instance, responsible for seeking such measures; however the Security Council may recommend appropriate procedures or methods of adjustment pursuant to Article 36(1). Further the Security Council has a fact-finding authority under Article 34 "in order to determine whether the continuance of the dispute or situation is likely to endanger the maintenance of international peace and security". Chapter VII of the UN Charter stipulates the action that may be taken by the Organisation if there are threats to peace, breaches of the peace, and acts of aggression. The Security Council also has the duty to determine the existence of the above-stated conditions and make recommendations *vis-à-vis* the same or to initiate measures in accordance with Articles 41 and 42.[8] Article 41 stipulates "measures not involving the use of armed force" including economic or diplomatic sanctions, and Article 42

---

[4]   Russia is considered to be a continuing State of the Soviet Union. Regarding distinction between continuity and succession of States, see Rein Mullerson, 'The Continuity and Succession of States, by Reference to the Former USSR and Yugoslavia', *ICLQ* 42, July 1993: 473-493. Also Roland Rich, 'Recognition of States: The Collapse of Yugoslavia and the Soviet Union', 4 *EJIL* 1993: 36-65. Therefore, a recommendation from the Security Council and acceptance by the General Assembly, which are procedures for admitting a new member, were not required. See Shaw, *International Law*, *supra* FN9 of Introduction, pp.677-678; and N. D. White, *Keeping the Peace: The United Nations and the Maintenance of International Peace and Security*, Manchester and New York: Manchester University Press, 2nd ed., 1997, p.24.

[5]   Article 24, the UN Charter.

[6]   Article 25, the UN Charter.

[7]   Article 33, the UN Charter.

[8]   Article 39, the UN Charter.

sets forth action by air, sea or land forces. However, since agreements between the Organisation and Member States on armed forces, assistance and facilities to be made available to the Organisation have not been signed, the Organisation in fact is not able to carry out enforcement action by UN forces under the Organisation's sole command as had originally been envisaged in the Charter.[9] Under Article 40, the Security Council may also take provisional measures before making recommendations or deciding measures referred to in Article 39.

Pursuant to Article 27(2), decisions of the Security Council require the affirmative vote of nine members, and on all matters except procedural ones, such an affirmative vote shall include the concurring votes of the permanent members.[10] Therefore it entitles any one permanent member to block the Security Council's decisions on non-procedural matters by a negative vote. This power of veto serves the purpose of preventing the permanent members "from being the potential objects of collective measures".[11] Practice has established that abstention by a permanent member on a substantive vote does not constitute a veto, and that a negative vote is required for a veto.[12] However, the power of veto is restricted by the proviso of Article 27(3), insofar that a party to the dispute shall abstain from voting in decisions under Chapter VI (pacific settlements of disputes), and under Article 52(3) (pacific settlement of local disputes through regional arrangements or regional agencies).

Any Member of the UN can call for a meeting of the Security Council to consider any issue, and the Secretary-General may also call for a meeting to consider any matter which may 'threaten the international peace and security'.[13] Upon such requests, the President of the Council convenes a meeting.

Any member state, which is not a member of the Security Council, may participate in the discussion at the Security Council if the Security Council considers that the interests of the former are specifically affected; however, they do not have a vote.[14] Also, the Security Council shall invite any member state which is not a member of the Security Council, or a non-member state,

---

[9]   For enforcement action carried out in a different mode with authorisation by the Security Council, see 1.1 'Legitimacy of Non-UN Multinational Forces Authorised by the Security Council' of Chapter 7.

[10]   Article 27(2) and (3), the UN Charter.

[11]   White, *op. cit.*, p.9.

[12]   *Ibid.* Also Shaw, *op. cit.*, p.826.

[13]   Article 99, the UN Charter.

[14]   Article 31, the UN Charter.

to participate in the discussion of a dispute to which the former is a party, provided that the former is not entitled to vote.[15]

During the Cold War, the world was polarised between the West and the East. The Security Council did not evade the bipolar division, and the use of the veto regularly paralysed its operation.[16] As it has been said: "[I]n any event, state decisions about power and policy constitute the primary force driving events at the UN."[17] Explaining the intention of the founders of the United Nations with respect to collective security, Dr. N.D. White states:

> ... to give collective interests primacy over national interests would be to have created a world government. In practice, the most that could be done was to give the world body, through the Security Council, greater powers for collective measures which might weigh more heavily on the scales against the counter-balance of national interests.[18]

2. THE GENERAL ASSEMBLY

Article 10 of the UN Charter provides that the General Assembly may discuss any questions or any matters within the scope of the Charter. Further, Article 11 states explicitly that the General Assembly may discuss any questions relating to the maintenance of international peace and security brought before it either by any Member State, the Security Council, or a non-Member State which is a party to the dispute concerned and accepts in advance the obligations of pacific settlement provided in the Charter for the purposes of the dispute. The General Assembly may make recommendations on such questions to the concerned State or States, or to the Security Council, or to both, unless the Security Council is exercising its functions

---

[15] Article 32, the UN Charter.

[16] Two hundred seventy-nine vetoes were cast from 1945 to 1990. Peter Malanczuk, *Akehurst's Modern Introduction to International Law*, 7th revised ed., Routledge, 1997, p.375. However, the vetoes' role can also be explained in a different way: "[B]y preventing action against a permanent member, the veto saved the organisation from wrecking itself in destructive operations against its most powerful members". Thomas G. Weiss, David P. Forsythe, and Roger A. Coate, *The United Nations and Changing World Politics*, Westview Press, 1994, p.25. Also see Leland M. Goodrich, Edvard Hambro and Anne Patricia Simons, *Charter of the United Nations: Commentary and Documents*, Third and Revised Ed., New York and London: Columbia University Press, 1969, p.291.

[17] Weiss *et al., op. cit.*, p.11

[18] White, *supra* note 4, p.4.

under the UN Charter in respect of the same dispute or situation.[19] The General Assembly may also call the attention of the Security Council to situations which are likely to endanger international peace and security.[20] In addition to Article 10, which confers general competence on the General Assembly,[21] Article 14 specifically refers to the General Assembly's role in regard to international peace and security:

> ... the General Assembly may recommend measures for the peaceful adjustment of any situation, regardless of origin, which it deems likely to impair the general welfare or friendly relations among nations, including situations resulting from a violation of the provisions of the present Charter setting forth the Purposes and Principles of the United Nations.

Besides the Charter provisions, the Uniting for Peace Resolution 377(V) is noteworthy in terms of the General Assembly's jurisdiction in the area of international peace and security. It was adopted in 1950 in the wake of the Korean crisis. When North Korean troops crossed the partition line between Soviet and US zones of occupation in June 1950, the US sought the Organisation's authorisation to take military action. Such an authorisation was not likely to be approved by the Security Council since the Soviet Union would have exercised her veto powers under the UN Charter. Taking advantage of the Soviet Union's absence from the Security Council,[22] a Security Council resolution recommending assistance to South Korea was adopted.[23] With the return of the Soviet representative to the Security Council, the Western States looked for an alternative means of taking collective measure in the event of the Security Council being blocked by the Soviet veto.[24] The consequent General Assembly Uniting for Peace Resolution had the purpose of allowing the General Assembly itself to authorise a military action:

---

[19]   Article 11(2) and Article 12(1), the UN Charter.

[20]   Article 11(3), the UN Charter.

[21]   See White, *supra* note 4, p.148, and Simma, *supra* note 3, p.14.

[22]   The reason for her absence was to protest at the failure to install the People's Republic of China in the Chinese permanent seat in the Security Council instead of the Republic of China.

[23]   SC Res. 83, 27 June 1950. SCOR, 474th mtg., UN Doc. S/1511. Seven in favour and one against. Two members, Egypt and India, did not participate in the voting, and the USSR was absent.

[24]   White, *supra* note 4, p.173. Dr. White uses the term 'collective security' in this context. It is questionable whether the terminology is appropriate, particularly as regards the Korean War, where neither North Korea nor South Korea was a member of the Organisation.

That if the Security Council, because of lack of unanimity of the permanent members, fails to exercise its primary responsibility for the maintenance of international peace and security in any case where there appears to be a threat to the peace, breach of the peace, or act of aggression, the General Assembly shall consider the matter immediately with a view to making the appropriate recommendations to Members for collective measures, including in the case of a breach of the peace or act of aggression the use of armed force when necessary, to maintain or restore international peace and security.[25]

Under the Uniting for Peace Resolution, the General Assembly, if not in session at the time, is entitled to hold an emergency special session upon the request by the Security Council on a vote of any nine members, or by a majority of the Member States, or by one Member if the majority of Members concurs.[26]

Regarding the limits of the General Assembly's power to establish a peacekeeping force, the World Court's conclusions in the *Certain Expenses* case provide several criteria. These will be discussed later in this chapter.[27]

---

[25] GA res. 337(V), 3 November 1950, 302nd mtg.

[26] The legality of this resolution was earnestly debated, as is explained by L. H. Woolsey: "It is said to be an attempt to by-pass the Security Council, to usurp its constitutional powers and relegate it to a secondary position in the United Nations structure, in other words, a back-door way of amending the Charter". L. H. Woolsey, 'The "Uniting for Peace" Resolution of the United Nations', *AJIL* 45, 1951: 129-137, p.133. As to the Uniting for Peace Resolution, in general, see Woolsey, *op. cit.*; F. A. Vallat, 'The General Assembly and the Security Council of the United Nations', 29 *BYIL*: 63-104, pp.96-100; Juraj Andrassy, 'Uniting for Peace', *AJIL* 50, 1956: 563-582; Keith S. Petersen, 'The Uses of the Uniting for Peace Resolution since 1950', 8 *International Organisation*, 1959: 219-232; and White, *supra* note 4, pp.172-178. The requirements for the convening of a special session are: at the request of the Security Council, of a majority of the Member States, or of one Member if the majority of Members concurs. In the post-Cold War era where the Security Council is functioning in relative harmony and where the General Assembly is not dominated by the Western States, this resolution had generally been considered outmoded. However, 10th emergency special session was held in April 1997 at the request of Qatar regarding the Occupied East Jerusalem and the rest of the Occupied Palestinian Territory. The 9th session was in 1982 and concerned the Occupied Arab Territories.

[27] *Infra* Section 5.

3.   THE ORIGINS OF UNITED NATIONS PEACE-KEEPING

The term 'peacekeeping' cannot be found in the UN Charter. The collective security system envisaged in the Charter was to have been based on an arrangement whereby States would make their forces available in accordance with agreements with the Security Council.[28] In political reality, where the Security Council lacked agreement among its Permanent Members, peace-keeping emerged "out of necessity and became the only practical method acceptable to the Council members for dealing with conflicts during the Cold War period".[29] The fact that peacekeeping is an *ad hoc* measure which had not been foreseen or envisaged by the founders of the Organisation makes it difficult to define the term. Marrack Goulding, ex-Under Secretary-General of the UN, gives the following definition:

> Field operations established by the United Nations, with the consent of the parties concerned, to help control and resolve conflicts between them, under United Nations command and control, at the expense collectively of the member states, and with military and other personnel and equipment provided voluntarily by them, acting impartially between the parties and using force to the minimum extent necessary.[30]

In the first instance, it should be noted that peacekeeping is a flexible mechanism and peacekeeping forces' mandate and composition varies from one mission to another. To understand the formation of a certain common understanding of peacekeeping such as in this definition presented by Goulding, we will revisit four early peacekeeping operations undertaken by the UN and analyse the constitutional basis and mandate for such operations.

3.1   United Nations Special Committee on the Balkans

The first observation mission of the UN during armed conflict was the United Nations Special Committee on the Balkans ('UNSCOB').[31]

---

[28]   Article 43, the UN Charter. See *supra* note 3.

[29]   Roy S. Lee, 'United Nations Peacekeeping: Development and Prospects', *Cornell International Law Journal*, 1995: 619-627, p.620.

[30]   Marrack Goulding, 'The Evolution of United Nations Peace-keeping', *International Affairs* 69(3), 1993: 451-64, p.455.

[31]   Regarding UNSCOB, see Karl Th. Birgisson, 'United Nations Special Committee on the Balkans,' in William J. Durch, ed., *The Evolution of UN Peace-keeping*, St. Martin's

Observation missions are not clearly distinguished from peacekeeping missions and are included within its broad definition. The distinctions can be found in their role and composition. The observers are usually unarmed, and assume a role of observation and reporting. They are drawn from various countries and do not operate as contingents.[32] Whereas, peacekeeping forces are lightly armed, and engage not only in observation and reporting but also in activities of more military nature such as the supervision of a cease-fire, patrol of border areas and deterrence of military incursions. They are composed of national contingents, "which retain a distinguishable national identity despite forming part of a UN institution".[33] Although UNSCOB is not always considered as a peacekeeping operation,[34] it was an experience that facilitated establishment and implementation of genuine peacekeeping operations by the Organisation.

On 3 December 1946, the Greek government brought complaints before the Security Council claiming that Albania, Yugoslavia and Bulgaria were assisting Communist guerrillas in northern Greece. The Security Council established a Commission of Investigation that went to the Balkans in early 1947.[35] The findings of the Commission confirmed the allegation. To circumvent the veto-stricken Security Council, the issue was removed from the Security Council's agenda by the US proposal and all records and documents in the case were placed at the disposal of the General Assembly by a Security Council resolution.[36] Since this resolution was considered as a procedural issue to transfer an agenda from the Council to the General Assembly, the Western bloc was able to avoid the Soviet veto.[37] UNSCOB was established in 1947 by a General Assembly resolution.[38] Owing to the refusal of the three Communist states to co-operate, the observer group only

---

Press, 1993, Chapter 5: 77-83; Alan James, *Peace-keeping in International Politics*, Macmillan, 1990: 87-92; and Rosalyn Higgins, *United Nations Peace-keeping: Documents and Commentary Vol.IV Europe 1946-1979*, Oxford University Press, 1981: 1-75.

[32] Simma, *supra* note 3, p.593.

[33] *Ibid.*

[34] See, for instance, *infra* note 39.

[35] SC Res. 339, 19 December 1946. SCOR, 87th mtg., UN Doc. S/339. Adopted unanimously.

[36] SC Res. 555, 15 September 1947. SCOR, 202nd mtg., UN Doc. S/555. Nine in favour, and two objections (Poland and the USSR).

[37] The Soviet view was that the convocation was a substantive matter, thus subject to the veto right. Simma, *supra* note 3, p.346; Goodrich, *supra* note 16, p.183; and White, *supra* note 4, pp.177-178.

[38] GA Res. 109(II), 21 October 1947, 100th mtg.

operated on the Greek side of the border.[39] By 1951, the situation in Greece had stabilised considerably and UNSCOB was terminated by the General Assembly by the end of that year.[40] Observers from the Balkan Sub-Commission of the Peace Observation Commission undertook the observation role; they ceased their operation at the end of 1953. The guerrilla activities were virtually ceased by mid-1950s.

3.2   United Nations Truce Supervision Organisation

In 1948, the Security Council established a Truce Commission for Palestine that comprised representatives from the Security Council, which had career consular officers in Jerusalem.[41] The General Assembly decided to support the Security Council by appointing a United Nations Mediator in Palestine and relieving the Palestine Commission of its responsibilities by Resolution 186 on 14 May 1948. On the same day, the proclamation of the establishment of the State of Israel was issued. The following day the United Kingdom terminated its mandatory administration of Palestine. Neighbouring Arab states intervened with armed forces, and intense fighting broke out. The Security Council succeeded in attaining a cease-fire on 29 May 1948, and took measures to provide the Truce Commission and the Mediator with "a sufficient number of military observers".[42] This was how United Nations Truce Supervision Organisation (UNTSO) was formed in order to supervise the 1948 truce in Palestine.[43] About one hundred military observers were deployed in June 1948, and the number was increased by three hundred in the summer of the same year, after which there was a further increase by

---

[39]   Alan James, formerly Professor of International Relations at the University of Keele, contends that UNSCOB cannot be categorised as a peacekeeping operation, because of: (1) its bias in favour of Greece; (2) its weak deterrent effect; (3) its not being of a wholly military character; and most importantly, (4) the lack of co-operation from the parties to the conflict. James, *supra* note 31, pp.89-91.

[40]   GA Res. 508, 7 December, 1951, 351ˢᵗ mtg. 48 in favour, 5 objections and 1 abstention.

[41]   SC Res. 48(1948), 23 April 1948. SCOR, 287ᵗʰ mtg. UN Doc. S/727. Eight in favour, and three abstentions (Colombia, Ukrainian Soviet Socialist Republic and USSR). Syria did not serve in the Commission although she satisfied this condition.

[42]   Operative Paragraph 6 of SC Res. 50(1948), 29 May 1948. SCOR, 310ᵗʰ mtg., UN Doc. S/801. The draft resolution was voted in parts.

[43]   Mona Ghali, 'United Nations Truce Supervision Organisation: 1948-Present', in Durch, *supra* note 31, Chapter 6: 84-103; and Rosalyn Higgins, *United Nations Peace-keeping 1946-1967: Documents and Commentary I The Middle East*, Oxford University Press, 1969: 1-217. For details of the Arab-Israeli Conflict from 1947 up to Operation 'Peace for Galilee' of 1982, see Istvan Pogany, *The Security Council and the Arab-Israeli Conflict*, Aldershot: Gower, 1984.

the same number.[44] Along with changes of political and military conditions, the mandate of the Truce Commission, and thus of UNTSO, evolved, ranging from supervising the truce, to the demarcation of armistice lines, mediation between the parties, the establishment and maintenance of demilitarised zones, and investigations of complaints regarding violations of agreements.[45] The United Nations Emergency Force I (UNEF I), which will be reviewed in the next sub-section, was set up by a group of military observers temporarily detached from UNTSO. There have also been three other UN peacekeeping forces established in the Middle East since 1973. These are the United Nations Emergency Force II (UNEF II), the United Nations Disengagement Observer Force (UNDOF), and the United Nations Interim Force in the Lebanon (UNIFIL), all of which were initially supported by UNTSO personnel. UNTSO is also known as a reliable source of personnel when new missions are set up or fact-finding or investigative missions are to be formed.[46] The Organisation remains operational to date.

3.3   The United Nations Emergency Force I

UNEF I was the first armed UN peacekeeping operation.[47] Its creation can be seen against a background of the increasing political significance of the Middle East to Great Britain and France when their powers were weakened in other parts of the world.[48] In the eyes of the West, President Nasser of Egypt, who refused to join a pro-Western alliance and who adhered to a nationalist ideology, was "inclining alarmingly toward the Soviet sphere".[49] After the US and Britain reversed their decision to finance the Aswan High Dam project in Egypt, Nasser announced the nationalisation of the Suez Canal Company. This gave Britain and France, who were the principal shareholders of the company, a pretext to take military action.[50] In coordination with these two powers, Israeli forces launched an attack on Egypt

---

[44]   James, *supra* note 31, p.153.
[45]   SC Res. 49, 22 May 1948. SCOR, 302nd mtg., UN Doc. S/773. Eight in favour and three abstentions (Syria, Ukrainian Soviet Socialist Republic and the USSR). Also *Instructions given by UN Mediator to UN observers engaged in supervision of the Truce in Palestine,* UN Doc. S/928, 28 July 1948.
[46]   Ghali, *op. cit.*, p.98.
[47]   Regarding UNEF I, see Mona Ghali, 'United Nations Emergency Force I', in Durch, *supra* note 31, Chapter 7: 104-130. Also James, *supra* note 31, pp.210-223.
[48]   Ghali, *op. cit.*, p.105.
[49]   *Ibid.*, p.106.
[50]   *Ibid.*, p.107.

on 29 October 1956. This was followed by an Anglo-French air offensive. Since two permanent members of the Security Council were directly involved in the conflict, it was the General Assembly which initiated the creation of the force, utilising the Uniting for Peace resolution.[51] The General Assembly recommended the immediate cessation of armed conflict and the withdrawal of foreign troops from the occupied areas,[52] and further requested the Secretary-General to submit to the General Assembly a plan for the setting up of an emergency international UN Force.[53] UNEF I's mandate included four responsibilities:

1. To secure and supervise a cease-fire by forming a buffer zone between Anglo-French-Israeli and Egyptian forces;

2. to supervise the withdrawal of foreign forces from Egyptian territory and the canal clearing operations;

3. to patrol border areas and deter military incursions; and

4. to secure the provisions of the Egypt-Israel Armistice Agreements".[54]

UNEF I also played a role in the exchange of prisoners, and in enquiries concerning missing personnel. The force operated over ten years, and then had to withdraw at the request of Egypt. In 1957, the size of UNEF I was at its authorised level of 6000, which for financial reasons was gradually reduced to less than 3400 at the time of its withdrawal in May 1967.[55] According to one account, the Egyptian request for UNEF's withdrawal was made as the result of false information given by the Soviet Union that Israel was preparing to invade Syria, and UN troops could not continue their presence against the will of the host state.[56] Since UNEF was not an operation under Chapter VII, consent of the host-state was a pre-condition for its presence in the region.[57] The decision of the then Secretary-General, U-Thant, to withdraw UNEF attracted widespread criticism, and the matter

---

[51] *Supra* note 26 and accompanying text.

[52] GA res. 997, 562nd mtg., ES-I, Doc A/RES/390, 2 November 1956. 64 in favour, 5 against (Australia, France, Israel, New Zealand and the UK), and 6 abstentions.

[53] GA res. 998, 563rd mtg., ES-I, Doc A/RES/395, 4 November 1956. 57 in favour with 19 abstentions including Egypt, France, Israel, the UK and the USSR.

[54] GA res. 1000, 5 November 1956, 565th mtg. 57 in favour with 19 abstentions including Egypt, France, Israel, the USSR, and the UK. Ghali, *op. cit.*, pp.112-3.

[55] Ghali, *op. cit.*, p.117.

[56] *Ibid.*, p.124.

[57] Consent of the host-state becomes one of the main principles of peacekeeping that will be discussed in Chapter 2.

was referred to the General Assembly, which had established the UNEF in the first instance. However, an affirmative decision by two thirds of the Member States was required to put the matter on the agenda of the General Assembly, and it was known that a large majority would have supported Egypt. One option available to the Secretary-General was to use Article 99 and summon the Security Council to consider the situation as a threat to international peace and security.[58] Since U-Thant foresaw an 'undignified brawl along East-West lines', he avoided this option.[59]

3.4   The United Nations Operation in the Congo

The last case study of this section is the United Nations Operation in the Congo (ONUC).[60] The Congo became independent from Belgium in 1960, but rivalry among local politicians and a lack of preparedness of the people for independence rapidly developed into civil war. In particular, the Province of Katanga, the wealthiest part of the country, sought secession with the support of Belgium. The Secretary-General received a request from President Kasavubu and Prime Minister Lumumba asking for the UN's military assistance. ONUC's first mandate was set forth in Security Council resolution 143 of 14 July 1960, as an authorisation to the Secretary-General:

> ... to take the necessary steps, in consultation with the govern-
> ment of the Republic of the Congo, to provide the Government
> with such military assistance as may be necessary until, ... the
> national security forces may be able, in the opinion of the
> Government, to meet fully their tasks.[61]

Despite Resolution 143, which also called for the withdrawal of Belgium, Belgian forces remained in Katanga. In Congo, the President and the Prime Minister dismissed each other. Being caught up in such chaos, an expansion of ONUC's mandate was unavoidable. Owing to political disagreements in the Security Council, the matter was transferred to the General Assembly

---

[58]   Article 99 of the Charter reads:
>   The Secretary-General may bring to the attention of the Security Council any
>   matter which in his opinion may threaten the maintenance of international peace
>   and security.

[59]   Brian Urquhart, *A Life in Peace and War*, W. W. Norton & Company, 1987, p.212.

[60]   William J. Durch, 'The UN Operation in Congo', in Durch, *supra* note 31, Chapter 19:
315-352; James, *supra* note 31, pp.291-299; and White, *supra* note 4, pp.254-261.

[61]   SC res. 143, 14 July 1960. SCOR, 873rd mtg., UN Doc. S/4387. Adopted by 8 votes to
none, with abstentions by China, France and the UK.

under the auspices of the Uniting for Peace Resolution, as in the case of UNEF I. However, the question returned to the Security Council after Lumumba's death. A General Assembly resolution on 20 September 1960 affirmed the Organisation's assistance to the Congolese Central Government and requested the Secretary-General to continue to take "vigorous action" to restore and maintain law and order and to safeguard the unity, territorial integrity and political independence of the Congo.[62] The Security Council declared that it was concerned about the fact that Lumumba and two other political leaders had been killed, the danger of widespread civil war, and the existence of a "threat to international peace and security". The Security Council accordingly urged:

> 1. That the United Nations takes immediately all appropriate measures to prevent the occurrence of civil war in the Congo, including arrangements for cease-fires, the halting of all military operations, the prevention of clashes, and *the use of force, if necessary, in the last resort* [emphasis added]; and
>
> 2. that measures be taken for the immediate withdrawal and evacuation from the Congo of all Belgian and other foreign military and paramilitary personnel and political advisers not under the United Nations Command, and mercenaries.[63]

This was the first resolution regarding the Congo that used the terms of Article 39 of the UN Charter. A finding in accordance with Article 39 of a threat to the peace, breach of the peace or act of aggression is a prerequisite for enforcement action under Article 42. With further explicit mention, in the same resolution, of "the use of force, if necessary, in the last resort" for preventing civil war, which is beyond self-defence, it may be argued that the operation shifted to enforcement. However, the general view of jurists is that the operation did not go so far, but remained under Article 40.[64]

---

[62]   GA res. 1474, ES-IV, 20 September 1960, 863rd mtg. 70 in favour, with 11 abstentions including France and the USSR.

[63]   SC res. 161, 21 February 1961. SCOR, 942nd mtg., UN Doc. S/4741. Nine in favour and two abstentions by France and the USSR.

[64]   See, e.g., Higgins, *op. cit.*, pp.57-58. Also Bowett, *United Nations Forces: A Legal Study of United Nations Practice*, Stevens & Sons, 1964, pp.175-180. Professor Bowett favours a broader basis in Article 39 in interpreting ONUC's operation, since ONUC's mandate was not limited to the supervision of compliance with the call for provisional measures. His comprehensive understanding is that ONUC's establishment was to achieve the general purpose of the Organisation set out in Article 1(1), in fulfilment of the Council's primary responsibility conferred by Article 24. The Council acted under Chapter VII following an implicit finding under Article 39. The purposes of the Force were

Security Council Resolution 169 of 24 November 1961 reaffirmed the policies and purposes of the United Nations with respect to the Congo as:

(a) To maintain the territorial integrity and the political independence of the Republic of the Congo;

(b) To assist the Central Government of the Congo in the restoration and maintenance of law and order;

(c) To prevent the occurrence of civil war in the Congo;

(d) To secure the immediate withdrawal and evacuation from the Congo of all foreign military, paramilitary and advisory personnel not under the United Nations Command, and all mercenaries; and

(e) To render technical assistance.[65]

ONUC was an important model of peacekeeping with several outstanding features: (1) at its peak, the force involved some 20,000 troops; (2) it was the first peacekeeping force which was composed of both civilian and military components; and (3) its mandate arguably crossed the threshold of enforcement action. The last two features will be discussed further in the next chapter. After the adoption of Resolution 169, large-scale fighting followed and it took approximately one year to end the secessionist movement. The Operation was terminated at the end of June 1964.

4. CONSTITUTIONAL BASIS OF UNITED NATIONS PEACEKEEPING OPERATIONS

Under which article of the UN Charter can a peacekeeping operation be established and implemented? As described in Section 1 above, Chapters VI and VII of the UN Charter provide for pacific settlement measures and action which may be taken with respect to threats to the peace, breaches of the peace, and acts of aggression, respectively. However, the provisions in Chapters VI and VII do not specifically mention or refer to peacekeeping

---

supervising and enforcing compliance with the provisional measures ordered under Article 40 and others which were consistent with the general powers of the Council under Article 39. As will be discussed later, the International Court of Justice also took a view in its Advisory Opinion in *Certain Expenses* case that ONUC was not an enforcement action. ICJ Rep. 1962, 163-4 and 166.

[65] SC res. 169, 24 November 1961. SCOR, 982nd mtg., UN Doc. S/5002. 9 votes to none, with 2 abstentions by France and the UK.

and it is not certain that it can be authorised under the Articles of these Chapters. In practice, the mandates and the scope of actions of peacekeeping operations cover a very wide spectrum, which will be discussed in detail in the subsequent chapters. However, at this point it may be noted that certain operations may be linked to pacific settlement measures thus invoking Article 36(1), whereas, supervision of cease-fires or the withdrawal of troops may fall under provisional measures in accordance with Article 40,[66] or, arguably, even measures under Article 41. Although Article 41 is hardly an obvious constitutional basis of a UN peacekeeping operation, the suggestion has been made by a leading specialist that an observer group or an inter-position force can be established under Article 41.[67] Professor Bowett affirms that, despite such a possibility, "this is clearly not the kind of measure which was contemplated as being appropriate to this Article at San Francisco" and that it is unlikely that the Security Council will rely solely on this Article as a constitutional basis. Furthermore, peacekeeping may occasionally be stretched "beyond Article 40, but not as far as Article 42".[68] Another possibility is to establish a peacekeeping force as a subsidiary organ of the General Assembly relying on Article 22, in conjunction with the proper power of the General Assembly under Articles 10, 11 or 14.[69] Likewise, the Security Council may establish peacekeeping forces as its subsidiary organs pursuant to Article 29. However, both Articles 22 and 29 are generally considered insufficient to be the sole legal basis for the establishment of peacekeeping forces.[70]

5.   COMPETENCE OF THE SECURITY COUNCIL AND THE GENERAL ASSEMBLY TO CREATE PEACEKEEPING FORCES

The four case studies referred to above illustrate that there has been no single procedure for establishing peacekeeping operations. In practice, peace-

---

[66]   White, *supra* note 4, p.228. The contrary view is that if Article 40 could obligate a State to facilitate the stationing of peacekeeping forces, it would constitute an evasion of Article 42. See Simma, *supra* note 3, p.619.

[67]   D. W. Bowett, *supra* note 64., pp.279-280.

[68]   *Ibid.*, p.280.

[69]   For example, the United Nations Emergency Force was regarded by the Secretary-General as a 'subsidiary organ of the General Assembly.' *Introduction to the Regulations for the United Nations Emergency Force*, UN Doc. A/3552. Also Agreement between the United Nations and Egypt, 8 February 1957, UN Doc. A/3527, pp.2 and 7.

[70]   Bowett, *op. cit.*, p.287.

keeping forces have been established both by the Security Council and the General Assembly. The power of the Security Council to take such measures cannot be questioned as it has primary responsibility for maintaining international peace and security (Article 24 (1)). The competence of the General Assembly to establish peacekeeping forces has been questioned, and the issue was examined in the *Certain Expenses* case by the International Court of Justice. The case was referred to the World Court in accordance with a General Assembly resolution asking for an Advisory Opinion concerning the question as to whether certain expenditures authorised by the General Assembly constituted expenses of the Organisation within the meaning of Article 17, Paragraph 2 of the UN Charter.[71] The expenditures in question were on UNEF and ONUC. The Soviet Union and France contested the legality of these expenditures, and refused to share the financial burden.

Article 11(2) of the Charter confirms the competence of the General Assembly to discuss any questions relating to the maintenance of international peace and security, as well as its recommendatory power in regard to such questions.[72] A restriction to its competence lies in the same paragraph, which reads:

> Any such question on which *action* is necessary shall be referred to the Security Council by the General Assembly either before or after discussion [emphasis added].

In the *Certain Expenses* case, the World Court considered the term 'action' in Article 11(2) as 'coercive or enforcement action':

> The word 'action' must mean such action as is solely within the province of the Security Council. It cannot refer to recommendations which the Security Council might make, as for instance under Article 38, because the General Assembly under Article 11 has a comparable power ...[73]

The responsibility conferred on the Security Council under Article 24 is "primary", not exclusive. This, in turn, meant that the General Assembly's powers were only limited by provisions in the UN Charter which explicitly prohibited such acts. Hence, although the General Assembly is not able to

---

[71] GA res. 1731(XVI), 20 December, 1961. Article 17(2) reads:
The expenses of the Organisation shall be borne by the Members as apportioned by the General Assembly.

[72] *Supra* note 19 and accompanying text.

[73] ICJ Rep. 1962, 151 at 164-5. See White, *supra* note 4, pp.151-2; Vallat, *supra* note 26, pp.97-99; and Andrassy, *supra* note 26, pp.566-568.

order enforcement action under Chapter VII, it is competent to create and mandate consensual, basically non-military peacekeeping operations. According to the Court, UNEF and ONUC were not enforcement actions, and could thus be established by the General Assembly.[74]

In the *Reparation* case, where the issue under consideration was whether the United Nations could bring an international claim against a responsible government on behalf of its representative, the World Court recognised the implied powers of the Organisation in its Advisory Opinion:

> Under international law, the Organization must be deemed to have those powers which, though not expressly provided in the Charter, are conferred upon it by necessary implication as being essential to the performance of its duties.[75]

In the *Namibia* case, the Court found that the General Assembly's termination of South Africa's mandate over Namibia was within its competence. The Court recognised a broad competence for the Assembly in its Advisory Opinion:

> For it would not be correct to assume that, because the General Assembly is in principle vested with recommendatory powers, it is debarred from adopting, in specific cases within the framework of its competence, resolutions which make determinations or have operative design.[76]

In regard to the Security Council's resolution which affirmed the General Assembly's decision to terminate South Africa's mandate,[77] the Court expressed its view regarding the "general powers" of the Security Council:

> ... Article 24 of the Charter vests in the Security Council the necessary authority to take action such as that taken in the present case. The reference in paragraph 2 of this Article to specific powers of the Security Council under certain chapters of the Charter does not exclude the existence of general powers to discharge the responsibilities conferred in paragraph 1. ...

---

[74]   ICJ Rep. 1962, 152, 163-4 and 166. See White, *supra* note 4, p.66.

[75]   *Reparation for Injuries Suffered in the Service of the United Nations*, ICJ Rep. 1949, 174 at 182.

[76]   *Legal Consequences for States of the Continued Presence of South Africa in Namibia (South Africa) Notwithstanding Security Council Resolution 276 (1970)*, ICJ Rep. 1971, 50.

[77]   SC res. 276, 30 January 1970. SCOR, 1529th mtg., UN Doc. S/RES/276(1970). Thirteen in favour and two abstentions by France and the UK.

> [T]he Members of the United Nations have conferred upon the Security Council powers commensurate with its responsibility for the maintenance of peace and security. The only limitations are the fundamental principles and purposes found in Chapter I of the Charter.[78]

Professor Seyersted argues in this regard that an intergovernmental organisation has an inherent power which allows the organisation to perform "a sovereign or international act not specifically authorised in its constitution".[79] Dr. White supports this idea of "inherent powers" by explaining the following two advantages.[80] Firstly, the doctrine of inherent powers allows the Organisation to fulfil its aims without having to concern itself with a literal interpretation of the Charter provisions. Secondly, Courts and commentators are able to review the Organisations' actions quickly and accurately through two real legal controls: "that the action in question aims to achieve one of the purposes of the Organisation, and that it is not expressly prohibited by any of the provisions of the constitution."[81]

Taking into account the opinions of the World Court referred to above recognising the broad powers of the Organisation and its organs, as well as the doctrine of inherent powers, the power of the General Assembly to create peacekeeping forces is deemed to have been ascertained.

6.   THE ROLE OF THE SECRETARY-GENERAL

The role of the Secretary General with respect to international peace and security needs to be analysed. The main provision in the UN Charter that stipulates the Secretary-General's authority in this regard is contained in Article 99.[82] In accordance with this Article, the Secretary-General may bring to the attention of the Security Council any matter that in his opinion may threaten the maintenance of international peace and security. The office holders have developed the range of their activities such as to include good offices, mediation, arbitration and fact finding.[83] The general view on the limits of the Secretary-General's power is that it does not go so far as to

---

[78]   ICJ Rep. 1971, 52.

[79]   F. Seyersted, *United Nations Forces*, 1966, pp.133-4.

[80]   White, *supra* note 4, p.67.

[81]   *Ibid.*

[82]   See *supra* note 58.

[83]   White, *op. cit.*, p.230. Also see Steven R. Ratner, *The New UN Peace-keeping: Building Peace in Lands of Conflict After the Cold War*, Macmillan, 1995, pp.68-71.

permit him to authorise an observer force or a peacekeeping force on his own initiative.[84] In case of UNEF I, the Secretary-General had an authorisation from the General Assembly to issue all regulations and instructions essential to the effective functioning of the force.[85] The United Nations Good Offices Mission to Afghanistan and Pakistan, which consisted of fifty military observers, is considered as an exceptional case in so far as the Secretary-General established the force.[86] The Geneva Agreement of 14 April 1988 provided that the UN should offer its good services to the parties.[87] The Secretary-General's notification of this provision[88] was subsequently approved by the Security Council by its Resolution 622 of 31 October 1988.[89] In Central America, a team of civilian observers for the elections in Nicaragua was appointed by the Secretary-General in 1989, while a subsequent military mission, the United Nations Observer Group in Central America, was created by the Security Council.[90] In the former case, the Secretary-General, Javier Perez de Cuellar, informed the General Assembly that he was setting up the UN Observer Mission to Verify the Electoral Process in Nicaragua (ONUVEN),[91] and the Secretary-General's decision was supported by the General Assembly, as well as by the Security Council.[92] The latter was a mission for the purpose of monitoring compliance with the security commitments under the Esquipulas II Agreements by the five parties, namely, Nicaragua, Honduras, Costa Rica, El Salvador, and Guatemala. This illustrates the distinction of competence between the Secretary-General and the Security Council, that the former is not able to establish a peacekeeping operation of a military nature unless authorised to do so by the latter, even when the force's function is limited to observation.[93]

---

[84]   Simma, *supra* note 3, p.592, and White, *supra* note 4, p.230.

[85]   Simma, *op. cit.*, p.593.

[86]   *Ibid.*, p.592.

[87]   *Letter dated 22 April 1988 from the Secretary-General addressed to the President of the Security Council*, UN Doc. S/19835.

[88]   *Letter dated 14 April 1988 from the Secretary-General to the President of the Security Council*, UN Doc. S/19834, 14 April 1988; and *Secretary-General's Letter*, UN Doc. S/19835, *supra* note 87.

[89]   SC res. 622, 31 October 1988. SCOR, 2828th mtg., UN Doc. S/RES/622(1988). Adopted unanimously.

[90]   SC res. 644, 7 November 1989. SCOR, 2890th mtg., UN Doc. S/RES/644(1989). Adopted unanimously.

[91]   *Letter dated 6 July 1989 from the Secretary-General Addressed to the President of the General Assembly,* 6 July 1989, UN Doc. A/44/375.

[92]   GA res. 44/10; and SC res. 637, 27 July 1989.

[93]   Simma, *supra* note 3, p.581.

With respect to the operation in the field of peacekeeping forces, the Secretary-General is not only the administrator of such forces but is also responsible for their executive direction and command.[94]

7. REGIONAL ARRANGEMENTS OR AGENCIES

The possibility of establishing a peacekeeping operation is not confined to the Organisation. Chapter VIII of the UN Charter refers to regional arrangements or agencies that may undertake efforts towards the pacific settlement of local disputes.[95] Such efforts are encouraged as far as those arrangements or agencies, as well as their activities, are consistent with the Purposes and Principles of the United Nations. However, if they are to take any enforcement action, authorisation by the Security Council is required pursuant to Article 53(1).[96] Also, they have the duty to keep the Security Council fully informed of their activities for the maintenance of international peace and security as provided for in Article 54.[97]

One example of a peacekeeping operation under Chapter VIII was a peace force established in Liberia by the Economic Community of West African States (ECOWAS), the ECOWAS Cease-fire Monitoring Group (ECOMOG). Although this operation was generally regarded as a peacekeeping operation, there were some problems as regards its legitimacy. The force, consisting of troops from Gambia, Guinea, Sierra-Leone and Nigeria, was constituted for the purpose of, "keeping the peace, restoring law and order and ensuring that the cease-fire was respected" in Liberia.[98] Liberia had been stricken by civil conflict since the end of 1989, when Charles Taylor and a group of rebels launched attacks against the existing regime led

---

[94] *Supplement to an Agenda for Peace: Position paper of the Secretary-General on the occasion of the fiftieth anniversary of the United Nations*, UN Doc. A/50/60 (S/1995/1), 3 January 1995, para.38.

[95] Article 52, the UN Charter.

[96] Article 53(1): "… no enforcement action shall be taken under regional arrangements or by regional agencies without the authorisation of the Security Council … until such time as the Organisation may, on request of the Governments concerned, be charged with the responsibility for preventing further aggression by such a state."

[97] Article 54: "The Security Council shall at all times be kept fully informed of activities undertaken or in contemplation under regional arrangements or by regional agencies for the maintenance of international peace and security."

[98] Final Communiqué of the First Session of the Community Standing Mediation Committee, ECOWAS, Banjul, Republic of the Gambia, August 6-7, 1990.

by President Samuel Doe.[99] When ECOWAS decided to dispatch ECOMOG, Taylor declared that such a force would be regarded as an invasion force.[100] First of all, the legitimacy of ECOMOG's operation was questioned because it lacked the consent of all of the parties to the conflict. Secondly, ECOMOG's impartiality was also questioned owing to the strong influence of Nigeria.[101] Initially most francophone members of ECOWAS opposed the operation for this reason.[102] Nigeria's president, Ibrahim Babangida, was a friend of Samuel Doe, and ECOMOG was clearly hostile towards Taylor's force.[103] Thirdly, ECOMOG's operation went beyond the generally accepted sphere of peacekeeping and it did involve itself in enforcement actions without authorisation from the UN Security Council.[104] The Organisation did not respond to the Liberian conflict until October 1992, when it approved ECOMOG action under Chapter VII by resolution 788 of 19 November 1992.[105] Later the Security Council established United Nations Observer Mission to Liberia (UNOMIL) to work with ECOMOG pursuant to the Cotonou Agreement of 1993.[106]

The example of ECOMOG shows that the mechanism to entrust peace-keeping operations to regional arrangements or agencies is yet to be developed. Since the Charter does not specify the details of this mechanism, the potential of this mechanism is to be explored.

---

[99] For historical background of Liberian conflict, see W. Ofuatey-Kodjoe, 'Regional Organizations and the Resolution of Internal Conflict: The ECOWAS Intervention in Liberia', *International Peace-keeping* 1(3), Autumn 1994: 261-302, and David Wippman, 'Enforcing the Peace: ECOWAS and the Liberian Civil War', in Lori Fisler Damrosch, ed., *Enforcing Restraint: Collective Intervention in Internal Conflicts*, Council on Foreign Relations, Inc., 1993, Chapter 4: 157-203.

[100] Ofuatey-Kodjoe, *op. cit.*, p.274; Wippman, *op. cit.*, p.178; also Wippman, 'Military Intervention, Regional Organizations, and Host-State Consent', *Duke Journal of Comparative and International Law*, Fall 1996: 209-239, p.225.

[101] Wippman (1993), p.172; Wippman (1996), p.227; and Ofuatey-Kodjoe, *op. cit.*, p.288.

[102] Wippman (1993), pp.167-168.

[103] *Ibid.*, pp.191-192. However, Wippman is of the view that Nigeria did not impose its will on Liberia and ECOMOG has indeed been a "Community enterprise". *Ibid.*, p.192.

[104] "Most Council delegates appear to have intentionally avoided the need for an explicit authorization of ECOMOG's use of force by accepting at face value the ECOWAS characterization of ECOMOG as a 'peace-keeping force'". Wippman (1993), p.185.

[105] SC res. 788, 19 November 1992. SCOR, 3138th mtg., UN Doc. S/RES/788(1992).

[106] SC res. 866, 22 September 1993. SCOR, 3281st mtg., UN Doc. S/RES/866(1993). Regarding problems experienced by UNOMIL in this co-operation, see Funmi Olonisakin, 'UN Co-operation with Regional Organizations in Peace-keeping: The Experience of ECOMOG and UNOMIL in Liberia', *International Peace-keeping* 3(3), Autumn 1996: 33-51.

CONCLUSION

This Chapter has analysed the Organisation's mechanism for maintaining international peace and security by reviewing the roles of the Security Council, the General Assembly, the Secretary-General, and other regional arrangements and agencies. We have also reviewed and illustrated four case-studies of peacekeeping during the earlier days of the Organisation, demonstrating that the form and scope of such operations have not been explicitly laid down in the UN Charter and that the shape they might assume differs from case to case. We then examined the constitutional basis and mandate for peacekeeping and confirmed the competence of the Security Council and the General Assembly to establish such operations.

In the next Chapter, we will examine the evolution of peacekeeping and seek dividing lines between peacekeeping and enforcement action, and between "peace-enforcement" and enforcement action. Also it will be argued that peacekeeping increasingly contains peacemaking and peace-building elements.

Chapter 2

Evolution of United Nations Peacekeeping

1. HISTORICAL OVERVIEW OF UNITED NATIONS PEACEKEEPING

The development and implementation of peacekeeping was through *ad hoc* policies and decisions taken by the UN and thus there is no single authoritative definition for the same. Therefore, it is useful to present a historical overview of peacekeeping before examining various theories and definitions of peacekeeping which have been discussed by commentators.

Wiseman divided the history of peacekeeping into five periods: a *Nascent Period* (1946-56); an *Assertive Period* (1956-67); a *Dormant Period* (1967-73); a *Resurgent Period* (1973-78); and a *Maintenance Period* (1978-85).[1] To these periods, A. B. Fetherston, of the Peace Research Centre at the Australian National University has added a sixth, an *Expansion Period* (1988-93). We will briefly review the history of UN peacekeeping by using these chronological divisions.

During the *Nascent Period*, several observer missions and commissions were set up. Two of them are still in place: the United Nations Truce Supervision Organisation (UNTSO) which has served in Palestine since 1948;[2] and the United Nations Military Observer Group in India and Pakistan (UNMOGIP) which has been deployed on the border between India and Pakistan since 1949.[3]

---

[1] Wiseman, in UNITAR, 1987, summarised and cited in A. B. Fetherston, *Towards a Theory of United Nations Peace-keeping*, Macmillan, 1994, p.16-19.

[2] See 3.2 'The United Nations Truce Supervision Organisation', Chapter 1.

[3] Kashmir became a battlefield after the independence of India and Pakistan from Britain on 15 August 1947. The Security Council resolved on 20 January 1948 (Resolution 39), to establish a United Nations Commission on India and Pakistan (UNCIP), consisting of three member states mainly for the purpose of mediating between the two parties. Its membership was later increased to five (Security Council resolution 47) and was authorised to use observers under Security Council resolution 726 of 21 April 1948. UNMOGIP was established upon the signing of the Karachi Agreement on 27 July 1949, to observe the cease-fire in Kashmir under the UNCIP. The number of military observers of UNMOGIP ranges from less than thirty to over one hundred. UNMOGIP remains in

The *Assertive Period* saw the establishment of seven new missions. Four of them were observer missions: the United Nations Observation Group in Lebanon (UNOGIL, 1958);[4] the United Nations Yemen Observation Mission (UNYOM, 1963-64);[5] the Mission of the Special Representative of the Secretary-General in the Dominican Republic (DOMREP, 1965-66);[6] and the United Nations India-Pakistan Observer Mission (UNIPOM, 1965-66).[7] The other three were larger-scale operations: the United Nations Operation in Congo (ONUC, 1960-64);[8] the United Nations Temporary Executive Authority and the United Nations Security Force in West New Guinea (West Irian) (UNTEA/UNSF, 1962-63),[9] and; the United Nations Force in Cyprus (UNFICYP, 1964-).[10] ONUC, as a multidimensional operation, and UNTEA/

---

place, despite termination of UNCIP in 1950, with a strength of 45 military observers as of 31 August 2001. http://www.un.org/Depts/DPKO/Missions/unmogip/unmogipF.htm (visited on 4 November 2001).

[4]   In response to a complaint by Lebanon that the United Arab Republic was instigating a revolt in Lebanon, UNOGIL was established by the Security Council under resolution 128 of 11 June 1958 with a mandate "to ensure that there is no illegal infiltration of personnel or supply of arms or other *materiel* across the Lebanese borders". The size of the observer group increased from approximately 100 to 650 along with the expansion of the observing area. UNOGIL left by 9 December following the withdrawal of US troops from Lebanon and UK troops from Jordan, as well as the withdrawal of the complaint by Lebanon from the agenda of the Security Council.

[5]   The Security Council established UNYOM by Resolution 179 of 11 June 1963. Its mandate, in accordance with the disengagement agreement between the UAR, Saudi Arabia and Yemen, was to verify Egyptian withdrawals and the cessation of Saudi arms aid to Royalists of Yemen.

[6]   DOMREP was established to observe the situation and to report on breaches of the cease-fire between the *de facto* authorities in the Dominican Republic. Its strength was two military observers who were provided to the military adviser to the representative of the Secretary-General.

[7]   Despite the presence of UNMOGIP, the Karachi Agreement broke down in August 1965. The Security Council resolution 215 of 5 November 1965 mandated UNIPOM to supervise the cease-fire and withdrawals in the area outside of Kashmir, and a further agreement in January 1966 gave it additional functions. UNMOGIP and UNIPOM were requested to ensure implementation of the agreements, and it was stipulated that their decision would be final and binding. UNIPOM withdrew upon the withdrawals of Indian and Pakistani armed forces, which were provided for in the said agreement.

[8]   See, 3.4 'The United Nations Operation in the Congo', Chapter 1.

[9]   UNTEA operated on the basis of the General Assembly's endorsement of the 15 August Dutch-Indonesian accord, dated 21 September 1962, aiming at the transfer of former Dutch New Guinea to Indonesia. UNSF assisted local police in maintaining law and order.

[10]   UNFICYP was established in accordance with Security Council resolution 186 of 4 March 1964, "in the interest of preserving international peace and security, to use its best efforts to prevent a recurrence of fighting [between the Greek Cypriot and Turkish Cypriot Communities] and, as necessary, to contribute to the maintenance and restoration

UNSF as a transitional authority, are both precedents of a 'new' type of peacekeeping which will be discussed later in this chapter.

After the active period, no new operations were established for seven years in what Wiseman describes as the *Dormant Period*. Then three operations followed during the *Resurgent Period*, all in the Middle East: the United Nations Emergency Force II (UNEF II, 1973-79) in the Sinai;[11] the United Nations Disengagement Observer Force (UNDOF, 1974-) in the Golan Heights,[12] and; the United Nations Interim Force in the Lebanon (UNIFIL, 1978-).[13] The latter two are still in operation. The *Maintenance Period* was then a period of quiescence which lasted for ten years.

---

of law and order and a return to normal conditions". Its presence continues in the absence of a political settlement, with a strength of 1,251 troops and 35 Civilian Police, supported by some 145 civilian staff, as of 31 August 2001. http://www.un.org/Depts/DPKO/Missions/unficyp/unficypF.htm (visited on 4 November 2001).

[11] Establishment of UNEF II was recommended by the Security Council in its resolution 340 of 25 October 1973. Its mandate was designed in accordance with the *Report of the Secretary-General on the implementation of Security Council resolution 340* (1973), as an observation of the cease-fire, prevention of a recurrence of the fighting, and co-operation with the International Committee of the Red Cross in its humanitarian endeavours. UN Doc. S/11052/Rev.1 of 27 October 1973. The mandate was approved by the Security Council in resolution 341 of 27 October 1973. Its force strength was some 7000 military personnel.

[12] UNDOF was created as a consequence of the Yom Kippur War, by Security Council resolution 350 of 31 May 1974. Its mandate was set forth in the *Protocol to the Agreement on Disengagement between Israeli and Syrian Forces concerning the United Nations Disengagement Observer Force*, to maintain the cease-fire and to see that the Agreement is scrupulously observed. UN Doc. S/11302/Add.1 Annex II of 30 May 1974. This interposition force between the two parties was 'a compromise between the Syrian insistence that the UN presence be merely an Observer Group and the Israeli desire for a UN Force". Urquhart, *A Life in Peace and War, supra* FN59, Chapter 1, p.249. UNDOF's strength is 1,039 troops assisted by some 80 military observers of UNTSO and some 125 civilian staff, as of 31 August 2001. http://www.un.org/Depts/ DPKO/Missions/undof/undofF.htm (visited on 4 November 2001).

[13] In mid-March 1978, Israeli forces invaded Lebanon in retaliation to a commando attack on 11 March 1978 in Israel which caused a significant number of casualties. Responsibility for the attack was claimed by the Palestine Liberation Organisation. The Lebanese Government protested to the Security Council maintaining that it had no connection with the Palestinian raid. In response, UNIFIL was established under Security Council resolution 425 of 19 March 1978. The resolution states its mandate as "confirming the withdrawal of Israeli forces, restoring international peace and security and assisting the Government of Lebanon in ensuring the return of its effective authority in the area". As of 31 August 2001, 4,486 troops are deployed assisted by some 470 civilian staff. http://www.un.org/Depts/DPKO/Missions/unifil/unifilF.htm (visited on 4 November 2001).

The official count of UN peacekeeping operations between 1945 and 1987 is thirteen;[14] forty-one new operations have been created since then.[15] Professor Adam Roberts suggests three reasons for the expansion of the number of peacekeeping operations.[16] Firstly, the capacity of the Security Council to agree on action in particular crises has increased, as is symbolised by the decline in the use of the veto. Secondly, there has been "a widespread mood of optimism that the UN can have a much more central role in international security and that peace-keeping can tackle a very wide range of urgent problems".[17] Thirdly, the end of the Cold War has led to situations where peacekeeping operations are called for: (i) the conclusion of regional peace agreements in Afghanistan, Angola, Namibia, Central America and Cambodia; (ii) the decline and collapse of two large communist-cum-federal states, namely, the Soviet Union and Yugoslavia; and (iii) the increased preference of major powers to respond to conflicts in distant countries within a UN framework over unilateral military action.

The *Expansion Period* started with the United Nations Iran-Iraq Military Observer Group (UNIMOG, 1988-91)[18] and includes: the United Nations Transitional Authority in Cambodia (UNTAC, 1992-93);[19] the United Nations Protection Force I and II (UNPROFOR in Croatia and in Bosnia-Herzegovina, 1992-95);[20] as well as the United Nations Operation in Somalia

---

[14]   Boutros Boutros-Ghali, *An Agenda for Peace: Preventive Diplomacy, Peacemaking and Peace-keeping*, New York: United Nations, 1992, para.47.

[15]   As of 15 September 2001 based on information available at <http://www.un.org/Depts/dpko>.

[16]   Adam Roberts, 'The Crisis in UN Peace-keeping', *Survival* 36(3), Autumn 1994:93-120, p.96.

[17]   *Ibid.*

[18]   An unarmed military observer force on the Iran-Iraq border was called for by Security Council resolution 598, and UNIMOG's mandate was approved by Resolution 619 of 9 August 1988. UNIMOG was given the tasks of monitoring and maintaining a cease-fire between the two parties as well as monitoring the withdrawal of the respective forces. The force consisted of some 400 military personnel.

[19]   Establishment of UNTAC was authorised by Security Council resolution 745 of 28 February 1992. It was a large-scale peacekeeping operation where some 22,000 international personnel were involved. It consisted of seven components: human rights, electoral, military, civil administration, police, repatriation and rehabilitation. For details, see Chapter 4.

[20]   A peacekeeping operation in the former Yugoslavia was 'considered' in Security Council resolution 721 of 27 November 1991. However, Security Council resolution 724 of 15 December 1991 endorsed the position of the Secretary-General that "the conditions for establishing a peace-keeping operation in Yugoslavia still do not exist". Yet a small group of personnel was sent to the former Yugoslavia for preparations for the possible deployment of a peacekeeping operation. UNPROFOR was finally established by Security

(UNOSOM I, 1992-93).[21] Dr. Fetherston calls into question whether the following missions are peacekeeping:[22] the United Nations Good Offices Mission in Afghanistan and Pakistan along with the Office of the Secretary-General in Afghanistan and Pakistan (UNGOMAP/OSGAP; 1988-90/1990-);[23] the United Nations Iraq-Kuwait Observation Mission (UNIKOM, 1991-);[24] the United Nations Security Guards (UNSG)[25] which provided security for the humanitarian operation of the Office of the United Nations Disaster Relief Coordinator (UNDRO); and UNOSOM II (1993-95).[26] OSGAP consisted of ten monitors and was actually a symbolic United Nations presence. As to UNIKOM and UNOSOM II, the lack of consent by the concerned parties renders it questionable as to whether they qualify as peacekeeping operations. UNOSOM II has further problems concerning the principle of non-use of force and, arguably, impartiality. UNSG is difficult

---

Council resolution 743 of 21 February 1992. It consisted of three parts, operations in Croatia, Bosnia-Herzegovina and Macedonia, respectively, involving over 38,000 military personnel, some 800 civilian police and over 2,000 other civilian staff. For details of UNPROFOR, see Chapter 6.

[21] UNOSOM I was established by Security Council resolution 751 of 24 April 1992, to guarantee some security for a major humanitarian assistance operation by a group of 500 military personnel. Its strength was later augmented to 50 military observers and 3,500 security personnel. Later UNOSOM's mandate was expanded and renamed UNOSOM II. See note 26 below.

[22] A. B. Fetherston, *supra* note 1, pp.30-31.

[23] Regarding the establishment of UNGOMAP, see 6 'The Roles of the Secretary-General', Chapter 1, FN86 and accompanying text. OSGAP, which has a Military Advisory Unit of ten military advisers, was established upon termination of UNGOMAP on 15 March, 1990.

[24] In the aftermath of the liberation of Kuwait, the Security Council established a demilitarised zone to be monitored by a UN observer unit in accordance with Resolution 687 of 3 April 1991. UNIKOM was created for that purpose under Security Council resolution 689 of 9 April 1991. Despite its start as an unarmed observation mission, UNIKOM's strength was increased in February 1993 following a series of incidents. As of 31 August 2001, it comprises 1,099 military personnel supported by some 220 civilian staff. http://www.un.org/Depts/DPKO/Missions/unikom/unikomF.htm (visited on 4 November 2001).

[25] UNSG was based on a Memorandum of Understanding on humanitarian assistance dated 18 April 1991, signed by the Foreign Minister of Iraq and the Executive Delegate of the Secretary-General for the United Nations Humanitarian Programme for Iraq, Kuwait, and the Iraq/Iran and Iraq/Turkey Border Areas.

[26] UNOSOM II was established under Security Council resolution 814 of 26 March 1993. UNOSOM II's mandate included monitoring of the cessation of hostilities, prevention of a resumption of violence, protection of UN personnel and other aid workers, as well as the repatriation of refugees and displaced persons. It comprised 28,000 military and police personnel and was involved in serious fighting. See *infra* 2.3 '*Third-Generation Peacekeeping*'.

to define as peacekeeping because it was run from UNDRO not from DPKO[27] and "was for purely humanitarian purposes, i.e. it had no political function".[28]

As is evident from the forgoing accounts, a question arises primarily as to whether a particular operation qualifies as peacekeeping, because there has been no consensus on a particular definition of peacekeeping and practice has evolved without a definitional context or laid down policy parameters. The *Expansion Period* did not only see an increase in the number of operations but also an expansion of the range of activities performed by peacekeeping missions. There is a need to examine various evolving theories and definitions of peacekeeping in order to ascertain and determine the desirable direction of development of peacekeeping in the future.

2. DEFINITIONS AND PRINCIPLES OF PEACE-KEEPING

2.1 First-Generation Peacekeeping

The proliferation of peacekeeping after the end of the Cold War had brought a new categorisation which divides peacekeeping into two types: *traditional* or *first-generation* or *Cold War peacekeeping*, on the one hand, and *new* or *second-generation* or *multidimensional peacekeeping* on the other. Preference as to which term depends on individual scholars.[29] This author does not favour the generational approach because some peacekeeping operations before 1988 had features of "second-generation" peacekeeping. However, to avoid confusion, and keeping in perspective the complexity of

---

[27] DPKO: Department of Peace-keeping Operations. It was created by Boutros-Ghali in 1992, and is headed by an Under-Secretary-General for Peace-keeping. Since November 1993, two Assistant-Secretaries-General run the Office for Operations and the Office for Planning and Support, respectively. Regarding details of recent reform on DPKO, see William J. Durch, 'Structural Issues and the Future of UN Peace Operations' in Donald C. F. Daniel and Bradd C. Hayes, eds., *Beyond Traditional Peace-keeping*, Macmillan, 1995.

[28] Fetherston, *supra* note 1, p.31.

[29] Generational approach was taken by, for instance, John Mackinlay, Jarat Chopra and Steven R. Ratner. See J. Mackinlay and J. Chopra, 'Second Generation Multinational Operations', *The Washington Quarterly* 15, Summer 1992; and Ratner, *The New UN Peace-keeping, supra* FN83 of Chapter 1. For a critique of the generational approach, see Charles Dobbie, 'A Concept for Post-Cold War Peace-keeping', *Survival* 36(3), Autumn 1994: 121-48; and Alan James, 'Peace-keeping in the post-Cold War era', *International Journal*, vol.L, no.2, Spring 1995:241-265.

its evolution, the theories of peacekeeping will be analysed by using the divisions into three generations.

In the previous Chapter, as well as in the previous section, we have reviewed a number of UN peacekeeping operations before the end of the Cold War. Most of these operations belong to first-generation peacekeeping. Steven R. Ratner, of the University of Texas School of Law, previously legal adviser to the US delegation to the Cambodian peace talks, defines first-generation peacekeeping as follows:

> First-generation operations represent those where a political organ of the UN deploys a military force between two or more armies, with their consent, pending, and in the absence of, a political settlement.[30]

Marrack Goulding explains the aim of first-generation peacekeeping as being "to support peacemaking efforts by helping to create conditions in which political negotiation can proceed."[31]

Despite the lack of a universally agreed definition, the concept of peacekeeping during the first-generation contained certain principles, which derive from five principles listed by a former Secretary-General, Dag Hammarskjold, and a Canadian diplomat, Lester Pearson, in regard to UNEF I:[32]

1) consent of the parties to the dispute for the establishment of the mission;[33]

2) non-use of force except in self-defence;

3) voluntary contributions of contingents from small, neutral countries to participate in the force;[34]

---

[30] Ratner, *op. cit.*, p.17.

[31] Goulding uses the term *"traditional peace-keeping"*, and this is one of six categories he introduces as will be discussed below. Goulding, 'The Evolution of United Nations Peacekeeping', *supra* FN30 of Chapter 1, pp.456-460.

[32] Urquhart, *supra* note 12, p.133. These principles are obviously not legal requirements as the peacekeeping itself is not explicitly determined in the Charter.

[33] Although this is a widely accepted key principle, according to Charles Dobbie, author of the British Army Field Manual *Wider Peace-keeping*, there are two definitions of peacekeeping without reference to the consent of the parties in conflict: one by the International Peace Academy and the other by NATO. See Dobbie, *supra* note 29, p.122.

[34] This was the opposite to what the drafters of the Charter anticipated. The great powers were expected to supply the main portion of the forces necessary for UN action. Goodrich *et al.*, *Charter of the United Nations*, *supra* FN16 of Chapter 1, p.632. This principle obviously does not apply any longer. For example, in the United Nations Iraq-Kuwait Observation Mission (UNIKOM, 1991-), all five permanent members are sending military observers.

4) impartiality and non-intervention; and

5) day-to-day control of peace-keeping operations by the Secretary-General.

Principles 1 (consent of the parties to the dispute), 2 (non-use of force), and 4 (impartiality) have been essential principles, at least during the first forty years of the history of UN peacekeeping. Nevertheless this does not mean that in reality all the principles are satisfied for every case of peacekeeping. For instance, parties to a conflict who once signed a peace agreement and gave consent to the presence of a peacekeeping mission may withdraw their co-operation at any time during the course of the implementation of the agreement. In such cases, options available for the mission are either to withdraw the peacekeeping forces, which happened in the case of UNEF I at the request of the Egyptian government, or to consider another step in enforcement.[35]

As to the principle of the non-use of force except in self-defence, its interpretation is not simple. In general, a wide definition of self-defence has been taken since UNEF II:

> Self-defence would include resistance to attempts by forceful means to prevent it from discharging its duties under the mandate of the Security Council.[36]

If all the parties abide by their peace accords or a cease-fire agreement, a peacekeeping force would not need to use force. Commanders on the spot are rather cautious in resorting to the use of force as they are aware of the risk to lightly armed peacekeepers. Also, the impact of a clash with one of local disputing parties is taken into account, as such incidents may be perceived as prejudicing the impartiality of the peacekeeping force and the operations as a whole may be dragged into the conflict.[37] Consequently if either party to the conflict considers that UN peacekeepers are partial, they may withdraw their consent to the peacekeeping operation.

It is apparent from the above that consent, impartiality and the use of force in peacekeeping operations are intertwined. Professor James points out that "what is at issue is not the motives of the peacekeepers, or even what

---

[35]   As a generally accepted principle, a subsidiary organ established by the General Assembly cannot operate in the territory of a state without that state's consent for the interference with the domestic jurisdiction referred to in Article 2(7). See Goodrich, *et al.*, *op. cit.*, p.190.

[36]   *Report of the Secretary-General on the implementation of Security Council resolution 340 (1973)*, UN Doc. S/11052/Rev.1 of 27 October 1973, para.4.

[37]   See, e.g., Marrack Goulding, 'The Use of Force by the United Nations', *International Peace-keeping* 3(1), Spring 1996:1-18, pp.8-9 and A. Roberts, *supra* note 16, p.102.

they do, but the local perception of what they do".[38] In the light of the evolution of peacekeeping, whether these principles are still valid is a critical question, as will be discussed below.

2.2 Second-Generation Peacekeeping

There are arguably two different interpretations of the concept of "second-generation" peacekeeping. One interpretation focuses on the political aspect of peacekeeping, while the other is concerned with the level of force used during the operations.

Ratner defines "second-generation" peacekeeping from a political viewpoint:

> Second-generation operations, or "the new peace-keeping," are best defined as UN operations, authorized by political organs or the Secretary-General, responsible for overseeing or executing the political solution of an interstate or internal conflict, with the consent of the parties.[39]

The main function of second generation peacekeeping for Ratner is, thus, implementation of a political solution. Ratner lists the following characteristics of second-generation peacekeeping:[40]

- Second-generation peace-keeping operations can have a substantial or predominantly non-military mandate and composition;

- Second-generation peace-keeping has complex agendas as it includes the broad notion of peace-building;

- Second-generation peace-keeping responds not only to interstate conflicts but also to intrastate conflicts;

- Second-generation peace-keeping involves numerous types of actors such as guerrilla movements, domestic political parties, regional organisations, non-governmental organisations and foreign investors; and

- Second-generation peace-keeping is a "fluid phenomenon" and the mandate of an operation may be adjusted to respond to the political situation on the ground.

---

[38] James, *supra* note 29, p.252.

[39] Ratner, *supra* note 29, p.17.

[40] *Ibid.*, pp.22-24.

Comparing the two generations of peace-keeping, Ratner contends that there is "a clear shift in the purpose of the operations - from provisional to permanent peace, and from primarily military-centred missions to predominantly political ones".[41]

John Mackinlay and Jarat Chopra, Senior Research Associate, and Research Associate and Lecturer in international law at the Thomas J. Watson, Jr. Institute for International Studies, Brown University, discuss 'second generation' operations from the military viewpoint.[42] They consider the "enlarging span of legitimate military tasks" of the UN to be represented by the following continuum:[43] (a) conventional observer missions; (b) traditional peace-keeping; (c) preventive peace-keeping; (d) supervising a cease-fire between irregular forces; (e) assisting in the maintenance of law and order; (f) protecting the delivery of humanitarian assistance; (g) the guarantee of rights of passage; (h) sanctions; and (i) enforcement. They think that "[p]eace-keeping cannot be stretched any further to meet second generation contingencies", and claim that "[t]here is pressing need for a new category of international military operations somewhere between peace-keeping and large scale enforcement".[44]

In addition to two distinctly different interpretations of second-generation peacekeeping, there are some other terms and categorisations for new types of peacekeeping. For instance, Mackinlay introduces another categorisation of UN forces according to their particular size, which determines their different military capabilities and limitations.[45] Firstly, there are the high-level forces consisting of some hundreds of thousands of troops that operate against a designated aggressor to enforce certain objectives, therefore without the consent of parties to the conflict.[46] Secondly, the mid-level or 'multifunctional' forces consisting of tens of thousands of troops which are deployed along with civil elements of the UN. Such forces must be used impartially. Thirdly, there are the low-level forces or 'supervisory presence' of up to several thousand troops, which represent "a largely symbolic military deployment".[47] Regarding the second category, Mackinlay argues that the operation's success "probably relies more on the ability of the UN's

---

[41]   *Ibid.*, p.17.

[42]   Mackinlay and Chopra, *supra* note 29.

[43]   *Ibid.*, pp.116-117.

[44]   *Ibid.*, p.118.

[45]   John Mackinlay, 'Improving Multifunctional Forces', *Survival* 36(3), Autumn 1994: 149-73, p.158.

[46]   This category falls under the third-generation to be discussed below.

[47]   Mackinlay, *op. cit.*

civil elements to achieve a long-term political plan than its military strength".[48] This category therefore may overlap with Ratner's second-generation peacekeeping.

Charles Dobbie, the author of the UK Army Field Manual, *Wider Peace-keeping*, advocates the term "wider peace-keeping". The term describes "the wider aspects of peace-keeping operations carried out with the consent of the belligerent parties but in an environment that may be highly volatile".[49] "Wider peace-keeping" is based on a distinction "between 'operational' and 'tactical' levels of consent". Overall consent for an operation must be maintained continuously, and only a tactical use of force is permissible for the purposes of defending the mission which the UN force has been assigned, as well as for self-defence, so far as such use of force is appropriate, proportionate and reasonable.[50] Dobbie lists Cold War operations which involve such functions as conflict prevention, demobilisation and humanitarian aid as falling under the category of wider peacekeeping and affirms:[51]

> [I]ndeed, the 'Cold War' label given to those peace-keeping operations undertaken between 1948 and 1988 is misleading because it degrades their apparent relevance. When examined closely, the essential characteristics of contemporary wider peace-keeping operations differ little from the characteristics of those that went before.[52]

Professor Alan James, in common with Dobbie, prefers the term 'wider peace-keeping' to 'second-generation peace-keeping'. Prof. James contends that "expanded responsibilities and a tougher approach to executing them ... arguably, are not necessarily connected".[53] He points out that it is not clear

---

[48]   *Ibid.*

[49]   *Wider Peacekeeping*, HMSO, 1995, pp.2-5.

[50]   John Gerard Ruggie, 'The UN and the Collective Use of Force: Whither or Whether?', *International Peace-keeping* 3(4), Winter 1996: 1-20, p.10.

[51]   Dobbie, *supra* note 29, pp.129-130.

[52]   *Ibid.*, p.130. Note however that not all the proponents of the term, "second-generation" peacekeeping deny such relevance. Ratner, for example, classifies UNTEA/UNSF as a second-generation peacekeeping operation. He considers that ONUC includes traits of second-generation missions. Furthermore, UNFICYP and UNIFIL are given as examples of missions that deployed uniquely on the territory of one state, albeit with the explanation that the underlying disputes were interstate in nature. UNGOMAP is classified by Ratner as first-generation peace-keeping, but with traits of second-generation missions in terms of the task allotted to the Force of supervising the execution of a political settlement. Ratner, *supra* note 29, pp.12-23.

[53]   James, *supra* note 29, p.247.

how to strike a balance between different functions encompassed by second-generation peacekeeping, that is, between the common factors with the traditional peacekeeping operations and the new activity characterised as second-generation. Furthermore, Prof. James questions the concept's internal coherence.[54] The internal incoherence observed by Prof. James, in the present writer's view, is caused by the widespread use of the term, "second-generation", without probing what it really means. This confusion can be avoided, as shown in the examples below, by using more explanatory terminology.

In contrast to the division into traditional and new forms of peacekeeping, Marrack Goulding presents six types of peacekeeping according to their respective functions:[55] (i) "the *preventive deployment* of United Nations troops before a conflict has actually begun, at the request of one of the parties and on its territory only"; (ii) *traditional peace-keeping* "to support peacemaking efforts by helping to create conditions in which political negotiation can proceed", (iii) "operations set up to support *implementation of a comprehensive settlement* which has already been agreed by the parties"; (iv) "operations *to protect the delivery of humanitarian relief supplies* in conditions of continuing warfare"; (v) "*the deployment of a United Nations force in a country where the institutions of state have largely collapsed*"; and (vi) "*ceasefire enforcement*". Goulding's intention in presenting this taxonomy of peacekeeping was to reflect the evolution of peacekeeping since 1988. He mentions that Type Five is "arguably not peace-keeping at all" and that Type Six "is not really peace-keeping", since both involve enforcement. Type Five contains peacemaking and post-conflict peace-building elements as well, and its examples are ONUC in the Congo and UNOSOM in Somalia. Type Six can be seen in the context of the operation in Bosnia-Herzegovina where consent of the parties to the deployment of the force existed, but the force could open fire in situations other than self-defence.

Dr. William J. Durch, Senior Associate at the Henry L. Stimson Centre, introduces four basic types of "peace operations": traditional peacekeeping, multidimensional peace operations, humanitarian intervention, and peace enforcement.[56] Dr. Durch's "humanitarian intervention" corresponds to Goulding's Types Four and Five, and "peace enforcement" may cover Types One and Six. An example of Goulding's Type One is the operation in

---

[54]   *Ibid.*, pp.247-248.

[55]   Goulding, *supra* note 31, pp.456-460.

[56]   William J. Durch, ed., *UN Peace-keeping, American Politics, and the Uncivil Wars of the 1990s,* Macmillan, 1997, pp.3-7.

Macedonia[57] and Dr. Durch prefers to label it as "deterrent deployment," while he thinks that it can be considered as "a latent form of enforcement."[58] Dr. Durch probably deliberately used the term "peace operations", since he included peace enforcement as one category.

The categorisations by Goulding and Dr. Durch represent expanding activities of so-called peacekeeping operations. Have the principles of peace-keeping, which had been maintained during the first-generation, been altered along with this expansion? During his tenure as UN Secretary-General, Boutros Boutros-Ghali defined peacekeeping in his report, *Agenda for Peace,* as follows:

> *Peace-keeping* is the deployment of a United Nations presence in the field, hitherto with the consent of all the parties con-cerned, normally involving United Nations military and/or police personnel and frequently civilians as well. Peace-keeping is a technique that expands the possibilities for both the preven-tion of conflict and the making of peace. [59]

This short quotation shows us the flexibility of "peacekeeping" as a concept that can even be described as ambiguous. The word 'hitherto' implies the possibility that the condition of obtaining the consent of all the parties may be dropped.[60] The particular difficulty in securing the consent of the parties to the dispute has been proven in recent cases of intra-State conflicts. The Organisation's position in early peacekeeping operations was to obtain the consent of the legitimate government. This was because the negotiation with leaders of factions could be construed as recognition of their authority. However, in recent intra-State conflicts such as the case in Yugoslavia and

---

[57] The Security Council authorised establishment of a presence of the UNPROFOR in Macedonia under Resolution 795 of 11 December 1992. U.N. SCOR, 3147th mtg., UN Doc. S/RES/795(1992). Adopted unanimously. The mission was renamed to UNPREDEP by Security Council resolution 983 of 31 March 1995. U.N. SCOR, 3512th mtg., U.N. Doc. S/RES/983(1995).

[58] *Ibid.*, p.7.

[59] Boutros-Ghali, *supra* note 14, para.20.

[60] It is said that the word "hitherto" was added by Bourtros-Ghali to take account of the UN's preventive mission in Macedonia (established on 11 December 1992 as a part of UNPROFOR by Security Council resolution 795 and changed into UNPREDEP on 31 March 1995 pursuant to Security Council resolution 983), which was not deployed with the consent of the Serbs. Donald C. F. Daniel and Bradd C. Hayes, 'Securing Observance of UN Mandates Through the Employment of Military Force', *International Peace-keeping* 3(4), Winter 1996: 105-125, p.107.

Cambodia, consent of the factions was also sought.[61] The case of UNPROFOR in the former Yugoslavia nonetheless showed the great difficulty in making such consent effective when the consenting parties do not have sufficient control over the factions. UNTAC in Cambodia was an example of a peacekeeping force which continued its operation despite withdrawal of co-operation by one faction. This situation occurred because the operation concerned an intra-state conflict.[62] If it had been an operation related to an inter-state conflict, the presence of a UN force without the consent of the host state would have interfered with the provisions of Article 2(7) of the Charter, non-intervention in matters which are essentially within the domestic jurisdiction, unless the Security Council had decided to apply enforcement measures under Chapter VII.

Marrack Goulding's definition, which was cited in the previous Chapter, maintains the requirement of consent:

> Field operations established by the United Nations, with the consent of the parties concerned, to help control and resolve conflicts between them, under United Nations command and control, at the expense collectively of the member states, and with military and other personnel and equipment provided voluntarily by them, acting impartially between the parties and using force to the minimum extent necessary.[63]

Furthermore, it should be noted here that the word 'hitherto' in the above definition by Boutros-Ghali was omitted in his subsequent report to the 48th session of the General Assembly on 14 March 1994. The painful experience of UNOSOM II, which abandoned another traditional principle of peacekeeping, non-use of force except in self-defence, must have encouraged this restoration of the principle.

---

[61] White, *Keeping the Peace, supra* FN4 of Chapter 1, p.233. Although it can be argued that the conflict in the former Yugoslavia transformed into an international conflict, this analysis is valid in terms of the conflict within Croatia.

[62] Although the Party of Democratic Kampuchea suspended its co-operation with UNTAC, it did not resort to military action against the peacekeeping operation. David Wippman of Cornell Law School argues that the right to withdraw consent arises when all the communities jointly wish to do so. David Wippman, 'Treaty-Based Intervention: Who Can Say No?', *University of Chicago Law Review*, Spring 1995: 607-687, pp. 646-653.

[63] Goulding, *supra* note 31, p.455.

2.3 Third-Generation Peacekeeping

Flourishing images of post-Cold War peacekeeping gave rise to discussions on peacekeeping and increased the expectations with regard to maintenance of international peace and security by this method. A phrase in the UN Chronicle in 1993 shows the optimism then prevailing in the United Nations:

> UNOSOM II is the first UN peace-keeping operation authorized by the Council, under Chapter VII of the UN Charter, to use force in the crucial task of disarming Somali factions. In fact, with this enforcement mandate, UNOSOM II may well repres-ent the emergence of a third generation of peace-keeping operations, it has been said.[64]

UNOSOM was first established mainly for the purpose of humanitarian assistance in accordance with Security Council resolution 751 of 24 April 1992.[65] Owing to the deterioration of the situation in Somalia, the United Task Force (UNITAF) led by the United States was authorised to carry out a peace-enforcement operation by Security Council resolution 794 of 3 December 1992.[66] UNOSOM II then took over the UNITAF as a Chapter VII operation. Its mandate included a task "to prevent any resumption of violence and, if necessary, take appropriate action against any faction that violates or threatens to violate the cessation of hostilities".[67] The coercive demilitarisation operation of UNOSOM II raised the tension and 25 Pakistani soldiers were killed by General Aidid's faction. The UN continued the operation and suffered further serious casualties, including 18 deaths, and the coercive methods were abandoned through Security Council resolution 897 of 4 February 1994.[68]

Due to the optimism before the setback of UNOSOM II, further new theories and terms of peacekeeping came forward with their emphasis on greater use of force. As we have already discussed, second-generation peace-keeping, for those who used this term from a military perspective, meant a tougher approach to peacekeeping. It was, however, arguable that second-

---

[64] 'UN operations: Not only expanding, but breaking new ground', *UN Chronicle*, Vol.30, No.3, September 1993, p.44.

[65] SCOR, 3069th mtg., UN Doc. S/RES/751(1992). Adopted unanimously.

[66] SCOR, 3154th mtg., UN Doc. S/RES/794(1992). Adopted unanimously.

[67] *Report of the Secretary-General*, 3 March 1993, UN Doc. S/25354, SCOR 48 Supp. January-March 1993, pp.200-208.

[68] SC res. 897, 4 February 1994. SCOR, 3334th mtg., UN Doc. S/RES/897(1994). Adopted unanimously.

generation peacekeeping stretched the wider interpretation of self-defence to the limit. Third-generation peacekeeping, in contrast, envisages the use of military force beyond the principle of self-defence.

A new term preferred in the USA is "muscular peace-keeping",[69] under-pinned by the expectation of the greater role of peacekeeping operations with a higher level of military force. Dobbie has criticised the tendency in the USA to link peacekeeping and peace-enforcement [70]on a unitary scale:

> Indeed, the perception of a spectrum linking peace-keeping and peace-enforcement appears to dominate US thinking at all levels ... Peace-keeping is depicted as a scaled-down version of peace-enforcement. The pig is, in effect, regarded as a small species of parrot.[71]

Dobbie calls such arguments 'middle-ground theory', whichever term is used for describing operations, if characterised as being in between peace-keeping and enforcement, either 'Chapter VI 1/2', 'aggravated peace-keeping' or 'Level Two'.[72]

Goulding also warns of the danger of a grey-area linking peacekeeping and enforcement.[73] He emphasises the difference between operations which deploy with the consent and co-operation of the parties, on the one hand, and those without consent but with powers to use force to compel the parties, on the other hand.

Furthermore, Professor Adam Roberts affirms the difference in purpose and character between enforcement and peace-keeping.[74] Yet Prof. Roberts elsewhere argues that "[F]orce, and the threat of force, have a role in the new peace-keeping operations". It is conditioned, however, by situation, timing and manner.[75]

The other strong opponent of this grey-area is John Gerard Ruggie, Kirkpatrick Professor of International Affairs at Harvard University:

---

[69]   A. James, *supra* note 29, p.250.

[70]   Dobbie uses this term based on the definition of the Army Doctrine Publication, 'Operations': "operations carried out to restore peace between belligerent parties who do not all consent to intervention and who may be engaged in combat activities". Cited in Dobbie, *supra* note 29, p.122.

[71]   *Ibid.*, p.142.

[72]   *Ibid.*

[73]   Goulding, *supra* note 31, p.461.

[74]   Adam Roberts, 'From San Francisco to Sarajevo: The UN and the use of force,' *Survival* 37(4), Winter 95-96:7-28, p.7.

[75]   A. Roberts, *supra* note 16, p.104.

> The United Nations has entered a domain of military activity - a vaguely defined no-man's land lying somewhere between traditional peace-keeping and enforcement - for which it lacks any guiding operational concept. It has merely ratcheted up the traditional peace-keeping mechanism in an attempt to respond to wholly new security challenges.[76]

For Professor Ruggie, the political objective of UN forces is to deny military victory to any one side so that the combatants understand negotiated settlement as the only viable alternative. Thus the military objective is "to deter, dissuade and deny (D3)".[77]

The US Army Field Manual, FM100-23 of December 1994, distinguishes between peace operations and war-fighting; the former is subdivided into peacekeeping and peace enforcement. In peace enforcement, consent is not absolute and the use of force is permissible to coerce or compel, but not to defeat any belligerent.[78]

Donald C. F. Daniel and Bradd C. Hayes also affirm the existence of a third category in addition to peacekeeping and enforcement.[79] The third category, named "inducement", aims at containing a crisis. It does not have to have a targeted adversary and it functions only when "diplomatic efforts are underwritten by credible military force".[80] Daniel and Hayes recognise the criticism directed against such 'grey area' measures, but contend that it is the reality:

> Those who would ignore it, partly because they fear 'mission creep', are simply wishing the world were a less messy place in which to live.[81]

In terms of the provisions of the UN Charter, Daniel and Hayes mention that any 'inducement' operation must be sanctioned under Chapter VII of the UN Charter. If so, 'inducement' measures presumably are either measures recommended by the Security Council pursuant to Article 39 or provisional measures under Article 40, and 'full-fledged enforcement' action is under Article 42.

---

[76] John Gerard Ruggie, 'Wandering in the Void: Charting the U.N.'s New Strategic Role', *Foreign Affairs* 72(5), Nov/Dec 1993: 26-31, p.26.

[77] *Ibid.*, p.29.

[78] J. G. Ruggie, *supra* note 50, p.11.

[79] Daniel and Hayes, *supra* note 60, pp.108-110.

[80] *Ibid.*, p.110.

[81] *Ibid.*

3.   PEACEKEEPING AND ENFORCEMENT ACTION

The line between peacekeeping and enforcement action is not as clear as it may seem under superficial scrutiny. Yet it is important to distinguish the two, as, in the author's view, they are essentially different types of operation as regards objectives, means and their nature. We will take two steps to understand the distinguishable line between peacekeeping and enforcement. First, we will focus on enforcement action *per se*. Second, we will endeavour to draw the line between the enforcement action and peacekeeping operation.

3.1   Enforcement Action

The enforcement measure involving use of force envisaged by the drafters of the Charter was action pursuant to Article 42, although there is the possibility to take such measures under Articles 39 or 40. If the Charter provisions are interpreted literally however, no enforcement measures may be implemented under Article 42 of the UN Charter until armed forces become available to the Organisation in accordance with Article 43, which stipulates special agreements between the Organisation and its Member States on armed forces, assistance, and facilities. This was the argument made by the Soviet Union against the legality of UNEF and ONUC in the *Certain Expenses* case mentioned in the previous Chapter.[82] In its Advisory Opinion in the *Certain Expenses* case, the International Court rejected the Soviet view, stating:

> It cannot be said that the Charter has left the Security Council impotent in the face of an emergency situation when agreements under Article 43 have not been concluded.[83]

Also, the discussions at San Francisco made it clear that it was not a prerequisite for the implementation of Chapter VII that all the agreements under Article 43 should have been concluded.[84] The following represents the general view of jurists on this issue:

> The purpose of Article 43 was to *facilitate* action by the Security Council; it would be wholly alien to that purpose to

---

[82]   See 5 'Competence of the Security Council and the General Assembly to Create Peace-keeping Forces', Chapter 1, FN71-74 and accompanying text.

[83]   ICJ Rep. 1962, 151 at 167.

[84]   Goodrich *et al.*, *supra* note 34, pp.319 and 630-631.

argue that the absence of agreements under Article 43 should prevent action by the Security Council. In other words, Article 43 provides a procedure by which the Security Council *may* act, but it does not prevent the Security Council from choosing an alternative procedure.[85]

Professor Bowett refers to the importance of Article 43 in this context:

> The wording of Article 42 is broad, leaving open both the method of recruiting the Forces and the precise nature of their command. The absence of agreements under Article 43 merely ensures that States cannot be compelled to contribute to United Nations action under Article 42; but action under Article 42 may be recommended by the Security Council, pursuant to a finding under Article 39.[86]

We can therefore conclude that the absence of the agreements pursuant to Article 43 of the Charter does not prevent the Security Council from taking action under Article 42.[87]

Despite the legal possibility for the Security Council to resort to enforcement action, such practice has hardly been carried out. During the Cold War period, the only example of collective use of force under the flag of the Organisation was in the Korean War. On 25 June 1950, North Korean troops crossed the 38th parallel, which had been the partition line between North and South Korea since the Second World War. The Security Council, which was convened at the request of the United States, adopted Resolution 82 on 25 June.[88] This determined that the armed attack by North Korea constituted

---

[85] Malanczuk, *Akehurst's Modern Introduction to International Law, supra* FN16 of Chapter 1, p.417. Dr. White presents a similar view: "It would appear acceptable for the Council to use the power granted to it in Article 42 without the mechanisms that were designed to make the imposition of military coercion a practical option". White, *supra* note 61, p.117. Also see Shaw, *International Law, supra* FN9 of Introduction, p.868; and H. Kelsen, 'Collective Security and Collective Self-Defense under the Charter of the United Nations', *AJIL* 42, 1948: 783-96, p.786.

[86] Bowett, *United Nations Forces, supra* FN 64 of Chapter 1, p.277. Also see Higgins, *United Nations Peace-keeping 1946-1967: Documents and Commentary*, Vol.III, Africa, Oxford University Press, 1980, pp.176-177; and Shaw, *op. cit.*, p.868.

[87] From this analogy, authorisation to voluntary Member States to use force for a particular action, which has been the measure repeatedly taken by the Security Council recently, may be an option available to the Security Council. The problems pertaining to this practice will be discussed in Chapter 7.

[88] UN Doc. S/1501, SCOR, 473rd mtg. The vote was nine in favour and one abstention by Yugoslavia.

a 'breach of peace' under Article 39. Security Council resolution 83 of 27 June recommended "that the Members of the United Nations furnish such assistance to the Republic of Korea as may be necessary to repel the armed attack and to restore international peace and security in the area".[89] The legal basis of this operation has been construed in various ways. For example, Dr. White is of the opinion that it derives from Article 39 and possibly 42.[90] Professor Higgins more categorically states that it was an enforcement action taken under Articles 39 and 42, as far as the action was directed *against* North Korea.[91] Measures taken *against* any State was a criterion applied by the World Court in the *Certain Expenses* case for distinguishing enforcement from peacekeeping.[92] Professor Bowett regards the action as "enforcement action authorised by recommendations under Article 39".[93] Both Higgins and Bowett take into account that the participating States regarded their action as essentially UN action under the authority of the Security Council, but not as collective self-defence. Another view is that the Security Council, acting under Article 39, recommended participation in collective self-defence, so that the operation itself was collective self-defence pursuant to Article 51.[94] The author finds the last view the most tenable, since the operation was not actually under the command and control of the Organisation.[95] The same point applies to the Gulf crisis that started in 1990. In addition, the phrasing of Security Council resolution 82, "furnish such assistance to Korea ..." appears consistent with this view.

In the case of Iraqi aggression against Kuwait in August 1990, the United States and various Allies were already gathering in Saudi Arabia for the purpose of collective self-defence, in accordance with Article 51, when Security Council resolution 678 of 29 November 1990 authorised the following action:[96]

---

[89]   UN Doc. S/1511, SCOR, 474th mtg. The vote was seven in favour and Yugoslavia cast a negative vote.

[90]   White, *supra* note 61, p.123.

[91]   Higgins, *supra* note 86, p.177.

[92]   ICJ Report, 1962, p.30.

[93]   Bowett, *supra* note 86, p.34.

[94]   Simma, ed., *The Charter of the United Nations*, *supra* FN3 of Chapter 1, p.614.

[95]   See Bowett, *supra* note 86, pp.41-45. Also Shaw, *supra* note 85, p.867: "... although termed United Nations forces, the contingents from the sixteen states ... were not in any real sense directed by the United Nations other than operating under a general Security Council authorisation."

[96]   SCOR, 2963rd mtg., UN Doc. S/RES/678(1990). The vote was 12 in favour, 2 against (Cuba and Yemen), and one abstention by China.

Acting under Chapter VII of the Charter, ...

> 2. *Authorizes* Member States co-operating with the Govern-
> ment of Kuwait, unless Iraq on or before 15 January 1991 fully
> implements, as set forth in paragraph 1 above, the above men-
> tioned resolutions [Resolutions 660-662, 664-667, 669, 670,
> 674 and 677], to use all necessary means to uphold and
> implement resolution 660 (1990) [withdrawal of Iraqi force and
> start of negotiations between Iraq and Kuwait] and all sub-
> sequent relevant resolutions and to restore international peace
> and security in the area; ...".

This resolution resulted in "a relentless forty-three day air campaign against
Iraq in which the total tonnage of bombs dropped was in excess of that
exploded by the US in Indo-China over eight and a half years".[97] 'To take
necessary means/measures' is the typical phrase in Security Council
resolutions when military action is envisaged. The operation casts doubt on
the adherence to the principle of proportionality in the use of force, as well
as on the nature of the operation, that is, whether it was collective self-
defence or enforcement action under Chapter VII.

When the military operation in accordance with Security Council
resolution 678 started, the Organisation lost control over the operation,
although it received reports from the Allies subsequent to the events. The
Allied states gathered in Saudi Arabia were prepared to exercise their right
to collective self-defence under Article 51. For example, a UK Government
spokesman stated in the House of Lords:

> ... the multinational force deployed in the Gulf is not a United
> Nations force. The question of United Nations command does
> not arise, therefore. British and other forces have been deployed
> at the request of Saudi Arabia and other countries in accordance
> with the inherent right of individual or collective self-defence
> under Article 51 of the United Nations Charter.[98]

However, in accordance with the Charter, the right envisaged under Article
51 is subject to suspension when the Security Council takes measures
necessary to maintain international peace and security. Security Council
resolution 661 of 6 August 1990 called for sanctions within the ambit of

---

[97]   Kaiyan Homi Kaikobad, 'Self-Defence, Enforcement Action and the Gulf Wars, 1980-88
       and 1990-1991', *BYIL* 63, 1992: 299-366, p.333. See FN 128 citing the figures.
[98]   HL Debs., vol.523, cols. 775-6, *passim*: 22 November 1990, cited in 'United Kingdom
       Materials on International Law 1990', *BYIL* 1990, p.630.

Article 41 under Chapter VII after mentioning the right of self-defence in its preamble:[99]

> Affirming the inherent right of individual or collective self-defence, in response to the armed attack by Iraq against Kuwait, in accordance with Article 51 of the Charter, ...

The previously mentioned Resolution 678, which was interpreted as an authorisation for the use of force against Iraq, did not make any determination under Article 39, which is a prerequisite for a Chapter VII operation. If the adoption of sanctions under Resolution 661 suspended Kuwait and its Allies' right of self-defence, Resolution 661 is self-contradictory. Professor Oscar Schachter affirms that Kuwait's right of self-defence had never been suspended. Therefore he is of the view that the use of force was neither enforcement action under Chapter VII in general nor pursuant to Article 42 in particular, but rather collective self-defence under Article 51.[100] This view is supported by the fact that the Organisation had no control over the operation. Professor Schachter drew this conclusion despite his awareness that if the operation was self-defence the Security Council's authorisation was unnecessary, explaining that Resolution 678 served the political purpose of underlining the support of the United Nations for the military measures.[101] Dr. Kaiyan Homi Kaikobad, of the University of Durham, contends that the existence of the right is a fact, but that it is different from the exercise of the right. Resolution 661, he continues, merely confirmed the existence of the right. However, on the grounds that self-defence does not require the Security Council's authorisation, Dr. Kaikobad considers that the Allies' operation was "a species of UN action authorised by the Council under Chapter VII".[102] Dr. Kaikobad further contends:

> There is nothing in the Charter or Chapter VII which suggests that joint military measures effected by States on the basis of an express authorization by the Council cannot constitute enforcement measures, either because they are not expressly based in Article 42 or because the Council is not in actual command of the operations.[103]

---

[99]   SCOR, 2933rd mtg., UN Doc. S/RES/661(1990). 13 in favour and two abstentions, by Cuba and Yemen.

[100]   Oscar Schachter, 'United Nations Law in the Gulf Conflict', 85 *AJIL* 1991: 452-473, pp. 458-460.

[101]   *Ibid.*

[102]   Kaikobad, *supra* note 97, pp.351-354.

[103]   *Ibid.*, p.360.

The author disagrees with the interpretation of Dr. Kaikobad. Interpretation of Article 42 in conjunction with Article 106, which stipulates temporary measures pending the coming into force of Article 43, provides the possibility that the Security Council is able to take enforcement action without the agreements stipulated under Article 43.[104] However, an enforcement action authorised by, but beyond the command and control of, the Security Council, is utterly different from the collective security measures envisaged in the Charter. In contrast to the case of the Korean War, the participating States in the Gulf action maintained that their actions were collective defence. It may be argued that, as the Security Council was not equipped with the means to implement a large-scale military operation of the type carried out by the Allies, at least Kuwait's right to self-defence had not been suspended by resolutions of the Security Council which, in any event, endorsed the action. Yet it does not mean that the measures taken by the Security Council, authorising an operation involving a significant use of force without exerting any control over it, was desirable for an organ which has the primary responsibility for the maintenance of international peace and security. The Security Council ended up being a mere observer in a case involving considerable violations of international law by Iraq. In the light of the collective security mechanism envisaged in the Charter, it was desirable that the Security Council had fulfilled its role by executing control and command of an enforcement action in such a case. If the Security Council considers the Allied forces' operation as one under Chapter VII, or specifically under Article 42, the author would argue that the Security Council gravely failed in discharging its responsibility under the Charter.

3.2 Legal Distinction between Peacekeeping and Enforcement Action

There are several factors which make it difficult to draw a clear line between peacekeeping and enforcement action. Firstly, as peacekeeping itself developed out of the practice of the United Nations' mechanism for international peace and security, we are not able to rely on explicit provisions of the Charter to define it. Secondly, because of the absence of the agreements pursuant to Article 43, the Security Council has actually employed an alternative procedure in regard to enforcement action which is to authorise states

---

[104] But note the view of Professor Bowett that the failure to implement Article 43 cannot be said to have extended Article 106's application indefinitely. Bowett, *supra* note 86, p.277. In any case, the provisions of Article 42 can be interpreted as allowing flexible measures to set up a force.

to voluntarily carry out particular enforcement operations. We thus have the burden of distinguishing something with undefined contours from something else which is taking on a different form from the procedure envisaged by the Charter. Thirdly, UN resolutions tend not to identify any specific article on which they are based. This promotes political compromise and flexibility in the implementation of the relevant resolutions, but makes an already complex legal analysis even harder. Finally, it is common for the mandate of a peacekeeping mission to be expanded or changed according to the altering situation. UN forces have therefore been entrusted with both functions of peacekeeping and enforcement as in the case of UNOSOM.

As referred to above, the World Court's criterion for distinguishing enforcement action in the *Certain Expenses* case was whether the measures were taken *against* a State. The military actions taken in the Korean War and the Gulf crisis were against North Korea and Iraq respectively, although the possibility of considering these operations as collective self-defence remains.[105] To put it differently, no lawyer would argue that these operations were peacekeeping.

The core question to be asked regarding the recent discussion on third-generation peacekeeping is whether it is actually peacekeeping. From what we have examined, we may conclude that third-generation peacekeeping identifies itself with peace-enforcement, and from now on this term will be used instead of third-generation peacekeeping. If we consider that peace-enforcement is one category of peacekeeping, then one of the main traditional principles of peacekeeping, limitation of the use of force to self-defence is not valid any more. Legally speaking, it is the Security Council which has to decide on how to describe the measures they have selected for maintenance of international peace and security as far as the description is consistent with the Charter. Thus "peace-enforcement" can be named "third-generation peacekeeping" if the Security Council so wishes. Politically or strategically, we may argue that by dropping this principle, we will lose the merits of peacekeeping which have proved its validity through history. The present writer supports this view, but this is a different discussion from the legal one which we are trying to evolve here.[106]

---

[105] *Supra* FN 94 & 95 and accompanying text.

[106] This view is quite common among those who worked as peacekeepers. See, for example, Sir Michael Rose, 'Field Coordination of UN Humanitarian Assistance, Bosnia, 1994', in Jim Whitman and David Pocock, eds., *After Rwanda: The Coordination of United Nations Humanitarian Assistance*, Macmillan, 1996: 149-160, pp.150-151; Bertrand de Lapresle, 'Principles to be Observed: for the Use of Military Forces Aimed at De-escalation and Resolution of Conflict': 137-152, pp.141 & 147; and Wolfgang Biermann and Ole Frederik Ugland, 'Lessons Learned in the Field: A Survey of UNPORFOR Officers': 81-

The recent UN practice regarding the use of force has been described in two different ways. One is to say that peace-enforcement is an enforcement measure which fall short of enforcement actions and that it belongs to one of the various categorisations referred to in relation to the third-generation peacekeeping above.[107] According to this argument, the Article 42 operation is war-fighting, but peace-enforcement is use of force to coerce or compel, not to defeat (US Army Field Manual).[108] The other way is, as some leading legal scholars do, to affirm the existence of enforcement elements in recent peacekeeping.[109]

It is noteworthy that prominent legal scholars affirm that peacekeeping and enforcement should be clearly distinguished. For instance, Professor Higgins states:

> Enforcement should remain clearly differentiated from peace-keeping. Peacekeeping mandate should not contain an enforcement function. To speak of the need for more "muscular peace-keeping" simply evidences that the wrong mandate has been chosen *ab initio*.[110]

Professor Malanczuk also asserts:

> 'Mixed peace-keeping' trying to incorporate enforcement elements confuses the different legal basis and functions of enforcement action, on the one hand, and peacekeeping, on the other. The two forms of UN action should remain clearly differentiated.[111]

4. PEACEKEEPING, PEACEMAKING AND PEACE-BUILDING

The Security Council considers an increasingly broad range of factors in reviewing international peace and security. In a statement issued by the President of the Council subsequent to a meeting on the responsibility of the

---

122, pp.91-94, both in Wolfgang Biermann and Martin Vadset, eds., *UN Peacekeeping in Trouble: Lessons Learned from the Former Yugoslavia: Peacekeepers' Views on the Limits and Possibilities of the United Nations in a Civil War-like Conflict*, Ashgate, 1999.

[107] *Supra* 2.3 'Third-Generation Peace-keeping'.

[108] *Supra* note 78 and accompanying text.

[109] For instance, Malanczuk, *supra* note 85, p.416; and Shaw, *supra* note 85, pp.870 & 876.

[110] Rosalyn Higgins, 'Second-Generation Peacekeeping', *ASIL Proceedings*, 1995, p.279.

[111] Malanczuk, *supra* note 85, p.425.

Security Council in maintaining international peace and security, held at the level of heads of State and Government on 31 January 1992, it was affirmed that:

> The absence of war and military conflicts amongst states does not in itself insure international peace and security. The non-military sources of instability in the economic, social, human-itarian and ecological fields have become threats to peace and security. The United Nations membership as a whole needs to give the highest priority to the solution of these matters. The members of the Council pledge their commitment to inter-national law and to the United Nations Charter. All disputes between states should be peacefully resolved in accordance with the provisions of the Charter. The members of the Council reaffirm their commitment to the collective security system of the Charter to deal with threats to peace and to reverse acts of aggression.[112]

The recognition that various non-military sources of instability may threaten peace and security is consistent with the wider range of reasons to set up peacekeeping operations. In the case of Somalia it was "human suffering" and "human tragedy" which was the threat to international peace and security.[113]

Adam Roberts warns that "[T]here is a much more interventionist element in peace-keeping today and this is at the heart of the crisis".[114] He points out the downgrading of the importance of consent in peacekeeping, by giving examples of Iraq and the former Yugoslavia. In northern Iraq, the Kurd-inhabited 'safe havens' were established without the consent of the state government,[115] whereas Security Council resolution 743 of 21 February 1992 mandated UNPROFOR a Chapter VII operation with reference to Article 25.[116] It should be noted that Chapter VII operations evade the

---

[112] *Statement of the President of the Security Council*, UN Doc. SCOR, 3046th mtg., 31 January 1992.

[113] SC res. 767, 27 July 1992, SCOR, 3101st mtg., UN Doc. S/RES/767(1992); and SC res. 794, SCOR, 3154th mtg., UN Doc. S/RES/794(1992). Both resolutions were adopted unanimously.

[114] Roberts, *supra* note 16, p.99.

[115] This was, however, not a UN peacekeeping operation.

[116] SC res. 743, 21 February 1992. SCOR 3055th mtg., UN Doc. S/RES/743(1992). Adopted unanimously.

restriction of Article 2(7), non-intervention in matters which are essentially within the domestic jurisdiction of any state. Article 2(7) reads:

> Nothing contained in the present Charter shall authorize the United Nations to intervene in matters which are essentially within the domestic jurisdiction of any state or shall require the Members to submit such matters to settlement under the present Charter, but this principle shall not prejudice the application of enforcement measures under Chapter VII.

Once the Security Council decides to invoke Chapter VII in regard to a peacekeeping operation, the targeted state is not able to rely upon its domestic sovereignty in order to refuse the action of the Organisation.

Michael Barnett, of the Department of Political Science at the University of Wisconsin, distinguishes juridical sovereignty and empirical sovereignty, in other words, external and internal sovereignty. Based on juridical sovereignty, "states recognise each other's existence and honor the principle of non-interference".[117] Empirical sovereignty means that "states have some degree of legitimacy and control over their society and within their borders".[118] Barnett explains that there has been a cognitive shift from juridical sovereignty to empirical sovereignty and that the shift has altered the UN's peacekeeping duties.

> Peace-keeping operations were invented to deal with problems emerging from decolonization and the globalization of sovereignty and, in this respect, reflected the understanding that juridical sovereignty and territorial integrity further international order.[119]

Barnett argues that the contemporary international community is more concerned with empirical sovereignty, noting that new peacekeeping operations such as UNTAG in Namibia, UNTAC in Cambodia, ONUSAL in El Salvador or UNOSOM in Somalia dealt with internal security and domestic order.[120]

In the Security Council President's statement mentioned above, the UN peacekeeping operations were reviewed in the following terms:

---

[117] Michael Barnett, 'The New United Nations Politics of Peace: From Juridical Sovereignty to Empirical Sovereignty', *Global Governance* 1, 1995:79-97, p.80.

[118] *Ibid.*

[119] *Ibid.*, p.81.

[120] *Ibid.*, pp.91-92.

The members of the Council note that United Nations peace-keeping tasks have increased and broadened considerably in recent years. Election monitoring, human rights verification and the repatriation of refugees have in the settlement of some regional conflicts, at the request or with the agreement of the parties concerned, been integral parts of the Security Council's effort to maintain international peace and security. The members of the Council welcome these developments.[121]

This is exactly the evolution of peacekeeping from a political viewpoint which was examined above as one of the two interpretations of the "second-generation" peace-keeping. Such multifunctional peacekeeping contains elements of peacemaking and peace-building. Boutros Boutros-Ghali presented the definition of peacemaking as:

Peacemaking is action to bring hostile parties to agreement, essentially through such peaceful means as those foreseen in Chapter VI of the Charter of the United Nations.[122]

The concept of post-conflict peace-building was explained as:

... action to identify and support structures which will tend to strengthen and solidify peace in order to avoid a relapse into conflict.[123]

A peace agreement or a cease-fire agreement is usually concluded before deployment of a peacekeeping operation. However, in case the agreement is broken or more detailed agreements are required, peacekeepers support the negotiation of conflicting parties. Furthermore, peacekeepers often promote reconciliation at community levels, which can be a part of peacemaking efforts and at the same time peace-building. As a principle of the Organisation, peaceful settlement of a conflict is always preferred to enforcement. The various peacekeeping measures, including peacemaking and peace-building, which are often conducted by civilian components of peacekeeping operations have significant potentiality.[124] The more sources of

---

[121] *Supra* note 112.

[122] Boutros-Ghali, *supra* note 14, para.20.

[123] *Ibid.*

[124] For instance, UNOSOM II in Somalia, mainly known for its military action, involved much in peace-building activities including establishment of a police force, reopening of courts in the capital city as well as development of the judicial and penal systems in other areas. Sonia K. Han, 'Building a Peace that Lasts: The United Nations and Post-Civil War

threats to peace and security that are recognised, the wider the range of activities of peacekeepers can grow. In non-military peacekeeping measures, we still need to consider the issue of sovereignty when a peacekeeping operation is set up to deal with internal conflicts as suggested by Barnett.

The bulk of this book will focus on human rights functions of peace-keeping operations. Human rights functions in peacekeeping operations are not an entirely new enterprise. The United Nations Truce Supervision Organisation (UNTSO) observed compliance with the Arab Armistice Agreements that covered return of displaced civilians and rights of prisoners of war.[125] UNTSO reported to the UN Headquarters that the existing resources of UNTSO prevented it from investigating allegations about the treatment of civilian population.[126] The United Nations Peace-Keeping Force in Cyprus (UNFICYP) contributes to the maintenance and restoration of law and order as a part of its mandate and reported, for instance, "the excesses by individual policemen in the course of searching and seizing civilians".[127] The human rights functions of peacekeeping operations are certainly expanding their sphere. In some operations, a unit which exclusively deals with human rights issues was set up and their activities range from monitoring, investig-ating and reporting human rights violations, to human rights education as well as assistance of judicial reform. In the following four chapters, peace-keeping operations and one human rights field operation which worked along with a peacekeeping operation in four conflict areas will be studied, with special focus on their human rights functions.

The underlying questions running through the four case studies will be: how can a peacekeeping operation contribute to human rights protection and promotion in a (post-)conflict area? To examine this question, it is essential to clarify the reason why the operation was set up, the objective of the operation, and the means given to the operation. For this purpose, the mandate and the composition of the operation need to be scrutinised. In other words, the starting point is whether human rights problems are addressed in the mandate and whether the composition reflects the mandate. The next question then is how the mandate was carried out. Were there qualified personnel and proper training? What were the main human rights issues in the operation area? Did those issues change during the course of operation?

Peace-Building', *New York University Journal of International Law and Politics*, Summer 1994: 837-892, pp. 865-866.

[125] Higgins, *United Nations Peace-keeping 1946-1967, Vol.I*, *supra* FN43 of Chapter 1, pp.33-50.

[126] *Ibid.*, p.57. U.N. Doc. S/7930/Add. 14, 23 June 1967.

[127] Higgins, *United Nations Peace-keeping, Vol.IV*, *supra* FN31 of Chapter 1, pp.129-130.

What was the interaction with the host state? Did the co-operation inside the peacekeeping force and with outside agencies/organisations work? At the end of each case study, what that particular peacekeeping operation could actually achieve in terms of human rights functions will be discussed.

Chapter 3

Human Rights Functions of the United Nations Observation Mission in El Salvador

1.   HISTORICAL BACKGROUND

During the 1980s, El Salvador suffered a civil war which resulted in some 75,000 deaths and over 1 million refugees and internally displaced persons.[1] One of the root causes of the civil war was the extreme concentration of wealth: in El Salvador about 85 per cent of the land belonged to fourteen families.[2] Edelberto Torres-Rivas, Professor of Social Science at the University of Costa Rica, describes this war:

> It was not a civil war against a single, particular dictatorship, but rather a revolution against a political system and, as such, it had much in common with class wars, which history indicates is the bloodiest type of conflict.[3]

The major parties to the civil war were the Government, supported by the USA,[4] and Frente Farabundo Martí para la Liberación Nacional (FMLN),

---

[1]   *The United Nations and El Salvador 1990-1995* (hereinafter, *The UN and El Salvador*), The United Nations Blue Books Series, Volume IV, United Nations Department of Public Information, 1995, Section I, p.7, para.14.

[2]   Graciana del Castillo, 'The arms-for-land deal in El Salvador', in Michael W. Doyle, Ian Johnstone and Robert C. Orr, eds., *Keeping the Peace: Multidimensional UN Operations in Cambodia and El Salvador*, Cambridge University Press: 342-365, p.344.

[3]   Edelberto Torres-Rivas, 'Insurrection and civil war in El Salvador', in M. W. Doyle *et al.*, eds., *op. cit.*: 209-226, p.221.

[4]   The US policy was centred on anti-Communist ideology. The US Government supported the El Salvador Government by financial assistance as well as military advice. Owing to the US support, the Armed Forces of El Salvador expanded from 10,000 in 1979 to 24,000 in 1982, and further to 56,000 in 1987. Tommie Sue Montgomery, *Revolution in El Salvador: From Civil Strife to Civil Peace*, Westview Press, 2nd ed., 1995, p.149. After the end of the civil war, the need of demobilisation of a large number of soldiers became a major problem. For the military involvement of the USA in El Salvador beyond supplying weapons, see Montgomery, pp.164-174.

which was supported by Cuba, Nicaragua and the USSR.[5] Both sides were responsible for acts of brutality against civilians including arbitrary detentions, death-squad killings, and disappearances.

On 15 December 1980, the UN General Assembly adopted resolution 35/192 deploring the "murders, disappearances and other violations of human rights reported in El Salvador", and urged the Government to "take the necessary steps to ensure full respect for human rights and fundamental freedoms in that country".[6] The UN Commission on Human Rights appointed a Special Representative to report on the situation of human rights in El Salvador in 1983. Meanwhile the "Contadora Group", which consisted of Colombia, Mexico, Panama and Venezuela, initiated regional peace-making efforts through a series of consultations with five Central American Governments, namely Costa Rica, El Salvador, Guatemala, Honduras and Nicaragua. In 1985, the Contadora effort was strengthened by the creation of a Support Group composed of Argentina, Brazil, Peru and Uruguay.

In May 1986 a declaration, which is known as Esquipulas I, was issued to affirm the five Central American Presidents' commitment to peace, co-operation and national sovereignty.[7] On 7 August 1987, the Presidents signed the *Procedure for the Establishment of a Firm and Lasting Peace in Central America*.[8] This was the Guatemala Procedure, or Esquipulas II, by which the five Presidents undertook to launch a process of democratisation in their countries, to promote a national dialogue, to decree a general amnesty, to bring about a genuine cease-fire and to promote the holding of free, pluralistic and fair elections. The Governments of these five countries requested all the Governments concerned to terminate support for irregular forces or insurrectional movements and reiterated their commitment to prevent the use of their own territories for the destabilisation of other countries in the region. An International Verification and Follow-up Commission (CIVS) was set up in order to support these objectives, involving the

---

[5]   The FMLN was created on 10 October 1981 as a result of the extraordinary surge of the masses after the death of Archbishop Oscar Arnulfo Romero, a leading human rights advocate. His assassination on 24 March 1980, was one of the egregious incidents during the civil war. See The Commission on the Truth for El Salvador, *From Madness to Hope: The 12-year War in El Salvador* (hereinafter, *Truth Commission Report*), UN Doc. S/25500, 1 April 1993, IV.D. The FMLN was a union of five major revolution organisations. E. Torres-Rivas, *supra* note 3, p.220.

[6]   UN Doc. A/RES/35/192. Recorded vote of 70 to 12 with 55 abstentions. 10 out of the 12 countries who objected to the resolution were Central and South American countries, including El Salvador herself.

[7]   UN Doc. A/40/1119-S/18106. SCOR 41.

[8]   UN Doc. A/42/521-S/19085. SCOR 42.

Foreign Ministers of the Contadora and Support Groups and of the five Central American countries, as well as the Secretaries-General of the United Nations and of the Organisation of American States (OAS).[9] Further, in November 1989 the Security Council established the United Nations Observer Group in Central America (ONUCA), the first United Nations peacekeeping operation in the western hemisphere.[10] The primary mandate of ONUCA was to patrol the borders of the five countries in order to monitor their compliance with the security commitments made in the Esquipulas II Agreement.

The Government of El Salvador and the FMLN commenced a dialogue on 15 September 1989. The FMLN sought agreement on wide-ranging reforms, particularly of the army, before its own demobilisation, while the Government insisted that the FMLN should lay down its arms first. On 31 October 1989, an explosion in a trade union hall derailed negotiations.[11] On 11 November 1989 the FMLN launched a large-scale offensive which affected parts of the capital for the first time. On 16 November 1989, six Jesuit priests as well as their housekeeper and her daughter were assassinated.[12] Ironically, these incidents, which resulted in the loss of hundreds of lives, demonstrated the impossibility of a military victory by either party to the dispute, and as a consequence of this realisation serious negotiations were resumed.

The peace process in El Salvador consisted of a series of agreements. The first of these is the San José Agreement on Human Rights signed by the two

---

[9] OAS first used an observer group, the Inter-American Peace Force, in 1965 during the Dominican crisis. Simma, ed., *The Charter of the United Nations*, *supra* FN3 of Chapter 1, p.601.

[10] SC res. 644 of 7 November 1989. SCOR, 2890th mtg., UN Doc. S/RES/644(1989). Adopted unanimously. UN observation operations are quite often considered as types of peacekeeping operations and ONUCA has been regarded as a peacekeeping operation. See Chapter 1, FN32 & 33 and accompanying text. During the Cold War, no peacekeeping operation could be expected in this region where the US had dominant political influence. See Brian D. Smith and William J. Durch, 'UN Observer Group in Central America', in Durch, ed., *The Evolution of UN Peace-keeping*, St. Martin's Press, 1993: 436-362, p.436.

[11] *Truth Commission Report*, IV.B.2.(j). The explosion killed a prominent leader of the National Trade Union Federation of Salvadorian Workers among others.

[12] *Truth Commission Report*, IV.B.1. These incidents resulted in a change of the US policy which had supported the government and the armed forces of El Salvador. George R. Vickers, 'The Political Reality After Eleven Years of War', in Joseph S. Tulchin with Gary Bland, ed., *Is There a Transition to Democracy in El Salvador?*, Lynne Reinner Publishers, 1992: 25-57, p.37.

parties on 26 July 1990.[13] The United Nations Observation Mission in El Salvador (ONUSAL) was established in accordance with this agreement. Concluding an agreement on human rights at such an early stage suggests that the Government did not consider its likely impact to be significant.[14] Pedro Nikken, an advisor to the United Nations negotiating team, who was subsequently appointed by the UN Human Rights Commission as the Independent Expert, drafted the agreement. It has been argued that, as the parties were not expected to sign the agreement, it was drafted to include very ambitious provisions.[15] However, in comparison with other political agendas, especially the military reform, human rights proved to be a good concession.[16] The Government did not fully appreciate the implications of accepting a resident verification mission.

On 27 April 1991, the parties signed the Mexico Agreements which contained a package of reforms relating to the army, the public security, the judicial system and the electoral system.[17] On 25 September 1991 the parties also signed the New York Agreement. This concerned the establishment of the Comisión Nacional para la Consolidación de la Paz (National Commission for the Consolidation of Peace, a forum of political parties), reduction of the armed forces, determination of a new doctrine of the armed forces in conformity with the peace settlement, the process of establishing the National Civil Police, and land redistribution.[18] The entire package of peace accords was finally signed at Chapultepec Castle, Mexico, on January 16, 1992 (Chapultepec Agreement).[19] The Accords provided for a cease-fire that was to be effective as of 1 February 1992.

---

[13] *Note verbale dated 14 August 1990 from El Salvador transmitting text of the Agreement on human rights signed at San José, Costa Rica, on 26 July 1990 between the Government of El Salvador and the FMLN*, UN Doc. A/44/971-S/21541, 16 August 1990.

[14] Lawyers Committee for Human Rights, *Imposing History: A Critical Evaluation of the United Nations Observer Mission in El Salvador* (hereinafter *Lawyers Committee Report*), December 1995, pp.7-8.

[15] *Ibid.*

[16] Mark LeVine, 'Peacemaking in El Salvador', in M. W. Doyle *et al.*, eds., *supra* note 2: 227-254, p.235.

[17] *Letter dated 8 October 1991 from El Salvador transmitting the text of the Mexico Agreement and annexes signed on 27 April 1991 by the government of El Salvador and the FMLN*, UN Doc. A/46/553-S/23130, 9 October 1991. See *infra* note 47-52 and accompanying text.

[18] *Letter dated 26 September 1991 and 4 October 1991 from El Salvador transmitting texts of the New York Agreement and the Compressed Negotiations, signed on 25 September 1991 by the Government of El Salvador and the FMLN*, UN Doc. A/46/502-S/23082.

[19] UN Doc. A/46/864-S/23501, 30 January 1992.

2.   COMPOSITION AND MANDATE OF ONUSAL

In accordance with the San José Agreement, ONUSAL was intended "to investigate the human rights situation in El Salvador as regards acts committed or situations existing as from the date of its establishment and to take any steps it deems appropriate to promote and defend such rights".[20] ONUSAL was initially a human rights verification mission, which later became a multidimensional peacekeeping operation. It was the first attempt by the UN to deploy such a mission before a cease-fire.[21]

ONUSAL was instituted on 26 July 1991 and its international staff numbered 101 by 15 September,[22] of which 42 were human rights observers and advisers, legal advisers, educators and political affairs officers.[23] There were also 15 military advisers and 16 police advisers.[24] ONUSAL established four regional offices in San Salvador, San Vicente, San Miguel and Santa Ana, as well as two sub-offices in Chalatenango and Usultan.[25] A "human rights co-ordinator" headed each of the regional offices.

ONUSAL's mandate was set forth as follows:[26]

(a) To verify the observance of human rights in El Salvador;

(b) To receive communications from any individual, group of individuals or body in El Salvador, containing reports of human rights violations;

(c) To visit any place or establishment freely and without prior notice;

(d) To hold its meetings freely anywhere in the national territory;

(e) To interview freely and privately any individual, group of individuals or members of bodies or institutions;

---

[20]   San José Agreement, *supra* note 13.

[21]   Ian Johnstone, *Rights and Reconciliation: UN Strategies in El Salvador*, Lynne Reinner Publishers, 1995, p.19.

[22]   *First report of the United Nations Observer Mission in El Salvador* (hereinafter *ONUSAL First Report*), Annex to *Report of the Secretary-General on ONUSAL and first report of the ONUSAL Human Rights Division*, UN Doc. A/45/1055-S23037, 16 September 1991, para.9.

[23]   *Ibid.*

[24]   *Ibid.*

[25]   *Ibid.*, para.10. See Map 1.

[26]   Paragraph 14 of the *San José Agreement*.

(f) To collect by any means it deems appropriate such information as it considers relevant;

(g) To make recommendations to the Parties on the basis of any conclusions it has reached with respect to cases or situations it may have been called upon to consider;

(h) To offer its support to the judicial authorities of El Salvador in order to help improve the judicial procedures for the protection of human rights and increase respect for the rules of due process of law;

(i) To consult the Attorney-General of the Republic;

(j) To plan and carry out an educational and informational campaign on human rights and on the functions of the Mission itself;

(k) To use the media to the extent useful for the fulfilment of its mandate;

(l) To report regularly to the Secretary-General of the United Nations and through him to the General Assembly.

The human rights mandate of ONUSAL is precise when compared with that of other missions.[27] It nevertheless has its limitation. The first report of the Director of the Human Rights Division of ONUSAL notes:[28]

There are very high, and in some cases inordinate, expectations of the Mission. Vast numbers of Salvadorians right across the political spectrum believe that the Mission will be able to prevent, or at least punish, human rights violations. Even though the Mission will try to fulfil the expectations which the Salvadorian people have of it, it is worth remembering that while its verification possibilities are considerable, it does not have the power to prevent violations or to punish violators. As a result, far from attempting to replace the institutions responsible for ensuring the protection and promotion of and respect for human rights, the Mission will assist Salvadorians in the effort to ensure unrestricted exercise of those rights. ....

---

[27]　This point will be developed in the following chapters.

[28]　*First Report of the Director of the Human Rights Division* (hereinafter *Human Rights Division First Report*), Appendix to *ONUSAL First Report*, para.16. See *supra* note 22.

These are common problems among human rights monitoring/observation missions. When such missions start these investigations, the local population naturally expects that justice will be achieved by the relevant international organisation, in this case, the UN. However, monitoring/observation missions cannot replace national judicial systems. "Monitoring" or "Observation" are the terms favoured by the Organisation with respect to human rights operations. They have been safe technical terms to avoid giving the impression of interfering with the sovereignty of the states subject to such operations. The mandate of monitoring or observation implies that the missions do not intend to take actions on their own accord to redress the situation. The missions instead depend on the political influence they have over the national governments, to ensure compliance with international standards of human rights protection.

Another point of difficulty at the early stage of ONUSAL was the continuation of the armed conflict in El Salvador:

> The misconception of the Mission's mandate seems to derive from the expectation that ONUSAL will give its opinion on military actions or aspects which do not fall within its mandate. This expectation has arisen because ONUSAL began its verification work before the cessation of the armed conflict. ... Its mandate is to verify compliance with the San José Agreement and to report thereon to the Secretary-General; its mandate does not include making public statements on what it has observed.[29]

In view of the progress of the peace process, the Security Council decided by resolution 729 of 14 January 1992, upon the enlargement of ONUSAL's mandate to include the verification and monitoring of the implementation of all the agreements between the Government of El Salvador and the FMLN.[30] For this purpose, a Military Division and a Police Division were established. ONUSAL thus became a multidimensional peacekeeping operation. The two Divisions' tasks were set forth in the Peace Agreement between the Government of El Salvador and the FMLN, signed in Mexico City on 16 January 1992.[31] The Military Division was responsible for verifying the cessation of the armed conflict.[32] The tasks of the Police Division were to co-operate in

---

[29] *Second Report of the United Nations Observer Mission in El Salvador* (hereinafter *ONUSAL Second Report*), UN Doc. A/46/658-S/23222, 15 November 1991, para.4.

[30] SC res. 729 of 14 January 1992. SCOR, 3030th mtg., UN Doc. S/RES/729(1992). Adopted unanimously.

[31] UN Doc. A/46/864-S/23501, 30 January 1992.

[32] *Ibid.*, Cessation of the Armed Conflict, Chapter VII.

ensuring a smooth transition and in assisting police authorities, as well as to accompany officers and members of the National Police in the performance of their duties.[33] According to the *Report of the Secretary-General on ONUSAL,* on 25 February 1992, the number of staff in the Military and Police Divisions was 368 and 147, respectively.[34] The same report states that the Human Rights Division was staffed by 51 civilian professionals and 14 police observers assigned by the Police Division.[35]

Despite the creation of two other divisions, the Human Rights Division maintained a special autonomous status. The Human Rights Division sent periodic reports directly to the UN Secretary-General and, through him, to the General Assembly. However, the creation of other divisions affected the reporting structure of the mission. Therefore the human rights co-ordinators, under certain circumstances, had to report to the head of the mission, besides reporting to the head of the division. This unclear chain of command was amended only in July 1994, when the co-ordinators were renamed "regional chiefs".[36]

From late 1992, the central team of the Human Rights Division in San Salvador included a Case Verification Unit which was "responsible for tracking and reporting on cases and situations", and an Administration of Justice and Institution Building Unit, which provided "technical cooperation to the judicial system, the PNC [National Civil Police], the Human Rights Ombudsman, and the nongovernmental organisations".[37]

In November 1992, the Police Division was expanded to 303 observers, of whom 18 were seconded to the Human Rights Division.[38] By contrast, the Military Division was reduced to 290 as of May 1992,[39] to 226 as of Novem-

---

[33]   *Ibid.*, National Civil Police, Section 7, Transitional Regime, B.e.

[34]   *Report of the Secretary-General on ONUSAL*, UN Doc. S/23632, 25 February 1992, paras.2 & 3.

[35]   *Ibid.*, para.4. 14 police observers were included in 147 staff in the Police Division mentioned above.

[36]   *Lawyers Committee Report*, pp.16-17.

[37]   Reed Brody, 'The United Nations and Human Rights in El Salvador's "Negotiated Revolution"', *Harvard Human Rights Journal*, Spring, 1995: 153-178, p.160. Reed Brody was director of the Human Rights Division of ONUSAL from 1994 to 1995.

[38]   *Report of the Secretary-General on the activities of ONUSAL*, UN Doc. S/24833, 23 November 1992, paras.31 & 32.

[39]   *Letter dated 15 May 1992 from the Secretary-General to the President of the Security Council concerning ONUSAL military observers*, UN Doc. S/23987, 20 May 1992.

ber 1992,[40] and to 74 as of May 1993.[41] This change in composition of the mission reflects the general improvement of the security situation in El Salvador and, in turn, the shift of the mission's focus.

Upon the request of the Government of El Salvador, the Security Council decided in Resolution 832 of 27 May 1993, to further expand the mandate of ONUSAL to include observation of the electoral process leading up to the general elections which were scheduled for March 1994.[42] The Electoral Division was established in September 1993 and 36 professional staff were deployed in 6 regional offices. The primary task of the Electoral Division was to observe the following: the impartiality of all electoral authorities; the voters' registration process; the mechanisms preventing multiple voting; respect for freedom of expression, organisation, movement and assembly; and voters' education, as well as to examine, analyse and assess criticisms, objections and attempts aiming at illegitimatising the electoral process.[43]

ONUSAL ended its mission on 30 April 1995, and a mission with a limited role and staffing, the United Nations Mission in El Salvador (MINUSAL), was initiated and started functioning on 1 May 1995. It consisted of eleven professionals and seven civilian police consultants. MINUSAL was further followed up by the United Nations Office of Verification in El Salvador (ONUV; 1 May - 31 December 1996) and the Support Unit (1 January - 30 June 1997).[44] Both ONUV and the Support Unit were established pursuant to General Assembly resolutions.[45] Neither of them were peacekeeping operations but ONUV was a verification operation and the Support Unit consisted of a few officers who supported an envoy of the Secretary-General making periodic visits to El Salvador for the purpose of a good offices function. The systematic monitoring of human rights violations, however, has virtually ended with the closure of ONUSAL.[46]

---

[40] *Report of the Secretary-General on the activities of ONUSAL*, UN Doc. S/24833, 23 November 1992, para.83.

[41] *Report of the Secretary-General on all aspects of ONUSAL's operations*, UN Doc. S/25812, 21 May 1993, para.14.

[42] SC res. 832 of 27 May 1993. SCOR, 3223rd mtg., UN Doc. S/RES/832(1993). Adopted unanimously.

[43] *Report of the Secretary-General on the activities of the ONUSAL Electoral Division*, UN Doc. S/1994/304, 16 March, 1994, II.2.

[44] Teresa Whitfield, 'Staying the Course in El Salvador', in Alice H. Henkin, ed., *Honoring Human Rights: From Peace to Justice*, Washington: The Aspen Institute, 1998: 163-188, p.165.

[45] GA res. 50/226, 10 May 1996; and GA res. 51/199, 17 December 1996.

[46] Whitfield, *op. cit.*

3. INSTITUTIONAL REFORMS RELEVANT TO HUMAN RIGHTS

In addition to the human rights observation activities undertaken by ONUSAL, the peace process in El Salvador initiated several reforms related to human rights. A remarkable step was achieved within the Mexico Agreement, signed on 27 April 1991.[47] Among other features, the Agreement provided for the creation of the National Civil Police (Policia Nacional Civil: PNC);[48] a new procedure for the election of Supreme Court judges;[49] the creation of a National Counsel for the Defence of Human Rights;[50] an annual allocation to the judicial system of no less than 6 per cent from the State budget;[51] as well as the formation of a Commission on the Truth to investigate "serious acts of violence that have occurred since 1980 and whose impact on society urgently requires that the public should know the truth".[52] Although the detailed analysis of these reforms is beyond the scope of this book, it should be noted that these reforms were important measures for enhancing the promotion and protection of human rights in El Salvador, which could not have been achieved by ONUSAL alone. Some of these reforms will be briefly reviewed before an analysis is made of the human rights activities of ONUSAL.

3.1   The National Civil Police

The existing police organs in El Salvador at the time of the Mexico Agreement were the National Police, the National Guard, and the Treasury Police. They were all part of the armed forces. During the civil war, the armed forces and the security forces were the principal perpetrators of systematic and extensive human rights violations.[53] Therefore, the establishment of a police force under civilian control, completely independent from the armed forces, was an important element of the peace process. The Government and the FMLN agreed that the new force would receive training at a new police academy, the National Academy of Public Security

---

[47]   UN Doc. A/46/553-S/23130, 9 October 1991.

[48]   Article 1(b) of Part I.

[49]   Article 1(a) of Part II.

[50]   Article 1(c) of Part II.

[51]   Article 1(b) of Part II.

[52]   Part IV.

[53]   *Truth Commission Report*, IV.A.

(Academia Nacional de Seguridad Publica: ANSP). The ANSP's training was designed in accordance with modern civilian police doctrines and techniques, including respect for human rights.[54] During the transitional period, both former FMLN combatants and National Police members were allowed to enter the ANSP, each taking up to 20% of the places, while the remaining 60% was reserved for civilians who had not participated in the conflict. The police reforms did not take place as initially agreed, mainly due to the reluctance of the Government to enhance the reform process. For instance, the military tried to maintain the National Guard and the Treasury Police, which were supposed to be dissolved immediately, by changing their names to the Border Guard and the Military Police, respectively. The Government also tried to transfer a large number of personnel from the both units to the National Police.[55]

The Police Division of ONUSAL was responsible for the co-ordination and supervision of the international effort at the ANSP, as well as for monitoring the ANSP's compliance with the Peace Accords. However, advising and training at the ANSP was undertaken by an international technical team, separate from ONUSAL. The team consisted of five national contingents, namely Norway, Spain, Sweden, Chile and the US. Of these, Norway, Spain and Sweden joined the ANSP through the United Nations Development Programme (UNDP), while the latter two did so through a bilateral agreement between the US and the Salvadoran government.[56] A commentator has pointed out that some contingents were civilian while others were military: "This did not make much sense given that the ultimate purpose was to create an entirely new civilian police force."[57]

In cases of international assistance in the future as referred to above, it would be worth studying which international model of police system and doctrine is appropriate. It is also worth studying whether such assistance could be included in a peacekeeping operation, or would be better as a separate project of technical assistance.

---

[54] Article 6 of Constitutional Reform, amendment to the Constitution of El Salvador Article 168(17). Also Gino Costa, 'The United Nations and Reform of the Police in El Salvador', *International Peacekeeping* 2(3), Autumn 1995:365-90, p.366.

[55] *Report of the Secretary-General on the activities of ONUSAL since the cease-fire (1 February 1992) between the Government of El Salvador and the FMLN*, UN Doc. S/23999, 26 May 1992, para.30.

[56] Costa, *op. cit.*, p.383.

[57] *Ibid.*

3.2   The National Counsel for the Defence of Human Rights

The role of the National Counsel for the Defence of Human Rights (Ombudsman) was particularly important in relation to the human rights function of ONUSAL. The main functions of the National Counsel were set forth by an amendment of the El Salvador Constitution: to investigate cases of human rights violations, to promote judicial or administrative remedies, to monitor the situation of persons deprived of their liberty, to monitor state organs, to recommend legislation, and to propose systemic reforms.[58]

However, as Timothy A. Wilkins, an American attorney, remarks, the Ombudsman's authority was limited. Firstly, it lacked direct jurisdiction over any matters and it could only work through other State organs. Secondly, since the Ombudsman did not have political power, it relied on moral persuasion. Thirdly, its funding was controlled by the executive branch.[59] Despite such defects, the establishment of the Ombudsman was one of the most significant improvements realised by the El Salvador peace process in the area of human rights.[60]

3.3   The Commission on the Truth

The Commission on the Truth, consisting of three foreign dignitaries appointed by the UN Secretary-General after consultation with the Government of El Salvador and the FMLN, assumed responsibility for investigating past human rights violations in accordance with the Mexico Agreement, while ONUSAL Human Rights Division dealt with recent or present abuses.[61] The Commission was set up on 15 May 1992 and received 2,000 direct testimonies as well as information from secondary sources relating to more than 20,000 victims.[62] The Commission delivered its final report to the Secretary-General and to President Cristiani on 22 September 1992. The report of the Commission named perpetrators of crimes both on the side of the Government and of the FMLN. At the outset, military and civilian

---

[58]   Mexico Agreement, Constitutional reform, Article 16.

[59]   Timothy A. Wilkins, 'The El Salvador Peace Accords: using international and domestic law norms to build peace', in M. W. Doyle *et al.*, eds., *supra* note 2: 255-281, p.260.

[60]   Regarding interaction between the Counsel and ONUSAL Human Rights Division, see *infra* 4.7 'Institution-building'.

[61]   Regarding the activities of and reflections on the Commission, see Thomas Buergenthal, 'The United Nations Truth Commission for El Salvador', *Vanderbit Journal of Transnational Law*, October 1994: 497-544.

[62]   *Truth Commission Report*, I.I.

authorities pressured the Commission to identify the individuals responsible so that the institutions would bear no collective responsibility.[63] Later the Commission was pressured not to publish any names. The report includes a wide range of recommendations for administrative, legislative, and constitutional changes, but many were ignored or delayed. In particular, El Salvador's Legislative Assembly passed legislation granting total amnesty to those guilty of extra-judicial crimes during the war, soon after the release of the report.[64] However, one important achievement of the Commission was to secure acceptance by the Legislative Assembly, following the recommendation of the Commission, of the compulsory jurisdiction of the Inter-American Court of Human Rights over future human rights violations, and the ratification of the Optional Protocol to the International Covenant on Civil and Political Rights, as well as of the Optional Protocol to the American Convention on Human Rights concerning economic, social and cultural rights (San Salvador Protocol).[65]

Truth commissions have been used as a tool to recover truth in various countries in transitional period from conflict to peace.[66] Truth commissions are normally not given prosecutorial or judicial powers, but may serve for purposes of reconciliation, deterrence and social reform. Unlike the criminal justice system, truth commissions look into "various social or political factors which led to the violence, or the internal structure of abusive forces, such as death squads or the intelligence branch of the armed forces".[67] This tool of justice lacks the function of retribution. However, that is often the very reason why this tool is chosen, i.e., for the sake of avoiding the destabilisation of the society under transition. Professor Thomas

---

[63] *Ibid.*, I.F.

[64] *The UN and El Salvador*, Introduction, V, para.115.

[65] *Lawyers Committee Report*, pp.138-139.

[66] Regarding different settings of truth commissions, see, for example, Priscilla B. Hayner, 'Fifteen Truth Commissions – 1974 to 1994: A Comparative Study', *Human Rights Quarterly* 16, 1994: 597-655; Priscilla B. Hayner, 'Commissioning the truth: further research questions', *Third World Quarterly* 17(1), 1996: 19-29; Mark Ensalaco, 'Truth Commission for Chile and El Salvador: A Report and Assessment', *Human Rights Quarterly* 16, 1994: 656-675; and Geoffrey Robertson, *Crimes Against Humanity: The Struggle for Global Justice*, Allen Lane The Penguin Press, 1999, pp.248-259. Also regarding diverse mechanisms to seek accountability, see M. Cherif Bassiouni, 'Searching for Peace and Achieving Justice: The Need for Accountability', *Law and Contemporary Problems*, 1996: 9-28; Richard J. Goldstone, 'Justice as a Tool for Peace-Making: Truth Commissions and International Criminal Tribunals', *New York University Journal of International Law and Politics*, 1996: 485-503; and Steven Ratner, 'The Schizophrenias of International Criminal Law', *Texas International Law Journal*, 1998: 237-256.

[67] Hayner, *op. cit.*, p.21.

Buergenthal, one of the three members for the Commission in El Salvador, underlines the healing effect of the truth commission:

> One could not listen to them without recognising that the mere act of telling what had happened was a healing emotional release, and that they were more interested in recounting their story and being heard than in retribution. It is as if they felt some shame that they had not dared to speak out before and, now that they had done so, they could go home and focus on the future less encumbered by the past.[68]

Prof. Burgenthal also affirms that the presence of ONUSAL in El Salvador helped the work of the Commission not only by being a source of logistic support but also by stabilising the situation:

> ... the fact that ONUSAL's military, police, and civilian personnel had offices and could be seen all over El Salvador also had an important pacifying effect on the country. It kept the combatants and their supporters apart, it diffused dangerous situations, and gave both sides a feeling of relative security. By the time the commission arrived in El Salvador, ONUSAL had succeeded in creating a political and social climate that greatly facilitated the task of the Commission.[69]

3.4   The *Ad Hoc* Commission

The establishment of the *Ad Hoc* Commission was agreed within the terms of the New York Agreement.[70] Composed of three Salvadoran civilians appointed by the Secretary-General after consultation with the Government and the FMLN, the Commission was in charge of evaluating military officers. The criteria of the evaluation were (1) records of observance of human rights; (2) professional competence; and (3) capacity to function "in the new situation of peace, within the context of a democratic society".[71] The Commission was given only three months to evaluate more than 2,000 military officers, and therefore limited its evaluation to 232 of the most senior officers and issued its report on 22 September 1992, which was kept confidential. To many people's surprise, the Commission recommended the

---

[68]   Buergenthal, *supra* note 61, p.539.

[69]   *Ibid.*, p.542.

[70]   See *supra* note 18 and accompanying text.

[71]   Johnstone, *supra* note 21, p.30.

discharge of the entire senior military establishment. Despite strong resistance from the military, the recommendation was implemented, albeit with delay.

These measures of reforming the police and military, of creating a national mechanism to address human rights violations, and of redressing past human rights abuses, progressed along with ONUSAL's human rights work. Without such measures, ONUSAL would not have been able to see the change in the Salvadorian society as much as it did at the end of its operation.

4. ACTIVITIES OF ONUSAL'S HUMAN RIGHTS DIVISION

4.1 Recruitment and Education of Officers

Among 42 staff initially employed by the Human Rights Division, some 16 human rights monitors and legal officers were hired from the NGO community.[72] A criterion was set not to hire staff with previous work experience in El Salvador and to avoid citizens of the US or of neighbouring Central American countries.[73] The Division's senior staff discovered, on arrival, that many of those hired to be human rights observers, "had no knowledge either of law, human rights or fact-finding".[74] Before their deployment, the first contingent of monitors received one week of training, including briefings from Division Director, a Salvadoran Army officer, the then head of the government human rights office, and Supreme Court President.[75] Nevertheless a week's training was considered insufficient according to the assessment and recommendation of the senior staff.

4.2 Main Human Rights Abuses

Because of the continuing armed conflict in El Salvador, from the outset ONUSAL devoted special attention to the observance of certain rights, namely the right to life, to integrity and security of the person and to personal liberty. Protection of the civilian population and the right to

---

[72] *Lawyers Committee Report*, p.45.
[73] *Ibid.*, p.46.
[74] *Ibid.*
[75] *Ibid.*, p.47.

personal freedom of displaced persons and of returnees, and of all persons in conflict zones, were other matters of specific concern.[76]

In a report dated 15 November 1991, the Human Rights Division summarised its findings on each category of human rights violations and presented its recommendations.[77] The report underlined the defects in police work with regard to the right to life and the security of the person.[78] The report also referred to clandestine leaflets and the broadcasting on radio or television of threatening messages,[79] which were obviously against the peace process. To avoid a large number of complaints of disappearances, which did not always correspond with an enforced or involuntary disappearance, the Division recommended the establishment of flexible mechanisms to inform complainants of the whereabouts of the persons concerned.[80] Respect for legal norms, including international humanitarian law, was called for in order to prevent torture and cruel, inhuman or degrading treatment or punishment and for the protection of civilians.[81] The Division recommended an urgent proposal to the Legislative Assembly to adopt a special provisional law for the provision of proper documentation to displaced persons, returnees and all persons living in conflict zones.[82] Lack of identification, which otherwise can be the basis of legal rights, is a common problem in conflict areas. With respect to military recruitment, the Division recommended the prompt enactment of a special law regarding compulsory military service, as well as the dissemination of the Ministry of Defence regulations on military recruitment procedures and the granting of exemptions from compulsory military service.[83] Furthermore, the Division referred to the violation of the provisions of Protocol II by the FMLN regarding the recruitment of children under the age of 15, and requested the observance of the rules of international humanitarian law.[84] Mentioned at the end of the report was the need for structural reforms of the criminal justice system, while stating that it would be premature to make an overall evaluation of the judicial system.

---

[76]   *Human Rights Division First Report*, para.24.

[77]   *Report of the Director of the Human Rights Division* (hereinafter *Human Rights Division Second Report*), Annex to the *ONUSAL Second Report*, UN Doc. A/46/658-S/23222.

[78]   *Ibid.*, paras.149-151.

[79]   *Ibid.*, para.152.

[80]   *Ibid.*, paras.153-154.

[81]   *Ibid.*, paras.155-159.

[82]   *Ibid.*, paras.160-163.

[83]   *Ibid.*, paras.165-168.

[84]   *Ibid.*, paras.167-170.

This was the result of the observation of ONUSAL's Human Rights Division during the initial three months. The real value of the Division's work, however, lies in its efforts to implement its own recommendations, as we will see below, following an overview of the change in human rights situation.

4.3 Change in the Human Rights Situation

The cease-fire established in February 1992 resulted in a decline in the number of allegations of human rights violations, particularly in former conflict zones.[85] The Human Rights Division of ONUSAL stated in its report for the period from 1 May to 31 July 1993 that there had been no reports of enforced disappearances during a period of 13 months.[86] However, the Division reported at the same time that grave violations involving the right to life, such as politically motivated arbitrary executions and torture, persisted and had even grown worse.[87]

When the election was approaching, a number of murders raised fears about the possible resurgence of illegal armed groups, including the so-called death squads. In responding to the concern that the situation may gravely hamper the peace process, a Joint Group for the Investigation of Politically Motivated Illegal Armed Groups was established. The Group consisted of four members: two representatives of the Government, the National Counsel for the Defence of Human Rights, and the Director of the Division of Human Rights of ONUSAL.[88] The Group issued its report at the end of July 1994, without naming any responsible individuals. The report confirmed the existence of the death squads, but denied the involvement of the state.[89]

The last report of ONUSAL's Human Rights Division stated that the number of complaints of arbitrary executions was gradually decreasing, and

---

[85] *Report of the ONUSAL Human Rights Division for the period from 1 January to 30 April 1992*, UN Doc. A/46/935-S/24066, 5 June 1992, para.2.

[86] *Report of the ONUSAL Human Rights Division for the period from 1 May to 31 July 1993*, UN Doc. A/47/1012-S/26416, 15 September 1993, para.6.

[87] *Ibid.*

[88] *Principles for the establishment of a joint group for the investigation of politically motivated illegal armed groups*, Annex to *Letter dated 7 December 1993 from the Secretary-General to the President of the Security Council concerning implementation of the recommendations of the Commission on the Truth regarding the investigation of illegal groups*, UN Doc. S/26865, 11 December 1993.

[89] For more details on the Joint Group, see Ian Johnstone, 'Rights and reconciliation in El Salvador', in Doyle *et al.*, eds., *supra* note 2: 312-341, pp.323-325.

that cases of a politically motivated nature had reduced in number.[90] The report did, however, refer to the continuing existence of organised crime networks in El Salvador, which could threaten political and social stability.[91]

Owing to the fundamental change from a conflict to a post-conflict situation, the issues of concern *vis-à-vis* human rights violations had also changed. The legal focus had shifted from humanitarian law to human rights law in general, and continuing efforts were required in institution-building of the judicial system as well as of the rule of law.[92]

4.4   Relationship with State Agencies

During the period from 26 July to 30 September 1991, the Human Rights Division of ONUSAL started its work by liaising with various organs of the State and their auxiliary services, as well as with the Public Prosecutor's Office, the armed forces and local authorities.[93] Contacts were also secured with the FMLN.[94]

From 1 October 1991, the Human Rights Division stepped up its activities by pursuing the investigation of cases and of situations involving human rights violations and also by following-up such cases and situations

---

[90]   *Report of the ONUSAL Human Rights Division covering the period from 1 July to 30 September 1994*, UN Doc. A/49/585-S/1994/1220, 31 October 1994, para.107.

[91]   *Ibid.*, para.110.

[92]   Professor Theodor Meron points out that the term "international humanitarian law" is somewhat misleading as it consists not only of "the law of Geneva" but also of "the law of The Hague". Theodor Meron, 'International Humanitarian Law and Human Rights Law', in Daniel Warner, ed., *Human Rights and Humanitarian Law: The Quest for Universality*, Martinus Nijhoff Publishers, 1997: 97-195, p.99. A part of international humanitarian law provides for protection of human rights through regulations of the armed conflicts. There is, therefore, an overlap between international humanitarian law and international human rights law. However, human rights treaties are subject to derogations in state of emergency except for certain non-derogable rights. Commentators increasingly underline the complementarity of the two systems of law, particularly in the situations of internal armed conflicts. See, for instance, Meron, *op. cit.*, Rosemary Abi-Saab, 'Human Rights and Humanitarian Law in Internal Conflicts'; and Cornelio Sommaruga, 'Humanitarian Law and Human Rights in the Legal Arsenal of the ICRC', both in Warner, ed., *op. cit.*: 107-123 and 125-133, respectively. Also David Petrasek, 'Moving Forward on the Development of Minimum Humanitarian Standards', *AJIL* 92, 1998: 557-563; and David Weissbrodt, 'Ways International Organizations Can Improve Their Implementation of Human Rights and Humanitarian Law in Situations of Armed Conflict', in Lutz *et al.*, eds., *New Directions in Human Rights*, *supra* FN9 of Introduction: 63-90. Regarding the derogations, see *infra* FN120 of Chapter 4.

[93]   *Human Rights Division First Report*, para.2.

[94]   *Ibid.*, para.3.

with the competent State organs.[95] Regular working meetings were held with an inter-agency group of the Salvadorian Government. The group was co-ordinated by the Executive Secretary of the governmental Human Rights Commission and consisted of representatives of the Supreme Court of Justice, the Armed Forces General Staff, the Office of the Attorney General and the Ministry of Foreign Affairs.[96] Periodic co-ordination meetings were also held with the FMLN Political and Diplomatic Commission in Mexico City or Managua.[97] Human rights officers made frequent visits to mayors' offices, departmental governments, military and police units, law courts and other public entities.[98] It is one thing to secure a forum of dialogue between a UN peacekeeping operation and host state agencies, whereas the fruitfulness of such dialogue is quite another matter.

ONUSAL applied a policy of frankness and transparency in dealing with the Government and the FMLN. It informed them of cases of alleged human rights violations attributed to them, and also gave them ONUSAL's views and assessments as to how the parties were fulfilling their commitments under the San José Agreement.[99] ONUSAL's self-assessment was optimistic:

> This direct dialogue has served to build mutual trust and has
> allowed ONUSAL to make recommendations in the hope that
> these will lead to an improvement in the human rights situation
> in the country.[100]

Their optimism was clearly misplaced. Their initial strategy of "avoiding confrontations with Salvadoran officials"[101] did not secure the mutual trust and co-operation they sought. Instead it raised criticism from international commentators that ONUSAL was compromising its own objectives in the name of co-operation.[102]

ONUSAL later attempted to change its strategy and to apply a more aggressive and critical approach. For example, the Human Rights Division gave the El Salvador Supreme Court a list of judges who had acted improperly, for investigation and disciplinary purposes. The ONUSAL's

---

[95] *Human Rights Division Second Report*, para.4.

[96] *Ibid.*, para.5.

[97] *Ibid.* The continuing armed conflict was the reason to set up meetings outside El Salvador.

[98] *Ibid.*

[99] *Ibid.*, para.6.

[100] *Ibid.*

[101] This was the instruction in the orientation session for new ONUSAL staff. *Lawyers Committee Report*, p.21.

[102] *Ibid.*, p.25.

action met with a strong reaction by President Calderón Sol, who took it as an insult to "national dignity".[103] Their relationship with the judiciary was seen to be an extremely uncooperative one: "judges were frequently defensive about ONUSAL inquiries into legal cases; in extreme instances, a judge would refuse to share copies of papers bearing on a case."[104] Supreme Court President Mauricio Gutiérrez himself publicly expressed the view that the judiciary, as an independent branch of government, is not bound by the peace accords, which were signed by the executive branch and the FMLN.[105] ONUSAL, thus, did not receive the full co-operation of the local public institutions in regard to its mandate "to collect by any means it deems appropriate such information as it considers relevant".[106]

The effectiveness of any UN peacekeeping operation always depends on a balance between receiving co-operation from host agencies and unilaterally pursuing mission objectives. The first step to ensure the co-operation is to have a written agreement that sets out the mandate of the operation between the Organisation and the host state. However, at the level of implementation of the agreement, one major determining factor can be the sincerity of the host government that signed the agreement. Another vital factor is the actual control the host Government exercises over its own agencies. In case of ONUSAL's Human Rights Division, although the agreement was sufficiently precise and the mandate was clearly set out, the operation faced various problems during its implementation.

4.5   Investigation

By November 1991, ONUSAL had received over one thousand complaints of alleged human rights violations.[107] By May 1992, the number reached

---

[103] *Ibid.*, p.110.

[104] Americas Watch, *El Salvador - Peace and Human Rights: Successes and Shortcomings of the United Nations Observer Mission in El Salvador (ONUSAL)*, 2 September, 1992, p.20.

[105] *Ibid.*, p.10. Similar situation was found in police work as well. Sub-Director for Operations advised his agents to disregard human rights doctrine taught at the ANSP (Police Academy). William Stanley and Robert Loosle, 'El Salvador: The Civilian Police Component of Peace Operations', in Robert B. Oakley, Michael J. Dziedzic, and Eliot M. Goldberg, eds., *Policing the New World Disorder: Peace Operations and Public Security*, Institute for National Strategic Studies, text available at: http://www.ndu.edu/inss/books/policing/chapter4.html (visited on 4 November 2001), 14/19.

[106] *San José Agreement*, Para 14(f).

[107] *Ibid.*, para.12.

4,528, of which 3,307 were declared "admissible".[108] The number of complaints does not necessarily represent the number of actual human rights abuses. However, the increase in the number of complaints shows the local population's knowledge of and trust in the work of ONUSAL.

The Human Rights Division of ONUSAL elaborated a method of "active verification". This was "a systematic investigatory procedure designed to gather objective evidence to corroborate the existence of human rights violations".[109] The procedure consisted of four phases. Firstly, the Mission received complaints or reported a violation on the Mission's own initiative. Secondly, the investigation or inquiry proper was carried out including a detailed follow-up of the facts, as well as police and judicial investigations and the exercise of the Mission's fact-finding powers. Thirdly, if the finding concluded that there was no violation of human rights, the case was closed. If verification revealed the opposite, recommendations were made either for compensation for the injury or for rectifying the situation which had caused the violation. Fourthly, the Mission used its good offices throughout the process in order to contribute to the transparency and efficiency of police investigations, due process, safety of witnesses, etc.

ONUSAL probably set its own limits to its investigations. Legal officers in one regional office attempted to assume an attorney/client relationship with persons coming in to file a complaint. However, the regional co-ordinator, who had no human rights experience, considered that his staff should limit themselves to merely recording cases. In a UN peacekeeping operation where a clear hierarchy exists, the decision of a higher ranking officer, in this case the regional co-ordinator, prevails. Even during the late stage of ONUSAL, staff were instructed "to verify that a violation had occurred, not to solve the crime".[110] This is the typical approach of the Organisation based on the mandate of human rights "monitoring" or "observation". The victims were instructed to go to the courts, and the Division used its 'good offices' for verification.[111] Yet one of the attorneys rightly affirmed that "[i]f the system was not working, then that *is* [sic] the violation".[112] It is important to encourage those alleging human rights

---

[108] *Report of the ONUSAL Human Rights Division for the period from 1 May to 30 June 1992*, U.N. Doc. A/46/955-S/24375, 12 August 1992, para.79.

[109] *Report of the ONUSAL Human Rights Division for the period from 1 July 1992 to 31 January 1993* (hereinafter *Human Rights Division Sixth Report*), UN Doc. A/47/912-S/25521, 5 April 1993, para.41.

[110] *Laywers Committee Report*, p.73.

[111] *Human Rights Division Sixth Report*, para.41.

[112] *Lawyers Committee Report*, p.73.

violations to use the local judicial system. After all, a UN presence does not last forever, so that the local population needs to learn how to cope with the existing system. What a human rights division of a peacekeeping operation can do is to monitor the function of the domestic system, to support those alleging human rights violations, and to encourage necessary reforms to the domestic system. The point is that one can interpret 'good offices' in a limited sense or accord it a more expansive function.

In addition to case investigations, ONUSAL also took an active interest in El Salvador's judicial system. They analysed the documentation of recently decided cases to discern whether or not the due process of law had been followed. They also analysed the day-to-day practice of the courts.[113] In November 1992, the Human Rights Division carried out a simultaneous and unannounced verification of twenty-six municipal and police jails throughout the country.[114] This was deemed necessary by ONUSAL because of the massive and systematic practice of arbitrary detention in El Salvador. A series of irregularities were identified as a result of checking "the entry-book information for each of the detainees, their dates of detention, the reason for their detention, and the time they had spent in detention".[115] Approximately 3,500 to 5,000 persons were being detained per month for minor offences such as drunkenness or vagrancy and were held incommunicado, without access to defence counsel.[116] These verification activities undertaken by the Human Rights Division was one of the factors that was used to identify the existing problem and to formulate solutions.

4.6   Reporting

Certain uniform reporting criteria were established in November 1992, some 15 months after the launch of the Human Rights Division, with the elaboration of a Methodological Guide.[117] Until that time, each regional office developed its own approach and style without any co-ordination. Even the classification of cases was carried out differently in the various offices.[118]

---

[113] *Human Rights Division Second Report*, para.171.

[114] Diego García-Sayán, 'Human Rights and Peace-keeping Operations', *University of Richmond Law Review*, 1994: 41-65, p.57. Diego García-Sayán was director of the Human Rights Division of ONUSAL from October 1992 to 1994.

[115] *Ibid.*

[116] Americas Watch, *supra* note 104, p.22.

[117] *Guía Metodológica para el Trabajo de la División de Derechos Humanos de la Misión de Observadores de las Naciones Unidas para El Salvador,* 6 November 1992. *Ibid.*, p.70.

[118] *Lawyers Committee Report*, p.71, also Americas Watch, *supra* note 104, p.19.

ONUSAL issued thirteen reports in total. The number of copies printed in El Salvador was 1,500, which automatically limited the number of potential readers.[119] The reports were submitted to the Chief of Mission before being sent to New York. At the early stage of ONUSAL's work, particularly before the January 1992 cease-fire, cases were dropped for political reasons in this process.[120]

Despite ONUSAL's mandate that explicitly sets forth the right to make use of the media, the main publications of ONUSAL were a series of reports to the UN Secretary-General and, through him, to the General Assembly. The reports obviously were not addressed to the people of El Salvador. This approach by ONUSAL was criticised:

> ONUSAL's reticence to make frequent public declarations on specific human rights cases was a significant missed opportunity. By broadly publicising its findings, the mission could have conveyed to Salvadorans a clearer sense of international and domestic criteria for human rights, and clarified a number of cases that initially appeared to be politically motivated but which proved otherwise upon further investigation. Had it clarified such cases, the mission might have increased public confidence in the early phases of the peace process and might also have had greater impact when it reported on other cases that were, in fact, political in nature.[121]

The reason for ONUSAL's reluctance to use the media with regard to its findings in cases of human rights violations was assumed to have been political sensitivity. Friction often existed between the human rights function and the political negotiation function in the same peacekeeping mission. In the early stages of the mission, radio and television colloquia prepared in New York announced the presence of the mission and promoted human rights in generic terms. These attempts were not well received by the local NGOs, as the programmes were not directly related to the Salvadoran

---

[119] *Lawyers Committee Report*, p.65. Reed Brody, ex-director of the Human Rights Division of ONUSAL, has a different view: "The Division made a major effort to distribute the report locally and to use its publication as an opportunity to comment to the Salvadoran public on the state of human rights". Brody, *supra* note 37, p.164.

[120] *Lawyers Committee Report*, p.88.

[121] William Stanley and David Holiday, 'Peace Mission Strategy and Domestic Actors: UN Mediation, Verification and Institution-building in El Salvador', *International Peacekeeping* 4(2), Summer 1997: 22-49, p.34.

situation.[122] In 1993, the Division also used the media by organising radio and television campaigns on human rights.[123] The campaigns aimed to "speak to ordinary citizens about their everyday problems". García-Sayán believes that "[i]t helped the population not only to become more aware of its rights, but also how to defend them".[124]

4.7   Institution-building

In 1993, the focus of the Human Rights Division gradually shifted from investigation of alleged human rights violations to supporting local institution-building involved in the promotion and protection of human rights.[125] On July 29, 1993, ONUSAL signed an agreement with the Office of the National Counsel for the Defence of Human Rights (Ombudsman) on co-operation in human rights monitoring and investigation techniques. These techniques included procedures for processing, organising and storing information, fund-raising, institution-building and outreach.[126] In mid-1994, the Division reported a decrease in complaints received by the Division during a period from 1 March to 30 June 1994, while the number of complaints received by the Ombudsman's office had increased.[127] The Office opened regional offices in early 1993.[128] The more active operation of the Office was due directly to the Division's efforts. Initially, ONUSAL had accompanied complainants to the Ombudsman's office, and joint initial interviews had been conducted. The two bodies had then classified the case,

---

[122] *Lawyers Committee Report*, p.51. Similar criticism was made by Americas Watch, *supra* note 104, pp.25-27.

[123] García-Sayán, *supra* note 114, p.61.

[124] *Ibid.*

[125] But see Whitfield, *supra* note 44, p.167: "... throughout 1993, efforts were concentrated on case work, while institution building was for the most part limited to the organisation of seminars and training activities."

[126] *Lawyers Committee Report*, p.108.

[127] *Report of the ONUSAL Human Rights Division covering the period from 1 March to 30 June 1994* (hereinafter *Human Rights Division Twelfth Report*), UN Doc. A/49/281-S/1994/886, 28 July 1994, para.11. The number of complaints received by the Division from March to June was 100, 90, 82 and 61 in each month. A subsequent report of the Division reported that the number of complaints received by ONUSAL in September 1994 was 58. According to the same report, ONUSAL declared 119 complaints of arbitrary detention admissible in September 1991, but only 13 in September 1994. *Report of the ONUSAL Human Rights Division covering the period from 1 July to 30 September 1994*, UN Doc. A/49/585-S/1994/1220, 31 October 1994, para.106.

[128] *Report of the Secretary-General on all aspects of ONUSAL's operations*, UN Doc. S/25812, 21 May 1993, para.9.

agreed on a list of investigatory steps and assigned responsibilities for the investigation. The Division later systematised its work with the Office and two attorneys and two UN policemen worked directly with staff at the Office.[129] Towards the end of the mission, representatives of the two organisations began to meet weekly for co-ordination of the investigation of individual cases, which also helped skill-transfer and training.[130] The Division considered the change as "a natural and desirable transfer of the tasks of verification to that Office".[131] In September 1994, the Ombudsman began issuing 'trenchant' monthly reports on the human rights situation.[132]

Approaching the end of the mission, the Division made clear the importance of local institutions in the improvement of the human rights situation in El Salvador:

> The human rights situation in El Salvador will remain precarious until State institutions are efficient enough to prevent and punish human rights violations. The impunity of the perpetrators is, in fact, still the main cause of human rights violations in El Salvador. It is therefore essential to accelerate the reform of the judicial system.[133]

However, ONUSAL's effort to strengthen the state institutions which were dealing with human rights violations started only towards the end of the operation, by which time it was very late to make any significant impact on the system. According to some commentators, the delay was caused by the weakness of the UN. Further, ONUSAL, according to the commentators, lacked an explicit mandate for institution-building:

> This lacuna in ONUSAL's mandate reflected the fact that the UN has more experience in interpreting human rights law than in working with state institutions to improve the actual practice and implementation of human rights norms.[134]

Institution-building cannot be achieved without effective co-operation between the UN mission and local institutions. With respect to the Ombudsman's office, the personal reluctance of the first Ombudsman, Carlos Molina

---

[129] *Lawyers Committee Report*, p.42.

[130] *Ibid.*, p.109.

[131] *Report of the Secretary-General on all aspects of ONUSAL's operations*, UN Doc. S/25812, 21 May 1993, para.9.

[132] Brody, *supra* note 37, p.173.

[133] *Human Rights Division Twelfth Report*, para.131.

[134] Stanley and Holiday, *supra* note 121, p.37.

Fonseca, is said to have caused the distance between the two organisations.[135] The reform of the judicial system has not developed as expected by ONUSAL despite repeated recommendations by ONUSAL as well as by the Truth Commission. The Human Rights Division conducted a survey of the judicial status of the 75 most significant cases. Twenty-five per cent of these cases never reached the court. Of those submitted to the court, the police have not investigated more than half the cases.[136]

There is criticism that ONUSAL should have worked with Salvadoran investigators and prosecutors, as well as with governmental and non-governmental advocates, from the beginning.[137] However, human rights investigations are frequently very sensitive, particularly in terms of the safety of victims and witnesses.[138] Without knowing the working partners well, and without establishing to a certain extent a trusting relationship with the partners, it would have been too risky to start sharing information regarding cases.

In mid-1993, the Government and ONUSAL agreed to establish executive machinery to implement agreements reached through the peace process and subsequently, in order to conduct the joint periodic evaluations at the highest political level.[139] This was a step forward to implement a large number of recommendations made or reaffirmed by ONUSAL.

ONUSAL made efforts to leave behind a series of technical assistance projects in El Salvador.[140] The projects were funded by individual donor countries and ONUSAL was involved only at the planning phase. Nonetheless, ONUSAL's opinions and recommendations based on its experience in El Salvador contributed significantly to the policy orientation and functions of these projects. Further, it also assisted in incorporating the actual needs of El Salvador in the objectives of these projects.

---

[135] *Ibid.*, p.40.

[136] *Lawyers Committee Report*, p.82.

[137] *Ibid.*, p.92.

[138] Even ONUSAL itself could do harm to those people. In one murder case, an ONUSAL police investigator visited the workplace of a witness in uniform and driving a marked ONUSAL car. This carelessness of ONUSAL dismayed an NGO. *Ibid.*, p.99.

[139] *Report of the ONUSAL Human Rights Division for the period from 1 February to 30 April 1993*, UN Doc. A/47/968-S26033, 2 July 1993, para.329.

[140] For details, see *Lawyers Committee Report*, pp.114-115.

4.8 Human Rights Education

Five staff members of the Human Rights Division were initially designated as human rights educators and were based in San Salvador. After a while, the five were redeployed to the regional offices. One successful programme carried out by an educator was to have the text of the Universal Declaration of Human Rights made into a large wooden puzzle, with a separate piece for each article of the Declaration. The puzzle was used in talks with "popular teachers" who worked in zones to which Ministry of Education employees were not assigned, with trade unionists and at the local military post.[141] Despite this fruitful attempt, such community education projects were eventually dropped due to leave or reassignment of the educators.

Another innovative effort at human rights education by ONUSAL was the Unit on Cooperation with the Armed Forces. The Unit was directed by a Spanish Colonel, Prudencio García, from April 1993. Col. García taught courses on human rights and "military sociology" at the Salvadoran Military Academy as well as at army bases around the country.[142]

The Division also provided courses for judges, prosecutors, and other court officials, and co-operated with the judicial training school to enhance the competence and professionalism of judges.[143] The Division also trained legal advisers to the National Civil Police (PNC).[144] Nevertheless, the workshops for judges and prosecutors, each lasting two-and-a-half days, revealed a "near-complete" ignorance of human rights law. Most participants failed even to cite the Salvadoran Constitution in deciding a case.[145] In light of the fact that the Salvadoran Constitution stipulates that international law takes precedence over domestic law, reform of the curriculum for the country's Judicial School was required. However, ONUSAL had to leave El Salvador before its realisation. The Constitution sets forth in Article 144:

> The international treaties formalised [celebrados] by El Salvador with other states or international organisms constitute laws of the Republic once they enter into effect, in conformity with the dispositions of the same treaty and of this constitution.

---

[141] *Ibid.*, p.54.
[142] *Ibid.*
[143] Johnstone, *supra* note 21, p.72.
[144] *Ibid.*
[145] *Lawyers Committee Report*, p.106.

> ... In case of conflict between the treaty and the law, the treaty shall prevail.[146]

A commentator notes that it should be questioned whether the time and resources of ONUSAL might have been more profitably directed to the training of human rights teachers.[147] "Train the trainers" is a common lesson for human rights function of peacekeeping operations taking into account the limited time and resources and potential long-lasting effect.

4.9   Co-operation inside ONUSAL

As mentioned previously, a certain number of police observers were seconded from the Political Division to the Human Rights Division of ONUSAL. The co-operation between the two Divisions, however, was not as good as it could have been. Staff of the Human Rights Division complained that ONUSAL police did not consistently pass on information that they had obtained on the performance of the Salvadoran police, as they were afraid of harming their collegial relationship with the Salvadorian police. Human rights investigators in regional offices also complained that some police conducted their own investigations of acts of violence, refusing any co-ordination with, or direction from, the human rights staff or regional co-ordinator. In one instance, the lack of co-ordination resulted in two conflicting reports on the same case being submitted by Human Rights and Police personnel. They were rejected by the Chief of Mission, who urged his staff to agree on a single version of events.[148] The Lawyers Committee for Human Rights refers to this issue:

> Some police conducted parallel investigations rather than take direction from a civilian human rights attorney - ironic indeed, given that El Salvador's central problem was the lack of civilian control over the military and security forces.[149]

From this author's own experience, it is clear that there tends to exist a rivalry between a civilian component and a civilian police or military component inside a peacekeeping operation. From the civilian component's viewpoint, police or military officers often lack basic knowledge about the

---

[146] *Constitution of El Salvador*, text available in Gisbert H. Franz, ed., *Constitutions of the Countries of the World: Republic of El Salvador*, Booklet 1, Translated by Reka Koerner, Dobbs Ferry, New York: Oceana Publications, Inc., 1998.

[147] Whitfield, *supra* note 44, p.180.

[148] *Lawyers Committee Report*, p.31. Also see Stanley and Loosle, *supra* note 105, 6/19.

[149] *Ibid.*, p.17. Also see Whitfield, *supra* note 44, p.169.

political situation of the country or sensitivity to the host community. From a police or military point of view, they strongly resist the "interference" by civilian officers in their "professional" field. In fact, the quality of the work mostly depends on each individual, and the co-operation between a civilian officer and a police or military officer also varies on a personal level. Looking back on the ONUSAL experience, Chief of Mission Enrique ter Horst has stated:

> In the future I would not set up a separate police division. And I would make sure that none of the police were treated like second-class functionaries. I would have mixed teams from the beginning.[150]

The co-ordination between agents in the field and headquarters was also problematic. The Lawyers Committee for Human Rights has noted: "[m]any had little or no sense of if or how their information was used or evaluated by ONUSAL headquarters".[151]

4.10 Co-operation with Other UN Agencies

The UN Human Rights Commission had designated Professor Pastor Ridrujelo as Special Representative to El Salvador in 1981. Although he served in this capacity until 1992, no co-operation existed between him and ONUSAL. The involvement of the UN Centre for Human Rights with ONUSAL was only during the preliminary mission in March 1991.[152]

The relationship with the standing UN agency, the United Nations Development Programme (UNDP), affected ONUSAL's work as referred to above in relation to the training of the Police Academy. Even after its departure, the work initiated by ONUSAL was not free from UNDP's influence. The joint investigations of the Ombudsman's office and of the UN were discontinued after ONUSAL was taken over by the United Nations Mission in El Salvador (MINUSAL). It was "in large part due to inadequate follow-up and infighting between UNDP and MINUSAL".[153] It is a very disappointing reality that UN infighting loses sight of the needs of the society which it is trying to help.

---

[150] *Lawyers Committee Report*, p.39.

[151] *Ibid.*, p.71.

[152] *Ibid.,* p.55. Also Whitfield, *supra* note 44, p.182.

[153] Stanley and Holiday, *supra* note 121, p.39. Based on interview with ONUSAL officials, May and July 1995.

4.11   Co-operation with Local NGOs

ONUSAL also failed to develop an effective relationship with local human rights NGOs in El Salvador. Although the Division's reports from time to time contain praise of such NGOs,[154] the actual collaboration with the NGOs was very little. One major reason was that, especially at the beginning of the mission, ONUSAL was cautious about the political alignment of local NGOs.[155] Limited co-operation included the preparation of materials for human rights education, which the national organisations could distribute, and some seminars held in 1994.

Co-operation with local NGOs is important for two major reasons. Firstly, local NGOs have established contacts with, or means of access to the local population, which can also be a source of valuable information. Secondly, they will continue to work in the same societies in the longer term, that is, after the UN peacekeeping operation has withdrawn. The interaction between a UN peacekeeping operation and local NGOs is to be considered as a part of the process of institution-building.

CONCLUSION

ONUSAL is generally considered to be a successful UN peacekeeping operation. The question is whether the general opinion stands if we focus on its human rights activities. At the outset ONUSAL was an exclusively human rights mission. Ian Johnstone, Second Officer in the Executive Office of the Secretary-General of the United Nations, remarks that this early deployment contributed to the broader peace process as a confidence-building measure.[156] The UN presence signified that both sides had given up on seeking a military victory. Also the presence raised the political costs to either party of breaking the peace process.[157] However, an observation of ONUSAL by the Lawyers Committee for Human Rights is probably correct:

> Above all, the UN had an overriding desire to achieve a political settlement and to keep the peace process on track, with all that this entailed in terms of compromise and adapting to political realities.[158]

---

[154] For instance, *Human Rights Division Second Report*, paras.9 & 10.

[155] Whitfield, *supra* note 44, p.177.

[156] Johnstone, *supra* note 89, p.314.

[157] *Ibid.*

[158] *Lawyers Committee Report*, p.18.

Thus the Human Rights Division was inevitably "subordinate to the political division and political concerns".[159] The staff of the Human Rights Division agrees on this point:

> At that time [when two experienced legal officers angrily left ONUSAL at an early phase] many of us still thought it was a human rights mission. Later we saw that it was only a political mission with a human rights coating so people would accept it more.[160]

This comment supports the view that the San José Agreement on human rights, the first of a series of peace agreements signed by the El Salvador Government and the FMLN, played a role of concession, and was not the major concern of the parties.[161] Another officer of ONUSAL stated:

> During the first six months it was easier, but once the other divisions arrived, it was more difficult. It was clear that human rights was no longer a priority for anyone. ... In truth, nobody any longer was interested in human rights, but for purposes of public discourse, we needed to say we were still monitoring human rights.[162]

ONUSAL's cautious approach in monitoring human rights violations by the PNC (National Civil Police) demonstrates the political consideration of ONUSAL. An officer of the Human Rights Division stated in an interview with the Lawyers Committee for Human Rights:

> The PNC did not become a subject until the 11th report, and even then the treatment was way too soft. They said we couldn't be too harsh because the PNC was the pillar of the peace accords. Highlighting their violations would do more harm than good, and put weapons in the hands of the anti-accords folks.[163]

Yet it should be noted that the Human Rights Division may benefit from its status as a part of multifunctional peacekeeping. Diego García-Sayán, Human Rights Division director, affirms:

---

[159] *Ibid.* Also see Americas Watch, *supra* note 104, p.24.

[160] *Lawyers Committee Report*, p.18.

[161] *Supra* note 16 and accompanying text.

[162] *Lawyers Committee Report*, p.19.

[163] *Ibid.*, p.37.

> From within the mission you can pressure the government .... Standing alone, a human rights division would lack influence, room for manoeuvre and status (*presencia*). The risk is that it would become one more NGO. Being within the mission gives it very direct standing as an interlocutor.[164]

An important effect of human rights monitoring and reporting is to pressurise the responsible government. One observer notes that "the Salvadoran government always stepped things up before a report went out". The same observer claims:

> And the reports are effective as a point of pressure to the extent that they are credible to donor governments.[165]

Ian Johnstone affirms the importance of keeping human rights verification and peacekeeping functions together:

> ... separating the functions ["finger-pointing" and "honest broker" roles, i.e., human rights verification and peacekeeping] could undermine both the status of human rights monitors and the moral authority of the rest of a peacekeeping mission.[166]

The very fact that human rights monitors, investigators or educators are deployed as a part of a peacekeeping operation illustrates that the society in question has quite serious, probably institutionalised, problems in terms of human rights. Therefore all the means available need to be utilised, including political pressure, economic incentives, public education, as well as direct condemnation of human rights abuses. The Lawyers Committee for Human Rights reports that "[i]nterviews with ONUSAL officials confirm that they viewed their primary responsibility to *las partes*, the signatories to the accords". The Lawyers Committee then renders the criticism that:

> [I]n failing to communicate consistently with the population, the UN missed an important opportunity to help move Salvadoran society forward.[167]

Human rights functions of a peacekeeping operation are aimed not only at the government of the host State but also at the people living within those States. Society expects justice through the human rights functions of the UN

---

[164] *Ibid.*, pp.20-21.

[165] *Ibid.*, p.91.

[166] Johnstone, *supra* note 89, p.338.

[167] *Ibid.*, p.41.

and to show that impunity prevailed during the conflict is no longer tolerated. One strategy which can be used to meet the real demands of the people and society is the effective reporting of human rights work in a peacekeeping operation. The UN's priority is usually the confidentiality of specific cases, either for the security of the persons involved, or for avoiding a counter-productive political effect. However, if the UN can promptly release the information on any reform resulted from its human rights work, this would significantly encourage the local community, providing it with the substantial hope that the lawless regime is being tackled by the international community. The fundamental aim of the peacekeeping operation must remain the benefit of the local community.

ONUSAL's human rights work was not exclusively that of the Human Rights Division, but also included reforms of the police and the judicial system, to which some other agencies including the Truth Commission, the *Ad Hoc* Commission, and the UNDP contributed significantly. The UN peace effort in El Salvador was certainly an innovative attempt in terms of its peace-building elements.[168] It is obvious from the analysis of the work done by ONUSAL in El Salvador, that it made major contributions to the reform of Salvadoran society. However the exact nature of the work undertaken and accomplished by ONUSAL became clear only towards the end of the operation. The mission was a process of learning what was required and what could be done for peace-building, such as: the reform and restructuring of judicial systems, which would then be able to prosecute perpetrators of human rights violations; civilian police, to keep the security and order of the society solely under the civilian control; domestic institution to monitor and promote human rights, and; dissemination of human rights to the entire society. Learning from the experience of ONUSAL, particularly its institution-building efforts, subsequent UN missions will be able to plan from their initial stage, comprehensive measures to transform the host society to one which enhances human rights protection.

---

[168] "It [UN's involvement in El Salvador] is the first in a new generation of United Nations operations whose purpose is post-conflict peacebuilding. In addition to the verification of respect for human rights, the United Nations is variously involved in a complex and integrated set of tasks". *Report of the Secretary-General concerning the formal end of the arms conflict in El Salvador*, UN Doc. S/25006, 23 December 1992.

Chapter 4

Human Rights Functions of the United Nations Transitional Authority in Cambodia

1. HISTORICAL BACKGROUND

Cambodia had been under French control since 1863. The French adminis-tration was defeated in 1945 by the Japanese forces, which had been occupying the Indo-Chinese Peninsula during the World War II, but France soon recovered the control. Cambodia became independent in 1953. From independence until the 1970 *coup d'état* by General Lon Nol, Sihanouk ruled Cambodia. Lon Nol regime was supported by the USA, which was involved in a lengthy armed conflict with North Vietnam. The Vietnam war caused serious damage in Cambodia in terms of the economy and human losses, as well as mass displacement. With support from Sihanouk who was in exile in Beijing, a Cambodian communist group led by Pol Pot, known as the Khmer Rouge, captured Phnom Penh in April 1975. Under the Pol Pot regime, which lasted until 1979, massive human rights violations took place.[1] The Pol Pot regime ended by the intervention of Vietnamese troops and the People's Republic of Kampuchea (PRK),[2] a government backed by Vietnam was established. In 1982, three groups opposing the PRK formed a coalition party, CGDK, led by Prince Sihanouk. The three groups were: the Front uni national pour un Cambodge indépendant, neutre, pacifique et

---

[1] Regarding atrocities committed under the Pol Pot regime, see, for example, Hurst Hannum, 'International Law and Cambodian Genocide: The Sounds of Silence', *Human Rights Quarterly* 11, 1989: 82-138; David P. Chandler, *The Tragedy of Cambodian History: Politics, War, and Revolution since 1945*, Yale University Press, 1991; and François Ponchaud, *Cambodia Year Zero*, Penguin Books, 1977. In contrast, Michael Vickery contests what he calls "the Standard Total View", which includes the total annihilation of intellectuals, the widespread starvation, and absence of medical treatment under the Pol Pot regime. According to Vickery, there was significant variance in administrative practices under the Pol Pot regime depending on time and place. For the results of his detailed research, Michael Vickery, *Cambodia: 1975-1982*, South End Press: Boston, 1984. His emphasis that rural-urban antagonisms had existed prior to the 1975 revolution is particularly interesting.

[2] The PRK changed its name to the State of Cambodia (SOC) in 1989.

coopératif (United National Front for an Independent, Neutral, Peaceful and Cooperative Cambodia; FUNCINPEC),[3] the Khmer People's National Liberation Front (KPNLF)[4] and the Party of Democratic Kampuchea (PDK, known as the Khmer Rouge). The civil conflict between the Phnom Penh Government and the coalition party resulted in several hundred thousand refugees and a larger number of internally displaced persons.

Despite the atrocities committed by the PDK, it held Cambodia's seat in the United Nations until 1982 due to antagonism towards the PRK backed by Vietnam. From 1982, the CGDK represented Cambodia in the United Nations although the PRK had *de facto* control of most of the territory.[5]

To find a solution to the Cambodian conflict, diplomatic efforts started as early as 1981. In July 1981, the United Nations General Assembly convened the International Conference on Kampuchea in New York. However, no dialogue between the conflicting parties had taken place until December 1987, when Prince Sihanouk and Hun Sen, Prime Minister of the Phnom Penh Government met in France. One year later, the dialogue and negotiation accelerated at the Jakarta Informal Meeting. In February 1989, Indonesia hosted a second Informal Meeting. A further step was taken at the initiative of the French Government by convening the Paris Conference on Cambodia from 30 July to 30 August 1989. Nineteen countries including five permanent members of the Security Council, four Cambodian factions and the Secretary-General of the United Nations attended the meeting. In January 1990, the five permanent members began a series of high-level discussions on the settlement process with a vision of significant UN involvement. At the end of August 1990, the Five succeeded in announcing an agreement on a settlement framework,[6] which was accepted by the four Cambodian factions in the following month. Pursuant to the framework, the Supreme National Council (SNC), a unique legitimate body in which the independence, national sovereignty and unity of Cambodia were to be enshrined throughout the transitional period, was established. The SNC consisted of six members from the SOC and two each from the three other factions. Following further consultations, the Paris Peace Agreements were

---

[3] A royalist party led by Sihanouk and, subsequently, by his son Prince Ranariddh.
[4] A republican non-communist group led by Son Sann, a former prime minister.
[5] Catherine Hughes, *UNTAC in Cambodia: The impact on human rights*, Singapore: Institute of Southeast Asian Studies, 1996, p.20.
[6] *Framework for a Comprehensive Political Settlement of the Cambodia Conflict*, UN Doc. A/45/472-S/21689, 31 August 1990.

signed by 19 states on 23 October 1991.[7] The Agreements consist of a Final Act and three instruments: the *Agreement on a Comprehensive Political Settlement of the Cambodia Conflict* (hereinafter, the "*Comprehensive Agreement*"); the *Agreement concerning the Sovereignty, Independence, Territorial Integrity and Inviolability, Neutrality and National Unity of Cambodia*; and the *Declaration on the Rehabilitation and Reconstruction of Cambodia*.[8]

During the final negotiations toward the Paris Agreements, Prince Norodom Sihanouk, President of the SNC, requested that the United Nations send observers to Cambodia "in order to assist the SNC in controlling the cease-fire and the cessation of foreign military assistance, as a first step within the framework of a comprehensive political settlement".[9] Responding to this request, the establishment of the United Nations Advance Mission in Cambodia (UNAMIC) was approved by the Security Council by resolution 717 on 16 October 1991.[10]

The Security Council decided to establish the United Nations Transitional Authority in Cambodia (UNTAC) in resolution 745 on 28 February 1992.[11] It was envisaged that UNTAC would contribute to the restoration and maintenance of peace in Cambodia, to the promotion of national reconciliation, to the protection of human rights and to the assurance of the right to self-determination of the Cambodian people through free and fair elections.[12]

---

[7] Dated 23 October 1991. UN Doc. A/46/608-S/23177 of 30 October 1991. The Signatories were the States that participated in the Paris Conference on Cambodia, namely, Australia, Brunei Darussalam, Cambodia, Canada, the People's Republic of China, the French Republic, the Republic of India, the Republic of Indonesia, Japan, the Lao People's Democratic Republic, Malaysia, the Republic of the Philippines, the Republic of Singapore, the Kingdom of Thailand, the Union of Soviet Socialist Republics, the United Kingdom of Great Britain and Northern Ireland, the United States of America, the Socialist Republic of Vietnam and the Socialist Federal Republic of Yugoslavia.

[8] For an excellent analysis of these Agreements, see Steven R. Ratner, 'The Cambodia Settlement Agreements', *AJIL*, January 1993:1-41.

[9] *Final communiqué of the Supreme National Council of Cambodia*, I.1; Annex to *Letter dated 23 September 1991 from the President of the Supreme National Council transmitting final communiqué of the Council's meeting in Pattaya, 26-29 August 1991*, UN Doc. A/46/494-S/23066, 24 September 1991.

[10] SC res. 717, 16 October 1991. SCOR, 3014th mtg., UN Doc. S/RES/717(1991). Adopted unanimously.

[11] SC res. 745, 28 February 1992. SCOR, 3057th mtg., UN Doc. S/RES 745(1992). Adopted unanimously.

[12] Para.4 of the preamble, SC res. 745.

2. COMPOSITION AND MANDATE OF UNTAC

Special Representative of the Secretary-General, Yasuhi Akashi (Japan), and the UNTAC Force Commander, Lieutenant-General John M. Sanderson (Australia), arrived in Phnom Penh on 15 March 1992. However, it took many months for the full deployment of UNTAC international staff which numbered some 22,000; such a large contingent for a peacekeeping operation was unprecedented.[13] It was also peculiar in regard to its multi-dimensional characteristics.[14] UNTAC consisted of seven components: the Human Rights Component, the Electoral Component, the Military Component, the Civil Administration Component, the Police Component, the Repatriation Component and the Rehabilitation Component.

The relationship between the host state, Cambodia, and UNTAC was based on the *Comprehensive Agreement*. UNTAC was established at the request of the Signatories to the *Agreement*.[15] Under Article 3 of the *Agreement*, the Supreme National Council (SNC) was recognised as "the unique legitimate body and source of authority in which, throughout the transitional period, the sovereignty, independence and unity of Cambodia are enshrined". Article 6 set out the relationship between the SNC and the UN:

> The SNC hereby delegates to the United Nations all powers necessary to ensure the implementation of this Agreement, as described in annex I. ...

In Annex I, it was provided that "UNTAC will exercise the powers necessary to ensure the implementation of this Agreement"[16] and that "[T]he SNC offers advice to UNTAC, which will comply with this advice provided there is a consensus among the members of the SNC and provided this advice is consistent with the objectives of the present Agreement".[17] It was the Special Representative of the Secretary-General who had the responsibility of determining whether the advice or action of the SNC was

---

[13] Ratner, *The New UN Peacekeeping, supra* FN83 of Chapter 1, p.166.

[14] *The United Nations and Cambodia 1991-1995* (hereinafter, *The UN and Cambodia*), The United Nations Blue Book Series, Volume II, 1995, p.3; Michael W. Doyle, *UN Peacekeeping in Cambodia: UNTAC's Civil Mandate*, Lynne Rienner Publishers, 1995, p.26; and James A. Schear, 'Riding the Tiger: The United Nations and Cambodia's Struggle for Peace', in William J. Durch, ed., *UN Peacekeeping, American Politics, and the Uncivil Wars of the 1990s*, Macmillan, 1997, p.135 & p.175.

[15] Article 2(1) of Part I. See *supra* note 7.

[16] Section A, 1.

[17] Section A, 2(a).

consistent with the present Agreement.[18] Thus, although the State of Cambodia was under the *transitional authority* of the Organisation, the sovereignty enshrined in the SNC was exercised by the Cambodian people. The establishment of the SNC, an organ consisted of four conflicting parties, was necessary to introduce UN temporary administration, since a UN Trusteeship of a Member State was prohibited under Article 78 of the UN Charter.[19] The SNC was granted a special legitimacy as embodying Cambodia's sovereignty, hence the SNC became competent to represent Cambodia externally.[20] That competence was the basis of the SNC's authority to grant powers to the United Nations.

The main mandate of UNTAC was set forth in the *Comprehensive Agreement* and its annexes. The mandate of each component will be reviewed briefly.

The Civil Administration Component was responsible for exercising direct control over the existing administrative structures of Cambodia in the field of foreign affairs, national defence, finance, public security and information (Article 1, Section B). Also, the Component was assigned direct supervision or control of other agencies, bodies and offices which would be determined by the Special Representative (Article 2, Section B). By mid-July 1992, the Civil Administration Component had established offices in all 21 provinces.[21] By September, over 800 members (some 200 international and 600 locally recruited staff) of the Civil Administration Component had been deployed.[22] The Component, however, could not always satisfy the required control due to *de facto* continuity of the SOC administration. For example, the SOC individually negotiated and signed an aviation treaty with Malaysia, despite the fact that the sovereign rights were allocated to the SNC during the transitional period pursuant to the Paris Agreements.[23]

---

[18] Section A, 2(e).

[19] Article 78:

> The trusteeship system shall not apply to territories which have become Members of the United Nations, relationship among which shall be based on respect for the principle of sovereign equality.

[20] Ratner, *supra* note 8, p.10.

[21] *Report of the Secretary-General on Cambodia containing his proposed implementation plan for UNTAC, including administrative and financial aspects* (hereinafter the *Implementation Plan*), UN Doc. S/23613, 19 February 1992, para.128.

[22] *Second progress report of the Secretary-General on UNTAC* (hereinafter *Second Progress Report*), UN Doc. S/24578, 21 September 1992, para.26.

[23] Michael W. Doyle and Nishkala Suntharalingam, 'The UN in Cambodia: Lessons for Complex Peacekeeping', *International Peacekeeping* 1(2), Summer 1994, pp.117-147, p.146, EN23.

The mandate of the Civilian Police Component was to supervise the existing police in order to ensure that law and order were maintained effectively and impartially, and that human rights and fundamental freedoms were fully protected (Article 5, Section B). The total number of civilian police monitors was planned to be about 3,600.[24]

The Military Component had four functions: verifying the withdrawal of all foreign forces; supervising the cease-fire, cantonment, and demobilisation of the military forces of the four factions; confiscating the caches of weapons and monitoring the cessation of all outside military assistance; and training in mine clearance (Section C and Annex 2). By mid-July 1992, 14,300 troops had been deployed.[25]

The Electoral Component assumed the task of organising and conducting a national election, including the establishment of a system of laws, procedures and administrative measures necessary for holding a free and fair election (Section D and Annex 3). Some 150 international staff of the Electoral Component had been deployed at UNTAC headquarters and 400 United Nations Volunteers of the same component almost fully deployed to the district level by September 1992.[26]

The Repatriation Component was led by UNHCR and was in charge of the repatriation and relief of Cambodian refugees and displaced persons (Annex 4). By the end of the mission, the Repatriation Component repatriated some 364,000 individuals. In addition, approximately 23,000 Cambodians returned spontaneously or under the auspices of the Thai authorities.[27]

The Rehabilitation Component, headed by the Rehabilitation Co-ordinator who had been appointed by the Secretary-General, engaged in the co-ordination of international, regional and bilateral assistance. The humanitarian needs, the resettlement needs and essential restoration, maintenance and support of basic infrastructure and utilities were considered to be urgent requirements.[28]

The Human Rights Component was responsible for fostering an environment in which respect for human rights shall be ensured by (a) developing and implementing a programme of human rights education to promote respect for and understanding of human rights; (b) overseeing human rights

---

[24] *Implementation Plan*, para.128.

[25] *Ibid.*, para.128.

[26] *Implementation Plan*, UN Doc. S/23613, 19 February 1992, para.12.

[27] *The UN and Cambodia*, Section 1, VII, p.40, para.96.

[28] *Implementation Plan*, II, G; and *Declaration on the rehabilitation and reconstruction of Cambodia*, UN Doc. A/46/608-S23/77, 30 October 1991.

in general during the transitional period; and (c) investigating human rights complaints, and where appropriate, taking corrective action (Article 16 of the Agreement and Section E of Annex 1). Compared with ONUSAL's human rights mandate, this mandate is less precise. For example, it refers neither to UNTAC's authority to freely visit any place, nor to its information gathering function. The only point that goes further than ONUSAL's mandate is the "corrective action".

At the beginning the Human Rights Component was going to have only 10 officers in total. Compared with the number of international staff in other components mentioned above, it is clear how small the Human Rights Component was. From the outset, UNTAC's focus was on the election. Human rights were considered as an element to support the creation of an environment to hold democratic elections. The reason for the modest number of human rights officers was explained by the Secretary-General:

> ... since all UNTAC staff operating in all areas of the mandate,
> would be charged with carrying out human rights functions, as
> an integral part of their primary duties.[29]

However, it was soon recognised that one officer should be appointed for each province.[30] By 18 September 1992, human rights officers had been deployed in 15 of the 21 provinces.[31]

UNTAC had an unprecedented authority: (1) to issue directives which would bind all Cambodian parties to the administrative structures under its direct control; and (2) to appoint UNTAC officials within the factional administrations and to require the assignment or removal of any officials.[32] Whether this authority helped UNTAC carry out its mandate will be analysed below.

3.   LEGAL REFORMS RELEVANT TO HUMAN RIGHTS

On 20 April 1992, the Supreme National Council (SNC) signed instruments of accession to the International Covenant on Civil and Political Rights and

---

[29]   *Implementation Plan,* para.21.

[30]   Yasunobu Sato, 'Lessons from UNTAC Human Rights Operation: Human Rights for Peace and Development', *Technology and Development*, No.10, January 1997:45-53, p.47.

[31]   *Second Progress Report,* para.7.

[32]   Articles 1 & 4, Section B of Annex 1 to *Agreement on a comprehensive political settlement of the Cambodia conflict.*

the International Covenant on Economic, Social and Cultural Rights.[33] On 10 September, the SNC also resolved that Cambodia should accede to the Convention against Torture and Other Cruel, Inhuman or Degrading Treatment or Punishment; the International Convention on the Elimination of All Forms of Discrimination against Women; the Convention on the Rights of the Child; and the Convention and Protocol relating to the Status of Refugees.[34] Although genuine implementation of international human rights norms is quite a different matter from accession of those treaties, this was a significant step forward for Cambodia towards a guarantee of human rights.

As the Secretary-General remarked, the human rights functions of UNTAC were not exclusively carried out by the Human Rights Component.[35] The Civil Administration Component of UNTAC drew up and proposed to the SNC operating procedures for the exercise of the right of assembly and freedom of association. SNC substantially agreed on them.[36] The Civil Administration Component also reviewed lists of laws of three political parties, the SOC, FUNCINPEC and KPLNF. The PDK failed to meet the request of Special Representative of the Secretary-General to submit the list.[37] One of the peculiar difficulties for UNTAC in dealing with legal matters in Cambodia was that it had to take into account four jurisdictions and four different legal systems inside the internationally recognised territory of Cambodia, since four factions had been governing the divided territory of Cambodia. The zones controlled by FUNCINPEC and KPLNF did not have any legal system comparable to the western countries and therefore UNTAC appointed judges in the territories to facilitate dispute resolution.[38]

In September 1992, the SNC approved a set of principles relating to the legal system, penal law and penal procedure, *Provisions Relating to the Judiciary and Criminal Law and Procedure Applicable in Cambodia During the Transitional Period* (hereinafter, *Transitional Criminal Provisions*).[39]

---

[33] *First progress report of the Secretary-General on UNTAC* (hereinafter *First Progress Report*), UN Doc. S/23870, 1 May 1992, para.14. Cambodia signed these treaties in 1980.

[34] *Second Progress Report*, para.8.

[35] See *supra* note 29 and accompanying text.

[36] *Second Progress Report*, para.33.

[37] *Second special report of the Secretary-General on UNTAC and phase II of the case-fire*, UN Doc. S/24286, 14 July 1992, para.16.

[38] Stephen P. Marks, 'The New Cambodian Constitution: From Civil Law to a Fragile Democracy', *Columbia Human Rights Law Review*, Fall 1994: 45-110, p.87.

[39] *Second Progress Report*, para.28.

The Provisions had a significant impact on the work of the Human Rights Component as will be discussed later.

The Information/Educational Division under the Civil Administration Component drafted a media charter in co-operation with the Human Rights Component. The principal aim of the charter was to lay down principles for the exercise of freedom of the press and the rights and obligations of media organisations and administrative agencies in the context of elections.[40] The freedom of the press was an important issue to be addressed in Cambodia since freedom of expression had been severely repressed under the Lon Nol regime, Pol Pot regime or the SOC.[41]

4. ACTIVITIES OF UNTAC HUMAN RIGHTS COMPONENT

4.1 Recruitment and Education of Officers

UNTAC was planned with clear awareness that specific training was required for its personnel. In addition to general orientation regarding the mandate, structure, and procedures of UNTAC, procedures and techniques to be applied for human rights supervision received special attention.[42] The Human Rights Component organised training programmes for UNTAC police monitors as early as April 1992.[43] This training, however, may have been inadequate, as one commentator describes:

> Other than the briefest of human rights awareness classes once members arrived in Cambodia, the officers received no training.[44]

The recruitment policy of UNTAC was probably flexible. There was at least one person who was transferred from the Civil Administration Component to the Human Rights Component of his own accord. With respect to this

---

[40] *Ibid.*, para.36.

[41] William Shawcross, *Cambodia's New Deal*, Contemporary Issues Paper #1, Washington D.C.: Carnegie Endowment for International Peace, 1994, pp. 63-64.

[42] *Implementation Plan*, para.165.

[43] *First Progress Report*, para.13.

[44] Ratner, *supra* note 13, p.172. Based on an interview with UNTAC CIVPOL official.

specific case, since the person concerned was a lawyer, his qualifications met the requirements of both assignments.[45]

4.2   Main Human Rights Abuses

By the *Second Progress Report* dated 21 September 1992, the Human Rights Component had received more than 250 complaints of harassment and intimidation, arbitrary arrest, wrongful death, destruction of property and wrongful injury.[46] One hundred and thirty of these were referred to other components of UNTAC, 13 were found to be unsubstantiated, and the Human Rights Component investigated the remainder.[47]

In the *Third Progress Report*, the Secretary-General noted three categories of threats to public order in Cambodia: "politically motivated attacks on political party offices and staff; attacks on Vietnamese-speaking persons; and killings which seem to have no particular political motivation but which spread a climate of fear and intimidation."[48] The former two are relevant to human rights abuses. The issue of violence against ethnic Vietnamese will be discussed here, and the politically motivated attacks will be dealt in the following sub-section.

In November 1992, Vietnamese-speaking villagers and fishermen were killed in Tuk Meas village and in Koh Kong province. UNTAC investigations indicated that responsibility lay with National Army of Democratic Kampuchea (NADK; under Khmer Rouge) units in both incidents.[49] In October and November 1992, four other incidents against victims of Vietnamese origin took place.[50] In mid-December the dead bodies of three fishermen of Vietnamese origin were found floating in the Mekong. They had been reported as being missing since 8 December. UNTAC investigations established that the murders had been committed by NADK soldiers.[51] On 27 December a group of about 24 soldiers attacked Taches village in Kompong Chhnang Province and killed 14 people and wounded 14 others,

---

[45]   Interview with Mr. Yasunobu Sato, former UNTAC Human Rights Officer, London, 18 February, 1999.

[46]   *Second Progress Report*, para.10.

[47]   *Ibid.*

[48]   *Third progress report of the Secretary-General on UNTAC* (hereinafter *Third Progress Report*), UN doc. S/25154, 25 January 1993, para.95.

[49]   *Report of the Secretary-General on the implementation of Security Council resolution 783 (1992) on the Cambodia peace process*, UN Doc. S/24800, 15 November 1992.

[50]   *Third Progress Report*, para.97.

[51]   *Ibid.*, para.98.

including women and children. The soldiers first asked villagers to identify "Vietnamese" and then committed the assaults.[52] At the scene of the murder, a printed message was left calling UNTAC not to support Vietnamese who killed the Khmers.[53] On 10 March 1993, 33 ethnic Vietnamese including 12 children were massacred by some 20 armed men in a floating village in Siem Reap Province. UNTAC investigations concluded that the perpetrators were PDK soldiers.[54] In this case, the Human Rights Component asserted that those authorising such acts could be held liable under international law for crimes against humanity, as well as for genocide or complicity in genocide, in accordance with the Genocide Convention.[55] Further attacks against ethnic Vietnamese followed this incident on 24 and 29 March 1993, in Kompong Chhnang Province and Phnom Penh. Out of fear caused by such attacks and killings, thousands of ethnic Vietnamese, mostly fishermen and their families living along Cambodia's Tonle Sap (Great Lake) moved down-river towards Vietnam. Many of them were second- or third-generation residents in Cambodia.[56] By the end of April 1993, more than 21,000 ethnic Vietnamese crossed the border into Vietnam.[57]

The Secretary-General noted:

> The issue of the status of ethnic Vietnamese resident in Cambodia had not been provided for in the Paris accords, and some within UNTAC's leadership were inclined to think of the situation as an internal security issue for Cambodian authorities to resolve.[58]

Yet one Human Rights Officer recalls the event:

> I felt the frustration of being in Cambodia to help promote international standards of human rights while at the same time being helpless in the face of larger historical and political events. ...

---

[52] *Ibid.*

[53] Yasunobu Sato, 'Cambodia dayori: Pandora no hako wo aketa UNTAC (Letters from Cambodia: UNTAC opened the Pandora's box)', *Hogaku Seminar* (Seminar of Legal Studies), No.460, April 1993, p.19. Yasunobu Sato was Human Rights Officer appointed to Kompong Chhnang.

[54] *Fourth progress report of the Secretary-General on UNTAC*, UN Doc. S/25179, 3 May 1993, para.116.

[55] Stephen P. Marks, 'Forgetting "the Policies and Practices of the Past": Impunity in Cambodia', *Fletcher Forum of World Affairs*, Summer/Fall 1994: 17-43, p.35.

[56] *Fourth Progress Report*, para.119.

[57] *Ibid.*, para.120.

[58] *The UN and Cambodia*, Section 2, VII, p.42, para.99.

In part, the job was simply too vast, the ethnic and historical conflict too deep for the U.N. to address. In part, the U.N. feared undermining public perceptions of its neutrality by siding too openly with the Vietnamese victims, and often was accused of partiality.[59]

The spontaneous action taken by the UNTAC was to have its naval units and civilian police monitor the movements of fleeing Vietnamese and try to ensure that the local authorities assumed their responsibility to protect the displaced persons.[60]

The issue of the ethnic Vietnamese is related to the political history of Cambodia. Under French colonial rule of Cambodia, Vietnamese were employed as bureaucrats controlling Cambodians. In December 1978, it was the Vietnamese invasion which ousted the repressive regime of the Khmer Rouge. However, there has been a widespread belief that the Vietnamese were planning to destroy Cambodia as a nation. Cambodians often mention the former Cham empire of the Mekong Delta, which had been overrun by the Vietnamese in the sixteenth century.[61] During UNTAC's administration, the PDK kept insisting that UNTAC must investigate the existence of "foreign forces", which clearly meant Vietnamese forces.[62] The failure of UNTAC to meet this requirement, according to the PDK, was one of the two main reasons of the PDK's suspension of co-operation with UNTAC. In May 1992, UNTAC established Strategic Investigation Teams (SITs) to follow up allegations of the continued presence of such forces.[63] On 1 March 1993, UNTAC announced that three persons had been identified as "foreign forces" within the meaning of the definition approved by the SNC at a meeting on 20 October 1992. Two of the men were serving with the Cambodian People's Armed Forces (CPAF; the military force of SOC), and the third was a former member. UNTAC asked the Phnom Penh authorities to discharge the two from their armed forces, and to withdraw the identity cards

---

[59] Jamie Frederic Metzl, 'The Vietnamese of Cambodia', *Harvard Human Rights Journal*, Spring 1995: 269-275, pp.274-275.

[60] *The UN and Cambodia*, Section 2, VII, p.42, para.99.

[61] Metzl, *op. cit.*, p.272.

[62] The anti-Vietnamese campaign was not only carried out by the PDK, but also by KPNLF and FUNCINPEC. See Sydney Jones and Dinah PoKempner, 'Human Rights in Cambodia: Past, Present, and Future', in Frederick Z. Brown, ed., *Rebuilding Cambodia: Human Resources, Human Rights, and Law*, Arlington: Public Interest Publications, 1993: 43-68, pp.57-60.

[63] *Fourth Progress Report*, para.43.

of all three.[64] UNTAC also asked the Government of Vietnam to accept the three men back as Vietnamese nationals.[65] They were all married to Cambodian women and had children, and UNTAC made it clear that "there was no suggestion that they were in any way under the control of the Vietnamese authorities".[66] In other words, they were not active members of a "foreign force".

The reluctance of UNTAC to look into the issue of Vietnamese in Cambodia allowed the new Constitution to be drafted in a way which does not sufficiently protect minorities' rights:

> ... most of the articles in the chapter ["The Rights and Duties of Cambodian Citizens"] use language that clearly excludes aliens and visitors, and is probably intended to exclude certain ethnic groups whose citizenship has not been firmly established under a nationality and citizenship law.[67]

The same view was presented by Justice Michael Kirby, then Special Representative of the UN Secretary-General for human rights in Cambodia in the post-UNTAC period:

> In the historical context of the relationship between ethnic groups in Cambodia, the provisions of the Constitution relating to human rights as they are presently worded may give rise to risk that they could be used to justify discrimination against non-Khmer ethnic groups, such as Cambodians of Vietnamese or other non-Khmer ethnic origin.[68]

To foster a neutral political environment, UNTAC had announced that it would give priority to protecting three freedoms: freedom from intimidation, freedom of party affiliation and freedom of action for political parties.[69] However it is pertinent to note that UNTAC's attention to human rights was not neutral but political. UNTAC showed sympathy to the PDK by setting up the Strategic Investigation Teams and trying to deport three long term

---

[64] *Ibid.*, para.46.

[65] *Ibid.*

[66] *Ibid.*, para.47.

[67] Marks, *supra* note 38, p.71.

[68] *Report of the Special Representative of the Secretary-General, Mr. Michael Kirby, on the situation of human rights in Cambodia submitted pursuant to Commission on Human Rights Resolution 1993/6*, Commission on Human Rights, 50th Sess., Agenda Item 19, at 35. UN Doc. E/CN.4/1994/73, E/CN.4/1994/73/Add. 1 (1994).

[69] *Third Progress Report*, para.101.

Vietnamese settlers, while avoiding addressing the issue of minorities rights. However, this does not mean that UNTAC had a single position on this issue. The Human Rights Component even categorised one case as a crime against humanity and genocide.[70] Unfortunately, senior members of UNTAC did not share this view.

4.3   Change in the Human Rights Situation

By February 1992, a broad view of human rights violations became clear to UNTAC. While the killings of Vietnamese-speaking persons had generally been attributed to NADK elements, the great majority of attacks on political party offices and members were attributed to soldiers, police or supporters of the SOC.[71] Politically motivated murders, abductions, bombings, threats and other forms of intimidation increased. Most of them were carried out by soldiers, the police or supporters of the SOC against the FUNCINPEC, the Buddhist Liberal Democratic Party and other political parties.[72] Incidents of violence and intimidation peaked in December 1992, after rising through October and November. The number of such incidents reduced significantly in January 1993.[73] This reduction in the number of incidents of politically motivated violence continued up to April.[74]

4.4   Relationship with State Agencies

Since the peace process of Cambodia involved four parties, the operation of UNTAC was necessarily complicated. The major obstacle was the suspension of co-operation by the PDK (Khmer Rouge). As a result of this, UNTAC did not have access to the area controlled by the PDK, with one exception being access by the electoral staff to certain zones.[75]

Although the three other factions basically maintained co-operation with UNTAC, there were some critical moments. For instance, in the wake of politically motivated attacks against the FUNCINPEC, most of which were attributed to the SOC, Prince Sihanouk informed the Special Representative

---

[70]   See *supra* note 55 and accompanying text.

[71]   *Report of the Secretary-General on the implementation of Security Council resolution 792 (1992)*, UN Doc. S/25289, 13 February 1993, para.13.

[72]   *The UN and Cambodia*, Section 1, VI. p.34. para.82. Also *Third Progress Report*, 96.

[73]   *Report of the Secretary-General on the implementation of Security Council resolution 792 (1992)*, UN Doc. S/25289, 13 February 1993, para.13.

[74]   *Fourth Progress Report*, para.126.

[75]   *The UN and Cambodia*, Section 1, VI, p.29, para.69.

of the Secretary-General that he was obliged to cease co-operation with UNTAC and the SOC.[76] Also Prince Norodom Ranariddh, leader of the FUNCINPEC, announced his intention to cease all working relations with UNTAC.[77] However, subsequent discussions with the Special Representative secured the continuation of co-operation from both Princes.

In terms of human rights functions, UNTAC did not enjoy the full co-operation of local authorities, to say the least. Owing to the increase in politically motivated violence, UNTAC had to take a firm stand with regard to the local authorities. In November 1992, UNTAC Provincial Directors informed the Phnom Penh administration officials responsible for each province, their deputies and heads of districts or communes, that they could be held personally responsible by UNTAC for all acts of intimidation, all threats and all violent actions perpetrated against the agents of the parties active in their province, if investigation so warranted.[78]

Another action of UNTAC that had significant implications in terms of human rights was a directive issued by the Special Representative on 6 January 1993 and endorsed by the Security Council on 8 March 1993 by resolution 810.[79] The directive established procedures for the prosecution of persons responsible for human rights violations, and vested UNTAC with powers to arrest, detain and prosecute suspects in cases involving serious human rights violations.[80] Such powers would be exercised in accordance with the *Transitional Criminal Provisions*, which were adopted by the SNC

---

[76] *Third Progress Report*, para.14.

[77] *Letter dated 5 January 1993 from Prince Norodom Ranariddh, member of the Supreme National Council, to the Secretary-General concerning the political situation in Cambodia*, text in *The UN and Cambodia*, Section 2, IV, p.251.

[78] *Third Progress Report*, para.102.

[79] *Third Progress Report*, para.103. The directive was issued pursuant to Articles 6 and 16 and Sections B and E of annex I of the *Comprehensive Agreement*. Pursuant to Article 6, the SNC delegated to the UN "all powers necessary to ensure the implementation of the Paris Agreements". Article 16 sets forth the UNTAC's responsibility during the transitional period to foster "an environment in which respect for human rights shall be ensured". Section B provides that the Special Representative may issue binding directives. Section E sets forth the mandate of the Human Rights Component referred to above. See *supra* 2. 'Mandate and Composition of UNTAC'. SC resolution 810, 8 March 1993. SCOR, 3181st mtg., UN Doc. S/RES/810(1993). Adopted unanimously.

[80] Text of the directive is cited in J. Basil Fernando, *The Inability to Prosecute: Courts and Human Rights in Cambodia and Sri Lanka*, Hong Kong: Future Asia Link, 1993, pp.32-33.

on 10 September 1992.[81] The Government of Phnom Penh criticised this directive as interference with the sovereignty of Cambodia.[82]

The first case of arrest pursuant to this directive was of a police officer of the SOC, who had been charged with the murder of a FUNCINPEC party official. The second was of a member of NADK (the army of the Khmer Rouge), who was charged with the murder of 13 ethnic-Vietnamese Cambodians and 2 other Cambodians.[83] UNTAC, however, had to face unexpected resistance. The Phnom Penh municipal court refused to allow the proceedings of both cases on the ground that they were outside the jurisdiction of the Court.[84] In the latter case, the court even refused to issue an order of temporary detention under advice from the Ministry of Justice.[85] The UNTAC Prosecutor concluded that the accused, a member of NADK, could not enjoy a fair trial before the "competent" court which was under the control of the SOC. Directive 93/2 thus set forth that until such time as independent courts could conduct fair trials, the Special Prosecutors were not bound by the *Transitional Criminal Provisions*, and that the suspects who had been arrested and detained by UNTAC were to remain in custody.[86] UNTAC then opened its own jail and held the accused along with three SOC officials accused of gross violations of human rights.[87] Consequently, Directive 93/2 ignored the right to due process of law by maintaining detention without judicial review, which was contradictory to the *Transitional Criminal Provisions* prepared by UNTAC itself. In 1993, further warrants were issued by the UNTAC special prosecutor for the arrest

---

[81] Directive no.93/1 of 6 January 1993, *Third Progress Report*, para.103.

[82] Yasunobu Sato, 'Cambodia dayori: Risou to genjitsu no hazama de (Letters from Cambodia: Between the ideals and the reality)', *Hogaku Seminar* (Seminar of Legal Studies), No.461, May 1993, p.16.

[83] *Report of the Secretary-General on the implementation of Security Council resolution 792 (1992)*, UN Doc. S/25289, 13 February 1993, para.15.

[84] Sato, *supra* note 53, p.18. This directive had an unforeseen side effect as well. Japanese civilian police, who were dispatched by the Japanese government after intensive national arguments on a constitutional principle, announced that they could not execute warrants. Their participation in the peacekeeping operation was based on an understanding that their activities would not involve use of armed force or coercion. Consequently some Japanese CivPol monitors were demoted.

[85] Human Rights Watch, *The Lost Agenda: Human Rights and U.N. Field Operations*, 1993, p.62.

[86] Sato, *supra* note 30, p.49.

[87] Marks, *supra* note 55, p.34.

of 12 people in connection with cases of the abduction and subsequent disappearance, and of the murder of political party members.[88]

In early February 1993, UNTAC established a system to bring to the attention of the SOC "ministry of defence" cases where members of CPAF (the SOC's military force) were alleged to have taken part in illegal activity.[89] Upon the request of UNTAC, the ministry established a special committee to investigate these allegations. Although the ministry provided UNTAC with a list of CPAF personnel responsible for investigations in each province and each unit, the ministry admitted the guilt of its personnel in only a small number of cases, and punishments were rare.[90] With regard to the crimes involving political or ethnic implications, as appropriate, the Special Representative also raised the matter in the SNC and in private meetings with and letters to the leaders of Cambodian parties concerned.[91]

Official expressions of co-operation from the Cambodian side did not guarantee that this was actually forthcoming. Owing to continuing politically motivated violence, UNTAC issued another directive on 17 March 1993, prohibiting the possession and carrying of firearms and explosives by unauthorised persons. Confiscation of firearms pursuant to this directive helped in significantly reducing reported serious crimes in Phnom Penh.[92]

4.5   Investigation

In UNTAC, three components, the Human Rights Component, the Civil Administration Component, and the Civilian Police Component, were involved in Human Rights investigations. The Human Rights Component had a separate unit for the investigation and monitoring of human rights violations. In addition, human rights provincial officers (HRPOs) appointed for each province undertook investigations in their respective provinces. In case of political harassment and acts of political violence, a Special Task Force of the Civil Police consisting of selected investigators was also involved. Serious acts of violence were however investigated by joint teams composed of the human rights officers and the Special Task Force assisted by the Civil Police officers in the area.[93]

---

[88]   *Fourth Progress Report*, para.111.
[89]   *Ibid.*, para.65.
[90]   *Ibid.*
[91]   *Fourth Progress Report*, para.82.
[92]   *The UN and Cambodia*, Section 1, VII, p.42.
[93]   Fernando, *supra* note 80, p.30.

Unlike the United Nations Observation Mission in El Salvador, UNTAC Human Rights Component did not attempt to apply uniform methods of investigations. HRPOs were expected to handle cases based on individual judgement.[94] Unless the case was considered by the Headquarters to be too serious to be handled only at the provincial level, each officer was left alone.[95]

4.6   Reporting

UNTAC Human Rights Component did not employ a prescribed form for reporting of human rights cases. Usually each Human Rights Provincial Officer (HRPO) submitted monthly reports, and special reports were prepared when serious cases took place. The reporting styles of both monthly reports and special reports depended on the individual officer.[96] One former HRPO of UNTAC is positive about this discretion:

> A unified reporting form may restrict officers psychologically.
> If officers are really qualified, there is no need to use a unified form.[97]

At the headquarters level, the policy of Dennis McNamara, Director of the Human Rights Component, was to point out general issues in reports, but not specific cases. It was for the purpose of protecting victims and human rights officers.[98]

There was a monthly meeting in Phnom Penh to discuss about how to solve problems. For HRPOs deployed in isolated areas, it was also a good opportunity to ease the tension of their work.[99] Also, the meeting should have functioned as an occasion to exchange information between HRPOs, and that could provide important psychological support for officers working without specific guidelines or instructions. Wide discretion given to individual officers may have resulted in a flexible approach suitable in each case. However, the key condition to operate human rights functions in a highly flexible way is to ensure that each officer is sufficiently qualified and

---

[94] Interview with Mr. Saijin Zhang, former HRPO, Bihać, Bosnia-Herzegovina, 20 November 1998 and interview with Mr. Y. Sato.

[95] At least two former HRPOs were positive about this discretion to use their own initiative. The interviews referred to above.

[96] Interview with former HRPOs: Mr. Zhang and Mr. Sato.

[97] Interview with Mr. S. Zhang.

[98] Same as above.

[99] Same as above.

experienced. As regards the forms of reports, one option is to determine basic items to be included and leave the rest to the discretion of each officer.

4.7 Institution-Building

4.7.1 Reform of Criminal Procedures

One of the first activities that the Human Rights Component undertook was reform of the prison system. A Prisons Control Commission was established and its review led to the release of prisoners detained without trial. Such releases numbered 108 in May and a further 150 in August 1992.[100] A large majority of detainees in civilian prisons administered by the Phnom Penh authorities had not been enjoying due process, and some prisoners had been detained for up to 10 years without trial.[101]

Following the adoption by the SNC on 19 September 1992 of the *Transitional Criminal Provisions*, UNTAC launched a training programme for local magistrates, police officers, prosecutors and public defenders.[102] They were from three of the four Cambodian parties excluding the PDK, and numbered about 200. This was a joint programme of the Human Rights Component and Civilian Police Component.[103] Although the *Transitional Criminal Provisions* contained the principle of the independence of the judiciary, the training programme revealed that "the whole concept of independence of the judiciary was alien" to the trainees:

> Some of them even expressed the view that even if they wanted to be independent, they had no way of making orders against the police or administrative officers as those persons are in fact more powerful than the judiciary.[104]

As the arrival of UNTAC had not changed the power structure of Cambodian society, the *Transitional Criminal Provisions* were virtually ignored by the Cambodian courts.[105]

In 1993, UNTAC commenced a programme of bringing prisoners before the courts for the determination of the legality of their detention. It was an

---

[100] *Second Progress Report*, para.10.

[101] *Third Progress Report*, para.21.

[102] *Ibid.*, para.63. Also *Fourth Progress Report* para.66.

[103] *Third Progress Report*, para.63.

[104] Fernando, *supra* note 80, p.10.

[105] *Ibid.*

endeavour to break the control of the security forces over issues of detention.[106] For prisoners held for long periods without trial, applications for their release were made in Phnom Penh and in several provincial courts. The major obstacle of this programme was the lack of appellate courts. In some cases, administrative authorities were approached for the release of long-term prisoners.[107]

4.7.2 Technical Assistance in Drafting a Constitution

Technical assistance in drafting a new Constitution was an important part of UNTAC's institution-building activity. Nevertheless, in comparison with some foreign governments or NGOs who were keen on influencing the legal system,[108] UNTAC was wary about being paternalistic. In September 1992, Mr. Akashi distributed at a SNC meeting, a brief, factual analysis prepared by Professor Reginald Austin, the head of the Electoral Component,[109] with respect to the drafting of a constitution. As noted by Stephen P. Marks, School of International and Public Affairs of Columbia University:

> Prof. Austin's draft deliberately avoided any suggestion that UNTAC intended to write the constitution or to propose draft texts. The text merely set out in general the issues that must be addressed when drafting a constitution, such as name, flag, delimitation of territory, form of government, etc.[110]

In November 1992, UNTAC sponsored a seminar for party representatives of the Technical Advisory Committee on constitutional principles. In January 1993, international experts were invited to assist in discussions on this issue. A further six-day constitutional seminar was held from 29 March to 3 April 1993. The seminar focused on four topics: constitutions and conflicts; Cambodia's constitutional history; crucial issues facing the Constituent Assembly; and developing procedures for debate.[111] One UNTAC participant recalls regarding the seminar:

---

[106] *Fourth Progress Report*, para.69.

[107] *Ibid.*

[108] Marks, *supra* note 38, p.60.

[109] Prof. Reginald Austin is a professor of law and former dean of the law school of the University of Zimbabwe.

[110] Marks, *supra* note 38, p.60.

[111] *Fourth Progress Report*, para.30.

> While helpful in deepening participants' awareness of comparative approaches to key issues of governance and constitution drafting, the Seminar did not appear to have much of an impact on the persons who actually drafted the text.[112]

UNTAC's sensitiveness not to be regarded as a new colonialist operation is plausible. However, UNTAC could have exercised more influence by emphasising the principles of the rule of law and human rights. S. P. Marks argues that if the following three points had been included in the provisions of the new Cambodian Constitution, the enforcement of human rights could have been strengthened.[113] Firstly, the domestic incorporation of international law, on which point the new Constitution is silent except for Article 31:

> The Kingdom of Cambodia shall recognize and respect human rights as defined in the United Nations Charter, the Universal Declaration of Human Rights, and all treaties and conventions related to human rights, women's rights and children's rights.

The application of international law in domestic legal systems may take different forms. The two major doctrines are transformation and incorporation.[114] The doctrine of transformation is based on dualism, and maintains

---

[112] Marks, *supra* note 38, p.5.

[113] Marks, *supra* note 55, pp.93-98. Marks also mentions another point to be taken into account, which is judicial control of the administration. The Constitution has provisions setting forth the right of individuals to complain or demand compensation for damage caused by illegal acts of the State organs, mass organisations or state officials. The question is whether these provisions are to be implemented. Marks affirms that he has no knowledge of successful cases in this regard.

[114] See, in general, Antonio Cassese, 'Modern Constitutions and International Law', *Recueil des cours*, 1985 III: 335-473, pp. 368-412, Shaw, *International Law, supra* FN9 of Introduction, 99-128; Malanczuk, *Akehurst's Modern Introduction to International Law, supra* FN16 of Chapter 1, 63-71; Ian Brownlie, *Principles of Public International Law*, 4th ed., Clarendon Press, 1990, pp.43-52; Shinya Murase, 'Kokusaihou no doutai (Dynamism of Contemporary International Law)' in Murase *et al.*, *Gendai kokusaihou no shihyou (Characteristics of Contemporary International Law)*, Tokyo: Yuhikaku, 1994: 1-61, pp.51-58; Andrew Valden S. Vereshchetin, 'New Constitutions and the Old Problem of the Relationship between International Law and National Law', *EJIL* 7(1): 1996: 29-41; V.S. Vereshchetin, 'Some Reflections on the Relationship between International Law and National Law in the Light of New Constitutions', in Rein Müllerson, Malgosia Fitzmaurice and Mads Andenas, eds., *Constitutional Reform and International Law in Central and Eastern Europe*, Kluwer Law International, 1998: 5-13; J. Cunningham, 'The European Convention on Human Rights, Customary International Law and the Constitution', *ICLQ* 43, 1994: 537-567; Eric Stein, 'International Law in Internal Law: Toward Internationalization of Central-Eastern Constitutions?', *AJIL* 88, 1994: 427-450; and Yuji

that international law must be transformed into municipal law before becoming effective within domestic jurisdiction. According to the doctrine of incorporation, on the other hand, international law is considered part of the law of the land and enforced without any procedure of transformation. General rules of international law or customary international law may be treated differently from treaty law. Furthermore, some States give primacy to international law over their municipal law, whereas others give equal status to international law and municipal law, and yet some other Constitutions are silent about the status of international law in the domestic legal order.[115] International human rights norms are increasingly referred to in national constitutions, as Valden S. Vereshchetin, Judge at the International Court of Justice, notes:

> Several new constitutions expressly provide for the primacy of international human rights and for their direct application by the courts and other State's organs. In some other cases such a rule flow from the general provisions on the supremacy of international law or its constituent parts.[116]

The provision of Article 31 of the new Cambodian Constitution remains weak in terms of human rights protection because applicability of the relevant human rights law is not clear.[117] To express that the State would

---

Iwasawa, 'The Relationship between International Law and National Law: Japanese Experiences', *BYIL* 64, 1993: 333-390.

[115] Professor Cassese gives examples of Italy, Japan, the Federal Republic of Germany and Greece as the first group, and Austria, Portugal and possibly Ireland as the second group with respect to the customary international law. Cassese, *op. cit.*, pp. 369-370. As to treaties, a very limited number of Western European States and a group of former French colonies as well as some Latin American States are examples of the first group, while Kuwait, Algeria and the Republic of Korea belong to the second group. Cassese, *op. cit.*, p.405. Vereshchetin points out that new constitutions of several Eastern-European States provides for supremacy of international treaties over national law. Vereshchetin, *op. cit.*, p.33. Also see, Malanczuk, *op. cit.*, p.65.

[116] Vereshchetin, *op. cit.*, p.41.

[117] Cf. Masanori Aikyo of Nagoya University is of the view that this provision is more concrete and precise comparing with Article 50 of the Constitution of Vietnam (1992) and suggests that it was due to the influence of the UNTAC. Masanori Aikyo, 'The 1993 Constitution of Cambodia', in Masanori Aikyo and Kenji Yotsumoto, *Gendai Cambodia no hou to jinken ni tsuite* (*Law and Human Rights in Cambodia Today*), Nagoya daigaku houseironshu Vol.157, 1994: 159-179, p.173. Article 50 of the Vietnam Constitution reads:

> In the Socialist Republic of Vietnam human rights in the political, civic, economic, cultural and social fields are respected. They are embodied in the citizen's rights and are determined by the constitution and the law.

'recognise' and 'respect' human rights is not necessarily a definite commitment to abide by the relevant human rights law. The provision leaves the Cambodian government a large margin of discretion as to how human rights protection will be implemented. The provision on human rights treaties in the Czech Constitution, for example, is far more assertive:

> Ratified and promulgated international accords on human rights and fundamental freedoms, to which the Czech Republic has committed itself, are immediately binding and are superior to law.[118]

UNTAC actually suggested in its constitutional seminar, the following text:

> 1. International treaties to which Cambodia is or may become a party are applicable as law in Cambodia as soon as they have entered into force and are promulgated by the State.

> 2. In case of conflict between a Cambodian law or regulation and a rule of international law, the latter shall prevail.

> 3. Norms of international law may be invoked before the courts of Cambodia and applied by the judge.

> 4. Any person within the jurisdiction of Cambodia may invoke a provision of an international human rights treaty to which Cambodia is a party in order to seek redress for an alleged violation of human rights protected by the treaty in question. The application of such treaty provisions by the courts shall complement and reinforce similar provisions, if any, contained in the Bill of Rights of the Constitution.[119]

This is a model provision, which precisely sets forth the status of treaty law in domestic jurisdiction.

Secondly, the issue is whether the Constitution allows the citizens to question the validity of the law on grounds of its constitutionality. Although the Constitution provided for the establishment of a Constitutional Court, citizens are able to appeal only through their representative or the chairman of the Parliament.

Text available at: http://www.batin.com.vn/vninfo/constitution/chaptr5c.htm (visited on 17 June 2000).

[118] Article 10, Constitution of the Czech Republic, adopted on 16 December 1992. Text available at http://www.uni-wuerzburg.de/law/ez00000_.html (visited on 17 June 2000). For more examples, see Stein, *supra* note 114, pp. 435-444.

[119] Text cited in Marks, *supra* note 55, p.94, FN 155.

Thirdly, provisions which strictly limit the derogations from human rights guarantees in case of public emergencies.[120] The actual provision incorporated in the new Constitution is:

> ... [w]hen the nation faces danger, the King shall publicly make an announcement declaring a state of emergency in the country after securing the consent of the prime minister and the chairman of the parliament.[121]

The provision does not specify what constitutes the "danger" and no mention is made regarding non-derogable human rights.

The Constitution was formally promulgated by Prince Sihanouk on 24 September 1993 and a constitutional monarchy, "The Kingdom of Cambodia" was established.[122] On the same day, Prince Sihanouk was elected King

---

[120] Regarding derogation of human rights during states of emergency in general, see Fitzpatrik, *Human Rights in Crisis*, *supra* FN10 of Introduction; Jaime Oràà, *Human Rights in States of Emergency in International Law*, Clarendon Press, 1992; Rosalyn Higgins, 'Derogations under Human Rights Treaties', *BYIL* 48, 1976-7: 281-320; Fionnuala Ni Aolain, 'The Emergence of Diversity: Differences in Human Rights Jurisprudence', *Fordham International Law Journal*, October 1995: 101-142; and Sara Stapleton, 'Ensuring a Fair Trial in the International Criminal Court: Statutory Interpretation and the Impermissibility of Derogation', *New York University Journal of International Law and Politics*, 1999: 535-609, pp.580-609.

[121] UNTAC suggested a model text on this point, too:

> 1. In time of war, famine, major natural catastrophe or other public emergency threatening the life of the nation, the Prime Minister [or other appropriate high official] may, after consulting the Council of Ministers, proclaim a State of Emergency. During the emergency, the government may take measures derogating from the human rights provisions of the constitution to the extent strictly required by the exigencies of the situation and necessary in a democratic society. These measures must be set out in the Proclamation of the State of Emergency.

> 2. No derogations may be made, regardless of the seriousness of the emergency, from the right to life; the prohibition against torture or other cruel, inhuman or degrading treatment or punishment; the prohibition of slavery or servitude; non-retroactivity of criminal legislation; freedom of thought, conscience and religion and any other rights that are not subject to derogation under this constitution or under any other provision of national or international law.

> 3. Any measures taken pursuant to this article shall be notified to the United Nations in accordance with Article 4 of the International Covenant on Civil and Political Rights."

Text cited in Marks, *supra* note 55, p.97, FN 167.

[122] *Further report of the Secretary-General on the implementation of Security Council resolution 745 (1992)*, UN Doc. S/26259, 5 October 1993, para.3.

of Cambodia by the Royal Council of the Throne.[123] Article 7 of the new Constitution sets forth that the King holds the throne but shall not hold power.[124]

4.8   Human Rights Education

The Human Rights Component organised training sessions for local organisations, teachers, school administrators and others.[125] Training programmes were later expanded to diverse audiences, including judges, police, defence lawyers, monks, public defenders, electoral supervisors, women's associations, health professionals and representatives of the Cambodian political parties.[126] Since virtually everyone with legal training had either fled or been murdered under the Pol Pot regime,[127] the education of legal experts was particularly important. For the general public, mobile video units were set up in each province to show videos on basic human rights concepts. A team of traditional singers was organised through the co-operation between UNESCO and UNTAC, to tour the provinces with a performance featuring human rights messages.[128] Formal human rights training was introduced into the Cambodian education system and curriculum materials were distributed to teachers in primary and secondary schools. A course of human rights studies started at Phnom Penh University for 210 law students.[129]

From 30 November to 1 December 1992, an International Symposium on Human Rights in Cambodia was also organised in Phnom Penh. It was participated in by representatives of each of the Cambodian human rights organisations and some 25 representatives of human rights organisations in

---

[123] The Royal Council of the Throne consists of the chairman of Parliament, the Prime Minister, two head monks, and the first and second Vice-Chairmen of Parliament. Marks, *supra* note 38, p.68.

[124] *Further report of the Secretary-General on the implementation of Security Council resolution 745 (1992)*, UN Doc. S/26259, 5 October 1993, para.3.

[125] *Second Progress Report*, para.9.

[126] *The UN and Cambodia*, Section 1, I., p.30, para.72. Besides the Human Rights Component, the Civilian Police Component (CIVPOL) also included human rights in its training courses for local police. *Fourth Progress Report*, para.86. Some of CIVPOL training was very successful and even united all four factions including the Khmer Rouge. Doyle, *supra* note 14, p.47.

[127] Marks, *supra* note 38, p.55. One commentator states that only five persons qualify if the Western definition of a lawyer were to be applied to Cambodia. Dolores A. Donovan, 'The Cambodian Legal System: An Overview', in Brown, ed., *supra* note 62: 69-107, p.87.

[128] *Third Progress Report*, para.18.

[129] *Ibid.*, para.17.

other areas of the world, as well as of the United Nations Centre for Human Rights and other United Nations agencies.[130] For Human Rights Day, 10 December, UNTAC organised various events in Phnom Penh and the provinces, including a nation-wide drawing contest for children.[131] In addition to educational materials, posters, leaflets, stickers and other printed materials, UNTAC printed 10,000 copies of a 400-page compilation of human rights instruments applicable in Cambodia.[132]

During the post-election period, UNTAC Human Rights Component redirected its human rights education programme towards "constitutional literacy". The programme was for Cambodian NGOs and the general public, with the aim of providing information on popular participation in constitution drafting with reference to examples from other Asian countries, and a basic understanding of constitutional concepts. The efforts of the Component led to the formation of a coalition of fourteen groups called Ponleu Khmer (Cambodian Illumination) which actively lobbied the Constituent Assembly in order to invest the Constitution with strong human rights provisions.[133] Despite the interest of the general public in the drafting of the new Constitution, the draft prepared in August 1993 by the Drafting Committee was kept secret, even from the other members of the Constituent Assembly.[134] The draft prepared by the Drafting Committee and another monarchical draft prepared by FUNCINPEC were brought before Sihanouk in Pyongyang who reportedly was there for health reason. It is said that Sihanouk made many hand-written amendments to the monarchical constitution shown to him for his approval.[135]

Human rights education probably formed a greater proportion of the whole human rights functions of UNTAC than in the case of ONUSAL in El Salvador. The dissemination of human rights is widely assessed as a successful part of UNTAC.[136] However, as it was not combined with strong emphasis on institution-building, UNTAC's achievement did not reach its full potential.

---

[130] *Ibid.*, para.23.

[131] *Ibid.*, para.25.

[132] *Fourth Progress Report,* para.19.

[133] Marks, *supra* note 38, p.61.

[134] *Ibid.*

[135] *Ibid.*, p.63.

[136] Doyle, *supra* note 14, p.46, Schear, *supra* note 14, pp.163-164, Shawcross, *supra* note 41, p.59.

4.9 Co-operation inside UNTAC

Human rights related activities in UNTAC were relatively complicated. The Human Rights Component, the Civil Administration Component and the Civilian Police were all involved in such activities. For example, prison visits were mainly conducted by the Civil Administration Component, with the co-operation of the Human Rights Component and the Civilian Police.[137]

There was internal discord between the Human Rights Component and the Civil Administration Component. It became clearer when an Action Cell was created following the issuance of the problematic Directive 93/2, which enabled the detention of suspects without judicial review.[138] The Action Cell was an advisory board comprised of representatives from each Component, and its approval was required for the issuance of new warrants. The Civil Administration Component tried to use the Action Cell as a buffer in persuading the government, while the Human Rights Component claimed that urgent measures were necessary to restrain severe human rights violations and to protect witnesses.[139] The discord was acute in the case of the kidnapping of four FUNCINPEC members by seven SOC (State of Cambodia) military officials in Battambang province. The Action Cell authorised the arrest of the suspects, but some members of the Action Cell insisted that the SOC should first be informed of the intended arrests and given a week to produce the suspects. The UNTAC military refused to permit the use of force in the arrest based on their narrow interpretation of its mandate. On the day of the arrest, the SOC military compound was deserted and the seven suspects had already been transferred to the Pailin front.[140]

Political consideration by the Civil Administration Component arguably jeopardised the neutrality of UNTAC in dealing with human rights issues. Commentators argue that UNTAC was soft with the SOC intransigence since losing SOC's co-operation meant UNTAC's failure.[141]

4.10 Co-operation with Other UN Agencies

As mentioned above, UNTAC had a joint programme of human rights education with the UNESCO. In addition, the UNHCR was an integral part of UNTAC as the Repatriation Component. UNHCR has established a

---

[137] *Fourth Progress Report*, para.66.

[138] *Supra* note 86 and accompanying text.

[139] Sato, *supra* note 30, p.49.

[140] Human Rights Watch, *supra* note 85, p.63.

[141] Hughes, *supra* note 5, p.32; and Jones and PoKempner, *supra* note 62, p.50.

countrywide mechanism for monitoring the condition of returnees, in co-operation with other components of UNTAC as well as UN agencies and NGOs. Its main objective was to survey the security situation and the reintegration of returnees.[142] This mechanism was accompanied with the training of local staff so that the system could be "Cambodianised" along with the gradual phasing out of UNHCR international staff.

4.11 Co-operation with Local NGOs

Unlike El Salvador, there had been no existing local human rights NGOs in Cambodia when UNTAC started its operation. The development of such organisations, however, was remarkable. By January 1993, five NGOs were in operation, with offices in nearly all provinces. Their combined member-ship was then reportedly approaching 50,000. UNTAC supported this development by providing them with materials, training and expertise as well as small grants for basic office expenses. UNTAC also set up a resource centre and library for collective use.[143] By the time of the election, the membership of Cambodian human rights non-governmental organisations, including Buddhist, student and women's groups, grew to some 150,000 persons.[144]

CONCLUSION

Balance between Political and Human Rights Functions

The general election for the constitutional National Assembly in Cambodia was held from 23 to 28 May 1993, with 89.56 per cent of the registered voters actually casting a vote.[145] The results of the election was as follows: FUNCINPEC won 45.47 per cent of the votes, the CPP came in second with 38.23 per cent, and the remainder was shared by 17 other parties.[146] A prominent international human rights NGO assesses the peace process in Cambodia:

---

[142] *Fourth Progress Report*, para.94.

[143] *Third Progress Report*, para.20.

[144] *The UN and Cambodia*, Section 1, VIII, p.50.

[145] *Report of the Secretary-General on the conduct and results of the election in Cambodia*, UN Doc. S/25913, 10 June 1993, paras.2 & 5.

[146] *Ibid.*, para.13.

> ... the emphasis on elections was so strong that other aims, including protection of basic human rights, became secondary.[147]

Tension between the political consideration and human rights activities existed in UNTAC as in the case of ONUSAL. For instance, prison visits and review of prisoners' cases by UNTAC resulted in the release of hundreds of prisoners during 1992. However, SOC media accused UNTAC of releasing dangerous criminals into society, and UNTAC changed its strategy to have SOC courts review arrests on their own. As a result, the prisons were once again full by March 1993.[148]

Yasushi Akashi, Special Representative of the Secretary-General for Cambodia, clearly affirms:

> I did not adopt the more radical measures urged by the UNTAC Human Rights Component, when they seemed to be based on unrealistically high standards in the context of Cambodian reality.[149]

That the Human Rights Component was unrealistic is arguable. Within the first week of the arrival of the Special Representative, a former political prisoner who had been detained by the SOC for attempting to form an opposition party was assaulted and later died of his wounds. UNTAC conducted an inconclusive inquiry, and declined to issue a full report on the incident or to continue the investigation. It was a detrimental precedent for human rights investigations in Cambodia.[150]

The subordination of human rights work to other Components may also be demonstrated by its logistics problem. There were no vehicles for the field staff of the Human Rights Component, and they were forced to rely on the co-operation of other components.[151] Field work of human rights monitors or investigators without vehicles, particularly in such a country where public transport can hardly be relied on, only invites doubts as to the seriousness of the operation.

---

[147] *Ibid.*, p.37.

[148] Human Rights Watch, *supra* note 85, p.54.

[149] Yasuhi Akashi, 'The Challenge of Peacekeeping in Cambodia', *International Peacekeeping* 1(2), Summer 1994: 204-215, p.210.

[150] Human Rights Watch, *supra* note 85, p.57.

[151] *Ibid.*, p.59. Also interview with Mr. Y. Sato.

Justice Package

Mark Plunkett, former UNTAC special prosecutor, points out another defect of the UNTAC human rights function. UN peace-building required a "justice package", a systematic, prepared combination of prosecutorial, police, and judicial capacities, together with a mandate to train.[152] Deprived of the means of prosecution, the UNTAC human rights function was inevitably limited. Although UNTAC had a mandate to draft Electoral Law, the other functions were to operate under the existing juridical system. An UNTAC Human Rights Officer also comments:

> In a society where a fair and independent judiciary is not guaranteed, due process is essentially meaningless. The situation highlighted the fact that the fundamental human rights to liberty (civil liberties) can only be ensured once the necessary judicial conditions are in place.[153]

Under the Constitution of the State of Cambodia, which was passed by the National Assembly on 30 April 1989 (1989 Constitution), the judiciary was subordinated to the executive power.[154] The Ministry of Justice administered the judicial process and held full power to make any decisions by even intervening prior to a hearing of a case.[155] The National Assembly had the powers to establish and dissolve the Supreme Court as well as the right to monitor the activities of the Supreme Court.[156] Before deciding on each case, judges had to request the advice of the Supreme Court and/or the Ministry of Justice. Instead of judicial review, this "advisory function" had played a role in the Cambodian justice system. There was no procedure for the public hearing of appeals, and the judges of the Supreme Court were not required to give reasons as to why a particular judgment given by the provincial court was considered incorrect. In two cases filed by the UNTAC Prosecutor at the Municipal Court of Phnom Penh, the Minister of Justice Uk Bun Chhoeum called the judge in charge and instructed him not to proceed with these

---

[152] Doyle, *supra* note 14, p.49.

[153] Sato, *supra* note 30, p.49.

[154] Fernando, *supra* note 80, p.1.

[155] Basil Fernando, 'Shinsei Cambodia ni okeru hou to jinken (Law and Human Rights in New Cambodia' (a lecture given on 7 March 1994 at Nagoya University. Translated into Japanese by Kenji Yotsumoto), in Aikyo and Yotsumoto, *supra* note 117, p.210.

[156] Article 48 of the 1989 Constitution.

cases.[157] Although Municipal Courts were functioning in the territory controlled by the SOC, no courts were functioning in other territories.[158]

J. Basil Fernando, head of the Human Rights Component, observed that the judicial power in Cambodia was generally exercised by the police. The police enjoyed vast powers of discretion – even as to whether to investigate a crime or not. The police were not required to give evidence in court.[159] Fernando concludes:

> The achievement of independence of the judiciary in Cambodia lies in reform of the police mainly and not mere reform of the judiciary.
>
> The reform of the police could not be achieved by mere police education; strict definitions of functions and account-ability to the court is essential to any rational functioning of the police.
>
> Till such a reform is achieved, the single most prominent threat to public security would be the police themselves.[160]

The Civilian Police Component of UNTAC did work in so far as it educated the local police. However, it apparently did not plan to fully undertake reform of the local police. The Component itself suffered significant defects in the eyes of commentators. Firstly, there were many monitors who spoke neither French nor English. The Military Component worked as national contingents, whereas the Police Component worked in mixed nationalities. Thus the problems with communication directly hampered the efficiency of their work. Secondly, some could not drive. This also obviously diminished the Police Component's capability. The third point relates to the nature of police work.[161] Particularly if community policing is the aim, local know-ledge, community trust, and expertise are required. Consequently cross-national police co-operation had to bear a heavy burden from the outset.[162]

---

[157] Cases of Em Chann and Than Theoun. Fernando, *supra* note 80, p.6.

[158] *Ibid.*, p.15.

[159] *Ibid.*, pp.7-8.

[160] *Ibid.*, p.8.

[161] Doyle, *supra* note 14, p.48. Also see Human Rights Watch, *supra* note 85, p.52.

[162] Doyle, *op. cit.* Also Alice Hills, 'International Peace Support Operations and CIVPOL: Should there be a Permanent Global Gendarmerie?', *International Peacekeeping* 5(3), Autumn 1998:26-41, p.32.

Accountability for Past Human Rights Abuses

In contrast with the former Yugoslavia and Rwanda, the Cambodian peace process, including the operation of UNTAC, did not seek accountability for past grave human rights violations.[163] The Paris Peace Agreements avoided the term "genocide" and instead referred to "the policies and practices of the past". Commentators regret the missed opportunity:

> The failure to address responsibility for the past in the interests
> of reaching an agreement with the four parties foreshadowed an
> unwillingness to address human rights abuses in the present for
> the same reasons of accommodation and served to diminish the
> importance of human rights more generally.[164]

Many commentators support the use of the term "genocide" as regards the atrocities committed by the Khmer Rouge.[165] This author, however, has reservations on this point. The Convention on the Prevention and Punishment of the Crime of Genocide (Genocide Convention) defines genocide as the following acts "committed with intent to destroy, in whole or in part, a national, ethnical, racial or religious group, as such":[166]

(a) Killing members of the group;

(b) Causing serious bodily or mental harm to members of the group;

(c) Deliberately inflicting on the group conditions of life calculated to bring about its physical destruction in whole or in part;

(d) Imposing measures intended to prevent births within the group; and

(e) Forcibly transferring children of the group to another group.

The policy of Khmer Rouge could not be the destruction of the Khmer, and thus it does not fall under the definition of genocide pursuant to the

---

[163] Regarding the International Tribunals for the former Yugoslavia and Rwanda, see, respectively, Chapter 6 and Chapter 5.

[164] Human Rights Watch, *supra* note 85, p.38. Also see Marks, *supra* note 55, p.27.

[165] See for example, Hannum, *supra* note 1, Marks, *supra* note 55, and Gregory H. Stanton, The Cambodian Genocide and International Law', in Ben Kiernan, ed., *Genocide and Democracy in Cambodia: The Khmer Rouge, the United Nations and the International Community*, New Haven: Yale University of Southeast Asia Studies, 1993: 141-161.

[166] GA resolution 260, UN Doc. A/810(1948).

Genocide Convention owing to the lack of an essential factor of the genocide, namely the *intention* to destroy the whole or a part of a particular group.[167] Burgler analyses Khmer Rouge's policy and concludes that:

> Democratic Kampuchea was not an attempt at auto-genocide by a group of lunatics. It was a conscious and rational, although very radical, attempt to create a classless and contradiction-free, modern and independent society.[168]

Furthermore, as will be discussed in the next chapter, the Genocide Convention does not refer to a political group as a possible target of genocide. If we are to consider Khmer Rouge's mass killings of certain ethnic groups or Buddhist monks, i.e. a religious group, the scale of killings become much smaller than if we consider the number of victims under the regime in total. This does not mean that the mass killings committed by the Khmer Rouge are insignificant. A large scale of human rights violations that were committed by the regime could be characterised as "crimes against humanity", and the efforts being undertaken to establish the truth in this regard are welcome. This author is of the view that it is more important to study how "conscious and rational" ideology allowed a belief that such atrocities were justifiable rather than to try to describe all the conduct of the Khmer Rouge as genocide. If we use the term, "genocide", regarding Khmer Rouge's atrocities against different ethnic or religious groups separately, we need to be aware that this term applies to a large number of situations in the world. Two international law scholars who were commissioned by the US Department of State to study legal issues relating to the implementation of the Cambodian Genocide Justice Act (1994) found:

> ... *prima facie* culpability for genocidal acts against religious and ethnic groups, including the Cham, Vietnamese, and Chinese ethnic groups and the Buddhist monkhood ...

but concluded that:

> ... the argument that acts against the Khmer national group constituted genocide remains problematic.[169]

---

[167] See, for example, Vickery, supra note 1; and Roel A. Burgler, 'The Case of Cambodia: the Khmer Rouge's Reign of Terror', in Albert J. Jongman, ed., *Comtemporary Genocides: Causes, Cases, Consequences*, PIOOM, 1996: 59-76.

[168] Burgler, *ibid.*, p.75.

[169] Jason S. Abrams and Steven R. Ratner, 'The Attempt to bring the Perpetrators of the Cambodian Genocide to Trial', in Jongman, *op. cit.*: 77-78, p.77. In July 2000, the Cambodian Government and the UN finally reached an agreement to establish a national

The reluctance of the UN and international community to address the issue of "genocide" was not significantly, but to certain extent, offset by the Human Rights Officers in the field.[170] In the teaching programme, the question of "genocide" and the crimes of the PDK were regularly included and discussed openly with all audiences including NGOs, students, and officials of parties and administrative structures.[171] One Human Rights Officer recalls:

> The human rights officers could at least be open and honest about the political realities of the Paris Agreements and the applicable provisions of international human rights law.[172]

Regarding the legal tradition of Cambodia, one commentator notes:

> It [Cambodia] lacks the legal traditions to expect courts to settle matters fairly and it has a religious tradition that teaches reconciliation without accountability.[173]

Another commentator analyses that Cambodia has two legal systems: "a formal legal system built around the courts and an informal one built around conciliation, with the latter only loosely attached to the state".[174] Kassie Neou, the director of the Cambodian Institute of Human Rights, affirms that the desirable way for Cambodia is "culturally related advocacy for national reconciliation". For instance, the current monuments to the genocide in several locations should be replaced by a centre with a stupa (Buddhist

---

tribunal with international participation in order to bring former Khmer Rouge leaders to justice. See, for instance, www.hrw.org/wr2k1/asia.cambodia.html. The National Assembly passed legislation on the tribunal on 2 January 2001, but the UN criticised the law as to the possibility of shielding suspects by amnesty. *Washington Post*, 3 February 2001.

[170] For the reaction of the UN Commission on Human Rights during the Khmer Rouge regime, see Jamie Frederic Metzl, 'The U.N. Commission on Human Rights and Cambodia, 1975-1980', *Buffalo Journal of International Law*, 1996: 67-98. The reluctance continued. On 21 June 1997, the Prime Ministers of Cambodia sent a letter to the United Nations Secretary-General requesting the establishment of an international tribunal to bring the Khmer Rouge to justice. China expressed its opposition on the ground that the matter was an internal affair, and the USA and the UK made it clear that they had no intention of funding such a tribunal. Brad Adams, 'UN Human Rights Work in Cambodia: Efforts to Preserve the Jewel in the Peacekeeping Crown', in Henkin, ed., *Honouring Human Rights, supra* FN44 of Chapter 3: 189-226, p.215.

[171] Marks, *supra* note 55, p.33.

[172] *Ibid.* Stephen P. Marks was head of human rights education, training, and information for the UNTAC.

[173] *Ibid.*, p.40.

[174] Donovan, *supra* note 127, p.92.

monument) that would be a place of remembrance but not of denunciation. Instead of displaying the skulls and bones of victims, the remains would be cremated, thus liberating the imprisoned souls.[175] Yet another commentator suggests the potential effectiveness in Cambodia of a mediation mechanism such as an ombudsman:

> Cambodia, like most Asian societies, has traditional methods of dispute settlement that are based on respect for elders, saving face, and family and clan sensitivities. ... This tradition of mediation provides fertile ground for informal procedures of resolving human rights problems through an ombudsman, human rights commissioner or and independent body consisting of persons who enjoy considerable prestige in the society.[176]

UNTAC experienced difficulty in implementing international standards of human rights in Cambodia. For example, despite the ban on shackles in Cambodian prisons, their use was continued in rural areas for the purpose of preventing prisoners escaping. Can we simply insist on the immediate abolition of the practice without considering an alternative to prevent prisoners' escapes? [177] When the World Food Program prepared plans for the distribution of food to prisoners in Cambodia, the idea had to be abandoned because of complaints that the prisoners would be better fed than the guards.[178] Studies of local conditions ought to be an integral part of human rights functions in peacekeeping operations. If UNTAC had taken into account cultural factors and local conditions from the time of planning, it could have left a stronger basis for Cambodian society to develop a human rights protection mechanism of its own style.

Overall Evaluation

Did UNTAC completely fail in its human rights functions? It certainly did not tackle the issue of ethnic minorities. Referring to the attacks against ethnic Vietnamese, one Human Rights Officer reflects:

---

[175] Marks, *supra* note 55, p.33. For example, at a genocide museum in Phnom Penh, skulls are displayed on the wall, forming a map of Cambodia. Some international election observers for the Cambodian election in 1998 commented upon visit of the museum, that it gives an impression of political propaganda rather than a genuine institution of historical records or memorial.

[176] Marks, *supra* note 38, p.92.

[177] Interview with Mr. Yasunobu Sato.

[178] Sato, *supra* note 30, p.49.

In eighteen months, my colleagues and I had hoped to tackle a millennium of hatred and the psychological insecurities of a traumatized nation. The job was impossible from the outset, and our failure allowed a post-election regime to be founded on the compromises made for the sake of preserving the electoral process.[179]

However, UNTAC did introduce human rights concepts to Cambodian society, and UNTAC was successful in developing a civil society in Cambodia. The problem in this regard is an assumption that UNTAC was prevented from addressing political or institutional sectors so that its energy was more devoted to grassroots actors, as one commentator suggested:

In the face of the government's hostility or indifference to the international presence after the elections, the range of international actors involved in rule of law promotion focused their attention on community groups and grassroots initiatives, but effectively ignored developments in the political sphere.[180]

UN peacekeeping operations do not usually last for a large number of years. In the case of UNTAC, it operated for only 18 months, in accordance with Security Council resolution 745 in which the Council decided to establish UNTAC.[181] If human rights functions of a peacekeeping operation have effect in the host society only as long as the peacekeepers are present, the post-peacekeeping period will easily suffer the resurgence of human rights abuses. Therefore it is desirable that the human rights functions of peacekeeping operations are designed to have longer-lasting effects by working on local institutions, training and educating local population through dialogue, not through imposition. After the departure of UNTAC, prison conditions have deteriorated again, and shackles reappeared. However, in some prisons, conditions remain reasonable, and the Minister of Justice demonstrated his willingness to implement reforms.[182] This illustrates the partial success of UNTAC in the area of human rights. On the one hand, UNTAC left police and military reforms mostly untouched. Both forces particularly affect the civil and political rights of individuals. On the other hand, UNTAC has made some part of the population, apparently including the then Minister of

---

[179] Metzl, *supra* note 59, p.275.

[180] Rama Mani, 'Conflict Resolution, Justice and the Law: Rebuilding the Rule of Law in the Aftermath of Complex Political Emergencies', *International Peacekeeping* 5(3), Autumn 1998: 1-25, p.7.

[181] *Supra* note 11.

[182] Shawcross, *supra* note 41, p.61.

Justice, conscious of the need for certain reforms. This consciousness may not necessarily be in the form of a human rights concept, but that can be something which will grow into the development of human rights awareness in the Cambodian society.

On 19 February 1993, the United Nations Commission on Human Rights adopted a resolution requesting the Secretary-General to ensure a continued United Nations human rights presence in Cambodia after the expiration of UNTAC's mandate.[183] This was an unprecedented decision of the Commission to authorise a field presence of the United Nations Centre for Human Rights. However, at the meeting of the UN Commission, the ASEAN countries strongly objected to the appointment of a Special Representative.[184] Consequently, it was decided that the new office of Special Representative would work for education and training in human rights. An office of the Centre for Human Rights in Cambodia was established on 1 October 1993.[185] Part of its 23 international and local staff were drawn from UNTAC Human Rights Component.[186] The purposes of the Centre for Human Rights were:

(a) To manage the implementation of educational and technical assistance and advisory services programmes, and to ensure their continuation;

(b) To assist the Government of Cambodia ... at its request, in meeting its obligations under the human rights instruments recently adhered to, including the preparation of reports to the relevant monitoring committees;

(c) To provide support to bona fide human rights groups in Cambodia;

(d) To contribute to the creation and/or strengthening of national institutions for the promotion and protection of human rights;

(e) To continue to assist with the drafting and implementation of legislation to promote and protect human rights; and

---

[183] UN Doc. E/CN.4/RES/1993/6, 19 February 1993.

[184] Shawcross, *supra* note 41, pp.59-60.

[185] *The UN and Cambodia*, p.50.

[186] *Further report of the Secretary-General pursuant to paragraph 7 of resolution 840 (1993)*, UN Doc. S/26360, 26 August 1993, para.29.

(f) To continue to assist with the training of persons responsible for the administration of justice.[187]

The human rights functions of the United Nations in Cambodia have thus been continuing after the departure of UNTAC.[188] A significant number of incidents of political violence, including the killings before the election in 1998, have demonstrated nevertheless that democracy is still far from having been reached.[189] One has to wonder what has changed in terms of political rights comparing the 1993 election under UNTAC with the 1998 election. It would be naive to expect that the human rights functions of a peacekeeping operation will be able to reform a society in a short period of time. However, what should be considered is how can such operations initiate human rights reforms that would be effective even without the presence of international organisations.

---

[187] *General Assembly resolution on the situation of human rights in Cambodia*, UN Doc. A/RES/154, 20 December 1993.

[188] For activities of the Centre for Human Rights, see B. Adams, *supra* note 170.

[189] Human Rights Watch, *Cambodia: Fair Elections not Possible*, Human Rights Watch Report, Vol.10, No.4, June 1998.

Chapter 5

The United Nations Human Rights Field Operation in Rwanda

1.   HISTORICAL BACKGROUND

Rwanda is a small hilly country in Central Africa. Before the genocide in 1994, Rwanda had a population of eight million, which was comprised of 85% Hutu, 14% Tutsi, and 1% Twa.[1] It was first colonised by Germany in 1890, and was subsequently placed under Belgian administration, first under the League of Nations Mandates System and, after 1946, under the United Nations International Trusteeship System. Some anthropologists have claimed that the Hutu and Tutsi were not ethnic groups, but rather that this is a social categorisation according to their occupation. In fact, social mobilisation was possible. When a Hutu acquires certain wealth, he/she could be considered as a Tutsi.[2] However, as colonisers used this categorisation for the division of the colonised, the criterion was absorbed in the local society itself.[3] Although the Tutsi were in the minority in terms of population numbers, they were favoured by the colonisers and gained higher occupational status, and property. In the wave of the nationalism in Africa, the Tutsi opted for independence and Belgium shifted to the side of the Hutu. In 1959

---

[1]   *The United Nations and Rwanda 1993-1996* (hereinafter *The UN and Rwanda*), The UN Blue Book Series, Volume X, 1996, p.7.

[2]   For the process of implanting "ethnic" division in Rwanda, see Gérard Prunier, *The Rwanda Crisis 1959-1994: History of Genocide* (hereinafter *The Rwanda Crisis*), Hurst & Company: London, 1995, especially pp.1-40.

[3]   The Cairo Declaration on the Great Lakes Region issued on 29 November 1995 as a result of a meeting among Presidents of Zaire, Uganda, Burundi and Rwanda, and a special Presidential envoy from Tanzania, refers to this point: "The Heads of State and delegations were convinced that the problems of Rwanda and Burundi were basically a consequence of a confluence of negative interests of colonialism and local opportunists who have fostered the ideology of exclusion that generates fear, frustration, hatred and tendencies to extermination and genocide". Annex to *Letter from the Permanent Representative of Rwanda to the United Nations addressed to the President of the Security Council, transmitting the Declaration of the Conference on the Great Lakes Region, signed in Cairo on 29 November 1995*, UN Doc. S/1995/1001, 30 November 1995.

political rivalry between "Tutsi" and "Hutu" parties developed into bloodshed. The Trusteeship Agreement for Ruanda-Urundi was terminated on 1 July 1962 and Rwanda and Burundi became two separate independent States. By the time of independence, 120,000 Rwandan refugees, mainly Tutsi, had taken refuge in neighbouring States.[4] Rwandans in exile attempted several times to come back to Rwanda with armed force, which caused renewed ethnic violence. For example, it has been estimated that between 10,000 and 14,000 Tutsi were killed during the 1963 massacres.[5]

In 1973, Major-General Juvénal Habyarimana, a Hutu from the northern part of Rwanda, seized power in a military coup d'état. His party, le Mouvement révolutionnaire national pour le développement (MRND) dominated the Government and institutionalised ethnic discrimination through a policy of ethnic and regional balance, which virtually marginalised the Tutsi.[6]

In Uganda, Rwandan refugees, mainly Tutsi, founded the Rwandese Patriotic Front (RPF) in 1988 for the purpose of securing the repatriation of Rwandans in exile and the reform of the Government in Rwanda. The RPF launched a military operation in 1990.

The international community, and especially the Organisation of African Unity (OAU) and the United Nations, started getting involved in the peace process in Rwanda from the beginning of 1990s. The purpose was to end the protracted civil war between the Hutu led by the President Habyarimana and the RPF exiles in Uganda. Under resolution 846 of 22 June 1993,[7] the Security Council established the United Nations Observer Mission Uganda-Rwanda (UNOMUR) with a mandate to ensure that no military assistance crossed the border into Rwanda. In August 1993, the two conflicting parties signed a cease-fire agreement, the Arusha Accords, and the Security Council decided to establish a peacekeeping operation, United Nations Assistance Mission for Rwanda (UNAMIR) under resolution 872 on 5 October 1993 in order to monitor the cease-fire.[8]

President Habyarimana was under increasing pressure from the international community to implement the Arusha Accords. On 6 April 1994, on

---

[4] *The Rwanda Crisis*, p.61.

[5] *Report by the Special Rapporteur on extrajudicial, summary or arbitrary executions on his mission to Rwanda, 8-17 April 1993*, E/CN.4/1994/7/Add. 1, 11 August 1993, para.16.

[6] A policy of ethnic quotas, which institutionalises limited representation of ethnic minorities, was also implemented in Rwanda particularly strictly in early 1970s. *The Rwanda Crisis*, pp.60-61.

[7] SC res. 846 of 22 June 1993. SCOR, 3244th mtg., UN Doc. S/RES/846(1993). Adopted unanimously.

[8] SC res. 872 of 5 October 1993. SCOR, 3288th mtg., UN Doc. S/RES/872(1993). Adopted unanimously.

the way back to his country from a regional summit held in Dar es Salaam, his aeroplane was shot down with the President of Burundi, Cyprien Ntaryamira, and others on board.[9] In a few hours, roadblocks had been installed and mass killings began.[10] The first targets were the Hutu politicians, including Prime Minister Agathe Uwilingiyimana, who were considered as moderate, and Tutsi. The killings of intellectuals, human rights activists and journalists followed. It was a long time before the international community and the Security Council recognised this situation as "genocide". Further, the reaction of the Security Council was to reduce the troops of the UNAMIR under resolution 912 of 21 April 1994.[11] Besides massacres of the Tutsi and the Hutu moderates, the fighting between the Government army and the RPF was aggravated as the RPF broke out the cantonment site determined under the Arusha Accords. With the advance of the RPF, the Hutu population fled *en masse* to neighbouring countries, partly because of the inflammatory propaganda put out by the paramilitary that they would be killed by the RPF if they stayed.

In May 1994, the United Nations High Commissioner for Human Rights (HCHR) suggested the appointment of a special rapporteur for Rwanda who would be supported by a field operation. The first five officers were fielded from June to August 1994, and the operation developed into a much larger operation, the Human Rights Field Operation for Rwanda (HRFOR). It was the first field operation under the auspices of the HCHR.[12] Unlike ONUSAL

---

[9] The most widely held view attributes the attack to Hutu extremists with the intent of blocking power-sharing with the Tutsi. Karhilo, 'The Establishment of the International Tribunal for Rwanda', *supra* FN17 of Introduction, p.685.

[10] The Commission of Experts concluded that the massacres were planned. The grounds for this conclusion are: (a) The campaign of incitement to exterminate the Tutsi orchestrated by both the public authorities and the media; (b) The distribution of weapons to the civilian population, particularly to members of the militias; (c) The exceptional speed of events at the outset including roadblocks set up all over Kigali just 30-45 minutes after the assassinations; and (d) The "screening" carried out at the roadblocks by militiamen and soldiers, and the lists drawn up by the public authorities with the aim of identifying Tutsi, after which they were immediately executed. *Report of the Special Rapporteur of the Commission on Human Rights on the situation of human rights in Rwanda*, A/50/709-S/1995/915, 2 November 1995, para.9. Also the Independent Inquiry later confirmed all these points. *Report of the Independent Inquiry into the actions of the United Nations during the 1994 genocide in Rwanda* (hereinafter, *Independent Inquiry Report*), 15 December 1999. Available at: http://www.un.org/News/ossg/rwanda_report.htm (visited on 4 November 2001).

[11] SC res. 912 of 21 April 1994, SCOR, 3368th mtg., UN Doc. S/RES/912(1994). Adopted unanimously.

[12] Mutoy Mubiala, 'L'opération des Nations Unies pour les droits de l'homme au Rwanda', *Hague Yearbook of International Law*, 1995:11-16, p.13.

(El Salvador) or UNTAC (Cambodia) analysed above, UNAMIR did not contain a component specialising in human rights activities, and HRFOR was established as an operation independent from an on-going peacekeeping operation under the Department of Peace-keeping Operation.

2. COMPOSITION AND MANDATE OF UNAMIR AND HRFOR

For the purposes of examining HRFOR as a human rights operation along with a peacekeeping operation, we will look at the composition and mandate of both UNAMIR and HRFOR in this section.

2.1 UNAMIR

United Nations Assistance Mission for Rwanda (UNAMIR) was a peace-keeping operation consisting of a military component, a civilian police component and a small civilian component. The civilian component had a total of 127 international staff, including 4 political officers, 2 public information officers, 1 human rights officer and humanitarian assistance officers.[13] Commencing with the arrival of the Force Commander, General Roméo A. Dallaire (Canada) on 22 October 1993, by late December the UNAMIR military force level reached 1,260.[14] The Civilian Police contingent of UNAMIR (CIVPOL) reached its authorised strength of 60 monitors in late December, consisting of a special investigation team, a liaison section and six police monitoring teams at its headquarters in Kigali.[15]

The initial mandate of UNAMIR was set forth in Security Council resolution 872 of 5 October 1993:[16] (a) To contribute to the security of the city of Kigali; (b) To monitor observance of the cease-fire agreement including the establishment of cantonment and assembly zones, and the demarcation of the new demilitarised zone and other demilitarisation procedures; (c) To monitor the security situation during the final period of

---

[13] *Report of the Secretary-General on Rwanda, requesting establishment of a United Nations Assistance Mission for Rwanda (UNAMIR) and the integration of UNOMUR into UNAMIR*, UN Doc., S/26488, 24 September 1993.

[14] *Report of the Secretary-General on UNAMIR*, UN Doc. S/26927, 30 December 1993, para.20.

[15] *Second progress report of the Secretary-General on UNAMIR for the period from 30 December 1993 to 30 March 1994*, UN Doc. S/1994/360, 30 March 1994, para.33.

[16] Operational Paragraph 3, SC resolution 872, 5 October 1993, UN Doc. S/RES/872(1993).

the transitional Government's mandate; (d) To assist with mine clearance; (e) To investigate and to report to the Secretary-General instances of alleged non-compliance with the provisions of the Protocol of Agreement on the Integration of the Armed Forces of the Two Parties; (e) To monitor the process of repatriation of Rwandese refugees and resettlement of displaced persons in order to verify that this is carried out in a safe and orderly manner; (g) To assist in the co-ordination of humanitarian assistance activities in conjunction with relief operations; and (h) To investigate and report on incidents regarding the activities of the gendarmerie and police.

The mandate of the Civilian Police (CIVPOL), which falls under item (h) above, was, in more detail, to assist in maintaining public security through the monitoring and verification of the activities of the gendarmerie and the communal police.[17] Further, in the absence of a component specialised in human rights activities, CIVPOL was the major actor of UNAMIR in relation to human rights issues. Its Special Investigation Team maintained contact with local human rights groups, followed cases involving ethnic or politically motivated crimes, together with complaints against the gendarmerie, while co-operating closely with the Government Prosecutor.[18] During the three months from January to March 1994, the Special Investigation Team dealt with 54 serious crimes, complaints and allegations of human rights violations.[19] Although CIVPOL was planned to be deployed in various parts of Rwanda, it could only operate in Kigali at this stage.[20]

UNAMIR's mandate was extended for six months until 29 July 1994 in accordance with Security Council resolution 909 of 5 April 1994, the day before the massacres started.[21] At the beginning of the genocide, the Belgian contingent lost 10 soldiers who were killed when they were guarding the Prime Minister of Rwanda.[22] As the Belgian contingent withdrew following this incident, UNAMIR military personnel stood at 1,515, decreasing from

---

[17] *Ibid.*, para.34.

[18] *Ibid.*

[19] *Ibid.*

[20] *Ibid.*, para.38.

[21] SC resolution 909, 5 April 1994. SCOR, 3358th mtg., UN Doc. S/RES/909(1994).

[22] UNAMIR had information regarding the strategy of the Interahamwe militia to provoke the killing of Belgian soldiers and the Belgian battalion's withdrawal as early as January 1994. This information was sent to the Department of Peace-Keeping Operation in New York, but was not taken seriously. See 'The 11 January Cable, I. Introduction', *Independent Inquiry Report*.

over 2,500 in late March, and Military Observers at 190, giving a total of 1,705 in late April when the genocide was ongoing.[23]

About two weeks after the beginning of the genocide, the Security Council, while "[A]ppalled at the ensuing large-scale violence in Rwanda", authorised reduction of the force level of UNAMIR to 270 and decided to change its mandate by resolution 912 of 21 April 1994. Because of the breakdown of the cease-fire, the conditions for peacekeeping no longer existed and there was no political will to strengthen the force in order to stop the massacres.[24] The mandate of UNAMIR was expanded to include the following functions:[25]

> (a) To act as an intermediary between the parties in an attempt to secure their agreement to a cease-fire;
>
> (b) To assist in the resumption of humanitarian relief operations to the extent feasible; and
>
> (c) To monitor and report on developments in Rwanda, including the safety and security of the civilians who sought refuge with UNAMIR, ...

The safety and security of civilians was to be monitored and reported, but the resolution made no reference to their protection. The Secretary-General, however, proudly pronounced to Rwandan people:

> I wish to remind you that I was the first to use the word "genocide" in the international assemblies in order to mobilize and sensitize international public opinion, in order to secure increased international assistance for your country, whether political, military, financial or technical.[26]

One has to ask why the warning from the Force Commander in the field informing the preparations for the massacres of Tutsi and his appeal for authorisation to act did not receive sufficient attention in the Secretariat in

---

[23] *Special report of the Secretary-General on UNAMIR, containing a summary of the developing crisis in Rwanda and proposing three options for the role of the United Nations in Rwanda*, UN Doc. S/1994/470, 20 April 1994, para.7.

[24] 'The continued role of UNAMIR, II. Description of Key Events', *Independent Inquiry Report*.

[25] SC res. 912, 21 April 1994. See *supra* note 11.

[26] *Statement delivered on 13 July 1995 by the Secretary-General to the Rwandan Parliament, inviting it and the Government to promote national reconciliation to help encourage the return of refugees*, UN Press Release SG/SM/5687, 20 July 1995.

January 1994.[27] According to the report of the Independent Inquiry, the Secretariat's primary concern was to avoid the use of force by UNAMIR, and very little thought was given to the possible disastrous consequences to the lives of the Rwandan people.[28] The decision by the Secretariat to consider the threats from the Hutu militia as negligible resulted in hundreds of thousands of deaths.

In the middle of the downsizing process of UNAMIR, the Security Council reconsidered the gravity of the situation and decided to amend the mandate once again with an increase of a force level of up to 5,500 under resolution 918 of 17 May 1994.[29] According to the report of the Independent Inquiry, the emphasis shifted "from viewing the role of the United Nations as that of neutral mediator in a civil war to recognising the need to bring an end to the massacres against civilians".[30] The force deployed under the amended mandate was known as UNAMIR II.

UNAMIR II's initial mandate included the following responsibilities in addition to the UNAMIR's mandate set forth in Security Council resolution 912:

(a) To contribute to the security and protection of displaced persons, refugees and civilians at risk in Rwanda, including through the establishment and maintenance, where feasible, of secure humanitarian areas;

(b) To provide security and support for the distribution of relief supplies and humanitarian relief operations.[31]

---

[27] Anne Mackintosh, 'Rwanda: beyond 'ethnic conflict'', *Development in Practice* 7(4), November 1997:464-474, p.470. Also Linda Melvern, 'Genocide behind the Thin Blue Line', *Security Dialogue* 28(3): 333-346, pp.336-338; and Michael N. Barnett, 'The Security Council, Indifference, and Genocide in Rwanda', *Cultural Anthropology* 12(4): 551-578, p.573. The Secretariat did not communicate UNAMIR's recommendations to the Security Council. The Secretary-General's justification is that such concerns as raised by UNAMIR and alarming reports from the field "are not uncommon within the context of peace-keeping operations". *The UN and Rwanda*, p.31.

[28] 'The 11 January Cable, II. Description of Key Events', *Independent Inquiry Report.*

[29] SC res. 918 of 17 May 1994, SCOR, 3377th mtg., UN Doc. S/RES/918(1994). The relevant part was adopted unanimously.

[30] 'New proposals on the mandate of UNAMIR, Description of Key Events', *Independent Inquiry Report.*

[31] SC res. 918, *supra* note 29. This resolution was adopted following separate votes on a particular part and the rest of the resolution. The cited part was adopted unanimously.

The responses of Member States were slow, and on 1 July 1994 the actual force level was 503, including 124 Military Observers.[32] This hesitation of the Member States led to Security Council resolution 929 of 22 June 1994 to authorise France to launch Operation Turquoise for solely humanitarian purposes.[33] The objectives of the Operation were the same as those of UNAMIR, i.e. "contributing to the security and protection of displaced persons, refugees and civilians in danger in Rwanda".[34] The operation, under Chapter VII, was carried out by France and Senegal for a period of two months as specified in resolution 929.

In mid-August 1994, CIVPOL initiated a training programme in order to provide trainees with a basic knowledge of routine and investigative police work.[35] UNAMIR II's mandate was further expanded by the Security Council resolution 965 of 30 November 1994 to include the protection of personnel of the International Criminal Tribunal for Rwanda (ICTR)[36] and to assist in the establishment and training of a new, integrated police force in Rwanda.[37] The force level of UNAMIR II reached 4,000 by October 1994[38]

---

[32] *The UN and Rwanda*, p.53.

[33] SC res. 929 of 22 June 1994, SCOR, 3392nd mtg., UN Doc. S/RES/929(1994). Ten in favour and five abstained (Brazil, China, New Zealand, Nigeria and Pakistan). Some States did not welcome the French initiative due to the perceived complex motivation of France. See *The Rwanda Crisis*, pp.103-106 & 110-111. Also Terry Terriff and James F. Keeley, 'The United Nations, Conflict Management and Spheres of Interest', *International Peacekeeping* 2(4), Winter 1995: 510-35, p.521. Operation Turquoise was one example of recent Security Council practice to authorise a non-UN multinational force to undertake a military operation under Chapter VII. This issue will be discussed in Chapter 7.

[34] *Letter dated 20 June 1994 from the Permanent Representative of France to the United Nations addressed to the Secretary-General*, UN Doc. S/1994/734, 21 June 1994.

[35] *Progress report of the Secretary-General on UNAMIR for the period from 3 August to 6 October 1994*, UN Doc. S/1994/1133, 6 October 1994, para.39.

[36] Formally, the International Criminal Tribunal for the Prosecution of Persons Responsible for Genocide and other Serious Violations of International Humanitarian Law Committed in the Territory of Rwanda and Rwandan Citizens Responsible for Genocide and other Such Violations Committed in the Territory of Neighbouring States, between 1 January 1994 and 31 December 1994 (hereinafter ICTR). It was established under Security Council resolution 955 of 8 November 1994. See *infra* 3.4 'International Criminal Tribunal for Rwanda'.

[37] SC res. 965, 30 November 1994. SCOR, 3473rd mtg., UN Doc. S/RES/965(1994). Adopted unanimously.

[38] *Secretary-General's Report*, UN Doc. S/1994/1133, *supra* note 35, para.30.

and over 5,700 in late January 1995, plus over 300 Military Observers and some 90 Civilian Police.[39]

When the focus on the Rwandan situation shifted from civil war settlement to rebuilding of the state, UNAMIR II's mandate was adjusted by Security Council resolution 997 of 9 June 1995. The new mandate was to provide good offices to help achieve national reconciliation within the framework of the Arusha Peace Agreement; to assist the Government in facilitating the voluntary and safe return of refugees; to support the provision of humanitarian aid; to assist in the training of a national police force; and to contribute to the security in Rwanda of personnel and premises of United Nations agencies, of the ICTR as well as those of human rights officers.[40] During the last three months of UNAMIR II, its mandate was to support efforts to restore peace and stability through the voluntary and safe repatriation of refugees and to contribute to the protection of the ICTR.[41] UNAMIR's mandate expired on 8 March 1996 and it withdrew upon the request of the government of Rwanda.

2.2 HRFOR

HRFOR was the first field operation deployed by the High Commissioner for Human Rights (HCHR).[42] The post of HCHR was created on the day before the beginning of the genocide in Rwanda, appointing José Ayala Lasso as the first HCHR. By the end of September 1994, 31 human rights officers had been deployed in Rwanda.[43] As of 1 April 1995, HRFOR was composed of 113 staff in 11 field offices, including 55 short-term staff, 30 United Nations Volunteers, 12 human rights officers from the European Union and 8 experts provided by the Governments of the Netherlands, Norway and Switzerland.[44] The observers were deployed in teams of four to eight persons per unit.[45] At the end of February 1996, the number of HRFOR

---

[39] *Progress report of the Secretary-General on UNAMIR for the period from 25 November to 6 February 1995,* UN Doc. S/1995/107, 6 February 1995, paras.23 & 34.

[40] SC res. 997, 9 June 1995. SCOR, 3542nd mtg., UN Doc. S/RES/997(1995).

[41] SC res.1029, 12 December 1995. SCOR, 3605th mtg., UN Doc. S/RES/1029(1995).

[42] See *supra* note 12.

[43] *Secretary-General's Report,* UN Doc. S/1994/1133, *supra* note 35, para.12.

[44] *Progress report of the Secretary-General on UNAMIR for the period from 7 February to 9 April 1995,* UN Doc. S/1995/297, 9 April 1995, para.11.

[45] *Report of the Special Rapporteur of the Commission on Human Rights on the situation of human rights in Rwanda,* UN Doc. A/50/709-S/1995/915, 2 November 1995, para.12.

human rights monitoring staff declined to 78.[46] This was due to constant uncertainty with regard to funding.

If we compare the size of HRFOR with the human rights component of ONUSAL and UNTAC, it was certainly a significant presence in a country as small as Rwanda. However, given the scale of the problems in Rwanda in the aftermath of the genocide and the continuing violent environment, even the level of over 100 observers could not be considered sufficient.

The main objectives and functions of HRFOR were defined in the Agreement between the United Nations High Commissioner for Human Rights and the Government of Rwanda as follows:[47]

- To carry out investigations into violations of human rights and humanitarian law;

- To monitor the ongoing human rights situation and, through the presence of human rights officers, help redress existing problems and prevent possible human rights violations from occurring;

- To co-operate with other international agencies in re-establishing confidence and thus facilitate the return of refugees and displaced persons and the rebuilding of civil society; and

- To implement programmes of technical co-operation in the field of human rights, particularly in the area of administration of justice.

With such broad objectives and planned functions, HRFOR's activities expanded in accordance with the needs recognised in the field.

HRFOR consisted of three units: Field Co-ordination Unit, Technical Co-operation Unit, and Legal Analysis and Co-ordination Unit. The Field Co-ordination Unit managed information gathering and field support, while the Technical Co-operation Unit supervised human rights promotion and assisted in the establishment of permanent structures that would safeguard human rights in Rwanda. For example, the Technical Co-operation Unit contributed judicial personnel and trained magistrates and other court officers. At the beginning of HRFOR, a Special Investigation Unit had existed instead of the Legal Analysis and Co-ordination Unit. Upon the establishment of an investigation unit of a judicial character within the

---

[46] *Report of the United Nations High Commissioner for Human Rights on the activities of the Human Rights Field Operation in Rwanda (HRFOR)*, UN Doc. E/CN.4/1996/111, 2 April 1996, para.53.

[47] *Ibid.*, para.9. The agreement entered into effect on 24 November 1994, subsequent to the actual deployment.

International Criminal Tribunal for Rwanda, the Special Investigation Unit was replaced by the Legal Analysis and Co-ordination Unit, which took charge of in-depth investigations into the genocide and present human rights violations, as well as carrying out analysis of the information coming from the field, in response to the needs of the Special Rapporteur.[48]

The HCHR described a new structure of HRFOR in his report of March 1997. There were the Office of the Chief of Mission, the Security and Communication Unit, the Operations and Documentation Unit, the Legal Unit, the Education and Promotion Unit, the Translation Unit and the Administrative Unit.[49] The Legal Unit undertook genocide trial monitoring, improvements in the penal administration and the training of the gendarmerie and the communal police. The Legal Unit also focused on the setting up of a national human rights commission, a parliamentary human rights commission and human rights departments in all government ministries.[50] The Education and Promotion Unit addressed vulnerable groups such as women and children, and NGOs. The Unit also had the objective of inculcating and fostering a human rights culture in the school system and the Rwandan public administration.[51] HRFOR also assisted local communities wishing to document and publish the history of the genocide in their communes.[52]

3. HUMAN RIGHTS FUNCTIONS UNDERTAKEN BY UN ORGANS OTHER THAN HRFOR

3.1 UNAMIR

UNAMIR did not contain a component exclusively in charge of human rights issues, unlike either ONUSAL or UNTAC. When the genocide started,

---

[48] *Report of the Secretary-General to the General Assembly on emergency international assistance for a solution to the problem of refugees, the restoration of total peace, reconstruction and socio-economic development in Rwanda*, UN Doc. A/50/654, 19 October 1995, para.54; and Annex III to *Report of the Special Rapporteur of the Commission on Human Rights on the situation of human rights in Rwanda*, UN Doc. A/50/709-S/1995/915, 2 November 1995, paras.15 & 17.

[49] *Report of the High Commissioner for Human Rights on the activities of Human Rights Field Operation for Rwanda (HRFOR)*, UN Doc. E/CN.4/1997/52, 17 March 1997, para.42.

[50] *Ibid.*, para.45.

[51] *Ibid.*, para.46.

[52] *Ibid.*, para.52.

UNAMIR could not continue to perform its mandate. The Secretary-General explained in his report that UNAMIR dedicated itself to the following efforts: (a) Securing an agreement on a cease-fire; (b) Protecting, as far as possible, United Nations civilian staff; (c) Protecting, as far as possible, other civilians, both foreign and Rwandese nationals; (d) Negotiating a truce with the two parties in order to enable the evacuation of expatriates to take place; (e) Assisting in the evacuation of non-Rwandese civilians, both United Nations and non-United Nations; (f) Rescuing individuals and groups trapped in the fighting; and (g) Providing humanitarian assistance to large groups of displaced persons under the protection of UNAMIR.[53]

Pending the formation and implementation of UNAMIR II, Operation Turquoise led by France commenced in Rwanda. On 2 July, France announced the establishment of a "humanitarian protected zone" in the Cyangugu-Kibuye-Gikongoro triangle in south-western Rwanda.[54] The Secretary-General claimed that UNAMIR had played a key role in providing protection to displaced persons and civilians at risk since the outbreak of the war.[55]

3.2 Special Rapporteur

On 25 May 1994, the Chairman of the Commission on Human Rights announced the appointment of Mr. René Dégni-Segui as Special Rapporteur on the human rights situation in Rwanda.[56] His mandate was to report on the root causes of the recent atrocities and on the ongoing human rights situation in Rwanda.[57] Theoretically, HRFOR was an operation to work for the Special Rapporteur, but practical co-operation failed to be achieved as will be discussed later.[58]

---

[53] *Secretary-General's Report,* UN Doc. S/1994/470, *supra* note 23, para.4.

[54] *Report of the Secretary-General on the situation in Rwanda,* UN Doc. S/1994/924, 3 August 1994, para.7.

[55] *Report of the Secretary-General to the General Assembly on emergency assistance for the socio-economic rehabilitation of Rwanda,* UN Doc. A/49/516, 14 October 1994, para.22.

[56] *Report to the Secretary-General on the investigation of serious violations of international humanitarian law committed in Rwanda during the conflict,* UN Doc. S/1994/867, 25 July 1994, para.25.

[57] *Secretary-General's Report,* UN Doc. S/1994/1133, *supra* note 35, para.12.

[58] See *infra* 4.10 'Cooperation with Other UN Agencies'.

3.3 Commission of Experts

In resolution 935 of 1 July 1994, the Security Council requested the Secretary-General to establish as a matter of urgency an impartial Commission of Experts in order to investigate the serious violations of international humanitarian law committed in Rwanda.[59] Its mandate was to examine and analyse information concerning grave violations of international humanitarian law committed in the territory of Rwanda.[60] The Secretary-General appointed the three members of the Commission.

The Commission reported that "the extermination of Tutsi by Hutu had been planned months in advance of its actual execution" and that the exterminations were carried out "primarily by Hutu elements in a concerted, planned, systematic and methodical way and were motivated out of ethnic hatred".[61] The Commission concluded: "there exists overwhelming evidence to prove that acts of genocide against the Tutsi group were perpetrated by Hutu elements in a concerted, planned, systematic and methodical way".[62]

3.4 International Criminal Tribunal for Rwanda (ICTR)

The Commission of Experts recommended the Security Council to amend the Statute of the International Criminal Tribunal for the former Yugoslavia so that the Tribunal's jurisdiction would cover international crimes committed in Rwanda.[63] On 8 November 1994, the Security Council, acting under Chapter VII of the Charter, decided to establish an international criminal tribunal under resolution 955.[64]

---

[59]   SC res. 935, 1 July 1994. SCOR, 3400th mtg., UN Doc. S/RES/935(1994). Adopted unanimously.

[60]   The information collected by HRFOR was made available to the Commission of Experts in accordance with Security Council resolution 935.

[61]   *Final report of the Commission of Experts established pursuant to Security Council resolution 935 (1994)*, UN Doc. S/1994/1405, 9 December 1994, para.58.

[62]   *Ibid.*, para.181.

[63]   *Preliminary report of the Independent Commission of Experts established in accordance with Security Council resolution 935 (1994)*, S/1994/1125, 4 October 1994, para.142. Regarding the ICTY, see Chapter 6.

[64]   SC res. 955, 8 November 1994, SCOR, 3543rd mtg., UN Doc. S/RES/955(1994). With the abstention of China and dissenting vote of Rwanda. Rwanda objected to the resolution for five reasons: (i) the absence of the capital punishment provision in the Statute; (ii) inadequate temporal jurisdiction; (iii) the ICTR not being independent from the International Criminal Tribunal for Yugoslavia and a small number of judges; (iv) the seat of the ICTR not being determined to be in Rwanda; and (v) inclusion of Common Article 3 to the four Geneva Conventions and Additional Protocol II. See Catherine Cisse, 'The

Owing to the limitations of space, a detailed analysis of the mandate, functions and jurisprudence of the ICTR is beyond the scope of this book.[65] HRFOR, it should be noted, was an investigative arm of the ICTR and the ICTR's work was intertwined with HRFOR's objectives. The ICTR was also relevant to the institution-building activities of HRFOR, since both were to support the Rwandan justice system. Todd Howland, former head of the Legal and Human Rights Promotion Unit of the HRFOR, and William Calathes of New Jersey City University, criticise the current position of the ICTR:[66]

> The ICTR's attempt to apply individual level justice to promote social order will not and cannot work. Individual level punishments can only affect a permanent change if the cause of the deviant behavior resides solely with the individual. In Rwanda, however, it is impossible to conclude that the causes of deviance reside with the individual. As the ICTR is focusing its attention on individual deviants, it is presenting the world, and the Rwandans, with the image of a person who needs correcting through punishment instead of a social system that needs reorganisation.[67]

This argument merits serious consideration when one looks into the human rights problems in post-genocide Rwanda.[68] The unprecedented difficulties

International Tribunal for the Former Yugoslavia and Rwanda: Some Elements of Comparison', *The Transnational Law and Contemporary Problems*, 1997:104-118, pp.107-108. Also see Payam Akhavan, 'The International Criminal Tribunal for Rwanda: The Politics and Pragmatics of Punishment', *AJIL* 90, 1996: 501-510, pp.505-508.

[65] For overview of the ICTR, see J. Karhilo, *supra* note 9. Regarding the ICTR, in general, also see Howland and Calathes, 'The U.N.'s International Criminal Tribunal, Is it Justice or Jingoism for Rwanda? A Call for Transformation', *supra* FN17 of Introduction; and Amann, 'Prosecutor v. Akayesu', *supra* FN17 of Introduction. Case documents are available at: <http://www.ictr.org/>. ICTR's judgments will be referred to below regarding genocide.

[66] Howland and Clathes, *supra* note 65, p.155.

[67] *Ibid.*, p.157. Also see Payam Akhavan, 'Justice and Reconciliation in the Great Lakes Region of Africa: The Contribution of the International Criminal Tribunal for Rwanda', *Duke Journal of Comparative and International Law*, Spring 1997:325-348, p. 342; and Jose E. Alvarez, 'Crimes of States/Crimes of Hate: Lessons from Rwanda', *Yale Journal of International Law*, Summer 1999: 365-483.

[68] Note, however, the work of the ICTR is widely appreciated in conjunction with the International Tribunal for the Former Yugoslavia for their contribution to development of international humanitarian law. See Antonio Cassese, 'On the Current Trends towards Criminal Prosecution and Punishment of Breaches of International Humanitarian Law', *EJIL* 9(1), 1998: 2-17; Goldstone, 'Justice as a Tool for Peace-Making: Truth

that Rwanda is facing require comprehensive measures, as will be discussed below.

4.   ACTIVITIES OF HRFOR

4.1   Recruitment and Education of Officers

When a former Head of the HRFOR states that "[t]here were in any event few mission officers in Rwanda with a strong background in human rights analysis and reporting",[69] one becomes sceptical about the recruitment policy of HRFOR. The recruitment of human rights observers for HRFOR was threefold: recruitment by the Centre for Human Rights, contribution from the European Communities (EC), and the United Nations Volunteers. The EC contributed a fully financed and equipped contingent of human rights field officers in accordance with the agreement with the High Commissioner for Human Rights (HCHR) concluded on 9 March 1995.[70] According to the agreement, the officers contributed were fully integrated in HRFOR. The EC nominated a co-ordinator of the contingent.[71] Although the official reports of the HCHR have never mentioned this, there were managerial tensions between the UN and the EC. The role of EC Co-ordinator was unclear in the managerial structure, and the EC proposed to change the arrangements in order to strengthen his role. HRFOR on the contrary sought to eliminate dual reporting lines. The EC abruptly terminated the contracts of the EC officers and despatched a fresh contingent in early 1996. Thereafter the EC was unenthusiastic about continued participation and withdrew from HRFOR in June 1997 following the worsening security situation.[72]

According to the Secretary-General's report, "all human rights officers in Human Rights Field Operation received comprehensive training to prepare them for their responsibilities in Rwanda".[73] Ian Martin, a former Head of

---

Commissions and International Criminal Tribunals', *supra* FN66 of Chapter 3, pp.498-501; Samantha I. Ryan, 'From the Furies of Nanking to the Eumenides of the International Criminal Court: The Evolution of Sexual Assaults as International Crimes', *Pace International Law Review*, 1999: 447-485, pp.468-469.

[69]   Ian Martin, 'After Genocide: The UN Human Rights Field Operation in Rwanda (hereinafter *After Genocide*)', in Henkin, ed., *Honouring Human Rights, supra* FN44 of Chapter 3: 97-132, p.116.

[70]   *HCHR's Report*, E/CN.4/1996/111, *supra* note 46, paras.45-47.

[71]   *Ibid.*

[72]   *After Genocide*, p.103.

[73]   *Secretary-General's Report*, UN Doc. S/1995/107, *supra* note 39, para.16.

HRFOR, gives us a different account. The training took place in Geneva and Kigali. Guidance notes entitled "Modus Operandi" were prepared in Geneva and provided to field officers, but "they were inadequate and little was done to improve them".[74] The formal training was developed only in December 1994, comprising briefings in Geneva (or Brussels, for field officers recruited by the European Union) and six days' training in Kigali. Martin states:

> The training gradually provided better background information, but remained weak in instructing officers in the methodology to be applied in their work. Efforts were made to address this weakness when the training program was revised and a field guidance manual developed in 1996.[75]

4.2   Main Human Rights Abuses

4.2.1. Genocide[76]

As referred to in the previous chapter, the definition of genocide under the Convention on the Prevention and Punishment of the Crime of Genocide requires evidence of an "intent to destroy, in whole or in part, a national, ethnical, racial or religious group, as such" as an essential element.[77] In Article 2(2), the Statute of the ICTR includes genocide amongst the offences over which it has competence. Genocide is defined in the same terms as in the Genocide Convention.[78] In *Prosecutor v. Akayesu*, a Trial Chamber of the Rwanda Tribunal affirmed:

> ... [t]he Genocide Convention is undeniably considered part of customary international law.[79]

---

[74]   *After Genocide*, p.103.

[75]   *Ibid.*

[76]   As for what happened in Rwanda in 1994, see African Rights, *Rwanda: Death, Despair and Defiance,* 2nd ed., 1995; Philip Gourevitch, *We wish to inform you that tomorrow we will be killed with our families*, London & Basingstoke: PICADOR, 1998; and *Prosecutor v. Jean-Paul Akayesu*, Case No.ICTR-96-4-T (2 September, 1998). Judgment, paras.106-129.

[77]   GA resolution 260, UN Doc. A/810(1948).

[78]   *Statute of the International Tribunal for Rwanda*, Annex to SC res. 955, 8 November 1994, SCOR, 3453rd mtg., UN Doc. S/RES/955(1994).

[79]   *Ibid.*, para.495.

The Trial Chamber considered that the group protected from Genocide is not limited to the four groups expressly mentioned in Article 2, but includes "any stable and permanent group".[80] The Chamber held that membership of such groups "would seem to be normally not challengeable by its members, who belong to it automatically, by birth, in a continuous and often irremediable manner".[81] Rejecting the argument that the massacre that took place in Rwanda in 1994 was only part of the war between the Rwandan Armed Forces (RAF) and the Rwandan Patriotic Front (RPF), the Chamber held that the genocide was indeed committed against the Tutsi as a group.[82]

Systematic rape was considered in details by a Trial Chamber of the ICTR in *Prosecutor v. Akayesu*. The Tribunal defined rape as "a physical invasion of a sexual nature, committed on a person under circumstances which are coercive".[83] The Chamber recognised that:

> ... the acts of rape and sexual violence, as other acts of serious bodily and mental harm committed against the Tutsi, reflected the determination to make Tutsi women suffer and to mutilate them even before killing them, the intent being to destroy the Tutsi group while inflicting acute suffering on its members in the process.[84]

The Chamber was of the opinion that:

> [rape and sexual violence] ... constitute genocide in the same way as any other act as long as they were committed with the specific intent to destroy, in whole or in part, a particular group, targeted as such. Indeed, rape and sexual violence certainly constitute infliction of serious bodily and mental harm on the victims and are even ... one of the worst ways of inflict harm on the victim as he or she suffers both bodily and mental harm.[85]

---

[80] *Ibid.*, para.516. See also the Chamber's consideration in paras.511-516. For a detailed discussion on the concept of genocide, see Johan D. van der Vyver, 'Prosecution and Punishment of the Crime of Genocide', *Fordham International Law Journal*, December 1999: 286-356.

[81] *Prosecutor v. Akayesu, supra* note 76, para.511.

[82] *Ibid.*, paras.126-127.

[83] *Ibid.*, para.688.

[84] *Ibid.*, para.733.

[85] *Ibid.*, para.731.

The act of "imposing measures intended to prevent births within the group" constitutes genocide if committed with that specific intent. The Chamber stated in interpreting the meaning of this measure:

> ... the Chamber holds that measures intended to prevent births within the group, should be construed as sexual mutilation, the practice of sterilization, forced birth control, separation of the sexes and prohibition of marriages. In patriarchal societies, where membership of a group is determined by the identity of the father, an example of a measure intended to prevent births within a group is the case where, during rape, a woman of the said group is deliberately impregnated by a man of another group, with the intent to have her give birth to a child who will consequently not belong to its mother's group.
>
> ...
>
> Furthermore, the Chamber notes that measures intended to prevent births within the group may be physical, but can also be mental. For instance, rape can be a measure intended to prevent births when the person raped refuses subsequently to procreate, in the same way that members of a group can be led, through threats or trauma, not to procreate.[86]

Thus the ICTR explicitly affirmed the possibility that large-scale rapes constitute genocide, showed a broad interpretation of rape and shed light not only on the physical but also on the mental aspects of this crime.

No one knows and no one will know the exact number of the victims of the genocide that took place in Rwanda in 1994. The number of people killed is estimated to be between 500,000 and 1 million.[87] A view of one ex-field officer of HRFOR is worth noting:

---

[86] *Ibid.*, paras.508-509.

[87] The Special Rapporteur of the Commission on Human Rights on the situation of human rights in Rwanda referred to "possibly reaching 1 million". Annex II to *Special Rapporteur's Report,* UN Doc. A/50/709-S/1995/915, *supra* note 48, para.8. The Independent Inquiry estimated the number of people killed at approximately 800,000 in a recent report. 'I. Introduction', *Independent Inquiry Report.*

What the world let happen in Rwanda will never be redressed, there is no possible solution to it. Actually, the international tribunal should not be entitled to use the word "justice".[88]

The main human rights abuses in post-genocide Rwanda can never be discussed as an issue separate from that experience. Thus the following points are all intertwined with the issue of genocide.

4.2.2. Refugees and Internally Displaced Persons (IDPs)

To the frustration of the new Tutsi-led Government and embarrassment of international organisations involved in humanitarian activities, refugee camps in the neighbouring countries of Rwanda became bases for cross-border incursions. For the deposed leaders, "the hapless refugee population" was "at once a political constituency, a source of income, and a territorial base for launching military offensives".[89] It was a situation that reminded us of the refugee camps for Cambodian refugees at the Thai borders where the Khmer Rouge maintained its control over the refugee population after 1979.[90] Todd Howland notes the exclusionary clause of the 1951 Convention that when there are serious reasons for considering that a person "has committed a crime against peace, a war crime, or a crime against humanity", he/she is excluded from protection.[91] Screening of such persons unqualified for protection was not applied to Rwandan refugees. When the Government ran out of patience, a crisis situation arose as the result of the forcible closure of IDP camps in south-western Rwanda.[92] HRFOR reinforced its teams in the area by deploying an additional 24 field officers. HRFOR encouraged the relevant government ministers to visit the affected areas and maintained close contacts with local authorities.[93]

---

[88] Roberto Ricci, *One Year of Human Rights Monitoring with the UN High Commissioner for Human Rights in Rwanda: Afterthoughts* (hereinafter *Afterthoughts*), Human Rights Centre, University of Essex, 1998, p.8.

[89] Akhavan, *supra* note 67, p.337.

[90] See, William Shawcross, *The Quality of Mercy: Cambodia, Holocaust and Modern Conscience*, London: Andre Deutsch, 1984.

[91] Todd Howland, 'Refoulement of Rwandan Refugees: The UNHCR's Lost Opportunity to Ground Temporary Refuge in Human Rights Law', *U.C. Davis Journal of International Law and Policy*, Winter 1998:73-101, pp.84-85.

[92] See *infra* 4.3 'Change in Human Rights Situation'.

[93] *Report of the Secretary-General on UNAMIR for the period from 10 April to 4 June 1995*, UN Doc. S/1995/457, 4 June 1995, para.27.

For the stabilisation and reconstruction of the country, the return of refugees and IDPs to their place of origin was a priority for the new Government of Rwanda. When the returns took pace in 1995, a database was created by HRFOR in co-operation with other United Nations agencies to provide accurate information on refugee movements. HRFOR monitored returnees by visiting transit centres and accompanying them to their home communes where feasible. After the returns, follow-up visits were made on a weekly basis. Field officers also visited the home communes prior to the arrival of returnees, when possible, in order to assess conditions for their reception and resettlement.[94]

Along with the progress of the return of refugees and IDPs, the issue of the right to property became increasingly important. In August 1994, the Inter-Ministerial Committee for urgent action on property and disputes over business establishments was established. The Committee experienced many difficulties in enforcing its decisions due to resistance by gendarmes and soldiers or the occupants. The stratagems used were: being absent on the day the eviction was to be carried out; leaving older people on the property at the time eviction was due to be carried out, which was intended to prevent forcible eviction, given the respect for older people in Africa in general and Rwanda in particular; appealing to groups of friends to provide physical opposition to the eviction; and seeking the protection of army officers, who sometimes ordered the arrest of the soldiers in charge of the eviction.[95] Even if property owners were relocated by the Committee, they had to leave the house and live in hiding after receiving threats from the evicted occupants. Moreover, there had been cases where reinstated individuals have been arrested, murdered, or have disappeared.[96]

4.2.3. Prisons and Detention Centres

A serious problem which genocide left in Rwanda was the issue of prisons. No country has ever faced such an enormous number of suspects that had to be detained. The number of arrested suspects was much more than the capacity of existing prisons. Furthermore, the judicial system had not resumed its former level of functioning. The situation automatically led to inhuman conditions of detention. For example, from September 1994 to May 1995, 902 of the 7,003 detainees held in one prison died mostly as the result

---

[94]   *Progress report of the Secretary-General on UNAMIR*, UN Doc. S/1995/848, 7 October 1995, para.20.

[95]   *Ibid.*, para.59.

[96]   *Ibid.*, paras.59-60.

of a lack of space.[97] By March 1996, 12 Rwandan prisons with a normal capacity of 12,250 had an estimated 70,000 persons incarcerated.[98] The number reached 99,300 by the end of January 1997,[99] and nearly 130,000 by 1998.[100]

Another problem related to prisons was the inhuman and degrading treatment of detainees.[101] The practice of beating was common in a large number of detention centres. In the Gisenyi prefecture, human rights observers reported receipt of 40 complaints from victims in January and February of 1995.[102]

4.3   Change in Human Rights Situation

In late November 1994, less than three months after the beginning of HRFOR's deployment, the Secretary-General reported:

> It is increasingly recognized that the mere presence and visibility of United Nations human rights personnel are having a positive effect in the communities where they are deployed, especially as a deterrent against human rights violations.[103]

The security situation, however, continued to be fragile, with persistent reports of summary executions, secret detention and torture, as well as banditry and other violent acts against civilians both in Kigali and in the

---

[97]   *After Genocide*, p.109.

[98]   *The UN and Rwanda*, p.102.

[99]   *Report of the High Commissioner for Human Rights on the activities of HRFOR*, UN Doc. E/CN.4/1997/52, 17 March 1997, para.8.

[100]   Mark A. Drumbl, 'Rule of Law and Lawlessness: Counselling the Accused in Rwanda's Domestic Genocide Trials', *Columbia Human Rights Law Review*, Summer 1998: 545-639, p.571.

[101]   Prohibition of inhuman and degrading treatment is provided for in several international human rights norms, including Article 5 of the *Universal Declaration on Human Rights* (adopted and proclaimed by General Assembly resolution 217A(III) of 10 December 1948), Article 7 of the *International Covenant on Civil and Political Rights* (adopted and opened for signature on 16 December 1966; and entered into force on 23 March 1976) and *Convention against Torture and Other Cruel, Inhuman or Degrading Treatment or Punishment* (adopted and opened for signature on 10 December 1984 and entered into force on 26 June 1987).

[102]   Annex III to *the Special Rapporteur's Report*, UN Doc. A/50/709-S/1995/915, *supra* note 48, para.75.

[103]   *Progress report of the Secretary-General on UNAMIR for the period from 7 October to 25 November 1994*, UN Doc. S/1994/1344, 25 November 1994, para.17.

countryside.[104] During February and March 1995, tensions increased. For example, the Prefect of Butare was murdered on 4 March.[105] On 22 April 1995, an outbreak of violence took place at the camp for IDPs in Kibeho, south-western Rwanda. It resulted in a considerable number of deaths. To investigate the incident, the Government established an Independent International Commission of Inquiry, inviting the participation of Belgium, Canada, France, Germany, the Netherlands, the United Nations and the Organisation of African Unity.[106] The Commission expressed its opinion that "the tragedy of Kibeho neither resulted from a planned action by Rwandan authorities to kill a certain group of people, nor was it an accident that could not have been prevented".[107] The Commission concluded that there was sufficient reliable evidence to establish that unarmed IDPs were subjected to human rights violations committed by both Rwandese Patriotic Army and armed elements among the IDPs themselves.[108] The Government of Rwanda recorded only 300 deaths as the number of victims of the Kibeho massacres, while other sources put the number at 8,000. UNAMIR suggested a figure between 1,500 and 2,000.[109]

On 12 September 1995, another serious incident took place at Kanama, in north-western Rwanda. Some 110 men, women and children were killed. Kanama was an area where reports of cross-border infiltration and sabotage from refugee camps in neighbouring Zaire had been increasing.[110]

In January 1996, the Special Rapporteur reported an apparent deterioration of the general human rights situation in Rwanda, in particular concerning violations of property rights and the right to freedom of expression.[111] The beginning of 1997 saw an increase in killings targeting genocide survivors and their associates.[112] In January 1997, HRFOR received reports of the killings of at least 424 persons in 55 incidents, the highest

---

[104] *Secretary-General's Report*, UN Doc. S/1995/107, *supra* note 39, para.7.

[105] *Secretary-General's Report*, UN Doc. S/1995/297, *supra* note 44, para.6.

[106] *Report of the Independent International Commission of Inquiry into the events at Kibeho in April 1995*, UN Doc. S/1995/411, 23 May 1995, paras.1-2.

[107] *Ibid.*, para.56.

[108] *Ibid.*, paras.60 & 61.

[109] Annex III to *the Special Rapporteur's Report*, UN Doc. A/50/709-S/1995/915, *supra* note 48, para.103.

[110] *Secretary-General's Report*, UN Doc. S/1995/848, *supra* note 94, para.26.

[111] *The UN and Rwanda*, p.102.

[112] HRFOR used the term "persons associated with genocide survivors" as to include family members of genocide survivors, old-caseload returnees [those left Rwanda as refugees in the years following 1959], persons involved in bringing the perpetrators of the genocide to justice, and persons who were perceived as supportive of genocide survivors.

record of killings since January 1996.[113] On 4 February 1997, five members of HRFOR were killed in an ambush on the way to a meeting.[114] Along with the increase in the number of returnees, the security situation was exacerbated particularly in the Ruhengeri prefecture in the north-west of Rwanda, bordering with Zaire and Uganda. There were armed attacks by groups of the ex-FAR and cordon-and-search operations by the Rwandese Patriotic Army, both involved violations of international human rights law and humanitarian law, causing a large number of civilian casualties.[115]

4.4 Relationship with State Agencies

Soon after HRFOR started deployment, Rwanda came under the control of new Tutsi dominated regime following the military success of the Rwandese Patriotic Front. The new Government did not have faith in UNAMIR, as can be seen from the following question put directly before the UN Secretary-General:

> Our people were massacred in the presence of very well armed United Nations forces. Instead of helping the population in distress, the United Nations force withdrew. ... when they [RPF] were going to drive it [the Government forces] from the country, the United Nations established a zone to save the murderers. ... Our people no longer trust the United Nations forces. How are you going to help us in order to restore their trust, which you need?[116]

Not surprisingly the relationship between UNAMIR and the Government of Rwanda was strained. UNAMIR did not always enjoy the freedom of movement set forth in the status-of-mission agreement. The Rwandese Patriotic Army denied UNAMIR access to parts of the country, searched and

---

[113] "Killings and other attacks against genocide survivors and persons associated with them from the beginning of January to mid February 1997", *Status report as at 27 February 1997*. Also see "Killings and other attacks against genocide survivors and persons associated with them January to December 1996", *Status report as at 24 January 1997*.

[114] "Five members of HRFOR killed in Karengera commune, Cyangugu prefecture, on 4 February 1997", *Status report as at 27 February 1997*.

[115] "Deterioration of the security and human rights situation in Ruhengeri prefecture, including killings of civilians during military operations, May-June 1997", *Status report as of 7 August 1997*.

[116] *Statement delivered 13 July 1995 by the Secretary-General to the Rwandan Parliament, inviting it and the Government to promote national reconciliation to help encourage the return of refugees*, UN Press Release SG/SM/5687, 20 July 1995.

seized UNAMIR vehicles and other equipment and participated in anti-UNAMIR demonstrations.[117] HRFOR faced the same problems. Despite the headquarters agreement governing the activities of the operation in Rwanda and the authorisations duly issued by the Minister of Justice, searches of human rights observers were carried out and observers were excluded from certain detention centres, including solitary confinement centres and military detention centres.[118] The searches of human rights observers could consequently put witnesses and complainants of human rights allegations in danger, when human rights observers were forced to let their documents be read by, for instance, the military.[119] Although the Government welcomed HRFOR's activities in genocide investigation and technical co-operation, it was nervous about HRFOR's activities in monitoring the human rights situation under the current regime.

According to the Special Rapporteur's report, the Rwandan authorities, both national and local, complained about the human rights observers:

> They accuse them of putting too much emphasis on the human rights violations being committed at present and accordingly neglecting the inquiry into the genocide. They maintain that the observers' action is "very police-oriented" and that the observers use legal terms such as "arbitrary arrests and detentions", the word "arbitrary" being, in the view of the authorities, equivalent to "unlawful".[120]

Nevertheless, in the period approaching the end of the mandate of UNAMIR, the Government of Rwanda made clear its wish to have the presence of HRFOR maintained after the mandate of UNAMIR expired.[121] The Government recognised "the importance of the monitoring of the human rights situation in the country as a factor contributing to the establishment of a climate of confidence".[122]

---

[117] *Secretary-General's Report*, UN Doc. S/1995/457, *supra* note 93, para.8.

[118] Annex III to *the Special Rapporteur's Report*, UN Doc. A/50/709-S/1995/915, *supra* note 48, para.26. Also *Report of the Special Rapporteur on the situation of human rights in Rwanda*, UN Doc. E/CN.4/1996/68, 29 January 1996, para.86; and *Afterthoughts*, p.10.

[119] *Afterthoughts*, p.14.

[120] Annex III to *the Special Rapporteur's Report*, UN Doc. A/50/709-S/1995/915, *supra* note 48, para.25.

[121] *Report of the Secretary-General outlining possible options for a United Nations role in Rwanda after the completion of UNAMIR's withdrawal*, UN Doc. S/1996/149, 29 February 1996, para.13.

[122] *Letter dated 1 March 1996 from the Minister for Foreign Affairs and Cooperation of Rwanda to the Secretary-General's proposal for the United Nations to maintain the office*

4.5   Investigation

In principle, investigation was supposed to be carried out by the Legal Analysis and Co-ordination Unit (LACU) based in Kigali. However, most of the work on genocide, such as the identification of eye-witnesses, material evidence and mass-grave sites, was conducted by the Human Rights Field Officers (HRFOs), especially during the first few months of the operation.[123]

After the establishment of the ICTR, the special investigation unit was placed to serve the Prosecutor of the Tribunal, with a view to pursuing the investigative work initiated under the mandate of the Special Rapporteur and the Commission of Experts.[124] The Special Investigation Unit created two teams: the Site Investigation Team and the Documentation and Evidence Team. While the Site Investigation Team conducted field investigations into massacres and mass-grave sites with the assistance of experienced forensic experts, the Documentation and Evidence Team gathered, catalogued, and supervised custody and control of all documents and evidence collected by the Special Investigation Unit.[125] The Commission of Experts credited the Special Investigation Unit's work as efficient in its final report.[126] However, Ian Martin comments that their work was not co-ordinated well with that of the field teams, since specialised personnel such as prosecutors, criminal investigators, police and forensic experts were seconded by several governments ,and they stayed only for short periods.[127]

4.6   Reporting

HRFOR did not have an explicit mandate to submit reports on the human rights situation in Rwanda, which is in clear contrast to the other human rights missions mandated by the Security Council or the General Assembly. The High Commissioner for Human Rights (HCHR) was asked by the General Assembly to report to the Commission on Human Rights and to the General Assembly "on the activities of HRFOR". It was the Special Rapporteur who was in charge of the reporting of the human rights situation

---

of the Special Representative in Kigali for a period of six months, UN Doc. S/1996/176, 7 March 1996, D.2.

[123] *Afterthoughts*, p.6.

[124] *Secretary-General's Report,* UN Doc. S/1994/1344, *supra* note 103, para.19.

[125] *Final report of the Commission of Experts*, UN Doc. S/1994/1405, *supra* note 61, para.24.

[126] *Ibid.*

[127] *After Genocide*, p.106.

in Rwanda.[128] The lack of a public statement as to the work done by HRFOR and significant delay in the functioning of the ICTR upset the local authorities.[129] At the request of the Commission on Human Rights, HRFOR's monitoring mandate was expanded in 1997 to report on the activities *and findings* of HRFOR.

Within HRFOR, each team of observers was headed by a team leader, who reported to the chief of the operation.[130] The team leader co-ordinated the work in the field, channelled the output to the Field Co-ordination Unit (FCU), and also reported to the team leaders' meeting held at the head-quarters every fortnight.[131] Field officers in the Monitoring Unit were assigned to report on the following:

(i)   Progress made towards national reconciliation;

(ii)   The existence of courts or magistrates responsible for settling disputes between Rwandan nationals;

(iii)   The availability of housing and other structures for persons returning to Rwanda;

(iv)   Measures taken by the local authorities or the Rwandan Patriotic Army concerning Rwandan returnees and the administrative practices to which the latter are subjected;

(v)   Security conditions in their zone;

(vi)   The availability of basic foodstuffs and services; and

(vii)   The formulation of education and information pro-grammes on human rights intended for Rwandan officials and the population as a whole."[132]

In October 1995, the newly-appointed Chief of HRFOR revised the monitoring and reporting procedures. Monthly or bimonthly reports were first submitted to the Presidency of Rwanda and to relevant Government ministries before being sent to Geneva. This was to provide the Government of Rwanda with the opportunity to supplement the reports with further

---

[128] *Ibid.*, p.115.

[129] *Afterthoughts*, p.9.

[130] *Special Rapporteur's Report*, UN Doc. S/50/709-S/1995/915, *supra* note 48, para.13.

[131] *Afterthoughts*, p.3.

[132] Annex III to *the Special Rapporteur's Report*, UN Doc. A/50/709-S/1995/915, *supra* note 48, para.16.

information and to correct factual inaccuracies.[133] This reporting system
induced positive actions from the Government of Rwanda, at least in the
aftermath of Kibeho incident.[134] The Minister of the Interior monitored
HRFOR's reports, and was personally involved in resolving problems.[135]
Starting in early 1997, these reports were released to the press at a briefing in
Kigali, but they neither had the status of official UN documents nor
circulated as such. HRFOR did issue "status reports" regarding its investigations of particular incidents, sets of incidents, or cases.

4.7 Institution-building

Professor William A. Schabas of the Université de Québec (Canada)
comments:

> ...the Rwandan legal system has never been more than a
> corrupt caricature of justice. ... In effect, there is almost
> nothing to "rebuild" or worth "rebuilding".[136]

Even prior to the genocide in 1994, out of 659 judges, only 34 had studied
law at an advanced level, and none of the cantonal court judges had had any
legal training. Out of 84 government procurators, only 18 held degrees in
law.[137] There were only about 40 lawyers in Rwanda and a bar association
did not exist.[138] The function of the rule of law was extremely limited, as
described in the Secretary-General's progress report:

> Owing to the lack of adequate finances to restore the public
> sector, the army continues to staff some civilian sectors of gov-
> ernance. It performs almost all police and gendarmerie

---

[133] *HCHR's Report*, UN Doc. E/CN.4/1996/111, *supra* note 46, para.23.

[134] See *supra* 4.3.

[135] William Clarance, 'The Human Rights Field Operation in Rwanda: Protective Practice Evolves on the Ground', *International Peacekeeping* 2(3), Autumn 1995:291-308, p.303.

[136] William A. Schabas, 'Justice, Democracy, and Impunity in Post-genocide Rwanda: Searching for Solutions to Impossible Problems', *Criminal Law Forum* 7(3), 1996:523-560, p.531.

[137] *Report by the Special Rapporteur on extrajudicial, summary or arbitrary executions on his mission to Rwanda 8-17 April 1993*, UN Doc. E/CN.4/1994/7/Add. 1, 11 August 1993, para.48. The Special Rapporteur of the Commission on Human Rights on the situation of human rights in Rwanda reported slightly different figures: Prior to the genocide, there were 708 judges and 45 recorded jurists; at the time of the report, less than 210 judges including only 60 trained jurists. Annex III to *the Special Rapporteur's Report*, A/50/709-S/1995/915, *supra* note 48, para.92.

[138] *Ibid.*, para.53.

functions, as well as prison services, in addition to manning some administrative posts in the provinces.[139]

The High Commissioner for Human Rights (HCHR) developed a programme of technical assistance in the administration of justice as a result of a needs-assessment mission undertaken in December 1994. The programme included the review of criminal cases of detainees, the improvement of prison administration, the establishment of civil dispute resolution mechanisms and the recruitment and training of civilian police.[140] The Technical Co-operation Unit of HRFOR issued a comprehensive programme addressing the needs of the Government of Rwanda in establishing a civil society based on respect for human rights. The programme included measures to facilitate the prosecution of suspects accused of serious human rights violations, together with a strategy for introducing human rights education into schools and government institutions.[141] A project was initiated to bring 50 international legal professionals to assist in the preparation of case files against those accused of having participated in the genocide. However, the Government of Rwanda later changed its opinion and recruited only 10 legal advisers to assist in the establishment of "special chambers" to handle genocide cases.[142] The Technical Co-operation Unit also assisted the Government to bring its legislation into closer conformity with international human rights law.[143]

An issue which attracted much attention in the international community was the large number of arrests and the overcrowded situation of prisons and detention centres under the new regime in Rwanda. Embarrassed by a speech of the Secretary-General, a government official commented:

> You seem to say that there will be peace in Rwanda only if there is justice and not vengeance. There is a sort of unfounded accusation in what you said ... In the current situation, there are

---

[139] *Secretary-General's Report,* UN Doc. S/1994/1344, *supra* note 103, para.8.

[140] *Secretary-General's Report*, UN Doc. S/1995/107, *supra* note 39, para.18.

[141] *Secretary-General's Report*, UN Doc. S/1995/297, *supra* note 44, para.14.

[142] *Secretary-General's Report*, UN Doc. S/1996/149, *supra* note 121, para.33. The Government preferred to use the same funding for providing over 1,000 judicial personnel with enhanced remuneration in order for the Ministry of Justice to attract qualified staff.

[143] *Secretary-General's Report*, UN Doc. S/1995/457, *supra* note 93, para.28.

indeed many prisoners; but if there was vengeance, there would not be any prisoners.[144]

The concern of the international community was not without reason, as most of the arrests that took place under the new Government did not satisfy the provisions of Rwandan criminal procedure. According to the prescribed procedure, the arrest of a person presumed to have committed an offence must be carried out with an arrest warrant issued by the government procurator. The lawful period of detention is 48 hours, which may be extended, but not beyond five days. If the prosecutor wishes to keep the arrested person in detention beyond that period, the person must be brought before the court of first instance. The court will decide, in chambers, on pre-trial custody, which may extend to one month, or order release on bail or unconditional release if the case is dismissed.[145] In the post-genocide period, the presence of international human rights officers ensured the continued attention for the hopeless situation of overcrowded prisons and also helped maintain the only contact for detainees to have with the outside world:

> ... they appear to prize it immensely for it makes them feel that they have not been forgotten, that they might, one day, be free again.[146]

HRFOR tackled this problem with a two-pronged strategy. On the one hand, the provision of humanitarian assistance to the prisoners and expansion of the prison capacity by 21,000 was sought. On the other hand, the strengthening of justice system was assisted through the organisation of seminars and training, as will be described in the sub-section "Human Rights Education" below, and through technical support to prosecutors and the courts.[147]

On 17 October 1995, six Supreme Court judges were appointed by the National Assembly, marking a positive development in the revival of the national judicial system.[148] Since 27 December 1996, court proceedings against persons accused of genocide were taking place in the domestic courts of Rwanda. HRFOR attended most court sessions, monitored the

---

[144] *Statement delivered 13 July 1995 by the Secretary-General to the Rwandan Parliament, inviting it and the Government to promote national reconciliation to help encourage the return of refugees*, UN Press Release SG/SM/5687, 20 July 1995.

[145] Annex III to *the Special Rapporteur's Report*, UN Doc. A/50/709-S/1995/915, *supra* note 48, para.66.

[146] *Afterthoughts*, p.11.

[147] *The UN and Rwanda*, p.103.

[148] *Report of the Secretary-General on UNAMIR for the period from 8 October to 1 December 1995*, UN Doc. S/1995/1002, 1 December 1995, para.8.

proceedings and reported several improvements, including more representation by defence lawyers, and the function of the Confessional and Guilty Plea Procedure.[149] However, such improvements were not necessarily the result of institution-building initiatives. For example, most of defence lawyers were from the Avocats sans Frontières (ASF), a Belgian NGO.[150] A concrete example of progress in institution-building was the training and deployment of 200 new *Inspecteurs de Police Judiciaire* in May and June 1997.

Rwanda has acceded to the International Covenant on Civil and Political Rights, but has not ratified the first and second optional protocols. According to a report of the UN Special Rapporteur on extra-judicial, summary or arbitrary executions, the provisions of the Covenant form part of the domestic law of Rwanda and take precedence in the event of conflict with another provision of domestic law.[151] The Trial Chamber of the ICTR noted in *Prosecutor v. Akayesu* that, since Rwanda acceded, by legislative decree, to the Convention on Genocide on 12 February 1975, the crime of genocide was punishable under the domestic law of Rwanda in 1994.[152] The accession to international human rights norms by a State does not necessarily guarantee that the relevant State government does abide by such norms, as the tragic events in Rwanda showed. Especially in a situation where a peace-keeping operation is required, intensified monitoring might enhance the implementation of human rights treaties. The lack of attention of UNAMIR in this regard is regrettable.

Rwanda is also a party to the following human rights and humanitarian treaties: the Convention on the Prevention and Punishment of the Crime of Genocide; the Convention on the Non-Applicability of Statutory Limitations to War Crimes and Crimes against Humanity; the Convention on the Rights of the Child; and the Convention relating to the Status of Refugees and the

---

[149] This is a procedure by which offenders in the second, third, and fourth categories benefit from a very substantial reduction in penalties in return for a full confession. See, Schabas, *supra* note 136, p.538.

[150] For more details on genocide proceedings in domestic courts, see "Genocide Trials to 30 June 1997", *Status report as of 15 July 1997;* "First genocide proceedings in Kibungo, Kigali, and Byumba on 27, 30, and 31 December 1996 and 3 January 1997", *Status reports as at 6 January 1997*; and "Genocide proceedings in Byumba, Butare, Gisenyi, and Kigali ville prefectures 8-20 January 1997", *Status report as at 24 January 1997*. Also see Drumbl, *supra* note 100.

[151] *Report by the Special Rapporteur on extrajudicial, summary or arbitrary executions on his mission to Rwanda, 8-17 April 1993*, para.25.

[152] *Prosecutor v. Akayesu, supra* note 76, para.496.

Protocol thereto; as well as to the four Geneva Conventions and their additional protocols.[153]

4.8 Human Rights Education

There was one officer in each HRFOR field team assigned to the activity of human rights education and promotion.[154] Human rights education played an important role in maintaining a good relationship with the Government of Rwanda:

> Technical co-operation was a major strength for the HRFOR. It was objectively but also strategically important. Together with the genocide work, it signified to the eyes of Rwandans that HRFOs were there not only to look and criticise, as monitoring is, at times, simplistically reduced, but also to assist.[155]

Training programmes set up by HRFOR were for "lay magistrates" and inspectors of the judicial police. Such programmes included seminars on arrest and detention procedures, techniques for the investigation of cases and respect for the rights of detainees and victims.[156] From June 1995 through to the end of 1996, about sixty such two-day workshops had been organised.[157] HRFOR also participated in training at the National Gendarmerie School in Ruhengeri and carried out training seminars for the gendarmerie and the RPA on the role of the armed forces and law enforcement officials in the protection and promotion of human rights.[158] Whereas the Ministry of Defence was dubious about this kind of training, it was the good relations between HRFOR teams and regional or local commanders that enabled a series of prefecture-level human rights seminars for the armed forces.[159]

In March 1997, HRFOR organised a seminar for high-level judicial officials on the Genocide Law and the relevant domestic and international legal procedures for the protection of the rights of the accused and civil

---

[153] Special Rapporteur's report, *supra* note 151, para.25.

[154] *Afterthoughts*, p.15.

[155] *Ibid.* Also see Clarance, *supra* note 135, p.299.

[156] *Report of the Special Rapporteur on the situation of human rights in Rwanda*, E/CN.4/ 1996/68, 29 January 1996, para.45.

[157] *After Genocide*, p.122.

[158] *HCHR's Report*, UN Doc. E/CN.4/1996/111, *supra* note 46, para.31. Also see "Seminar for the high command of the Rwandese Patriotic Army, 3-7 February 1997", *Status report as at 27 February 1997*.

[159] *After Genocide*, p.120.

claimants.[160] HRFOR also developed a project for the creation of centres to provide legal and other advice to women at commune level. The project was in co-operation with local legal associations and competent ministries. Human rights education was also conducted through radio broadcasts, newsletters and a weekly human rights club.[161]

4.9 Co-operation with UNAMIR

As HRFOR was independent from ongoing peacekeeping operation, HRFOR reported to the High Commissioner for Human Rights in Geneva. The Security Council, however, considered the Special Representative of the Secretary-General (SRSG) to be in charge of co-ordinating UN activities in Rwanda. In practice, the link between the SRSG and HRFOR was not strong.[162]

UNAMIR and HRFOR had overlapping monitoring functions. At the local level, co-operation was good in most regions, including the sharing of information and facilities, as well as some joint visits.[163] However, the military and Civilian Police components of UNAMIR "received no human rights training or guidance to assist them in their monitoring roles". Furthermore, "[M]ost CIVPOL members had no knowledge of UN human rights standards".[164] The SRSG and HRFOR eventually agreed that HRFOR would organise human rights training for peacekeepers toward the end of the UNAMIR mandate.

4.10 Co-operation with other UN Agencies

HRFOR worked in close co-operation with UNHCR in assisting the voluntary repatriation of refugees. UNHCR greatly appreciated the presence of HRFOR:

> In a country which was often subjected to human rights violations, as evidenced by the massacres which occurred during the

---

[160] *Ibid.*, pp.123-124.

[161] *HCHR's Report*, UN Doc. E/CN.4/1996/111, *supra* note 46, para.32.

[162] *After Genocide*, p.127.

[163] *Ibid.*

[164] *Ibid.*, p.128. As mentioned earlier, CIVPOL worked on human rights cases before the deployment of HRFOR. It is hard to speculate from the regular description in the Secretary-General's reports on what actually had been done by CIVPOL. See *supra* note 19 and accompanying text.

recent civil war, the presence of United Nations human rights monitors enhances confidence-building measures.[165]

UNHCR has protection officers whose work may well overlap with that of human rights officers. In case of Rwanda, as the number of protection officers were limited, the information from HRFOR must have been essential for the UNHCR.[166]

UNDP was involved in the reconciliation and rehabilitation programmes of the Government of Rwanda. In the area overlapping the mandate of HRFOR, UNDP had a programme to rehabilitate existing prison space and construct new detention centres in order to increase overall prison capacity. UNDP also provided for the training of Rwandan judicial and administrative personnel, and planned the deployment of 50 expatriates. There was some tension between UNDP and HRFOR, as UNDP regarded itself as the co-ordinating agency and channel for donor support to the justice sector, while HRFOR assumed that it was the principal agency in this matter.[167]

Theoretically, HRFOR was an operation to assist the Special Rapporteur. However, the Special Rapporteur made it clear in a rather extraordinarily straightforward way that the system of co-operation hardly worked:

> The relations between the operation [HRFOR] and the Special Rapporteur remain very theoretical and practically non-existent. They are filtered by the Special Procedures Branch, which forms a kind of screen blocking access to information needed by the Special Rapporteur.[168]

The Special Rapporteur's main criticism addressed the bureaucracy of the Centre for Human Rights:

> The operation is planned and executed, without any participation by the Special Rapporteur, by the Special Procedures Branch, which directs all activities from Geneva. Moreover, the hierarchical system in the Centre [Centre for Human Rights]

---

[165] *Update on the Rwanda emergency by the Executive Committee of the Programme of the United Nations High Commissioner for Refugees*, UN Doc. A/AC.96/825/Add. 1, 26 September 1994, para.12.

[166] For example, one ex-field officer of HRFOR recalls that in his sector HRFOR had two teams with 16 officers, while there was just one UNHCR protection officer. *Afterthoughts*, p.12.

[167] *After Genocide*, p.117.

[168] Annex III to *the Special Rapporteur's Report*, UN Doc. A/50/709-S/1995/915, *supra* note 48, para.27. Also see "Seminar for the high command of the Rwandese Patriotic Army 3-7 February 1997", *Status report as at 27 February 1997*.

requires that the observers and other investigators deployed in the field should address their reports not to the Special Rapporteur through the chief of mission, but along a chain which runs from the team leader to the High Commissioner and passes through the unit chiefs, the co-ordinators, the chief of mission and the chief of the Special Procedures Branch. In other direction, the Special Rapporteur is obliged to transmit his instructions to the operation through the Office of the High Commissioner, who forwards them via the Special Procedures Branch, going down through the various levels of the hierarchy. The chief of mission is forbidden, even in urgent situations, to contact the Special Rapporteur directly.[169]

The Special Rapporteur explains how this bureaucratic mechanism hampered efficient co-operation between him and HRFOR. Firstly, the delay in the flow of information: for example, he could not receive written reports on events which occurred at Kibeho on 22 April 1995 until 6 May 1995, when he finally received it from the chief of operation, bypassing the hierarchical procedure.[170] Secondly, a shifting of information within the Special Procedures Branch: the Branch communicated "only what it sees fit" to give to the Special Rapporteur.[171] Thirdly, some important documents disappeared. The Special Rapporteur comments:

It is as if there were a lack of willingness to cooperate with the Special Rapporteur, in breach of Commission on Human Rights resolution S-3/1 of 25 May 1994 on the situation of human rights in Rwanda.[172]

The HCHR's report on the co-operation with the Special Rapporteur displays a stark contrast with that which the Special Rapporteur presented:

As is the general practice with other rapporteurs, the Special Rapporteur has received at all times the full assistance of the Centre for Human Rights staff in Geneva as well as that of the

---

[169] Annex III to *the Special Rapporteur's Report*, UN Doc. A/50/709-S/1995/915, *supra* note 48, para.28.

[170] *Ibid.*, para.29.

[171] *Ibid.*

[172] *Ibid.*

Human Rights Field Operation in Rwanda in the preparation
and conduct of and follow-up to these visits [to Rwanda].[173]

The relationship between HRFOR and the ICTR was another uneasy issue.
HRFOR transmitted all information gathered since 1994 to the ICTR
through the HCHR.[174] Thereafter, the ICTR did not show any interest in a
collaborative relationship with HRFOR.[175] The ICTR's investigative capacity
was established only in late 1995, and its investigators did not have the
information handed over by HRFOR for their use. The information was
processed into a database outside Rwanda.[176] For the Rwandese, investigation by different UN organs into the genocide was confusing. Many
witnesses were interviewed by various institutions including the
Commission of Experts, HRFOR, humanitarian NGOs and governmental
agencies. Some people became even reluctant to speak to the ICTR's
investigators, as they had already recounted their experiences to other
interviewers.[177] The bureaucracy of the Organisation and the division
between UN organs undermined the situation of the people for whom all
those organs were assigned to work.

4.11 Co-operation with NGOs

HRFOR collaborated with the International Committee of the Red Cross
(ICRC) with regard to visits to persons deprived of their freedom in Rwanda.
HRFOR field officers accorded priority to ensuring respect for judicial
guarantees for the detainees, including the circumstances of arrest, the
duration of temporary detention, the establishment of individual legal files,
the release of arbitrarily detained persons and the confirmation of release.

---

[173] *Report of the United Nations High Commissioner for Human Rights on the Human Rights
Field Operation in Rwanda (HRFOR)*, UN Doc. A/50/743, 13 November 1995, para.28.

[174] *HCHR's Report*, UN Doc. E/CN.4/1996/111, *supra* note 46, para.43.

[175] *After Genocide*, p.107.

[176] *Ibid.* A massive database collected at the De Paul University's International Human
Rights Law Institute was transferred to the Office of the Prosecutor of the ICTY. See J.
Karhilo, *supra* note 9, p.693.

[177] Cisse, *supra* note 64, p.115. The present writer experienced a similar situation in the field
work. Interviewees of alleged human rights abuse cases expect international interviewers
to do something about their cases. When several organisations work in the same area, they
may be interviewed several times by different organisations between which the interviewees cannot necessarily distinguish well. If the interviewees think nothing has been
improved by telling their painful experiences to several foreigners one after another, they
start thinking that those foreigners are just collecting stories to report but are not trying to
help them.

The ICRC dealt primarily with conditions of detention in terms of physical and psychological treatment and material conditions. Representatives of HRFOR and ICRC had regular meetings at least once a week to enhance mutual co-ordination.[178]

Rwandese human rights NGOs had suffered extreme harm because of the genocide. Both Tutsi and Hutu human rights activists had been the victims of the genocide, while some others associated with the NGOs were accused of complicity in the genocide. The NGOs were partly divided on ethnic lines and the stance towards the new Government.[179]

CONCLUSION

Being the first field operation under the High Commissioner for Human Rights (HCHR), HRFOR was unique in being independent from a peace-keeping operation. In this regard, two questions need to be considered for future operations. Firstly, why was UNAMIR not designed to include a human rights component? Secondly, what are the merits and demerits of a human rights operation independent from but alongside a peacekeeping operation, in cases where both operations are under the United Nations?

As regards the first question, it is assumed that the politicians did not pay much attention to human rights issues. Comparing the Arusha Accords and San José Agreement in El Salvador,[180] the difference is manifest. The San José Agreement was exclusively on human rights, while the Arusha Accords were primarily political agreements. The reconnaissance mission headed by General Roméo A. Dallaire, later Force Commander of UNAMIR, was even not aware of the report published by the Special Rapporteur of the Commission on Human Rights on Summary and Extrajudicial Executions about the situation in Rwanda.[181] The report already discussed the possibility of genocide being committed in Rwanda. It was only after the occurrence of genocide that the HCHR suggested:

> The Commission on Human Rights may further wish to endorse the suggestion that future United Nations efforts aimed at conflict resolution and peace-building in Rwanda should be

---

[178] *HCHR's Report*, UN Doc. E/CN.4/1996/111, *supra* note 46, paras.27-28.

[179] *After Genocide*, p.124. The division of NGOs was also on political party lines. See *Rwanda Crisis*, p.131 including FN8.

[180] See *supra* FN13 of Chapter 3. The San José Agreement was one of a series of peace agreements in El Salvador.

[181] '2. The inadequacy of UNAMIR's mandate', III, *Independent Inquiry Report*.

accompanied by a strong human rights component and that this process should be effectively supported by a comprehensive programme of human rights assistance.[182]

Three Special Rapporteurs of the commission on Human Rights on the human rights situation in Burundi, Rwanda and Zaire, respectively, held a co-ordination and consultation meeting in January 1996, and they also recommended that the field observers of HRFOR should be deployed in all three countries:

> [... these] operations should receive appropriate financing from the United Nations. They [Special Rapporteurs] consider that human rights must form an integral part of a global United Nations strategy and must not be used as a sop for the conscience of the international community.[183]

When the genocide took place in Rwanda, UNAMIR did not have a component specialised in human rights issue, and the deployment of HRFOR came afterwards. It would be naive or simplistic to say that the existence of such human rights specialists could have prevented the tragedy. However, there is a possibility that their presence could have given more warnings regarding the tensions arising in Rwanda and that such warnings might have led to some preventive measures, or at least a much swifter reaction from the Organisation. The report of the Independent Inquiry underlines "a costly error of judgment" made by the Secretariat, the leadership of UNAMIR and the Security Council members, to view the situation in Kigali after the death of the President "as one where the cease-fire had broken down and therefore needed to be restored through negotiations, rather than one of genocide in addition to the fighting between the RGF and RPF".[184] It is the case that in any event the international community was reluctant to be involved in the confused situation in Rwanda. The proof was that, even after the situation on the ground came to be known around the world, the Member States showed great reluctance in contributing troops to UNAMIR II.[185] Even if the

---

[182] *Report of the United Nations High Commissioner for Human Rights on his mission to Rwanda of 11-12 May 1994*, UN Doc. E/CN.4/S-3/3, 19 May 1994, para.38.

[183] *Report on the coordination meeting, held in Geneva, on 18 and 19 January 1996, of Special Rapporteurs on the situation of human rights for three countries of the Great Lakes region*, UN Doc. E/CN.4/1996/69, 15 February 1996, para.16(f).

[184] '8. Focus on achieving a cease-fire, III. Conclusions', *Independent Inquiry Report*.

[185] For the reasons of the initial indifference of the international community regarding the ongoing genocide in Rwanda, see A. Mackintosh, *supra* note 27, pp.465-466. For example, the focus of politicians and journalists on the election in South Africa is mentioned.

presence of human rights experts did not deter the genocide, nor alleviate the atrocities, they could record the ongoing human rights violations for the subsequent processes to seek accountability.

Assuming the positive effects of a human rights specialists' presence, what were the merits and demerits of HRFOR as an independent operation? Firstly, HRFOR might have had an advantage by distancing itself from UNAMIR, since UNAMIR lost the local population's confidence through its failure to take action at the time of the genocide.[186] Secondly, the office of HCHR may stress the expertise in human rights work. However, field officers were recruited on an *ad hoc* base for the operation. HRFOR must have had some highly competent staff, whereas it has been already noted that some officers lacked experience.[187] Taking these factors into account, the expertise of HRFOR to be distinguished from the human rights component of other peacekeeping operations is unfounded. Furthermore, the indirect link with New York undermined the use of information collected by the operation. After departure of UNAMIR, the patience of the Government of Rwanda ran out with regard to the growing Hutu insurgency from eastern Zaire. HRFOR's reporting was highly relevant for the policymakers in New York, but the information reached New York belatedly via Geneva.[188]

As a unique operation under the HCHR, HRFOR could not rely on any experience from the outset. There was no advanced planning team, neither was use made of the experience at New York . Ian Martin rightly comments:

> The Centre for Human Rights later argued that the situation in post-genocide Rwanda was so unique that prior experience would not have been transferable. But given the acknowledged lack of experience in the Centre, the development of HRFOR would have benefited from the involvement of a planning team familiar with the experience of other operations.[189]

Being independent from UNAMIR, HRFOR constantly suffered from its unstable financial basis. The number of officers never reached the target figure of 147. Short-term contracts due to uncertain funding resulted in inefficiency of the operation, as those who had started to familiarise

---

[186] William Clarance, 'Field Strategy for the Protection of Human Rights', *International Journal of Refugee Law* 9(2): 229-254, p.245.
[187] *Supra* note 69 and accompanying text.
[188] *After Genocide, p.128.*
[189] *Ibid.*, p.102.

themselves with the work had to leave.[190] HRFOR also lacked certain equipment. Some regional offices had neither telephones nor fax, which disrupted communications between a number of offices and headquarters.[191] Eventually UNAMIR provided communications, vehicle maintenance, and procurement, financial, and personnel services to HRFOR. After the departure of UNAMIR, HRFOR arranged with UNDP for financial services, with the ICTR for communications, and with UNHCR for vehicle maintenance.[192] The question naturally arises as to whether it is worth complicating the operation by separating human rights functions from the multifunctional peacekeeping operation.

In addition to the above, the lack of co-ordination between Geneva and HRFOR was acute. With regard to technical co-operation, HRFOR, the Centre for Human Rights and UNDP tried to co-ordinate the plan. Assessment missions from the latter two visited Rwanda and made separate reports. The Centre followed up the issue slowly and approached the technical co-operation programme in Rwanda, setting aside HRFOR.[193] Then the Chief of HRFOR objected to Geneva's attempt to undertake direct control:

> ... I wish to insist that the bureaucratically centralised procedures by which the Centre micromanages such services from Geneva are inappropriate – indeed dysfunctional – for a major human rights field operation in a situation as complex and often fast moving as the post genocide Rwanda of today.[194]

The link between the field and headquarters and, at a higher level, to Geneva is also an important factor for a human rights operation. For field officers, the link between one's work with the higher level of the mission is essential to maintain their motivation.[195] Needless to say, to tackle human rights problems in a post-genocide society is not an easy task even for experienced HRFOs. If the operation can assure HRFOs that their work is contributing or will contribute to improvements in the situation, many qualified officers will overcome immense difficulties on the ground. One ex-HRFO expressed

---

[190] Annex III to *the Special Rapporteur's Report*, UN Doc. A/50/709-S/1995/915, *supra* note 48, paras.20-21.

[191] *Ibid.*

[192] *After Genocide*, p.150.

[193] *Ibid*, p.117.

[194] Clarance, *Statement*, 1 October 1995.

[195] See, for instance, *Afterthoughts*, pp.13-14.

feeling upset that it seemed as if reports from field offices simply disappeared into thin air.[196] If so, HRFOR unfortunately failed this test.

The importance of the UN presence in the field of human rights in Rwanda must have been widely recognised. The General Assembly commended the efforts of HCHR and requested the Secretary-General to ensure adequate financial and human resources and logistical support for HRFOR.[197] However, the same General Assembly did not approve the request for regular budgetary funding for HRFOR.[198] It was a missed opportunity to support the promotion of human rights in Rwanda, taking into account that the Government of Rwanda even welcomed the strengthening of HRFOR to 300 monitors.[199] Ian Martin claims that he has no doubt that:

> [... the] presence of HRFOR's teams in the prefectures had a significant short-term impact: The incidence of human rights violations would have been greater in their absence.[200]

However, he casts doubts on long-term trend for human rights in Rwanda, as this depends on the security situation. He criticises the hasty withdrawal of HRFOR thus:

> While human rights field operations should be planned with an exit strategy, donor insistence that HRFOR have an early exit strategy, even before the major refugee return had occurred, was either naive, or evidence of their desire to taper off funding.[201]

It should be noted that HRFOR was subject to severe criticism from outside assessment. The Joint Evaluation team that visited Rwanda in April-June 1995 referred to:

> [... a] broad and ambiguous mandate, poor preparations prior to deployment, limited logistics and resource support, inept leadership, absence of a coherent strategy, poor coordination between headquarters and field staff, bureaucratic infighting within the

---

[196] Anonymous interview conducted by the present writer, June 1999.

[197] *General Assembly resolution on the situation of human rights in Rwanda*, UN Doc. A/RES/50/200, 22 December 1995, Operational Paragraphs 9 & 22.

[198] *Secretary-General's Report*, UN Doc. S/1996/149, *supra* note 121, para.15.

[199] *HCHR's Report*, UN Doc. E/CN.4/1996/111, *supra* note 46, para.58.

[200] *After Genocide*, p.130.

[201] *Ibid*. HRFOR ended its operation on 28 July 1998 as the Government of Rwanda terminated its agreement with the HCHR.

UN system, apathy if not hostility of the Rwandese government,
and a highly politically-charged environment.[202]

The challenge that Rwanda is facing after the genocide is extraordinary. The
return of refugees and internally displaced persons was an essential factor for
rebuilding the State. However, many insurgents, including those who
participated in the genocide, have returned and continued destabilising the
society. The number of arrests overwhelmed the capacity of both the prisons
and detention centres and of the justice system. To keep adhere to its
commitment of respecting human rights, the new Government is required to
ensure due process and fair trial. Many lawyers were killed during the
genocide, and others fled. There are lawyers who had been refugees of 'old
case loads'. Most of them have been trained in the common law systems of
various east African states, whilst Rwandan criminal law follows the
continental model. In addition, those 'new' lawyers are often not able to
speak and read French, the language in which Rwandan legislation and most
legal commentary is written.[203] Many property cases have to be solved
between old-case returnees and returnees who fled in 1994. In sum, in the
worst of conditions resulting from the devastation caused by the genocide,
Rwanda is having to pay at once the debt of its long historical problems.
Professor Schabas rightly commented:

> It should be kept in mind that no judicial system, anywhere in
> the world, has been designed to cope with the requirements of
> prosecuting crimes committed by tens of thousands, and
> directed against hundreds of thousands. ... Even a prosperous
> country, with a sophisticated judicial system, would be required
> to seek special and innovative solutions to criminal law pro-
> secutions on such a scale.[204]

As a human rights operation in such conditions, a comprehensive approach
combining monitoring and technical assistance was plausible, as Ian Martin
affirms:

> ... monitoring identified needs for training and resources, while
> technical assistance provided means of addressing those needs.

---

[202] Joint Evaluation of Emergency Assistance to Rwanda, *The International Response to
Conflict and Genocide: Lessons from the Rwanda Experience*, Study 4, Rebuilding Post-
War Rwanda, pp.76-82.

[203] Schabas, *supra* note 136, p.533.

[204] *Ibid.*, p.534. Regarding the difficulty of the domestic genocide trials in Rwanda, see also
Drumbl, *supra* note 100.

In turn, monitoring would provide feedback on the effectiveness of the technical cooperation projects in improving human rights. Where institutions have been destroyed or have never existed, to criticise human rights violations while offering no linkage to assistance would invite dismissal; to pursue technical co-operation while ignoring serious ongoing violations would be naïve and unacceptable.[205]

HRFOR's serious defect was that the many organisational problems mentioned above prevented the HRFOs from concentrating on the work they were sent to do. Much HRFOR energy was wasted as the result of bureaucracy and a lack of experience in field operations. If the HCHR plans to establish a large-scale field operation such as HRFOR, it is necessary to reconsider the advantages and disadvantages of such an operation working independently of an ongoing peacekeeping operation. HRFOR did not prove the merits of carrying out a field operation under the HCHR. To have a separate human rights field operation alongside with a peacekeeping operation certainly complicate the work as a whole, for instance, from the viewpoint of logistics and co-ordination, and there would surely be redundancy. What is a cause for concern is that no UN evaluation took place, nor was any systematic debriefing of staff undertaken.[206]

The current situation in Rwanda is in fact another test of the international community's commitment to human rights norms. In addition to political instability, the human rights of tens of thousands of people are at stake. A commentator appeals:

> Whatever improvements may have been made in the quality of trials, only 300 out of 130,000 prisoners were adjudged from 1994 to early 1998. Any legal system which, in over three

---

[205] *After Genocide*, p.119.

[206] *Ibid*, p.131. William Clarance suggests that the Centre for Human Rights might best not be involved in providing operational support to human rights activities on the ground other than with small monitoring missions and mechanisms. Clarance believes that field operations should fall to "more appropriately orientated UN agencies". However, he does not think that the Department of Peace-Keeping Operations (DPKO) is the appropriate one, or the Department of Political Affairs or the United Nations Development Programme, but possibly the UNHCR. Clarance, *supra* note 186, pp.251-253. This is an interesting suggestion. However, since human rights issues are not always relevant to refugees, this author does not particularly support this idea. Furthermore, it is important to strengthen human rights orientation within the DPKO.

years, has only determined the guilt or innocence of 0.2% of all detainees cannot be said to be dispensing "justice".[207]

If no drastic measures are taken, many prisoners may spend their lives in prison without standing trial. The world is curiously silent about the fate of those people, while the light is shone on the "justice" of the small number of people who did enjoy a fair trial before the International Tribunal. Also, we should be aware that the continuing violence mainly caused by insurgents consisting of Rwandese Armed Forces has killed many, and even today threatens more lives.[208]

---

[207] Drumbl, see *supra* note 100, p.630.

[208] See African Rights, *Rwanda: the Insurgency in the Northwest*, available at: http://www. unimondo.org/African Rights/insurgency.html (visited on 14 May 2000).

Chapter 6

Human Rights Functions of the United Nations Peace-keeping Operations in the Former Yugoslavia

1.   HISTORICAL BACKGROUND[1]

In the early sixth century, the Slavonic-speaking peoples began migrating to the Balkans. A Serbian state under the Nemanjić Empire, founded in the 1160s, was a major military power in the Balkans. In 1389 the Ottoman Empire defeated the Serbs and began 500 years of its reign. While under Ottoman rule, the Serbs maintained Eastern Orthodox faith. The Serbs gained autonomy within the Empire in early 19th century. By 1699, most of the territory of current Croatia fell under the control of the Catholic Habsburgs. Although the Croatians were only given the status of second-class citizens, they enjoyed a certain amount of freedom. The Treaty of Berlin placed the two provinces of Bosnia-Herzegovina under Austria-Hungarian administration in 1878, albeit that the territories were still legally under Turkish sovereignty. The Declaration of Corfu of 1917 was the basis for the unification of Serbia, Croatia and Slovenia. By the end of the World War I, the Kingdom of the Serbs, Croats, and Slovenians was recognised by the international community. The post-war settlement overseen by the victorious Western powers was supposedly based on the principle of national self-determination. Nevertheless it left minorities within new state borders.

---

[1]   For the history of the former Yugoslavia, see for example, Leonard J. Cohen, *Broken Bonds: Yugoslavia's Disintegration and Balkan Politics in Transition*, 2nd ed., Westview Press, 1995; Marcus Tanner, *Croatia: A Nation Forged in War*, Yale University Press, 1997; Tim Judah, *The Serbs: History, Myth and the Destruction of Yugoslavia*, Yale University Press, 1997; Laura Silber and Allan Little, *The Death of Yugoslavia*, Penguin Books, 1995; Steven L. Burg and Paul S. Shoup, *The War in Bosnia-Herzegovina: Ethnic Conflict and International Intervention*, Armonk & London: M. E. Sharpe, 1999; David Campbell, *National Deconstruction: Violence, Identity, and Justice in Bosnia*, Minneapolis & London: University of Minnesota Press, 1998; and Noel Malcolm, *Bosnia: A Short History*, Papermac, 1996.

One historian estimates that one fourth of the average east European state's national population consisted of ethnic minorities.[2]

In 1941, the Kingdom of the Serbs, Croats and Slovenians was occupied by Germany, and the Serbs fled the German oppression. Germany created a puppet state, the Independent State of Croatia, and Croatian Fascists, called Ustashe, led the massacre of Jews, Serbs, and Roma. A resistance movement loyal to the Yugoslav royal family in exile was called Četniks. The two terms, Ustashe and Četniks, were used again in the recent conflict.

After World War II, the Federative People's Republic of Yugoslavia was established under the leadership of Marshal Tito, half-Croat and half-Slovenian, who had led a Communist-partisan organisation. The Federative People's Republic of Yugoslavia became the Socialist Federal Republic of Yugoslavia (SFRY) in 1963. The SFRY consisted of six Republics - Bosnia-Herzegovina, Croatia, Macedonia, Montenegro, Serbia and Slovenia - and two autonomous regions, Kosovo and Vojvodina. The Federal Government was controlled by a Presidential Council. The chairmanship of the collective presidency rotated among the leadership of the republics and autonomous territories. The SFRY led by Tito did not follow the Stalinist model and became a leading force in the non-aligned movement. The death of Tito in 1980, however, weakened the unity of the SFRY. The economic disparity between the republics was clear, and caused a flare-up of nationalism .

In a referendum held on 23 December 1990, a significant majority of the Slovenian people opted for independence. Also, in Croatia, a referendum in May 1991 resulted in strong support for independence. Both Croatia and Slovenia declared independence on 25 June 1991. On 27 June 1991 the Yugoslav People's Army (JNA), which was dominated by the Serbs deployed its military forces in Slovenia to prevent secession. The war in Slovenia lasted only ten days. However, hostilities in Croatia spread, since Serbs in Croatia wanted to remain within the federation of Yugoslavia. Despite the UN Secretary-General's warning of the possible serious consequences of premature recognition, the European Political Co-operation

---

[2] Raymond Pearson, *National Minorities in Eastern Europe 1848-1945*, Macmillan, 1983, p.148. For example, Pearson presents a table showing that Poland in 1921 consisted of 69.2% Poles, 14.3% Ruthenes and 16.5% other minorities and that Rumania in 1930 consisted of 70.8% Rumanians, 8.6% Magyars and 20.5% other minorities, with a warning regarding inaccuracy of official censuses. Pearson, *op. cit.*, p.163. Also see Joseph Rothschild, *Return to Diversity: A Political History of East Central Europe Since World War II*, 2nd ed., Oxford University Press, 1993, pp.3 & 10-12; and Robert Bideleux and Ian Jeffries, *A History of Eastern Europe: Crisis and Change*, Routledge, 1998, p.426.

Ministerial Meeting declared their recognition of Slovenia and Croatia on 15 January 1992.[3]

During the initial stages of the formation of the new states of Slovenia and Croatia, the European Community assumed a monitoring and negotiating role in Croatia. The UN Security Council did not even convene its first meeting on the conflict in the Balkans until 26 September 1991, leaving the matter to be dealt by the regional peace efforts. The first measure taken by the Security Council was a call for a complete embargo on all deliveries of weapons and military equipment to Yugoslavia.[4] Cyrus R. Vance, the former U.S. Secretary of State, was appointed as the Secretary-General's personal envoy to Yugoslavia and worked for the achievement of a cease-fire agreement, which was necessary for the deployment of a peace-keeping operation.

The United Nations Protection Force (UNPROFOR) was established under the Security Council resolution 743 of 21 February 1992.[5] Its mandate was initially limited to the situation in Croatia, and it was deployed in certain

---

[3]   *Statement by the Presidency on the Recognition of Yugoslav Republics,* Brussels, 15 January 1992, EPC Press Release 9/92. It is generally considered that the question of the recognition of states has become more a matter of political discretion than a legal issue based on criteria of statehood. Roland Rich, 'Recognition of States: The Collapse of Yugoslavia and the Soviet Union', 4 *EJIL,* 1993: 36-65; Malanczuk, *Akehurst's Modern Introduction to International Law, supra* FN16 of Chapter 1, p.85; and Shaw, *International Law, supra* FN9 of Introduction, pp.297-298 & 300. The arguably premature recognition of Croatia had a significant effect on the subsequent political solution to the conflict and on the rights of the 'minorities' in Croatia. See Shaw, *op. cit.,* p.309 including FN 65. The premature recognition can also be argued in the case of Bosnia-Herzegovina. Regarding the minority status, Fionnuala Ni Aolain, a former Special Representative of the Prosecutor of the International Criminal Tribunal for the Former Yugoslavia, rightly points out in the context of the Dayton Agreement:

>   This policy is not only a demotion in status from the principle of equality the international community allegedly sought to inject into the peace-making process, it is a thorough reversal of the pre-existing standing of peoples prior to the war. In the former Socialist Federal Republic of Yugoslavia these peoples were defined as belonging to constituent nations, to whom equal rights among and within the nations accrued. The war and the state entities which emerged from it, demoted these rights from those of nationhood and equality to minority status.

Fionnuala Ni Aolain, 'The Fractured Soul of the Dayton Peace Agreement: A Legal Analysis', *Michigan Journal of International Law,* Summer 1998: 957-1004, pp.975-976. The same can be discussed regarding Croatia.

[4]   SC res. 713, 25 September 1991. SCOR, 3009th mtg., S/RES/713(1991). Adopted unanimously.

[5]   SC res. 743, 21 February 1992. SCOR, 3055th mtg., UN Doc. S/RES/743(1992). Adopted unanimously.

areas of Croatia designated as United Nations Protected Areas (UNPAs), with its headquarters in Sarajevo. The UNPAs were areas in which Serbs constituted the majority or a substantial minority of the population.

Following the creation of Slovenia and Croatia, Bosnia-Herzegovina held a referendum on 1 March 1992 and the majority opted for independence, although many Serbs boycotted the poll. The European Community recognised Bosnia-Herzegovina on 6 April 1992.

In resolutions 981 (1995), 982 (1995) and 983 (1995) of 31 March 1995, the Security Council decided to establish three separate but interlinked peacekeeping missions in the former Yugoslavia: the United Nations Confidence Restoration Operation in Croatia (UNCRO); the United Nations Protection Force (UNPROFOR) in Bosnia and Herzegovina; and the United Nations Preventive Deployment Force (UNPREDEP) in the former Yugoslav Republic of Macedonia.[6] A theatre headquarters, United Nations Peace Forces headquarters (UNPF-HQ) was retained in Zagreb.

2. COMPOSITION AND MANDATE OF UNITED NATIONS PEACEKEEPING OPERATIONS IN THE FORMER YUGOSLAVIA

The development of the United Nations peacekeeping operations in the former Yugoslavia was a very complex process. Therefore, this chapter has to deal with four different operations, namely UNPROFOR, UNCRO, the United Nations Transitional Administration in Eastern Slavonia, Baranja and Western Sirmium (UNTAES), and the United Nations Mission for Bosnia and Herzegovina (UNMIBH) including the United Nations International Police Task Force (IPTF). Although there was another preventive operation in Macedonia,[7] this chapter will limit its focus to the current Republic of Croatia and Bosnia and Herzegovina.

---

[6] SC res. 981, 31 March 1995. SCOR, 3512th mtg., UN Doc. S/RES/981(1995). SC res. 982, 31 March 1995. SCOR, 3512th mtg., UN Doc. S/RES/982(1995). SC res. 983, 31 March 1995. SCOR, 3512th mtg., UN Doc. S/RES/983(1995).

[7] UNPROFOR's presence in the former Yugoslav Republic of Macedonia was authorised by the Security Council under resolution 795 of 11 December 1992. Its mandate was essentially preventive, to monitor and report any developments in the border areas. UNPROFOR within the former Yugoslav Republic of Macedonia was renamed the United Nations Preventive Deployment Force (UNPREDEP) in accordance with Security Council resolution 983 of 31 March 1995. SCOR, 3512th mtg., UN Doc. S/RES/983 (1995).

This chapter cannot deal with the details of the activities undertaken by the four peacekeeping operations mentioned above. The purpose and aim of this chapter is to highlight the various approaches adopted by the peace-keeping operations in conducting their human rights functions. For the purposes of clarity and an easier understanding of the complex evolution of the United Nations peacekeeping operations in the former Yugoslavia, this section deals with Croatia and Bosnia-Herzegovina separately.

2.1   United Nations Peacekeeping Operations in Croatia

2.1.1   United Nations Protection Force (UNPROFOR)

The United Nations Protection Force (UNPROFOR) was established pursu-ant to Security Council resolution 743 of 21 February 1992 as an "interim arrangement" to "create the conditions of peace and security required for the negotiation of an overall settlement of the Yugoslav crisis".[8] The resolution stated that the situation in Yugoslavia continued to constitute a threat to international peace and security as determined in resolution 713 of 25 September 1991.[9] The situation described in Resolution 713 was that the Security Council was concerned "by the fighting in Yugoslavia which is causing a heavy loss of human life and material damage and by the consequences for the countries of the region, in particular in the border areas of neighbouring countries...". Resolution 743 did not explicitly invoke Chapter VII,[10] and UNPROFOR was referred to as a peacekeeping operation. The authorised strength of UNPROFOR was originally some 13,000 troops, 100 military observers and approximately 530 police personnel.[11] The force deployed in United Nations Protected Areas (UNPAs): Sector North, Sector South, Sector West and Sector East. UNPROFOR was authorised to control access to UNPAs and to ensure that the UNPAs remained demilitarised. The civilian police component of UNPROFOR had the task "to monitor the maintenance of law and order by the existing police forces, with particular regard to the well-being of minority groups".[12] It should be noted that

---

[8]   SC res. 743, *supra* note 5.

[9]   See *supra* note 4.

[10]   However, the determination of a threat to international peace and security virtually means that the resolution was within the ambit of Chapter VII.

[11]   *The Blue Helmets: A Review of United Nations Peace-keeping* (hereinafter *The Blue Helmets*), The United Nations Department of Public Information, 3rd ed., 1996, p.514.

[12]   *Report of the Secretary-General*, 26 June 1992, S/24188 & Add. 1.

UNPROFOR's mandate was to "monitor" the maintenance of law and order, not to "maintain" it by themselves. Since UNPROFOR did not have a civilian component exclusively engaged in human rights activities, the main component which dealt with human rights issues was the Civilian Police. However, the peacekeeping plan did not function as expected, because of continuing armed conflict and expulsion, coercion and intimidation in the UNPAs.[13]

The mandate of UNPROFOR was enlarged first by Security Council resolution 762 of 30 June 1992, to undertake monitoring functions in the "pink zones". The "pink zones" were outside the UNPAs but largely populated by Serbs and had been controlled by the JNA (Yugoslavian National Army).[14] Further enlargement of UNPROFOR's mandate and strength in Croatia was authorised under Security Council resolution 769 of 7 August 1992, to enable it "to control the entry of civilians into the UNPAs and to perform immigration and customs functions at the UNPA borders at international frontiers".[15] As the Secretary-General stated in his report, the new mandate entailed "quasi-government functions which went beyond normal peace-keeping practice".[16] The third enlargement of UNPROFOR's mandate in Croatia pursuant to Security Council resolution 779 of 6 October 1992 added the responsibility for monitoring the demilitarisation of the Prevlaska Peninsula near Dubrovnik.[17] Along with the expansion of the mandate and area of deployment, the strength of UNPROFOR at the end of 1993 stood at 26,947 troops plus 675 Civilian Police and 578 Military Observers.[18]

In resolution 815 of 30 March 1993, the Security Council explicitly referred to the UNPAs as integral parts of the territory of the Republic of Croatia.[19] This virtually put an end to the possibility of independence for the Serbs who insisted on the sovereign "Republic of Serb Krajina". However, the conflicting views of the two sides continued. In May 1994, the Croatian Government requested the General Assembly to include an agenda item

---

[13] *Report of the Secretary-General*, 27 July 1992, S/24353 & Add. 1.

[14] SC res. 762, 30 June 1992. SCOR, 3088th mtg., UN Doc. S/RES/762(1992). Adopted unanimously.

[15] SC res. 769, 7 August 1992. SCOR, 3104th mtg., UN Doc. S/RES/769(1992). Adopted unanimously.

[16] *Report of the Secretary-General*, 27 July 1992, S/24353 & Add. 1.

[17] SC res. 779, 6 October 1992. SCOR, 3118th mtg., UN Doc. S/RES/779(1992). Adopted unanimously.

[18] *United Nations Year Book* (hereinafter *UNYB*) *1993*, p.434.

[19] SC res. 815, 30 March 1993. SCOR, 3189th mtg., UN Doc. S/RES/815(1993). Adopted unanimously.

entitled "The situation in the occupied territories of Croatia".[20] In responding to this request, Yugoslavia expressed anger, stating that the Serbs had constituted a majority in UNPAs for centuries and so that it did not constitute occupation.[21] In a resolution, the General Assembly clearly stated that it would respect Croatia's territorial integrity,[22] however it referred to the possibility of autonomy:

> *Urges* the restoration of the authority of the Republic of Croatia in its entire territory, and also urges the utmost respect for human and minority rights in the territory of Croatia, including the right to autonomy in accordance with the Constitution of the Republic of Croatia and established international standards.[23]

At the end of 1994, UNPROFOR consisted of 38,332 troops, 693 Military Observers, 764 Civilian Police, 483 civilian international staff and 1,496 international contractual staff.[24] As of mid-March 1995, UNPROFOR in Croatia was reduced to 14,825 troops and military support personnel, 256 military observers and 731 Civilian Police.[25] UNPROFOR was separated into three operations at the end of March 1995.[26]

2.1.2 United Nations Confidence Restoration Operation in Croatia (UNCRO)

The Security Council established the United Nations Confidence Restoration Operation in Croatia (UNCRO) by resolution 981 of 31 March 1995.[27] UNCRO had three main functions: to oversee the implementation of a cease-fire agreement of 29 March 1994; to advance the process of reconciliation and the restoration of normal life; and to maintain conditions of peace and security and to restore confidence.[28] The third function included activities "to

---

[20] Letter dated 27 May 1994 from Croatia, UN Doc. A/49/142.
[21] Letter dated 13 October 1994 from Yugoslavia, A/C.4/49/9.
[22] GA res. 49/43 of 9 December 1994, para.2. Adopted by 142 in favour, no objections and 18 abstentions. Abstaining states included China and the Russian Federation.
[23] *Ibid.*, para.7.
[24] *UNYB 1994*, p.497.
[25] *The Blue Helmets*, p.521.
[26] See *supra* note 6 and accompanying text.
[27] SC res. 981, 31 March 1995. SCOR, 3512th mtg., UN Doc. S/RES/981(1995).
[28] *The Blue Helmets*, p.548.

monitor the human rights situation of individuals and communities to ensure that there was no discrimination and that human rights were protected".[29]

On 1 May 1995, the Croatian Army launched a military offensive in the Sector West. Subsequent to this offensive, arrangements were made with the Croatian Government for the comprehensive deployment of UN Civilian Police and civil affairs personnel throughout Sector West. Their functions included the provision of humanitarian assistance, human rights monitoring, facilitating the voluntary return of refugees and displaced persons, and supporting local confidence-building measures between communities.[30] However, in early August, the Croatian Army carried out another offensive, Operation Flash, in Sectors North and South. The Special Representative established a humanitarian crisis cell, composed of UNPF staff, to collate information and co-ordinate responses. The cell communicated with all international agencies involved in humanitarian affairs and co-ordinated the work of four human rights action teams in the field led by officers of the Centre for Human Rights.[31]

As of 20 July 1995, the strength of the military component amounted to 11,059, including 296 military observers.[32] As of mid-November 1995, UNCRO consisted of 6,581 troops and military support personnel, 164 military observers and 296 civilian police.[33] As of 15 January 1996 the Security Council terminated the mandate of UNCRO.[34] The withdrawal of UNCRO drastically reduced the Organisation's capacity to monitor human rights in the former Sectors West, North and South. UN personnel responsible for human rights monitoring were limited to a small number of officers from the United Nations High Commissioner for Refugees (UNHCR) and two human rights officers from the Centre for Human Rights of the United Nations Secretariat.[35] The former Sector East, at the border with Serbia, became the area of transitional administration by the United Nations Transitional Administration for Eastern Slavonia, Baranja and Western Sirmium (UNTAES).

---

[29] *Ibid.*

[30] *Ibid.*, p.551.

[31] *The Blue Helmets*, p.553.

[32] *Report of the Secretary-General submitted pursuant to Security Council resolution 981 (1995)*, UN Doc. S/1995/650, 3 August 1995, para.3.

[33] *The Blue Helmets*, p.554.

[34] *Further report on the situation of human rights in Croatia pursuant to Security Council resolution 1019 (1995)*, UN Doc. S/1996/109, 14 February 1996, para.3.

[35] *Ibid.*

2.1.3 United Nations Transitional Administration for Eastern Slavonia, Baranja and Western Sirmium (UNTAES)

The United Nations Transitional Administration for Eastern Slavonia, Baranja and Western Sirmium (UNTAES) was established on the basis of the *Basic Agreement on the Region of Eastern Slavonia, Baranja and Western Sirmium* between the Government of the Republic of Croatia and the local Serbian community signed on 12 November 1995.[36] The decision for its establishment was taken by Security Council resolution 1037 of 15 January 1996.[37] According to the initial plan, UNTAES was composed of 5,000 contingent personnel, 600 civilian police, and 469 international civilian staff.[38] The purpose of UNTAES was "to achieve the peaceful re-integration of the region into the Croatian legal and constitutional system following four years of war and hostility".[39] The war drastically changed the ethnic composition of the region since 1991. Some 70,000 Croats and others left the region and some 75,000 Serbs, mostly displaced persons from other parts of Croatia, moved into the region.[40] Thus at the time when UNTAES was established, the region was mostly inhabited by a Serb population.

The Special Representative of the Secretary-General recommended the establishment of a transitional council for the transitional administration. The council was to be chaired by the transitional administrator, and was to include one representative each from the Croatian Government, the local Serb population, the local Croat population and other local minorities.[41] The idea was that the council would be advisory in nature and "the transitional administrator alone would have executive power and he would not have to obtain the consent of either the council or the parties for his decisions".[42] This condition should have been based on the lesson learned from UNTAC in Cambodia. In UNTAC, the Special Representative of the Secretary-General had to be advised by the Supreme National Council.[43] Although UNTAES covered only a part of the territory of a Member State of the

---

[36] UN Doc. S/1995/951, annex.

[37] SC res. 1037, 15 January 1996. SCOR, 3619th mtg., UN Doc. S/RES/1037(1996).

[38] *The Blue Helmets*, p.556.

[39] SC res. 1023, 22 November 1995. SCOR, 3596th mtg., UN Doc. S/RES/1023(1995).

[40] *Report of the Secretary-General pursuant to Security Council resolution 1025 (1995)*, UN Doc. S/1995/1028, 13 December 1995, para.6.

[41] *Ibid*, para.14.

[42] *Ibid*.

[43] See *supra* FN17 and accompanying text of Chapter 4.

Organisation, this was a considerable precedent in terms of authorising an absolute executive power to a UN mission.

The military component of UNTAES had the tasks of demilitarising the region, monitoring the voluntary and safe return of refugees and displaced persons, contributing to the maintenance of peace and security in the region, and otherwise assisting in the implementation of the Basic Agreement. At the planning stage of UNTAES, the Secretary-General stressed that UNTAES should operate under Chapter VII of the UN Charter.[44] Given the difficult experience of UNCRO in securing the opposing parties' co-operation, the Secretary-General should have expected a similar situation for UNTAES. Although UNTAES in fact became a UN peace-keeping force, the Secretary-General was of the view at the planning stage that the deployment and command of the force "would best be entrusted to a coalition of Member States rather than to the United Nations".[45]

The mandate of UNTAES's civilian component was, among other things, to establish, train and monitor a temporary police force, to undertake tasks relating to civil administration, to facilitate the return of refugees, to organise elections, to assist in the co-ordination of development and economic reconstruction plans of the Region, and to monitor the parties' compliance with their commitments to respect the highest standards of human rights and fundamental freedoms.[46] As in the case of UNCRO, the human rights mandate of UNTAES was limited to "monitoring". UNTAES was also supposed to co-operate with the International Criminal Tribunal for the Former Yugoslavia.[47]

The Basic Agreement, on the basis of which UNTAES was established, was not a detailed plan of the transitional administration. The Secretary-General himself observed that:

> The imprecise nature of the agreement, and the risk of differing interpretations of some of its provisions, also make it unwise to assume that compliance will be readily forthcoming.[48]

Therefore the actual scope and form of UNTAES depended on the planning on the ground during the process of implementation. The actual human rights activities undertaken by UNTAES will be analysed in Section 4 below.

---

[44] *Secretary-General's Report*, UN Doc. S/1995/1028, *supra* note 40, para.9.

[45] *Ibid*, para.23.

[46] SC res. 1037 of 15 January 1996. See *supra* note 37.

[47] *Ibid*.

[48] *Secretary-General's Report*, UN Doc. S/1995/1028, *supra* note 40, para.22.

Under resolution 1145(1997) of 19 December 1997, the Security Council authorised a Civilian Police Support Group of 180 officers to continue monitoring the local police forces after the withdrawal of UNTAES.[49] At the end of its mandate, UNTAES was aware of continuing concerns regarding the well-being of the minority population after the complete reintegration of the Region into Croatia. However, it was understood that, because of limited resources, the Organisation needed to prioritise its peace-keeping operations all over the world, and that the situation did not justify continuing operation of UNTAES according to that criterion. The establishment of the Support Group was an exit strategy for UNTAES, in order to maintain a certain monitoring function of the Organisation. The Support Group ended its mandate on 15 October 1998 and the Organisation for Security and Co-operation in Europe (OSCE) took over the responsibilities of monitoring the police on the following day. Again, these developments acted as an exit strategy for the Organisation. The replacement of the monitoring function of the Organisation by a regional organisation meant the continuance of inter-national monitoring and that alleviated the concern of the local minority population. Sixty of the 118 OSCE police monitors had previously served with the United Nations, which facilitated the immediate transfer of the monitoring function from the Organisation to the OSCE.[50]

2.2 United Nations Peace-keeping Operations in Bosnia-Herzegovina

2.2.1 UNPROFOR

UNPROFOR was expanded to cover not only Croatia but also Bosnia-Herzegovina in accordance with Security Council resolution 758 of 8 June 1992.[51] The new mandate included managing the operations of Sarajevo airport and escorting the humanitarian cargo. The responsibility for peace-making efforts taken since September 1992 by the Conference of Yugoslavia was handed over to the International Conference on the Former Yugo-slavia.[52] While escalation of the conflict in Bosnia-Herzegovina and 'ethnic

---

[49] SC res. 1145, 19 December 1997. SCOR, 3843rd mtg., UN Doc. S/RES/1145(1997).

[50] *Final Report of the Secretary-General on the United Nations Police Support Group*, UN Doc. S/1998/1004, 27 October 1998, para.2.

[51] SC res. 758, 8 June 1992. SCOR, 3083rd mtg., UN Doc. S/RES/758(1992). Adopted unanimously.

[52] Regarding European Community's peacemaking role, see Bertrand de Rossanet, *War and Peace in the Former Yugoslavia*, Kluwer Law International, 1997.

cleansing' had been reported, EC Envoy Lord David Owen and UN representative Cyrus Vance designed a peace plan to divide Bosnia-Herzegovina into ten semi-autonomous provinces. This plan was accepted only by the Croats, and even the Clinton Administration announced that it would not support the plan. UNPROFOR's mandate was limited to providing humanitarian assistance, and not to stop human rights infringements.

In response to the escalation in fighting, the Security Council imposed a no-fly zone over Bosnia-Herzegovina by resolution 781 of 9 October 1992.[53] Although this resolution did not explicitly refer to Chapter VII, it reaffirmed Security Council resolution 770 of 13 August 1992, which had determined the existence of a threat to international peace and security and had invoked Chapter VII.[54] The enforcement of the no-fly zone depended on the NATO air power, and not on UNPROFOR. On 16 April 1993, the Security Council decided to establish a safe-area in and around Srebrenica.[55] On 6 May 1993, the Security Council declared additional safe-areas, Sarajevo, Tuzla, Žepa, Goražde, Bihać and their surroundings.[56] Subsequently UNPROFOR's mandate was further expanded "to deter attacks against the safe areas, to monitor the cease fire, to promote the withdrawal of military or paramilitary units other than those of the Government of the Republic of Bosnia and Herzegovina and to occupy some key points on the ground".[57]

On 1 March 1994, Bosnian Muslims and Bosnian Croats signed two fundamental documents for the establishment of a federation in the territory controlled by the two parties: a *Framework Agreement establishing a federation in the Areas of the Republic of Bosnia and Herzegovina with a majority Bosnian and Croat Population*, and an *Outline of a Parliamentary Agreement for a Confederation between the Republic of Croatia and the Federation*.[58]

In late November 1994, the situation in Bosnia-Herzegovina was aggravated when the Bosnian Serbs entered the designated safe area of Bihać in response to an offensive launched in October from the Bihać pocket by the Bosnian Army. Upon the request of the Organisation, the North Atlantic

---

[53] SC res. 781, 9 October 1992. SCOR, 3122nd mtg., UN Doc. S/RES/781(1992). 14 in favour and one abstention by China.

[54] SC res. 770, 13 August 1992. SCOR, 3106th mtg., UN Doc. S/RES/770(1992).

[55] SC res. 819, 16 April 1993. SCOR, 3199th mtg., UN Doc. S/RES/819(1993). The issue of safeareas will be discussed *infra* 4.3.1 'Safe-Areas'.

[56] SC res. 824, 6 May 1993. SCOR, 3208th mtg., UN Doc. S/RES/824(1993).

[57] SC res. 836, 4 June 1993. SCOR, 3228th mtg., UN Doc. S/RES/836(1993). 13 in favour and 2 abstentions by Pakistan and Venezuela.

[58] *UNYB 1994*, p.550.

Treaty Organisation (NATO), responded by carrying out air strikes against air attacks by Krajina Serbs into the Bihać pocket.[59] However, the Special Representative of the Secretary-General secured a cease-fire agreement between the Bosnian Government and the Bosnian Serbs on 23 December 1994 and a cessation-of-hostilities agreement on 31 December 1994.[60]

On 31 March 1995, three separate peacekeeping operations were established by Security Council resolutions, and the so-called "UNPROFOR II" became exclusively responsible for Bosnia-Herzegovina.[61] As of mid-March 1995, UNPROFOR in Bosnia-Herzegovina included 21,994 troops and military support personnel, 305 military observers and 45 civilian police.[62]

The General Framework Agreement for Peace in Bosnia and Herzegovina was finally signed at a ceremony in Paris on 14 December 1995.[63] Based on a request from the parties, a multinational military Implementation Force (IFOR) of 55,000 troops and a United Nations International Police Task Force (IPTF) were established. IFOR was further taken over by a Stabilisation Force of 31,000 troops on 20 December 1996.[64]

2.2.2 United Nations Mission in Bosnia and Herzegovina (UNMIBH)

The United Nations Mission in Bosnia and Herzegovina (UNMIBH) is a new type of peacekeeping operation which consists of International Police Task Force (IPTF) and civilian officers who support the IPTF. Unlike ordinary peacekeeping operations, it does not contain a military component and it operates in co-operation with the Stabilisation Force, a NATO-led multinational force.[65] The establishment of the IPTF was decided upon under

---

[59] *Report of the Secretary-General pursuant to Security Council resolution 947 (1994)*, UN Doc. S/1995/222, 22 March 1995, para.19.

[60] *Ibid.*, para.20. For the process of negotiating these agreements, see General Sir Michael Rose, *Fighting for Peace: Bosnia 1994*, London: The Harvill Press, 1998.

[61] See *supra* note 6.

[62] *The Blue Helmet*, p.538.

[63] UN Doc. S/1995/999. Hereinafter referred to as the "Dayton Agreement". For the analysis of the Agreement, see Aolain, *supra* note 3; James Sloan, 'The Dayton Peace Agreement: Human Rights Guarantees and their Implementation', 7 *EJIL*, 1996:207-225; Elizabeth M. Cousens, 'Making Peace in Bosnia Work', *Cornell International Law Journal*: 789-818, 1997; and Zoran Pajić, 'The Dayton Constitution of Bosnia and Herzegovina – A Critical Appraisal of its Human Rights Provisions', in Rein Müllerson, Malgosia Fitzmaurice and Mads Andenas, eds., *Constitutional Reform and International Law in Central and Eastern Europe*, Kluwer Law International, 1998.

[64] Susan L. Woodward, 'Bosnia After Dayton: Year Two', *Current History* 96(608): 97-103, p.98.

[65] At the beginning UNMIBH co-operated with IFOR, SFOR's predecessor.

Security Council resolution 1035 of 21 December 1995 with the tasks set out in Annex 11 of the Dayton Peace Agreement:

> a) monitoring, observing and inspecting law enforcement activities and facilities, including associated judicial organisations, structures and proceedings;
>
> b) advising law enforcement personnel and forces;
>
> c) training law enforcement personnel;
>
> d) facilitating, within the IPTF's mission of assistance, the Parties' law enforcement activities;
>
> e) assessing threats to public order and advising on the capability of law enforcement agencies to deal with such threats;
>
> f) advising governmental authorities in Bosnia and Herzegovina on the organisation of effective civilian law enforcement agencies; and
>
> g) assisting by accompanying the Parties' law enforcement personnel as they carry out their responsibilities, as the IPTF deems appropriate.[66]

IPTF itself, as an unarmed monitoring and advisory force, was therefore not supposed to exercise any executive law enforcement functions.[67] By late March 1996, 789 civilian police officers were deployed and 260 were undergoing a mission-specific training programme, while the authorised number of officers was 1,721.[68] IPTF was given additional responsibilities relating to the investigation of human rights abuses by local police forces at the end of 1996 in accordance with Security Council resolution 1088 of 12 December 1996.[69] IPTF is an example of the increasing role played by UN civilian police in the human rights dimension of peacekeeping operations. The Security Council decided in resolution 1103 of 31 March 1997 to increase

---

[66] *Agreement on International Police Task Force*, Annex 11 to the Dayton Peace Accords, Article III.

[67] *Report of the Secretary-General pursuant to Security Council resolution 1026 (1995)*, UN Doc. S/1995/1031, 13 December 1995, para.27. Also *Report of the Secretary-General pursuant to Security Council resolution 1035 (1995)*, UN Doc. S/1996/210, 29 March 1996, para.35.

[68] *Secretary-General's Report,* UN Doc. S/1996/210, *supra* note 67, para.6.

[69] SC res. 1088, 12 December 1996. SCOR, 3723rd mtg., UN Doc. S/RES/1088(1996). This decision concurred with the conclusions of London Conference of the Peace Implementation Council held on 4 and 5 December 1996.

the authorised strength of IPTF to 2,027, along with the expansion of its responsibilities. IPTF carries out its activities through two main components: Operations Division and Development Division. The Operations Division monitors the local police in order to ensure freedom of movement, adherence to professional police procedures and respect for human rights. The Development Division assists the restructuring of police forces by the local authorities through downsizing and through the screening of the officers for criminal records.[70]

A United Nations Civilian Office was established together with IPTF under Security Council resolution 1035. A total of 49 Civil Affairs officers are deployed at UNMIBH headquarters, four regional headquarters (Sarajevo, Banja Luka, Mostar and Tuzla) and at a liaison office in Pale.[71] The task of UNMIBH's civil affairs officers was to support IPTF and provide their good offices for resolving problems among the parties on the ground; to monitor population movements and assess their political implications; to liaise with other international organisations including IFOR (later SFOR); and to monitor political events, developments and trends and prepare assessments for UNMIBH headquarters.[72] In the summer of 1997 UNMIBH set up a Human Rights Office.[73] The Human Rights Office consists of 120 IPTF monitors and 10 civilian staff.[74] The Office co-ordinates all the human rights activities of the Mission, including the maintenance of liaison with the other human rights organisations operating in the mission area.[75]

The Security Council decided in resolution 1144 of 19 December 1997 that UNMIBH and IPTF should be entrusted with additional tasks within the existing mandate. The tasks were:

(a) the creation of specialised IPTF training units to address key public issues, such as refugee returns; organised crime, drugs, corruption and terrorism; and public security crisis management (including crowd control); as well as training in the detection of financial crime and smuggling; and

---

[70] *Report of the Secretary-General on the United Nations Mission in Bosnia and Herzegovina,* UN Doc. S/1997/694, 8 September 1997, para.4.

[71] *Report of the Secretary-General pursuant to Security Council resolution 1088 (1996),* UN Doc. S/1997/224, 14 March 1997, para.15.

[72] *Secretary-General's Report,* UN Doc. S/1996/210, *supra* note 67, para.10.

[73] *Secretary-General's Report,* UN Doc. S/1997/694, *supra* note 70, para.22.

[74] *Report of the Secretary-General on the United Nations Mission in Bosnia and Herzegovina,* UN Doc. S/1997/966, 10 December 1997, para.16.

[75] *Secretary-General's Report,* UN Doc. S/1997/694, *supra* note 70, para.22.

(b) cooperation with the Council of Europe and OSCE, under the coordination of the High Representative, in a programme of judicial and legal reforms, including assessment and monitoring of the court system, development and training of legal professionals and restructuring of institutions within the judicial system.[76]

In accordance with Security Council resolution 1168 of 21 May 1998, UNMIBH recruited 30 specialist monitors to staff the Drug Control, Organised Crime, and Public Order and Critical Incident Management Units.[77] UNMIBH further established a Judicial System Assessment Programme in accordance with Security Council resolution 1184 of 16 July 1998.[78] UNMIBH, and in particular IPTF, is arguably expanding its role beyond the sphere of a peacekeeping operation by covering such activities which were categorised and undertaken within the objectives of technical assistance operations. The role envisaged for UNMIBH obviously extends to undertaking activities for peace-building. Since drug control or dealing with organised crime would stabilise the situation in the Balkans and contribute to the peace and security of the region, the expansion of peacekeeping activities are consistent with the recognition of a broader meaning of "peace and security". It is desirable, however, that the Organisation will also develop a theoretical design of peacekeeping based on case studies of conflict resolution. If the expanding activities of peacekeeping in the field challenge the root causes of conflicts, this is a more than welcome development. Nevertheless, without theoretical development, the creative efforts in the field can easily be hampered by difficulties created by changes in personnel and a shift of mission focus.

---

[76] *Report of the Secretary-General on the United Nations Mission in Bosnia and Herzegovina,* UN Doc. S/1998/227, 12 March 1998, para.35.

[77] *Report of the Secretary-General on the United Nations Mission in Bosnia and Herzegovina,* UN Doc. S/1998/862, 16 September 1998, para.11.

[78] *Ibid.,* para.26.

3. VARIOUS UNITED NATIONS HUMAN RIGHTS MISSIONS IN THE FORMER YUGOSLAVIA[79]

The conflicts in the Balkans since 1992 shocked the world through the atrocities committed by parties to the conflict against civilians, as will be discussed in the following section. The United Nations' actions against the human rights violations were mainly taken through organs other than peace-keeping forces as summarised below, although peacekeepers on the ground were in fact involved in activities that prevented the perpetuation of human rights violations.

3.1 Commission of Experts

Because of the reports of atrocities and violation of human rights and humanitarian law in the former Yugoslavia, the Security Council requested the Secretary-General to establish an impartial commission of experts by resolution 780 of 6 October 1992.[80] The Commission of Experts consisted of five members and was based in Geneva. The Commission designed a database in order to "provide a comprehensive, consistent and manageable record of all reported alleged grave breaches of international humanitarian law".[81] The Commission concluded its work in the spring of 1994, and the database and all the information compiled by the Commission was forwarded to the Office of the Prosecutor of the International Tribunal.[82] Although the establishment of the Commission did not deter further violations of humanitarian law, its role to preserve evidences of such violations including exhumation of mass graves and a major field investigation on rapes by teams of female lawyers and mental health specialists was significant.

---

[79] This section does not refer to non-UN missions or organs involved in human rights activities in the former Yugoslavia. For example, a European Community Monitoring Mission had been deployed in Croatia even before UNPROFOR was established. Their activities were mainly of a military intelligence nature, but also reported on human rights issues. For ECMM's activities, see, for instance, Sean M. Maloney, 'Operation Bolster: Canada and the European Community Monitor Mission in Former Yugoslavia, 1991-1992', *International Peacekeeping* 4(1), Spring 1997: 26-50.

[80] SC res. 780, 6 October 1992. SCOR, 3119th mtg., UN Doc. S/RES/780(1992). Adopted unanimously.

[81] *The Blue Helmets*, p.506.

[82] The Commission issued two interim reports and a final report: UN Docs. S/25274(1993), S/26545(1993), and S/1994/674(1994).

3.2 Special Rapporteur

The UN Human Rights Commission convened for the first time in its history a special session on the human rights situation in the former Yugoslavia on 13-14 August 1992. The Commission asked its Chairman to appoint a Special Rapporteur in its resolution 1992/S-1/1, and Mr. Tadeusz Mazowiecki, the former Prime Minister of Poland, was appointed. Mr. Mazowiecki and his successor, Ms. Elisabeth Rehn, submitted periodical reports to the Commission, which played an important role in informing the international community of the crisis *vis-à-vis* human rights violation in the former Yugoslavia.[83]

3.3 Centre for Human Rights

In March 1993 the Centre for Human Rights opened human rights field offices in Zagreb and in Skopje, and later in Sarajevo and Mostar. The Federal Republic of Yugoslavia and the local authorities of Bosnian Serbs did not allow field office operations in territories under their control until early 1996.[84]

After the signing of the Dayton Agreement, an integrated field operation in Bosnia and Herzegovina was maintained by the High Commissioner for Human Rights and the Centre for Human Rights. Their activities included the servicing of the mandates of the Special Rapporteur of the Commission on Human Rights and the expert on missing persons. They also provided technical expertise to the Office of High Representative and other international organisations.[85]

---

[83] Wiebe, 'The Prevention of Civil War through the Use of the Human Rights System', *supra* FN9 of Introduction, pp.432-433.

[84] *The Blue Helmets*, p.502.

[85] *Report of the Secretary-General pursuant to resolution 1035 (1995)*, UN Doc. S/1996/460, 21 June 1996, para.28. The High Representative has a task of mobilising and co-ordinating the activities of the organisations and agencies involved in the civilian aspects of the peace settlement pursuant to the Dayton Agreement. For more details, see Annex 10 to the Dayton Agreement, *Agreement on Civilian Implementation of the Peace Settlement*. See also Michael O'Flaherty, 'International Human Rights Operation in Bosnia and Herzegovina', in Alice H. Henkin, ed., *Honoring Human Rights from Peace to Justice*, The Aspen Institute, 1998: 71-95.

3.4 International Criminal Tribunal for the Former Yugoslavia (ICTY)

The Commission of Experts recommended the establishment of an *ad hoc* war crimes tribunal in its first interim report.[86] The Security Council decided by resolution 808 of 22 February 1993 that an international tribunal should be established,[87] and a final decision on its establishment was made through Security Council resolution 827 on 25 May 1993.[88] The tribunal has "the sole purpose of prosecuting persons responsible for serious violations of international humanitarian law committed in the former Yugoslavia between 1 January 1991 and a date to be determined by the Security Council upon the restoration of peace".[89]

Despite the duties of Member States to co-operate, the International Criminal Tribunal for the former Yugoslavia does not receive full co-operation in practice. For example, although the Prosecutor of the ICTY has requested access to documents captured during Operation Storm in Croatia, investigators have been denied an opportunity to inspect an inventory of that material. Croatia agreed that the Prosecutor would examine the dossiers prepared by its criminal authorities only as a result of their investigations into crimes allegedly committed by Croatian personnel during the

---

[86] *First interim report of the Commission of Experts*, UN Doc. S/25274.

[87] SC res. 808, 22 February 1993. SCOR, 3175th mtg., UN Doc. S/RES/808(1993). Adopted unanimously.

[88] SC res. 827, 25 May 1993. SCOR, 3217th mtg., UN Doc. S/RES/827(1993). Adopted unanimously. The tribunal consists of two Trial Chambers and an Appeals Chamber, the Prosecutor, and a Registry. There are rapidly growing studies on the system, function and jurisprudence of the Tribunal. See, for instance, James C. O'Brien, 'Current Developments: The International Tribunal for Violations of International Humanitarian Law in the Former Yugoslavia', *AJIL* 87, 1993: 639-659; Shraga and Zacklin, 'The International Criminal Tribunal for the Former Yugoslavia', *supra* FN17 of Introduction; Meron, 'War Crimes in Yugoslavia and the Development of International Law', *supra* FN17 of Introduction; Meron, 'International Criminalization of Internal Atrocities', *supra* FN17 of Introduction; Warbrick and Rowe, 'The International Criminal Tribunal for Yugoslavia', *supra* FN17 of Introduction; Greenwood, 'International Humanitarian Law and the *Tadic Case*', *supra* FN17 of Introduction; Sarooshi, 'The Powers of the United Nations International Criminal Tribunals', *supra* FN17 of Introduction; Turns, 'The International Criminal Tribunal for the Former Yugoslavia: The Erdemović Case', *supra* FN17 of Introduction; King and La Rosa, 'International Criminal Tribunal for the Former Yugoslavia', *supra* FN17 of Introduction; and Murphy, 'Progress and Jurisprudence of the International Criminal Tribunal for the Former Yugoslavia', *supra* FN17 of Introduction.

[89] SC res. 827, *supra* note 88.

Operation.[90] Although the ICTY had major difficulty in apprehending indictees, SFOR recently made a significant contribution.[91]

The ICTY and the ICTR for Rwanda are significantly contributing to the development of international humanitarian law as well as international criminal law. The *ad hoc* tribunals strengthened the jurisprudence governing such international crimes as crimes of genocide, crimes against humanity, and war crimes. This development will be continued by a permanent international criminal court, whose final Statute was adopted in July 1998.[92] The ICTY's case-law will be considered in sections below in the context of human rights abuses that occurred during the conflict in the former Yugoslavia.

4. HUMAN RIGHTS ACTIVITIES OF THE UN PEACEKEEPING OPERATIONS IN THE FORMER YUGOSLAVIA

4.1 Recruitment and Education of Officers

As mentioned above, UNPROFOR was essentially a military operation headed by a Force Commander, and did not contain any component which exclusively engaged in human rights issues. This is unfortunate, particularly as the Special Rapporteur had clearly mentioned in his report regarding the importance of field presence as early as 1993:

---

[90] *Report of the Secretary-General pursuant to Security Council resolution 1019 (1995)*, UN Doc. S/1996/456, para.42.

[91] As of 10 October 2001, 31 remain at large out of 80 indictees. Information available at http://www.un.org/icty/glance/indictlist-e.htm (visited on 4 November 2001). The extradition of Slobodan Milošević on 28 June 2001 was a significant recent development.

[92] *Rome Statute of the International Criminal Court*, UN Doc. A/CONF.183/9, 17 July 1998. Regarding the Statute, see the following articles in *AJIL* 93 (1999). Philippe Kirsch and John T. Holmes, 'The Rome Conference on an International Criminal Court: The Negotiating Process': 2-12; David J. Scheffer, 'The United States and the International Criminal Court': 12-22; Mahnoush H. Arsanjani, 'The Rome Statute of the International Criminal Court': 22-43; and Darryl Robinson, 'Defining "Crimes Against Humanity" at the Rome Conference': 43-57. Also regarding development of jurisprudence from the ad hoc courts to the permanent court, see Van der Vyver, 'Prosecution and Punishment of the Crime of Genocide', *supra* FN80 of Chapter 5, Jose E. Alvarez, 'Crimes of States/Crimes of Hate: Lessons from Rwanda', *Yale Journal of International Law*, Summer 1999: 365-483; Beth Van Schaack, 'The Definition of Crimes against Humanity: Resolving the Incoherence', *Columbia Journal of Transnational Law*, 1999: 787-850; and Danesh Sarooshi, 'The Statute of the International Criminal Court', *ICLQ* 48, 1999: 387-404.

> The presence of field officers would provide the Special
> Rapporteur with information in a more systematic manner and
> enable him to act more rapidly against violations.[93]

Also, the Human Rights Commission asked the Security Council to consider establishing a UN observer mission to investigate and report on alleged human rights violations in Kosovo, Sandjak and Vojvodina.[94] However, as the Secretary-General explained in his report of 11 March 1994, with its limited budget, UNPROFOR was spreading its resources very thinly, to the extent that modification of its mandates was required if its strength was not increased.[95]

In Bosnia and Herzegovina after the Dayton Agreement, the Organisation mandated IPTF, a UN police force, to monitor, advise and train local law enforcement agencies. The conditions of recruitment were: (i) eight years of policing experience; (ii) ability to communicate in English; and (iii) driving skills. Although these minimum qualifications had been notified to Governments in advance, a large number of prospective monitors had to be repatriated due to their failure to meet these conditions.[96] Upon arrival at the mission, police officers undergo a seven-day training and check-in process, during which a half-day is spent on human rights training.[97] IPTF conducted a human rights and humanitarian law training programme for its police monitors, in co-ordination with the UN Centre for Human Rights (later the Office of the United Nations High Commissioner for Human Rights). The Centre had run an eight-day "training of trainers" course and then IPTF held its own five-day human rights courses for monitors in each region.[98] According to the Head of Training and Projects Unit, UNMIBH Civil Affairs, Civil Affairs officers do not receive human rights training in particular, "nor do they need it as we have far too many human rights professionals".[99] The importance of the training and recruitment of officers are particularly

---

[93] *Report on the situation on human rights in the territory of the former Yugoslavia,* 10 February 1993, UN Doc. E/CN.4/1993/50, para.12.

[94] UN Doc. E/1993/23 of 23 February 1993.

[95] *Report of the Secretary-General,* 11 March 1994, UN Doc. S/1994/291 & Corr. 1.

[96] *Secretary-General's Report,* UN Doc. S/1996/210, *supra* note 67, para.8.

[97] Interview with Mr. Ali Halim, IPTF Human Rights Instructor/Trainer, Sarajevo, 25 June 1999.

[98] *Report of the Secretary-General pursuant to resolution 1035 (1995),* UN Doc. S/1996/460, 21 June 1996, para.12.

[99] E-mail interview with Mr. Graham Day, Head of Training and Projects Unit, Civil Affairs, UNMIBH, 5 May 1999.

recognised in IPTF, along with the expansion of its tasks. The Secretary-General noted:

> The role of IPTF is changing. Monitoring, observing and report-
> ing will continue, but the shift towards training and advising in
> the field, and in particular the selection of monitors who can
> work permanently alongside local chiefs of police or inside
> ministries of interior, will require officers with sound
> professional skills and a confident grasp of democratic policing
> principles.[100]

4.2　Main Human Rights Abuses

4.2.1 Ethnic Cleansing

During the armed conflict from 1992 to 1995, the forcible evacuation took place in a large number of places both in Croatia and Bosnia-Herzegovina. The methods used for this purpose included intimidation, harassment, discrimination, bombardment of civilian targets, forced displacement and murder. Arson and the destruction of properties often followed displacement so that those displaced would never return.[101]

4.2.1.a Ethnic Cleansing and Genocide

Regarding the situation in Bosnia-Herzegovina, the General Assembly refer-red to "ethnic cleansing" as genocide.[102] To support this view in legal terms, the proof of specific intent is required in accordance with the definition of genocide contained in the Statute of the ICTY.[103] Unlike the situation in Rwanda where the intent to destroy the Tutsi as a group was manifest, the burden of proof of genocidal intent in case of the former Yugoslavia is

---

[100] *Report of the Secretary-General on the United Nations Mission in Bosnia and Herzegovina,* UN Doc. S/1998/491, 10 June 1998, para.69.

[101] John Quigley rightly comments: "Ethnic cleansing is a term that does not define an act for which there is responsibility under international law. Rather, it is an umbrella term for a number of acts for which a state does bear responsibility under international law." John Quigley, 'State Responsibility for Ethnic Cleansing', *U.C. Davis Law Review,* Winter 1999: 341-387, p.346.

[102] GA res. 48/143 of 20 December 1993. Adopted without vote.

[103] Article 4(2) of the Statute of the ICTY (adopted on 25 May 1993, as amended on 13 May 1998). The definition of genocide is in accordance with that of the Genocide Convention as cited in *supra* FN166 and accompanying text of Chapter 4.

extremely complex. An accused may argue that, as regards the persons he/she had evicted, he/she did not care where they would go or what they would do. The accused may claim that their only purpose was to ensure that the village he/she lived in would be ethnically pure. This indifference to the fate of the other ethnic groups is different from a policy to eliminate them. However, such indifference cannot be claimed, for instance, in the case of the Srebrenica massacre, which will be discussed below.[104] The proof of genocidal intent depends on the definition of the destruction of a group. Eviction, for example, not only from the property but also from the community deprives a person of a means of making a living. If one ethnic group is forced to leave a village, the consequence is most likely the destruction of livelihood of the group members, which may threaten their survival, as well as lead to the destruction of community life, and furthermore the group may be dispersed. Whether this situation falls under the definition of genocide as the destruction of a part of a group would require the examination of all the conditions in each case. The difficulty of proving genocidal intent was demonstrated in *Prosecutor v. Goran Jelisić*. The Trial Chamber held:

> … the behaviour of the accused appears to indicate that, although he obviously singled out Muslims, he killed arbitrarily rather than with the clear intention to destroy a group. The Trial Chamber therefore concludes that it has not been proved beyond all reasonable doubt that the accused was motivated by the *dolus specialis* of the crime of genocide.[105]

As showed in this decision, various acts that constituted "ethnic cleansing" as a whole cannot be equated to genocide in a legal sense. Ethnic cleansing was achieved by diverse methods, such as harassment, intimidation and execution.[106] Even if some acts which aimed at ethnic cleansing did not constitute genocide, it does not in any way whatsoever diminish the seriousness of the large number of crimes committed in the process of ethnic cleansing. Furthermore, certain acts do amount to crimes of genocide, whereas others may be classified as war crimes and/or crimes against humanity.

---

[104] *Infra* 4.3.1 'SafeAreas'.

[105] *The Prosecutor v. Goran Jelisić*, Judgment of the Trial Chamber, ICTY, 14 December 1999, para.108.

[106] Regarding diversity of the methods, see Drazen Petrovic, 'Ethnic Cleansing – An Attempt at Methodology', 5 *EJIL*, 1994: 342-359.

4.2.1.b Rape as an International Crime

One of the methods used for ethnic cleansing was mass rape. We will take rape as an example to see how the ICTY defined different categories of international crimes. The Security Council described what was going on in the former Yugoslavia as "the massive, organised and systematic detention and rape of women".[107] The Special Rapporteur affirmed that rape in connection with ethnic cleansing was a grave breach of the Fourth Geneva Convention (article 27 (2) and article 147) and a war crime (Additional Protocol I).[108] The General Assembly affirmed that rape was used as a weapon of war:

> [The General Assembly] *Expresses its outrage* that the systematic practice of rape continues to be used as a weapon of war against women and children and as an instrument of ethnic cleansing, and recognizes that rape in this context constitutes a war crime.[109]

In the Statute of the ICTY, rape is explicitly included in the category of crimes against humanity.[110] The ICTY considered the definition of rape in *Prosecutor v. Anto Furundžija*.[111] While examining whether forced oral penetration should be classified as rape, the Trial Chamber held that such

---

[107] SC res. 798, 18 December 1992. SCOR, 3150th mtg., UN Doc. S/RES/798(1992). Adopted unanimously.

[108] Report on the situation of human rights in the territory of former Yugoslavia, 10 February 1993, UN Doc. E/CN.4/1993/50, para.89.

[109] GA res. 49/196 of 23 December 1994 by 150 in favour, no objection and 14 abstentions including China and Russian Federation. See also Theodor Meron, 'Rape as a Crime Under International Humanitarian Law', *AJIL* 87, 1993: 424-428; and Christine Chinkin, 'Rape and Sexual Abuse of Women in International Law', 5 *EJIL*, 1994, 326-341.

[110] Article 5(g) of the Statute of the ICTY, adopted 25 May 1993. The ICTY and the ICTR substantially expanded the jurisprudence on rape by considering it as an international crime. See, in general, Kelly D. Ashkin, 'Sexual Violence in Decisions and Indictments of the Yugoslav and Rwandan Tribunals: Current Status', *AJIL* 93, 1999: 97-123; Kelly D. Ashkin, 'The International War Crimes Trial of Anto Furundžija: Major Progress Toward Ending the Cycle of Impunity for Rape Crimes', *Leiden Journal of International Law* 12(4), 1999: 935-955; and Samantha I. Ryan, 'From the Furies of Nanking to the Eumenides of the International Criminal Court', *supra* FN68 of Chapter 5. A further development is that the Rome Statute of the International Criminal Court included as a crime against humanity, "rape, sexual slavery, enforced prostitution, forced pregnancy, enforced sterilization, or any other form of sexual violence of comparable gravity". Article 7(1)(g), Rome Statute.

[111] *Prosecutor v. Anto Furundzija*, Case No.IT-95-17/1-T10 (10 December 1998), Judgment, paras.174-186.

penetration constituted "a most humiliating and degrading attack upon human dignity".[112] The Chamber went on to state:

> The essence of the whole corpus of international humanitarian law as well as human rights law lies in the protection of the human dignity of every person, whatever his or her gender. The general principle of respect for human dignity is the basic underpinning and indeed the very raison d'être of international humanitarian law and human rights law; indeed in modern times it has become of such paramount importance as to permeate the whole body of international law.[113]

The emphasis on the psychological and mental harm caused by the act of rape is in consonance with the judgment in the *Akayesu case* given by the ICTR, as discussed in the previous chapter.[114] Numerous cases of rape in detention camps in Bosnia-Herzegovina were surely an attack against the victimised women's dignity.[115]

The Trial Chamber held that rape may constitute a grave breach of the Geneva Conventions, the violation of laws or customs of war, or an act of genocide.[116] Article 27(2) of the Fourth Geneva Convention reads:

> Women shall be especially protected against any attack on their honour, in particular against rape, enforced prostitution, or any form of indecent assault.

Article 147 of the Fourth Geneva Convention reads:

> Grave breaches ... shall be those involving any of the following acts, if committed against persons or property protected by the present Convention: wilful killing, torture or inhuman treatment, including serious injury to body or health, unlawful deportation or transfer or unlawful confinement of a protected person, compelling a protected person to serve in the forces of a hostile Power, or wilfully depriving a protected person of the rights of fair and regular trial prescribed in the present convention, taking of hostages and extensive destruction and

---

[112] *Ibid.*, para.183.

[113] *Ibid.*

[114] See *supra* FN83-85 and accompanying text of Chapter 5.

[115] See, for example, *Prosecutor v. Vukovic*, Case No.IT-96-23/1, Initial indictment, 26 June 1996.

[116] *Prosecutor v. Furundzija*, Judgment, *supra* note 111, para.172.

appropriation of property, not justified by military necessity and carried out unlawfully and wantonly.

Article 2 of the Statute of the ICTY sets forth a similar provision. Although not explicitly mentioned, rape would fall under two categories of grave breach: "wilfully causing great suffering or serious injury to body or health" and "torture or inhuman treatment".[117] Gross points out that recognising the crime of rape as constituting a grave breach or a war crime shifts the focus of attention from the massive and systematic resort to such acts towards repression of each individual act of rape, thus would be easier to prove than as crimes against humanity.[118] The argument made by Gross, however, faces difficulty in case of internal armed conflicts. The concept of grave breaches has not been widely recognised as applicable to internal armed conflicts, as the Appeals Chamber found in the *Tadić Case.* [119] The Chamber held that in the present state of development of the law, Article 2 of the Statute of the ICTY only applies to offences committed within the context of international armed conflicts.[120] The Chamber, however, referred to a "possible change in *opinio juris*" towards recognising the applicability of grave breaches in internal armed conflicts.[121] As to the crimes against humanity, on the other hand, the Appeals Chamber rejected a necessary connection between the existence of an international armed conflict and the existence of crimes against humanity by stating that:

> It is by now a settled rule of customary international law that crimes against humanity do not require a connection to international armed conflict. Indeed ... customary international law may not require a connection between crimes against humanity and any conflict at all. Thus, by requiring that crimes against humanity be committed in either internal or international armed conflict, the Security Council may have defined the crime in Article 5 more narrowly than necessary under customary international law.[122]

---

[117] See discussion on this issue of Oren Gross, 'The Grave Breaches System and the Armed Conflict in the Former Yugoslavia', *Michigan Journal of International Law*, Spring, 1995: 783-829, pp.820-824

[118] *Ibid.*, p.823.

[119] *Prosecutor v. Tadić*, Decision on the Defence Motion for Interlocutory Appeal in Jurisdiction, 2 October 1995, paras.79-85. Also see Greenwood, *supra* note 88, pp.275-276.

[120] *Prosecutor v. Tadić, op. cit.*, para.84.

[121] *Ibid.*, para.83.

[122] *Ibid.*, para.141. See further Schaack, *supra* note 92, pp.826-832.

The Chamber presented the requirement in determining a crime against humanity as:

> [... it] is the occurrence of the act within the context of a wide-spread or systematic attack on a civilian population that makes the act a crime against humanity as opposed to simply a war crime or crime against national penal legislation.[123]

Thus to demonstrate a crime against humanity, it must be proved that the perpetrator knew the broader context in which his/her act occurred, and furthermore, "the act must not be taken for purely personal reasons unrelated to the armed conflict".[124]

A Croatian doctor who looked into the mass rapes in Bosnia-Herzegovina is convinced that there were "orders to rape". He was of the opinion that the paramilitary groups directed from Belgrade were using rapes to build up a kind of "Serbian solidarity".[125] Alexandra Stiglmayer, a journalist, analyses this point:

> For one thing, the rapes and killings teach locals [sic] Serbs who is "good" and who is "contemptible". At the same time, by forcing them to go along they destroy the bonds of friendship that existed between them and their Muslim and Croatian neighbors.[126]

The doctor mentioned above adds another reason:

> The local Serbs are witnesses to crimes, and those from abroad want to silence them by making them culprits too.[127]

Arguably, this method of forcing locals to participate in the crimes applies not only to rapes but other means of ethnic cleansing taken in Bosnia-Herzegovina or Croatia. Further, this method could also have been used by other parties to the conflict. In order that it can be proved legally that such methods were used during the armed conflict in the former Yugoslavia, the prosecutors of the crimes would have to engage in and execute detailed and laborious fact-finding missions. In the process of proving the use of such

---

[123] *Prosecutor v. Tadić. op. cit.*

[124] *Prosecutor v. Tadić*, Opinion and Judgment, 7 May 1997, para.656. For criticism against these new criteria established by the ICTY, see Schaack, *supra* note 92, pp.832-840.

[125] Alexandra Stiglmayer, ed., *Mass Rape: The War against Women in Bosnia-Herzegovina*, University of Nebraska Press, 1994, p.160.

[126] *Ibid.*, p.161.

[127] *Ibid.*

methods, the ICTY would be able to determine the involvement of the people who were in positions of responsibility in the commission of the crimes. This author believes that the entire process will help in identifying the real and root causes of the conflict. The ICTY, which was established under the Chapter VII for international peace and security, would then fulfil its task.

4.2.2 Victor's Justice

The ethnic cleansing that occurred during the conflict in the former Yugoslavia has been well documented.[128] However, other tools of 'ethnic cleansing' employed subsequent to the end of the armed conflict are much less well known. The Parliament of Croatia passed a general amnesty law on 20 September 1996. The law applies to "persons accused of or sentenced for criminal acts committed in Croatia in connection with aggression, rebellion or armed conflict between 17 August 1990 and 23 August 1996".[129] The legislation exempts from its coverage the alleged perpetrators of war crimes provided for in articles 119 to 137 of the Basic Penal Code of Croatia.[130] The amnesty law, however, was not implemented in a fair and equitable manner. Out of 94 persons released from detention or imprisonment in accordance with the new amnesty law, more than 20 persons were re-arrested immediately or within days. In some cases the charge on which they were re-arrested was for the same acts for which they had previously been held, thus making the amnesty meaningless.[131]

During UNTAES's mandate, there were various lists of war criminals, either official or non-official. The number of 'war criminals' was over 2,000 at the beginning, which reduced to 25 near the end of the mandate. This reduction in the number of war criminals came about as the result of political negotiation rather than through the judicial process.[132] For people under the

---

[128] There are a large number of reports on this issue. Just to mention a few: Russell Watson *et al.*, 'Ethnic Cleansing', *Newsweek*, 17 August 1992: 13-14; Lara Marlowe, '"Cleansed" Wound', *TIME*, 14 September 1992: 34-35; J.F. O. Mcallister, 'Atrocity and Outrage', *TIME*, 17 August, 1992: 21-24; and Aryeh Neier, *War Crimes: Brutality, Genocide, Terror, and the Struggle for Justice*, Times Books, 1998, 140-142, 150-151, and 160-161.

[129] *Further report on the situation of human rights in Croatia pursuant to Security Council resolution 1019 (1995)*, UN Doc. S/1996/101, para.26.

[130] *Ibid.*

[131] *Ibid.*, para.28.

[132] Human Rights Watch criticised this point:

UN transitional administration waiting for reintegration into Croatia, the lists could create enormous psychological pressure. They did not believe in fair trial by the victors. Some of those who were on the lists chose to leave the Region, mainly to the Federal Republic of Yugoslavia. Since their families were likely to leave together, if 1,000 alleged 'war criminals' left the Region, assuming the average number of family members to be four, Croatia could get rid of 4,000 Serbs in this manner. A similar concern exists in Bosnia-Herzegovina in the context that the return of minorities is prevented. Fionnuala Ni Aolain of the Hebrew University Faculty of Law points out:

> After the signing of the Dayton Agreement the authorities in the Federation of Bosnia and Herzegovina and the Republika Srpska had started publicizing lists of persons whom they considered to be responsible for war crimes. Many of these compilations were based on questionable evidence and were also a mechanism to intimidate, discouraging refugees from returning to their homes which were under the control of another ethnic group.[133]

A particular concern pertaining to justice after an armed conflict is whether fair trial can be guaranteed. According to Croatian law, defendants will be provided with a court-appointed defence lawyer at their request only if a sentence of 10 years or more may be imposed for the crime with which they are charged.[134] The question of justice even goes into the courtroom, where human rights monitors can only observe the proceedings. An Austrian newspaper, *Die Presse,* reported on a case of 19 Serbs from a small village in

---

> If sound legal principles are to govern the indictment and trial of suspected war criminals, the Croatian government must indict those against whom sufficient evidence of such crimes is gathered, ...

Human Rights Watch describes the discomfort of the Croats, some of them lost their relatives during and after the siege of Vukovar, over the political negotiation between the Government and UNTAES regarding the length of the list of suspects. Human Rights Watch/Helsinki, *Croatia: Human Rights in Eastern Slavonia during and after the Transition of Authority*, A Human Rights Watch/Helsinki Report, Vol.9, No.6(D), April 1997, p.17. This is a legitimate concern. However, doubt on the credibility of those lists was prevailing at that time in UNTAES. If a list had been prepared based on sound investigation, the number of suspects should not have increased or decreased so easily. (An increase is of course possible when resulting from new investigation.) Also it was widely understood that most of those who committed war crimes had already left the Region.

[133] Aolain, *supra* note 3, p.999.

[134] *Further report on the situation of human rights in Croatia*, UN Doc. S/1996/109, *supra* note 34, para.31.

Eastern Slavonija indicted on a charge of having committed war crimes.[135] They were convicted and sentenced to terms of imprisonment from 8 to 18 years at the first instance court. In the conviction of one defendant, Judge Ante Budica emphasised that the defendant was "involved in political and military structures of the territorial defence of Serb extremists". The article reads:

> That was enough – and such claim goes for all Serbs who in the period between 1991 and 1995 lived in the Region. Between 70 and 80 Serbs are in Croatian jails for similar "war crimes". The purpose of the trial for war crimes actually presents individual-ization of the incorrectly presumed collective guilt, while the trials in Croatia generalize.[136]

The present writer interviewed two of the 19 Serbs indicted for war crimes during UNTAES mandate. Their names were on a so-called "final list" of 25 war criminals compiled by the Croatian government. One of them, repres-enting the 19, said that they were willing to go to The Hague. They claimed that they had nothing to do with war crimes since they had never taken weapons and had instead been on watch duty. As a field officer, what the present writer could do was to report their concern and to seek to bring this to the attention of the higher level of UNTAES. This issue was also reported by the Centre for Human Rights, and the action taken by UNTAES was the political negotiation with Croatian Government. UNTAES Civilian Police undertook court monitoring, which was continued by the Civilian Police Support Group after the withdrawal of UNTAES. Although the effect of court monitoring sometimes appears to be desperately limited, this

---

[135] *Die Presse*, translated and reported in *Glas Slavonije*, 17 November 1999. The translation into English was carried out by a person who is known to this author, but who remains anonymous for security reasons.

[136] *Ibid.* OSCE reports on the same case and another case of a man extradited from Germany in May 1997:

> ... it is apparent from the Sodolovci and Horvat verdicts that the courts base individual criminal responsibility for war crimes on the grounds that the defendants, being members of Serb territorial defence units, are by that fact alone participants in a criminal enterprise.

Report of the OSCE Mission to the Republic of Croatia on Croatia's progress in meeting international commitments since May 1999, 28 September 1999, para.16. Also see Amnesty International, *Croatia: Shortchanging Justice – the "Sodolovci" Group*, Amnesty International Report, EUR 64/006/1999, December 1999, available at http://web.amnesty.org/ai.nsf/Index/EUR640061999?OpenDocument&of=COUNTRIES¥ CROATIA (visited on 4 November 2001).

continuance of monitoring presence from UNTAES to the Support Group and then to the OSCE at least enabled the following-up of cases.

The ICTY has concurrent jurisdiction to prosecute persons for serious violations of international humanitarian law committed in the territory of the former Yugoslavia, and has primacy over national courts.[137] The expectation that ICTY would request to defer these cases, however, is not great, given the fact that ICTY's attention is directed to secure accountability when the national courts "shield the accused from international criminal responsibility".[138]

4.3   Change in the Human Rights Situation

4.3.1 Safe-Areas

As already mentioned, the Security Council established several safe-areas in Bosnia-Herzegovina during 1993.[139] The concept of a safe area, however, contained serious elements of confusion.[140] Prior to the designation of Srebrenica as a safe-area, the evacuation of the population from Srebrenica had continued. The Bosnian Government was worried, since its strategy was to pressurise the United Nations by using the peoples' plight so that Srebrenica would become a safe haven protected by UN forces. The Bosnian Army was of the opinion that the mass evacuation was "not in the interest of Bosnians and contradictory to their military goal".[141] The governing authorities forced the people not to flee from the areas where they were resident; this was a covert strategy for retaining control over the areas and to secure the support of the international community. It exposed the people living in these areas to danger because of the policies of the government on one hand and the ethnic cleansing by the Serbs on the other.

---

[137]   Article 9(1) of *Statute of the International Tribunal*, adopted 25 May 1993, as amended 13 May 1998.

[138]   Article 10 of the Statute of the International Tribunal.

[139]   See *supra* note 55 and accompanying text.

[140]   Some commentators explain that safe havens need not depend on the consent of the warring parties and could be enforced, while safe areas were based on consent. Jan Willem Honig and Norbert Both, *Srebrenica: Record of a War Crime*, Penguin Books, 1996, p.104. Concerning the safe havens established in Iraq for the protection of the Kurds, the UN Secretary-General was of the view that such operation would require the permission of Iraq. Peter Malanczuk, 'The Kurdish Crisis and Allied Intervention in the Aftermath of the Second Gulf War', *EJIL* 2, 1991: 114-32, p.129.

[141]   Honig and Both, *op. cit.*, p.92.

Safe areas had a detrimental effect on UNPROFOR's relationship with the Bosnian Serbs. In March 1994, the Secretary-General reported to the Security Council that the safe-areas were used by the Army of Bosnia-Herzegovina "as locations in which its troops can rest, train and equip themselves as well as fire at Serb positions thereby provoking Serb retaliation".[142] Because of this abuse of the safe areas by the Bosnian Army, the Bosnian Serbs thought that UNPROFOR was not an impartial and neutral observer. The Secretary-General affirmed that the concept needed redefining. To implement the safe-areas effectively, UNPROFOR needed more strength. If the co-operation of the fighting parties was not to be gained, then UNPROFOR would have to shift to "peace-enforcement mode".[143] Subsequently the Secretary-General recommended the demilitarisation of the safe areas so that they would be in compliance with the Geneva Conventions of 12 August 1949 and the Additional Protocols of 1977.[144] The Secretary-General explained the situation:

> When a safe area has strategic importance in ongoing military operations launched or provoked by the forces defending the area, it would be unrealistic to expect the other party to avoid attacking that area, even with full knowledge of the likely consequences of violating the relevant Security Council resolutions.[145]

On 6 July 1995, the Bosnian Serbs launched a full-scale assault on the safe area of Srebrenica and UNPROFOR positions were overrun. Srebrenica fell on 11 July, followed by fall of Žepa on 25 July. What was most disturbing for UNPROFOR was that the safe areas turned into extremely vulnerable places. After the fall of Srebrenica, thousands of Muslim men were executed by the Bosnian Serbs.[146] This was the largest single massacre to take place on

---

[142] *Report of the Secretary-General*, 16 March 1994, UN Doc. S/1994/300.

[143] *Ibid.*

[144] *Report of the Secretary-General*, 1 December 1994, UN Doc. S/1994/1389, para.52. Article 15 of the Fourth Geneva Convention provides for "neutralised zones" where "wounded and sick combatants or non-combatants" and "civilian persons who take no part in hostilities, and who, while they reside in the zones, perform no work of a military character" would be sheltered. Protocol I provides for "non-defended localities" in Article 59. The Parties to the conflict are prohibited to attack such localities.

[145] *Secretary-General's Report*, UN Doc. S/1994/1389, *supra* note 144, para.37.

[146] For review of the fall of Srebrenica, see *Report of the Secretary-General pursuant to General Assembly resolution 53/35: The Fall of Srebrenica* (hereinafter, *Srebrenica Report*), UN Doc. A/54/549, 15 November 1999; and *Report of the Secretary-General pursuant to Security Council resolution 1019 (1995) on violation of international*

European soil since the end of the World War II. We can consider several factors that caused the failure of the safe areas. First, UNPROFOR was not given the means to protect the areas designated as safe areas and consequently could not protect the people in the area. There were not enough troops, and a peacekeeping force was in any case not a combat force. The Dutch Battalion (Dutchbat) stationed in Srebrenica numbered 150, whereas there were 2,000 Serbs surrounding the area.[147] Secondly, the only potential means of protecting the areas, NATO's air support, was not used effectively as a result of communications problems between each layer of the chain of command. The emergency felt and perceived in the field was not recognised at a higher level.[148] Third, UNPROFOR did not prioritise the protection of civilians. After the fall of Srebrenica, the Dutchbat Commander did negotiate for the deployment of one soldier in each bus in which the civilians were "evacuated".[149] However, the speed with which the Bosnian Serb Army carried out the operation did not allow Dutchbat to carry this out. Furthermore, Dutchbat did not insist that the Muslim men should not be separated from women and children. The plea of the Bosnian Muslims not to hand them over to the Serbs was refused because Dutchbat believed that the Muslims would be treated in accordance with the Geneva Conventions.[150] It is hard to understand why Dutchbat could be of this opinion after so many violations of international humanitarian law by all the parties to the conflict in Bosnia-Herzegovina, and especially by the Serbs. If the Dutchbat was not aware of those violations, there was a fundamental problem as regards the information flow in UNPROFOR. To make the matter worse, the Special Representative of the Secretary-General ordered that human rights violations should neither be reported nor made public, the reasons put forward for this was the concern for the security of Military Observers in Srebrenica.[151] Also, only few accounts by Dutchbat who had witnessed signs of serious abuses were forwarded up the UNPROFOR chain of command.[152] The negligence of both the Special Representative and the Dutchbat as regards the fate of people from Srebrenica raises the question of the duty of the United Nations

---

humanitarian law in the areas of Srebrenica, Zepa, Banja Luka and Sanski Most, UN Doc. S/1995/988, 27 November 1995. Also J.W. Honig and N. Both, *supra* note 140.

[147] *Srebrenica Report,* para.472.

[148] *Ibid.,* paras.235, 243, 249, 252, & 282.

[149] *Ibid.,* para.320.

[150] *Ibid.,* para.348.

[151] *Ibid.,* para.353.

[152] *Ibid.,* para.358.

and peacekeepers to protect human rights. This point will be developed in the next chapter.

4.3.2 Broken Agreements

During the period of the mandate for UNPROFOR, the prospects for a peaceful solution sometimes improved around Sarajevo. Instances of this were a cease-fire agreement on 23 February 1994 between the Bosnian Army and the Croatian Defence Council,[153] an anti-sniping agreement, and an agreement for the use of the routes across Mount Igman for civilian and humanitarian traffic in March 1994.[154] However, by the end of May 1995 UNPROFOR had lost control of all the weapons collection points in the Sarajevo exclusion zone.[155]

4.3.3 Operation Flash and Operation Storm

In Croatia, the Croatian Army and police entered Sector West on 1 May 1995. The Croatian Government initially explained that this operation was a police action aimed at restoring security on the Zagreb-Belgrade highway, following the stabbing of a Serb by a Croatian refugee on 28 April and the subsequent retaliatory killing of three Croatian citizens by Serbs, and a further alleged attack on a Croat on 30 April.[156] However, it turned out to be Operation Flash, an operation to establish complete control over the Sector. The Croatian police had reportedly conducted themselves properly, but in their absence the remaining Serbs were subject to harassment and intimidation, including looting and the burning of houses.[157]

On 4 August 1995, the Croatian Army launched a military offensive, Operation Storm, in Sectors North and South. As a result of this military operation, more than 90 per cent of Serb inhabitants of these Sectors fled.[158] In November 1995, the Secretary-General wrote:

---

[153] *Report of the Secretary-General pursuant to Security Council resolutions 982(1995) and 987(1995)*, UN Doc. S/1995/444, 30 May 1995, para.42.

[154] *Ibid.*, para.44.

[155] *Ibid.*, para.50.

[156] *Report of the Secretary-General submitted pursuant to Security Council resolution 944 (1995)*, UN Doc. S/1995/467, 9 June 1995, para.5.

[157] *Ibid.*, para.15.

[158] *Report of the Secretary-General pursuant to Security Council resolution 1009 (1995)*, UN Doc. S/1995/835, 29 September 1995, para.5.

As if the savagery of the war in the Balkans since 1991 was not enough, the past few months have seen further despicable acts of cruelty and violence, as illustrated by the catalogue of reported atrocities ... evidence of a consistent pattern of summary executions, rape, mass expulsions, arbitrary detentions, forced labour and large-scale disappearances.[159]

The reports of looting, intimidation, killings and arson continued, and the Secretary-General strongly criticised Croatian Government's failure to implement effective security measures:

[...the] leading causes of continuing lawlessness in the region are the lack of an adequate professional police presence and the Croatian authorities' unwillingness to take firm preventive action against human rights violators.[160]

In some cases police officers had themselves taken part in criminal acts, while in other cases criminal acts were perpetrated by members of the Croatian army. Further, Croatian civilian police officers have been either unwilling or afraid to exercise their duties.[161]

4.3.4 Administrative Discrimination

After the cessation of military hostilities, new concerns regarding human rights began to emerge. Victor's justice mentioned above was a part of it. Another area of concern has been administrative discrimination. For instance, in September 1995, the Croatian Parliament decided to suspend temporarily several articles of a special constitutional law affecting the rights of national minorities, including articles that provided for special self-governing status for districts predominantly populated by a national minority.[162] Although the Security Council called for the decision to be rescinded by issuing a statement from the President of the Council,[163] the suspension was still effective in September 1999.[164]

---

[159] *Secretary-General's Report,* UN Doc. S/1995/988, *supra* note 146, para.74.

[160] *Further report on the situation of human rights in Croatia,* UN Doc. S/1996/456, *supra* note 90, para.13.

[161] *Ibid.*

[162] *Further Report on the situation of human rights in Croatia,* UN Doc. S/1996/109, *supra* note 34, para.26.

[163] UN Doc. S/PRST/1996/26. *Further Report on the situation of human rights in Croatia,* UN Doc. S/1996/456, *supra* note 90, para.38.

[164] *Report of the OSCE, supra* note 136, p.13.

In addition, the law on the temporary management of currently abandoned property in the formerly occupied territory, which came into effect on 3 December 1995, created a major obstacle for the recovery of their property by ethnic Serb Croats. The law allowed the Croatian Government to make abandoned homes and property available for the housing of displaced persons unless the owners claimed their property for their personal use by returning to Croatia.[165] Subsequently the Croatian Government suspended the time-limit for filing claims to property 'abandoned' during Operation Storm which would prevent the hand-over of the property to displaced persons for their temporary use.[166] However, this suspension did not apply to lease-holders who left rented property during Operation Storm.[167]

Discrimination was also found in the provision of social benefits:

> Reconstruction assistance was far more likely to be dispensed to citizens of Croat, as opposed to Serb origin. Utility services such as electricity and water, as well as transport lines to Croatian Serb communities, have been slow in materialising. ... Applications for documentation by Croatian Serb individuals, including for recognition of citizenship, are frequently stalled for bureaucratic and other reasons, while citizens of Croat origin find the process to be much swifter.[168]

The ethnic compositions of the former Sectors West, South and North of Croatia have changed not only by the Serb population fleeing *en masse* during Operation Flash and Operation Storm, but also by the influx of over 55,000 displaced Croats from elsewhere in the country, together with Croat refugees from Bosnia-Herzegovina and the Federal Republic of Yugoslavia. The number of Croatian Serbs who remained in the former sectors was some 10,000.[169] Responding to criticism expressed in Secretary-General's reports

---

[165] *Report of the Secretary-General pursuant to Security Council resolutions 981(1995), 982(1995) and 983(1995)*, UN Doc. S/1995/987, 23 November 1995, para.8.

[166] *Further report on the situation of human rights in Croatia*, UN Doc. S/1996/109, *supra* note 34, para.22.

[167] *Further report on the situation of human rights in Croatia*, UN Doc. S/1996/456, *supra* note 90, para.29.

[168] *Further report on the situation of human rights in Croatia pursuant to Security Council resolution 1019 (1995)*, UN Doc. S/1996/101, para.16. Regarding the difficulties faced by remaining Croatian Serbs, see also *Further report on the situation of human rights in Croatia*, UN Doc. S/1996/109, *supra* note 34, para.20; and *Further report on the situation of human rights in Croatia*, UN Doc. S/1996/456, *supra* note 90, paras.21-24.

[169] *Further Report on the situation of human rights in Croatia*, UN Doc. S/1996/101, *supra* note 168, para.18.

regarding the inadequacy of measures to enhance return of the Serbs, the Croatian Government stated:

> ... The Secretary-General should not overlook the fact that a mass and unmanaged return of Serbs to the liberated territories would promote an exodus of non-Serbs who have just returned there and would discourage the return of non-Serbs who are yet to return to the liberated areas. All of these people were expelled by the rebel Serbs in the first place.[170]

Neither UNPROFOR nor UNCRO had any mandate to advise the Government of Croatia on these issues. UNTAES could rely on the executive powers of the transitional administrator on issues in the Region. Civil Affairs officers in the field reported problems discovered on the ground, and some issues were discussed at a high level. However, UNTAES's executive powers were applicable only within the Region, and even if political negotiation had affected certain matters of policy, the Croatian Government could amend any legislation after the reintegration of the Region.

4.4 Relationship with State Agencies

The UN forces in the former Yugoslavia took pains to secure the co-operation of the conflicting parties. In Croatia, neither the Croatian Government nor local Serb authorities were satisfied with UNPROFOR's activities. The Croatian Parliament supported the termination of UNPROFOR's mandate and the Security Council was informed of this in a letter dated 24 September 1993.[171] The Croatian Government explained the reason:

> Croatia cannot accept any prolongation of the "peace-keeping" operation that is in fact not keeping peace but preserving the status quo, which is seriously undermining the sovereignty and territorial integrity of Croatia.

The Croatian Government did not oppose UNPROFOR's powers to perform immigration and customs functions at the UNPA borders and even invited international human rights monitors. What mattered to them was territorial integrity; the recovery of control over the areas where UNPROFOR was deployed. UNPROFOR was actually hampered from carrying out its

---

[170] *Further Report on the situation of human rights in Croatia*, UN Doc. S/1996/456, *supra* note 90, para.27.

[171] *Letter dated 24 September 1993 from the representative of Croatia to the President of the Security Council*, 24 September 1993, UN Doc. S/26491.

mandate by the continuing armed conflict between the Croatian Government force and the Serbs. Thus, under resolution 871 of 4 October 1993, the Security Council authorised UNPROFOR, "in carrying out its mandate in the Republic of Croatia, acting in self-defence, to take the necessary measures, including the use of force, to ensure its security and its freedom of movement".[172] As the Secretary-General stated that he had to face the choice of recommending either the withdrawal or a continuation of the Force before each renewal of UNPROFOR's mandate, the absence of any certainty as regards the co-operation of the Croatian Government and Krajina Serb authorities made it difficult for UNPROFOR to carry out its mandate.[173] There were restrictions on UNPROFOR's freedom of movement, and a large number of cease-fire agreement violations were perpetrated by both sides. The Croatian Government did not grant a broadcasting licence to UNPROFOR, either.[174] On 12 January 1995, President of the Republic of Croatia informed the Secretary-General that his Government had decided not to agree with a further extension of UNPROFOR's mandate beyond the existing mandate period. The President stated that it was an indisputable fact that "the present character of the UNPROFOR mission does not provide conditions necessary for establishing lasting peace and order in the Republic of Croatia, a sovereign State member of the United Nations".[175] One major reason to be noted why UNPROFOR's relationship with the Croatian Government was so difficult was that there had been no status-of-force agreement with the Government.[176] A status-of-force agreement with the Croatian Government was signed, belatedly, on 15 May 1995,[177] while the agreement with the Republic of Bosnia and Herzegovina, where UNPROFOR was deployed later than in Croatia, was concluded on 15 May 1993.[178] The Secretary-General affirmed that the establishment of UNPROFOR's headquarters and principal logistic bases in Croatia without the prior conclusion

---

[172] SC res. 871, 4 October 1993. SCOR, 3286th mtg., UN Doc. S/RES/871(1993). Adopted unanimously.

[173] *Report of the Secretary-General submitted pursuant to Paragraph 4 of Security Council resolution 947(1994)*, UN Doc. S/1995/38, 14 January 1995, para.3.

[174] *Ibid.*, para.24.

[175] *Letter from President Tudjman to Secretary-General*, UN Doc. S/1995/28, annex, 12 January 1995, para.4.

[176] *Report of the Secretary-General*, UN Doc. S/1994/1067, 17 September 1994.

[177] *Report of the Secretary-General submitted pursuant to Security Council resolution 994 (1995)*, UN Doc. S/1995/467, 9 June 1995, para.16.

[178] *Secretary-General's Report*, UN Doc. S/1995/222, *supra* note 59, para.56.

of a status-of-force agreement caused difficulties and additional costs to the mission.[179]

The Croatian Government, however, later moderated its hostile stance toward UNPROFOR, and even invited the deployment of a large number of UNCRO civilian personnel throughout Sector West to monitor Serbs' human rights.[180] Yet during the Operation Flash, a total restriction of movement was imposed on UNCRO in Sector West for the first seven days of May and vehement accusations of partiality were levelled against the personnel who were reporting on human rights during that period.[181] On the other hand, the Krajina Serb "Assembly" rejected the name of UNCRO, "on the grounds that it prejudged a political solution" and also rejected the parts of Security Council resolution 981 (1995) that treated the Serb-held territories as part of Croatia.[182] Nevertheless, the "Assembly" was ready to co-operate with the United Nations in the search for a peaceful and just solution to the conflict "based on principles of impartiality and equal honouring of the sovereign rights of the Serb nation in the Republic of Serb Krajina".[183]

Before the expiry of UNTAES's first twelve-month mandate, the local Serb Regional Assembly requested the Transitional Administrator to communicate to the Security Council its request for an extension of the duration of the mandate for an additional one year.[184] On the other hand, the House of Representatives of the Croatian Parliament unanimously adopted a non-binding resolution calling for the termination of UNTAES's mandate on 15 January 1997. There were hostile and aggressive statements against UNTAES both in the media and by the Government. The Minister of Defence even threatened military action if the region were not returned by April 1997.[185]

In Bosnia-Herzegovina, all the parties to the conflict frequently restricted UNPROFOR's freedom of movement. In vain, UNPROFOR repeatedly sought the deployment of Civil Affairs officers and civilian monitors into

---

[179] *Ibid.*, para.55.

[180] *Secretary-General's Report*, UN Doc. S/1995/467, *supra* note 156, para.16.

[181] *Ibid.*, para.17.

[182] *Ibid.*, para.18.

[183] *Ibid.*

[184] *Report of the Secretary-General on the United Nations Transitional Administration for Eastern Slavonia, Baranja and Western Sirmium*, 28 August, 1996, UN Doc. S/1996/705, para.11.

[185] *Report of the Secretary-General on the United Nations Transitional Administration for Eastern Slavonia, Baranja and Western Sirmium*, UN Doc. S/1996/883, para.2.

areas controlled by the Bosnian Serbs.[186] The removal of a newly installed
civil affairs presence in Banja Luka, where human rights protection of non-
Serbs were of particular concern, was demanded by the Bosnian Serbs on 25
February 1995.[187] In addition, the Bosnian Serbs objected to the deployment
of civilian police monitors on their territory.[188]

After the Dayton Agreement, the level of co-operation between the police
forces of the entities and IPTF varied significantly. IPTF and Civil Affairs'
intervention achieved the removal or transfer of several key police execut-
ives from their positions on the grounds of their non-compliance with agreements made by their political authorities on police restructuring.[189]

4.5   Investigation

Notwithstanding the lack of an explicit mandate, UNPROFOR became
involved in interviewing evicted individuals, organising patrols to protect
houses, and compiling data on those groups believed to be responsible for
the expulsions.[190] Since the Centre for Human Rights had a field presence,
human rights issues were not officially the mandate of UNPROFOR. However, on the basis of initiative of officers in the field, activities such as court
monitoring and prison visits were conducted.[191] After Operation Flash,
Civilian Police monitors interviewed released detainees who had been investigated as suspected perpetrators of war crimes.[192] UNCRO also gathered
information on possible human rights violations from statements made by
local residents of the Sector West to its own personnel and to representatives
of UNHCR and the officers of the Centre for Human Rights of the United
Nations Secretariat. UNCRO also examined information from reports from
its own military components and from humanitarian organisations.[193]

---

[186] *Secretary-General's Report*, UN Doc. S/1995/222, *supra* note 59, para.34.
[187] *Ibid.*, para.34.
[188] *Ibid.*
[189] *Report of the Secretary-General pursuant Security Council resolution 1035 (1995)*, UN Doc. S/1996/820, para.8; and *Report of the Secretary-General,* S/1998/491, *supra* note 100, paras.20-25.
[190] UNIC, UK, Doc.NS/21/92, 28 May 1992. Referred to in A. B. Fetherston, O. Rams-botham and T. Woodhouse, 'UNPROFOR: Some Observations from a Conflict Resolution Perspective', *International Peacekeeping*, Vol.1, No.2, Summer 1994: 179-203, p.183.
[191] E-mail interview with former Civil Affairs Officer in UNPROFOR and UNCRO on 16 November 1999.
[192] *Secretary-General's Report*, UN Doc. S/1996/820, *supra* note 189, para.28.
[193] *Ibid.*, para.31. See also T. Modibo Ocran, 'How Blessed Were the UN Peacekeepers in Former Yugoslavia? The Involvement of UNPROFOR and Human Rights Issues in

The Human Rights Office of UNMIBH initiates, assists and monitors investigations by local police, leaving independent investigations as a last resort.[194] In 1998 the Office started surprise prison visits, monitoring of selected trials and gathering of gender-related data.[195]

Peacekeepers are usually very cautious not to stray from their mandate. Whether a peace-keeping operation is explicitly determined as a subsidiary organ of the Security Council or not, it is clear that the scope of powers of the peacekeeping operation is determined by the Security Council, and such powers cannot exceed those assigned to the Security Council by the Member States.[196] In practice, when the interpretation of the mandate of a peace-keeping operation in the field is different from that in the Secretariat, there is not much room for the peacekeepers in the field to argue against the Head-quarters.[197] Human rights monitoring by UNPROFOR and UNCRO was possible because it was low-profile, whereas the Headquarters in New York would not have approved the use of force for the protection of civilians from human rights abuses.

4.6 Reporting

UNCRO continued to report the situation in Sectors West, North and South, after Operation Flash in April 1995 and Operation Storm in August 1995, this reporting including instances of human rights abuse and the destruction of property. UNCRO's Human Rights Action Teams co-operated with the

---

Croatia, 1992-1996', *Wisconsin International Law Journal*, Winter 2000: 193-255, pp.234.

[194] *Secretary-General's Report,* UN Doc. S/1998/227, *supra* note 76, para.21.

[195] *Ibid.*, para.24.

[196] Simma, ed., *The Charter of the United Nations, supra* FN3 of Chapter 1, p.486. In the event that the General Assembly is the parent organ of the peacekeeping operation, the analogous relationship applies between the operation and the General Assembly. The International Court of Justice held in its Advisory Opinion on the Effect of Awards Made by the UN Administrative Tribunal:

> The precise nature and scope of the measures by which the power of creating a tribunal was to be exercised, was a matter for determination by the General Assembly alone.

Effect of Awards of Compensation made by the UNAT, ICJ Reports (1954), p.58. See also Simma, *op. cit.*, pp.200-201.

[197] See, for example, the case of UNAMIR in Rwanda in the previous Chapter, FN27 and accompanying text. For more details, see *Report of the Special Rapporteur of the Commission on Human Rights on the situation of human rights in Rwanda,* A/50/709-S/1995/915, 2 November 1995.

United Nations High Commissioner for Human Rights in monitoring human rights.[198]

At the planning phase of UNTAES, noticeable consideration was given to human rights issues. In Article 6, the Basic Agreement provided that :

> The highest levels of internationally recognised human rights and fundamental freedoms shall be respected in the Region.[199]

The United Nations Task Force to Establish the Transitional Administration in Sector East included an active reporting system in its plan:

> Designing and implementing a human rights information system (HRIS) which quickly informs the press, embassies in Zagreb, NGOs, Croatian government and appropriate UN and Council of Europe institutions on HR violations. A daily report (embassies, press, NGOs) noting violations should be supplemented by a bi-monthly analytical human rights report (Security Council, Human Rights Committee of the Council of Europe and the Croatian government) identifying trends which could include the base line indicators.[200]

This system, however, was not implemented. The human rights aspect of the mandate was marginalised to some extent at the implementation phase. Some officers were employed for human rights posts, but were not assigned to any specific task on human rights. One possible explanation for this marginalisation is that since a significant number of civil affairs officers had experienced Operation Flash or Operation Storm in other Sectors before their work in UNTAES, most of them did not believe that UNTAES could do much.[201] When it comes to the implementation phase, prioritisation by an officer in charge is also important. If the person who makes decisions on the prioritisation of a working agenda does not recognise the importance of human rights work, this results in an insufficiency in human resources and attention in the area. In the UNTAES headquarters in Vukovar from autumn

---

[198] *Secretary-General's Report*, UN Doc. S/1995/222, *supra* note 59, para.14. Also see Ocran *supra* note 193.

[199] The "Region" meant the former Sector East, where the United Nations transitional administration was established.

[200] United Nations Task Force to Establish the Transitional Administration in Sector East, *Approaches to monitor and influence human rights observance in Sector East*, Annex Q to *Background Report on the Region of Eastern Slavonia, Baranja and Western Sirmium*, Zagreb, December 1995.

[201] E-mail interview with a former Civil Affairs Officer of UNPROFOR, UNCRO and UNTAES, 23 November 1999.

1997, there were a few officers who were exclusively assigned the work on human rights. This number of officers makes field-work difficult or even impossible. The opposite may also happen. UNTAES had several civil affairs regional offices taking on the responsibility for a particular geographical area.[202] This author worked in one of the regional offices and was assigned to the development and maintenance of a human rights database. The work included the collation of information primarily from Civilian Police's Incident Reports, but also from civil affairs field officers and military observers, together with complaints direct from the local population. This work inevitably went beyond the bounds of the area of responsibility (AOR) of the Regional Office. In principle, there was an implied rule not to intervene in other regional offices' AOR. This work, however, did receive co-operation from other regional offices, and the headquarters did not object such an initiative of one regional office. The initiative was taken by the Officer in Charge (OIC) of the particular regional office since, on the basis of his work experience in another Sector, he considered human rights to be a very important factor for the peace in the Region. The aim of the database was to produce periodical reports featuring the change in the human rights situation in the Region. The idea of the OIC was to use the reports exactly as planned by the Task Force quoted above. After a certain period of information gathering, the investigation of specific cases was also conducted for more detailed reporting. Unfortunately, for several reasons the periodic reports did not achieve the aim. Firstly, since it was an initiative from a regional office, as regards the use of the reports, lobbying at the headquarters level was necessary.[203] Secondly, changes in personnel were frequent, which made a consistent approach to the issue difficult. Thirdly, from time to time field officers were assigned urgent tasks by the headquarters and even if the OIC of the regional office was ready to prioritise human rights work, it was not always possible to maintain the prioritisation. UNTAES established a Human Rights Unit in early August 1997 and employed some new human rights officers. However, since the mission was to be closed in mid-January 1998 its establishment was too late. The policy insisted upon by the Office

---

[202] The number and locations of regional offices changed during the course of the mission.

[203] Eventually one report was sent from the headquarters to the Croatian local government side without the knowledge of our regional office. It was not by any means a pleasant report for the Croatian government. It was not in fact supported by officers undertaking human rights work at the headquarters, either, since such action was not discussed with them in advance. Those officers probably considered that more detailed examination of the style and contents of the report was required before making it public, and the present writer fully agrees with this. This event shows the difficulty inherent in a multi-layered and compartmentalised working and reporting system of a peacekeeping mission.

of the High Commissioner for Human Rights in Geneva to employ new officers was also questionable in terms of effectiveness, since a certain amount of time was inevitably required to them to familiarise themselves with the situation.

4.7   Institution-building

In 1995 Croatia ratified the Optional Protocol to the International Covenant on Civil and Political Rights, which enabled individuals to communicate to the Human Rights Committee alleged violations of their rights under the Covenant.[204] In November 1996, Croatia was formally admitted as a member of the Council of Europe, and the Government of Croatia ratified the European Convention for the Protection of Human Rights and Fundamental Freedoms and its Protocols on 5 November 1997. Therefore Croatia accepted the competence of the European Commission and the European Court of Human Rights. She also ratified the Framework Convention for the Protection of National Minorities and the European Convention for the Prevention of Torture and Inhuman or Degrading Treatment or Punishment on 11 October 1997.[205]

The UNTAES Civilian Police component took control of the prison in Beli Manastir with a view both to establishing a prison administration that was better integrated and to monitoring respect for human rights standards in the prison.[206] UNTAES Civilian Police also assisted establishment of multi-ethnic Transitional Police Force (TPF). The role of the Civilian Police, however, was limited to the 'monitoring' of the TPF. Under the transitional administration of UNTAES, the Joint Implementation Committee on Human Rights, consisting of Croatian Government representatives, representatives of local Serb authorities and UNTAES officers, was the mechanism for institution-building in the field of human rights. However, it was unable to achieve significant progress in institution-building.

As regards Bosnia-Herzegovina, the Dayton Agreement designed institutions in order to protect human rights: the Human Rights Commission, which consists of an Ombudsperson and a Human Rights Chamber.[207] The part played by the UN peacekeeping operation in the area of human rights is

---

[204] *Further Report on the situation of human rights in Croatia*, UN Doc. S/1996/109, *supra* note 34, para.29.

[205] *Further Report on the situation of human rights in Croatia*, UN Doc. S/1996/101, *supra* note 168, para.30.

[206] *Secretary-General's Report*, UN Doc. S/1996/705, *supra* note 184, para.26.

[207] For more details of these institutions, see F. N. Aolain, *supra* note 3, pp.984-988.

the rehabilitation of local police by IPTF. IPTF is currently actively involved in the democratisation of the local police force. Their policy is to introduce community policing in Bosnia-Herzegovina. IPTF designed three courses for the local police. Firstly, a two-day "information" course that explains the IPTF restructuring process and its aims. Secondly, a one-week "human dignity" course which introduces a modern view of the role of the police officer in a democratic society. Third, a three-week "transition" course which is "a condensed version of a police academy course and focuses on basic police skills".[208] IPTF also assists the local police in rehabilitating and developing proper police academies.[209] In 1998, the IPTF started co-locating selected IPTF monitors permanently with local chiefs of police or senior police officers in their place of work. The result of the monitoring is used for further reform of the local police.[210] The UNMIBH Legal Office worked with an international expert team on the re-drafting of the Criminal Code and the Code of Criminal Procedure for the Federation.[211]

4.8 Human Rights Education

In peacekeeping operations in the former Yugoslavia, human rights education has not enjoyed as much attention as it had received in ONUSAL in El Salvador or UNTAC in Cambodia. In the case of UNPROFOR both in Croatia and Bosnia-Herzegovina, as well as UNCRO, the continuation of the armed conflicts made it difficult for such a function to be carried out. Regarding the post-conflict period, one reason may be that the concept of human rights itself was not new to the local population. For example, on a number of occasions this author had the opportunity of interviewing alleged victims of human rights violations in the area under the administration of UNTAES, and many of them discussed their cases with reference to human rights and even international law. Also, there were some local NGOs specialised in human rights issues. UNTAES and UNMIBH both put particular emphasis on police training, not on civic education.[212]

---

[208] *Secretary-General's Report,* UN Doc. S/1997/966, *supra* note 74, para.8.

[209] *Ibid.,* para.9.

[210] *Secretary-General's Report,* UN Doc. S/1998/491, *supra* note 100, para.39.

[211] *Report of the Secretary-General on the United Nations Mission in Bosnia-Herzegovina,* UN Doc. S/1997/468, 19 June 1997, para.19.

[212] There were still some activities in this area. For example, during UNTAES administration, the Joint Implementation Committee on Human Rights organised and conducted a human rights training seminar sponsored by the Council of Europe and a local non-governmental organisation. *Report of the Secretary-General on the United Nations Transitional*

4.9   Co-operation within UN Peacekeeping Operations

After Operation Storm in Croatia, the Special Representative of the Secretary-General established a humanitarian crisis cell to collate information and co-ordinate responses. The Cell consisted of UNPF staff and communicated with all international agencies involved in humanitarian affairs. It also co-ordinated four human rights action teams.[213]

UNTAES organised weekly human rights co-ordination meetings. Participants included civil affairs, civilian police, military observers and border monitors within UNTAES, the UN Centre for Human Rights, UNICEF, the International Committee of the Red Cross (ICRC), the Organisation for Security and Cooperation of Europe (OSCE) and the European Community Monitoring Mission (ECMM).

4.10   Co-operation with Other UN Agencies

In mid-January 1995, UNPROFOR took the initiative to form an Inter-Agency Working Group on Human Rights Issues under the chairmanship of the Head of Civil Affairs. The agencies involved in the Working Group were UNHCR, the Centre for Human Rights and the ICRC, and representatives from OSCE and ECMM were also invited to participate when issues relevant to their activities were addressed.[214] The Working Group met on an as-needed basis and served to share resources, reduce duplication and co-ordinate ongoing efforts to promote pluralism in the local communities. With the agreement of the UN High Commissioner for Human Rights the Working Group also held a series of training sessions for field officers and developed an information package containing the primary international documents on human rights for dissemination to field officers.[215]

The United Nations involvement in the human rights field in Bosnia-Herzegovina after the Dayton Agreement consists of three agencies: the UNHCR to provide protection to newly returned refugees; the IPTF to monitor the local security forces' respect for human rights; and the United Nations High Commissioner for Human Rights to train personnel charged with human rights monitoring or other activities related to human rights, to

---

Administration for Eastern Slavonia, Baranja and Western Sirmium, UN Doc. S/1996/622, 5 August 1996, para.13.

[213] *Report of the Secretary-General submitted pursuant to Security Council resolution 1009 (1995)*, UN Doc. S/1995/730, para.16.

[214] *Secretary-General's Report*, UN Doc. S/1995/222, *supra* note 59, para.45.

[215] *Ibid.*, para.46.

provide the High Representative with experienced and trained human rights officers, and to support the work of the Special Rapporteur and of the Expert on the special process regarding missing persons.[216] The High Representative co-ordinates the activities of various organisations and agencies.[217]

4.11 Co-operation with NGOs

Since UNTAES was understaffed in the area of human rights, Civil Affairs officers often referred complainants in specific cases to local NGOs specialised in human rights area. UNTAES received special co-operation from the Civil Rights Project, an international NGO. The Civil Rights Project specifically looked into the problems faced by the Serbs in the Region in obtaining Croatian citizenship, identification cards and passports. Those whose applications were rejected consulted the Civil Rights Project, and many cases were taken to a court. This co-operation was particularly helpful for the local population, as UNTAES did not have the capacity to follow-up individual cases, although efforts were made to seek explanation and advice from the relevant ministries of the Croatian Government. Many cases are still pending as of 1999.

CONCLUSION

Correctly, Human Rights Watch, a prominent international human rights NGO, severely criticises the failure of UNPROFOR and the international community's response to the conflict in the former Yugoslavia:

> UN peacekeeping and other efforts in both Croatia and Bosnia-Herzegovina have been marked by timidity, disorganization, unnecessary delay and political indecision. Quite apart from the difficulties of negotiating among parties that are unwilling to cease fighting and are acting in bad faith, UN operations in the region have been hampered by competition between member states and the Secretary General; disputes between the Secretary General and UN personnel in the field; member states' unwillingness to commit necessary financial resources; and violations of the arms and trade embargoes by several nations.[218]

---

[216] *Secretary-General's Report*, UN Doc. S/1995/1031, *supra* note 67, para.32.

[217] See *supra* note 85.

[218] Human Rights Watch, *The Lost Agenda*, *supra* FN85 of Chapter 4, pp.85-86.

In comparison with ONUSAL in El Salvador or UNTAC in Cambodia, UNPROFOR, UNCRO and UNTAES have taken a different approach in dealing with human rights. Despite the large scale of human rights problems, the operations in the former Yugoslavia were not designed to contain a civilian component specialised in human rights work, and military and civilian police components had to undertake the task. One civil affairs officer in UNPROFOR commented:

> The presence of UN soldiers in the villages as well as regular patrols and visits by other components and other UN agencies proved to be a quite effective form of protection for the vulnerable groups.[219]

Since the effect of deterrence is difficult to prove, this role of UNPROFOR has not been appreciated. Many commentators regard UNPROFOR as a failed mission. While the information on egregious human rights abuses shocked the world, it was difficult for the general public to understand what the UN soldiers were there for. If we look into the mandate of UNPROFOR, however, the peacekeepers were not there to confront directly the perpetrators of human rights abuses. It was the decision of the Security Council, which means the decision of the Member States, not to give such a mandate to UNPROFOR. The United Nations' response to the reports of atrocities in the former Yugoslavia was mostly fact-finding and reporting through the establishment of a Commission of Experts and the appointment of Special Rapporteurs. The Organisation failed to utilise its field presence, the peacekeepers.

When a peacekeeping operation is deployed in an area where a cease-fire is not actually in place, as in the case of UNPROFOR, the deployment of civilian human rights officers might not be considered appropriate for security reasons. If a military component is to be more explicitly assigned human rights functions in the future, their training should be well designed. In the event that the international community is not ready to resort to enforcement action through the Security Council's decision, at least the recording and reporting of human rights abuses and violation of humanitarian law is necessary to seek accountability at a later stage.

When UNTAES was preparing a standardised reporting form for human rights cases, there was a discussion at a co-ordination meeting as to whether UN military and civilian police should be participants in this project. In

---

[219] Saijin Zhang, 'Victim Assistance in Peace-keeping Operations', a paper presented at the Expert Group Meeting on Victims of Crime and Abuse of Power in the International Setting held at Vienna, 18-22 November 1995, p.4.

many countries, military and police officers are often the perpetrators of human rights abuses. That was the motivation of some participants in the meeting to question whether military and police officers were qualified to be involved in human rights monitoring. In fact, the present writer had been already receiving essential co-operation from military observers and Civilian Police in order to collate information for the human rights database. The exclusion of UN military and Civilian Police from human rights activities was not acceptable for two reasons. Firstly, as a part of a UN operation, UN military and police components should have been actively practising international human rights norms. Second, in a peacekeeping operation with limited human resources, the exclusion of those two components would have seriously reduced the UN's capacity to collect information on the ground. At the end, their participation in the project was continued.

The disturbing reality is, however, that in some instances UN peacekeepers act against the protection of the human rights of local populations.[220] It is indeed an embarrassment that the Organisation could be charged with human rights violations as the result of the actions of its agents. The Organisation certainly needs more training of peacekeepers in human rights norms.

The structure of UNMIBH is an interesting example in terms of the co-operation between a police force and civil affairs. IPTF has the major role to play in enhancing the rule of law and law enforcement in Bosnia and Herzegovina, while civil affairs support them. The focus on training of local police is important in terms of institution-building. IPTF is introducing into Bosnia and Herzegovina community policing, which is even new to some of its own staff. This idea comes from the initiative in the field, not from New York.[221] The task is considered in the following context:

> The challenge is to convert the existing Local Police Forces into local police services. From police being servants of the State to being servants of the communities they live in.[222]

---

[220] For example, Italian soldiers from a UN peace-keeping mission in Somalia were alleged, by a representative of the Norwegian Save the Children agency, to have paid for sex with Mozambican girls as young as 12. *The Guardian*, 19 February 1994, p.12. It was also alleged that UNOSOM members had engaged in the torture of prisoners, detainment of suspected criminals without access to counsel, and targeting of civilians with firearms. Brian D. Tittemore, 'Belligerents in Blue Helmets: Applying International Humanitarian Law to United Nations Peace Operations', *Stanfrod Journal of International Law*, Winter 1997: 61-117, pp.89-90.

[221] Interview with Mr. Day, Sarajevo, 25 June 1999.

[222] E-mail interview with Mr. Day, 21 April 1999.

The UNMIBH is indeed conducting a new attempt by the Organisation as the Secretary-General confirms:

> UNMIBH has developed innovative forms of monitoring that involve both civil affairs officers and IPTF monitors. These include co-locating in police facilities and holding regular consultations with civilian authorities at all levels of government; working with police in criminal investigations aimed at uncovering organized crime and terrorism; devising a new approach to auditing police services in municipalities and cantons of the Federation; continuing investigation of police involvement in human rights abuses in areas of return; and new forms of court and trial monitoring. These innovative forms of monitoring will enable UNMIBH to oblige local law enforcement agencies, in the early stages of establishing the rule of law, to operate in a manner fully consistent with democratic practice.[223]

There are specific reasons as to why UNMIBH has managed to develop such a comprehensive endeavour. First, the length of the mission exceeds six years.[224] Second, UNMIBH operates in a relatively calm security situation. The Secretary-General stated in his report dated 11 June 1999 that "the country is no longer in an emergency situation and is decisively on the road to recovery".[225] Third, there are international staff who had served in UNPROFOR, UNCRO or UNTAES, and their experience and knowledge are valuable assets to the mission. Fourth, there are many other international organisations including UN agencies that co-operate with UNMIBH. In other words, there are significant investments of financial and human resources in Bosnia and Herzegovina by the international community.

The strength of the UNMIBH, and particularly IPTF, is the combination of training, assessment/monitoring, and means of inducing enforcement. For instance, IPTF has the power to carry out the certification of local police officers. If their assessment/monitoring confirms serious non-compliance, IPTF is able to decertify the officers concerned. Using such authority while developing a constructive relationship with local institution proves to be the most effective driving force for establishing the rule of law. However, the

---

[223] *Report of the Secretary-General on the United Nations Mission in Bosnia and Herzegovina*, UN Doc. S/1999/670, 11 June 1999, para.60.

[224] The current mandate is until 21 June 2002. Security Council resolution 1357, 21 June 2001, SCOR., 4333rd mtg., UN Doc. S/RES/1357(2001).

[225] *Secretary-General's Report*, UN Doc. S/1999/670, *supra* note 223, para.56.

line between co-operation and intervention is not always clear, as Fionnuala Ni Aolain warns:

> A particular problem in the early stages of IPTF deployment was a notable lack of sensitivity to and knowledge of IPTF domestic legal culture and rules ... External legal actors must avoid imbuing their contact community with a sense of their own cultural and legal superiority.[226]

In addition, the expansion of the area of operation of IPTF such as providing specialised training and advice in the area of drug control and organised crime, however, arguably goes beyond a peacekeeping role. It may become a test case to measure to what extent the Organisation needs to maintain its peacekeeping and peace-building presence in order to ensure sustainable peace in a post-conflict area.

---

[226] Aolain, *supra* note 3, p.991.

Chapter 7

Protection of Human Rights and United Nations Peace-keeping

1. THE FORCIBLE PROTECTION OF HUMAN RIGHTS

A review of recent UN peacekeeping operations demonstrates that ending or preventing deliberate and systematic human rights violations have hardly been the core or fundamental objective of peacekeeping operations.[1] In preceding chapters, we saw how UN peacekeeping forces failed in their attempts to protect civilians from massacres in Rwanda and in Srebrenica, Bosnia-Herzegovina. Firstly, the respective UN forces were not given the mandate to act for the protection of the civilians. Secondly, they did not have the means or the resources to do so. Thirdly, it is questionable whether a peacekeeping force, not an enforcement force, is suitable and necessary to achieve the above-mentioned objective.[2] Nonetheless, even with the limited means and resources available to them, the peacekeepers could have undertaken particular activities for the protection of civilians. In this chapter this

---

[1] See, e.g., David B. Steele, "Securing Peace for 'Humanitarian Aid?'", *International Peacekeeping* 5(1), Spring 1998:66-88, p.70. "The process of intervention starts with a call to end massive human rights violations and is then frequently limited to mandate to enforce humanitarian objectives". Also, Tonny Brems Knudsen, 'Humanitarian Intervention Revisited: Post-Cold War Responses to Classical Problems', *International Peacekeeping* 3(4), Winter 1996:146-165, p.147. "What we have seen in cases like Bosnia and Somalia has not been a whole-hearted attempt to stop or prevent genocide by full-scale use of force as prescribed by the Grotian doctrine of humanitarian intervention. Instead, outside interference has on most occasions attempted to limit it and provide relief after the damage has been done."

[2] See the discussion in Chapter 2. Traditional peacekeeping has three basic principles: the non-use of force except in self-defence, impartiality, and the consent of the parties to the conflict. This author supports two prominent legal scholars' view that peacekeeping and enforcement should be clearly distinguished. See Professors Rosalyn Higgins and Peter Malanczuk, *supra* FN110 & 111, and accompanying text of Chapter 2. The need to respect these three principles in peacekeeping operations was stressed by the Special Committee on Peacekeeping Operations, which was endorsed by the Fourth Committee of the General Assembly. UN Doc. GA/SPD/179, 22 May 2000.

particular aspect of the peacekeeping operations and the crucial role which peacekeepers can play for the protection of the civilians will be discussed.

1.1   Legitimacy of Non-UN Multinational Forces Authorised by the Security Council

If UN peacekeeping forces are unable to stop large-scale human rights abuses, who has the capacity to do so? The recent practice of the Organisation has been to authorise a multinational force not under the UN command to carry out certain military action when such action is beyond the capacity of a UN peacekeeping force. Examples are the Unified Task Force in Somalia,[3] the French-led Operation Turquoise in Rwanda,[4] and the US-led multinational force in Haiti.[5] None of these three operations had a mandate to confront human rights violations directly, but were all deployed in situations where human rights were seriously undermined.

In an extraordinary case of human rights abuses, nothing prevents the Security Council from taking measures under Chapter VII of the UN Charter.[6] When Chapter VII is invoked, the restriction under Article 2(7), non-intervention in matters which are essentially within the domestic jurisdiction, is no longer applicable to the operations of the Organisation.[7] The military action taken under Chapter VII by the Organisation is a collective measure pursuant to the UN Charter, and is clearly different from

---

[3]   The US-led Unified Task Force carried out Operation Restore Hope to secure the airfield and port in Mogadishu and several other places, together with relief centres. For the authorisation by the Security Council, see Security Council resolution 794 of 3 December 1992, SCOR, 3145th mtg., UN Doc. S/RES/794(1992). Adopted unanimously.

[4]   See supra FN33 & 34 and accompanying text of Chapter 5.

[5]   The authorization was granted by Security Council resolution 940 of 31 July 1994, after a UN peacekeeping force, the United Nations Mission in Haiti, was prevented from landing in Haiti. SCOR, 3413th mtg., UN Doc. S/RES/940(1994). Adopted by 12 in favour and 2 abstentions (Brazil and China). The relevant paragraph reads:

> Acting under Chapter VII of the Charter of the United Nations, *authorizes* Member States to form a multinational force under unified command and control and, in this framework, to use all necessary means to facilitate the departure from Haiti of the military leadership, consistent with the Governors Island Agreement, the prompt return of the legitimately elected President and the restoration of the legitimate authorities of the Government of Haiti, and to establish and maintain a secure and stable environment that will permit implementation of the Governors Island Agreement, ...

[6]   For instance, the safe-areas in Bosnia-Herzegovina were established by resolutions invoking Chapter VII. See supra FN55 & 56 and accompanying text of Chapter 6.

[7]   See discussion in 4 'Peace-keeping, Peacemaking and Peace-building' of Chapter 2.

"intervention".[8] The question is whether the Security Council can legitimately contract out military operations to certain States volunteering to carry them out.

Dr. Sarooshi raises two reasons why the Security Council cannot lawfully delegate to Member States an unrestricted power of command and control over a force carrying out authorised military enforcement action.[9] Firstly, the Council itself does not possess such a power, as States that contribute troops have the right to be consulted and to participate in the decisions as to how their troops are to be used.[10] This right derives from Article 44 of the Charter, which reads:

> When the Security Council has decided to use force it shall, before calling upon a Member not represented on it to provide armed forces in fulfilment of the obligations assumed under Article 43, invite that Member, if the member so desires, to participate in the decisions of the Security Council concerning the employment of contingents of that Member's armed forces.

The provision of Article 44 should be read in conjunction with Article 43, which refers to special agreements between Member States and the Organisation on the provision of contingents. Although Articles 43 and 44 *per se* do not apply in the case of the voluntary contribution of troops, the object and purpose of the provisions remain applicable. The second reason, according to Dr. Sarooshi, is that the Council must at all times retain overall authority and control over the exercise of its delegated Chapter VII powers.[11]

While Dr. Sarooshi emphasizes the conditionality of non-UN multinational forces, Professor John Quigley criticises the entire method of contracting out military operations by emphasizing the special role assigned to the Security Council:

> The U.N. Charter deprived states of the power to determine unilaterally when to use force by transferring that power to the

---

[8] "...it is only the Security Council which can decide on coercive measures against the will of a government. Hence, such sanctions are not 'interventions' in the traditional sense, but collective measures under a legal regime, which the State in question has accepted by ratifying the Charter". Reinhard Marx, 'A Non-Governmental Human Rights Strategy for Peacekeeping?', *Netherlands Quarterly of Human Rights* 14(2), 1996: 127-145, p.133.

[9] Danesh Sarooshi, *The United Nations and the Development of Collective Security: The Delegation by the UN Security Council of its Chapter VII Powers*, Clarendon Press: Oxford, 1999, p.34.

[10] *Ibid.*, p.35.

[11] *Ibid.*

> Security Council. The authorization technique arguably turns
> the Charter system on its head, in effect reverting to the League
> of Nations approach.[12]

Quigley further points out problems of the authorisation technique. Firstly, there is no assurance that any action will follow after the Security Council's decision to authorise a military action.[13] Secondly, the Security Council does not control the military action once it is underway.[14] Thirdly, States that undertake the military action may do so for their own self-interests.[15]

By contrast, Sean D. Murphy, Deputy Assistant Legal Adviser, US Department of State, argues that the method of authorising states to use force is appropriate as the major powers carry the major burden.[16] Some commentators argue that the problem lies in the decision-making process of the Security Council, not the authorisation *per se*, and suggests reforms in this regard.[17]

To preserve the collective security system envisaged in the UN Charter, it is essential that the Security Council maintains command and control of enforcement action. Authorisation of the use of force without overall command and control by the Security Council certainly relaxes the international norms of the non-use of force. As discussed below, some States, including some of the permanent members of the Security Council, now believe that, in certain circumstances, the use of force is permissible, relying on the doctrine of humanitarian intervention.

1.2 Humanitarian Intervention

According to the traditional theory of humanitarian intervention, a State is permitted to intervene forcibly in another State when the State subject to

---

[12] John Quigley, 'The "Privatization" of Security Council Enforcement Action: A Threat to Multilateralism', *Michigan Journal of International Law*, Winter 1996: 249-283, p.261.

[13] *Ibid.*, p.263.

[14] *Ibid.*, p.264.

[15] *Ibid.*, pp.270-271. For instance, see Prunier, *The Rwanda Crisis 1959-1994*, *supra* FN2 of Chapter 5, pp. 103-106, 110-111, and 148-149, regarding France's special interest in Rwanda; and Burns H. Weston, 'Security Council Resolution 678 and Persian Gulf Decision Making: Precarious Legitimacy', *AJIL* 85, 1991: 516-535, pp.523-524, as to "the great-power pressure diplomacy" used by the US regarding the Gulf Crisis.

[16] Sean D. Murphy, 'The Security Council, Legitimacy, and the Concept of Collective Security After the Cold War', *Columbia Journal of Transnational Law*, 1994, p.223 & 261.

[17] *Ibid.*, pp.257-269; and David D. Caron, 'The Legitimacy of the Collective Authority of the Security Council', *AJIL* 87, 1993: 552-588.

intervention "commits cruelties against and persecution of its nationals in such a way as to deny their fundamental human rights and to shock the conscience of mankind".[18] The State subject to intervention is considered to have abused its sovereignty so that it is regarded as "having made itself liable to action by any State which was prepared to intervene".[19]

The UN Charter, however, prohibits the unilateral use of force "against the territorial integrity or political independence of any state, or in any other manner inconsistent with the Purposes of the United Nations" under Article 2(4) with recognised exceptions for individual or collective self-defence under Article 51 and enforcement actions under Chapter VII authorised by the Security Council.[20] Therefore, any right of humanitarian intervention represents an additional, albeit controversial, exception to Article 2(4). The principle of non-intervention in essentially domestic issues as provided for in Article 2(7), enshrines respect for state sovereignty. On the other hand, the Charter holds respect for human rights as one of the principal objectives of the Organisation. Article 1(3) reads:

> To achieve international cooperation in solving international problems of an economic, social, cultural, or humanitarian character, and in promoting and encouraging respect for human rights and for fundamental freedoms for all without distinction as to race, sex, language, or religion; ...

Also, Article 55 must be taken into account in conjunction with Article 56. In accordance with Article 55, the United Nations has to promote "[U]niversal respect for, and observance of, human rights and fundamental freedoms for all without distinction as to race, sex, language, or religion" as one of its purposes. Under Article 56 all Member States have obligation "to take joint and separate action in cooperation with the Organization" to achieve the Organisation's purposes, including the above.

On the issue as to whether there exists a customary law rule permitting humanitarian intervention as an exception to the general prohibition laid down in Article 2(4), there have been two main schools of thought. One school argues that state practice does not support the existence of such a

---

[18] Sir Robert Jennings and Sir Arthur Watts, eds., *Oppenheim's International Law*, 9th ed., Vol.I Peace, p.442.

[19] Ian Brownlie, *International Law and the Use of Force by States*, Oxford University Press, 1963, p.338.

[20] See *supra* FN3 and accompanying text of Chapter 1.

customary law rule.[21] The other school, on the contrary, affirms the existence of the customary law of humanitarian intervention.[22] Furthermore, another school of thought, which recognises the emerging customary law of humanitarian intervention, may have to be added.[23]

Legal scholars who take a restrictive approach towards humanitarian intervention quote several General Assembly resolutions to support their position. Firstly, the *1965 Declaration on the Inadmissibility of Intervention in the Domestic Affairs of States and the Protection of their Independence and Sovereignty* sets forth in its operative paragraph 1:

> No State has the right to intervene, directly or indirectly, for any reason whatever, in the internal or external affairs of any other State. Consequently, armed intervention and all other forms of interference or attempted threats against the personality of the Sate or against its political, economic and cultural elements, are condemned.[24]

The *1970 General Assembly Declaration on Principles of International Law concerning Friendly Relations and Cooperation among States in accordance with the Charter of the United Nations* includes the following principles: "the principle that States shall settle their international disputes by peaceful

---

[21] See Ian Brownlie, 'Humanitarian Intervention', in John Norton Moore, ed., *Law and Civil War in the Modern World*, Baltimore: Johns Hopkins Press, 1974, especially pp.220-221; and Richard B. Lillich, 'Humanitarian Intervention: A Reply to Ian Brownlie and a Plea for Constructive Alternatives', in Moore, ed., *op. cit.* Brownlie's main point of criticism against Lillich was that the latter failed to provide examples of state practice which supported his argument. To discuss whether humanitarian intervention is legally justifiable, comprehensive research into state practice, which is beyond the scope of this book, is essential. For research on state practice, see, David J. Scheffer, 'Towards a Modern Doctrine of Humanitarian Intervention', *University of Toledo Law Review*, Winter 1992: 253-293, p.254 FN4; and Thomas M. Franck and Nigel S. Rodley, 'After Bangladesh: The Law of Humanitarian Intervention by Military Force', *AJIL* 67:275-300, pp.279-95. As discussion questioning the doctrine of humanitarian intervention, see Natalino Ronzitti, *Rescuing Nationals Abroad and Intervention on Grounds of Humanity*, Martinus Nijhoff, 1985; and Nigel Rodley, 'Collective intervention to protect human rights and civilian populations: the legal framework', in N. Rodley, ed., *To Loose the Bands of Wickedness: International Intervention in Defence of Human Rights*, Brassey's (UK), 1992.

[22] See, W. Michael Reisman, 'Sovereignty and Human Rights in Contemporary International Law', *AJIL* 84, 1990, 866-876; R. Teson, *Humanitarian Intervention: An Inquiry into Law and Morality*, Transnational Publishers, Dobbs Ferry, 1988; and Lillich, *supra* note 21.

[23] Antonio Cassese, *'Ex iniuria ius oritur*: Are We Moving towards International Legitimation of Forcible Humanitarian Countermeasures in the World Community?', 10 *EJIL* 1999: 23-30.

[24] GA resolution 2131(XX) of 21 December 1965.

means in such a manner that international peace and security and justice are not endangered"; "the principle concerning the duty not to intervene in matters within the domestic jurisdiction of any State"; "the duty of States to co-operate with one another in accordance with the Charter"; "the principle of equal rights and self-determination of peoples"; and "the principle of sovereign equality of States".[25] After stating the above principles, the Declaration reads:

> Nothing in this Declaration shall be construed as prejudicing in any manner the provisions of the Charter or the rights and duties of Member States under the Charter or the rights of peoples under the Charter, ...

It further stresses:

> [T]he principles of the Charter which are embodied in this Declaration constitute basic principles of international law ...

The *Declaration on the Inadmissibility of Intervention and Interference in the Internal Affairs of States* almost reiterates the previous two declarations.[26] It particularly states regarding human rights:

> (1) The duty of a State to refrain from the exploitation and the distortion of human rights issues as a means of interference in the internal affairs of States, of exerting pressure on other States or creating distrust and disorder within and among States or groups of States.[27]

Two Declarations of the General Assembly have been issued in the 1990s basically repeating the same views as those of the above three Declarations. One is resolution 46/130 of 17 December 1991, on respect for the principles of national sovereignty and non-interference with the internal affairs of States in their electoral processes.[28] It recalls Resolution 2625(XXV) and Article 2(7) of the Charter in its preamble. Nothing particularly new is found in this Declaration in terms of emphasis on the principle of non-interference. For instance, in its operative paragraph 5, the Assembly "[U]rges all States to respect the principle of non-interference in the internal affairs of States and the sovereign right of peoples to determine their political, economic and social system". Another declaration, General Assembly resolution 47/130 of

---

[25]   GA resolution 2625(XXV) of 24 October 1970.

[26]   GA resolution 36/103 of 9 December 1981.

[27]   *Ibid.*

[28]   The resolution was passed by a vote of 86 in favour, 40 against and 11 abstentions.

18 December 1992, on respect for the principles of national sovereignty and non-interference in the internal affairs of States in their electoral processes, is almost identical with the previous one.[29]

The rejection of humanitarian intervention as permissible under international law is supported by the developing countries, and the repeated General Assembly declarations of similar content are proof of the consistent attitude of those countries. In practice, countries in the South are likely to be targets of such intervention, whereas the major powers are unlikely to be the subjects of such action.[30] Although not related to the protection of human rights, the relationship between intervention and its abuse by powerful States was referred to by the International Court of Justice in the *Corfu Channel* case. Responding to the UK Government, who contended that their act could be justified by "a new and special application of the theory of intervention, by means of which the State intervening would secure possession of evidence in the territory of another State, in order to submit it to an international tribunal and thus facilitate its task",[31] the Court stated:

> The Court can only regard the alleged right of intervention as the manifestation of a policy of force, such as has, in the past, given rise to most serious abuses and such as cannot, what ever be the present defect in international organization, find a place in international law. Intervention is perhaps still less admissible in the particular form it would take here; for, from the nature of things, it would be reserved for the most powerful States, and might easily lead to perverting the administration of international justice itself.[32]

Particularly, military intervention based on human rights grounds continues to be objected to as an imposition of the Western value system or as premised upon a paternalistic attitude.[33] In its judgment in the *Nicaragua* case, the International Court rejected various US justifications for its use of force against Nicaragua. In particular, the Court held:

---

[29] The result of the vote was 99-45-16.

[30] Franck and Rodley, *supra* note 21, p.304.

[31] *ICJ Report 1949*, p.34.

[32] *Ibid.*, p.35.

[33] For instance, see Neta C. Crawford, 'Decolonization as an International Norm: The Evolution of Practices, Arguments and Beliefs', in Laura W. Reed and Carl Kaysen, eds., *Emerging Norms of Justified Intervention*, American Academy of Arts and Sciences, 1993, p.57.

... the use of force could not be the appropriate method to monitor or ensure such [human rights'] respect. With regard to steps actually taken, the protection of human rights, a strictly humanitarian objective, cannot be compatible with the mining of ports, the destruction of oil installations, or again with the training, arming and equipping of the *contras*.[34]

In contrast, the morality of humanitarian intervention is frequently explained in terms of globalisation, the development of human rights norms and the emergence of individuals as subjects of international law.[35] The following words of Javier Perez de Cuellar, a former Secretary-General of the United Nations, are quite often cited as proof of this new sense of morality and represent the view of interventionists:

We are clearly witnessing what is an irresistible shift in public attitude towards the belief that defence of the oppressed in the name of morality should prevail over frontiers and legal documents.[36]

In a different context, namely the conditions imposed on Iraq following the cease-fire between Iraq and Kuwait, Peter J. Formuth, Special Assistant for Policy Planning at the US Mission to the UN, also explains the decline of state sovereignty:

---

[34] *Case concerning Military and Paramilitary Activities in and against Nicaragua* (Nicaragua v. United States of America), Judgment of 27 June 1986, ICJ Report 1986, para.268.

[35] In general, see James N. Rosenau, 'Normative Challenges in a Turbulent World'; and Jarat Chopra and Thomas G. Weiss, 'Sovereignty Is No Longer Sacrosanct: Codifying Humanitarian Intervention'; both in *Ethics & International Affairs* 6, 1992.

[36] UN Press Release SG/SM/4560, 24 April 1991. Scheffer affirms this view: "To argue today that norms of sovereignty, non-use of force, and the sanctity of internal affairs are paramount to the collective human rights of people, whose lives and well-being are at risk, is to avoid the hard questions of international law and to ignore the march of history." Scheffer, *supra* note 21, p.259. Also see Philip Alston, 'The Security Council and Human Rights: Lessons to be Learned from the Iraq-Kuwait Crisis and its Aftermath', 13 *Australian Year Book of International Law*, 1992: 107-176, p.172: "..., recognition of the linkage between human rights violations on the one hand and threats to peace and security on the other is no longer merely a reflection of the optimism of human rights advocates, but has become an accepted part of the mainstream wisdom."

Several far-reaching steps taken by the Security Council have recently been adding momentum and credibility to the communitarian element in global security.[37]

He has further stated:

... a country that violates international law may have its sovereignty permanently - and uniquely - restricted in order to better secure interests of the wider international community.[38]

A similar view was presented by Professor Christopher Greenwood:

By the 1970s a considerable body of support existed for the view that grave violations of human rights were not a matter 'essentially within the domestic jurisdiction' of the state concerned, involving as they did breaches of that state's obligations under international law.[39]

There is also a view that by becoming a member of the United Nations, each state has in effect waived certain sovereign rights in the sense that Member States must abide by the provisions of the Charter.[40] This point conforms with the view of the International Court of Justice in the *Nicaragua* case. In its judgment of 27 June 1986, the World Court affirmed the possibility of a State binding itself by agreement in relation to a question of domestic policy, such as that relating to the holdings of free elections on its territory:

[T]he Court cannot discover, within the range of the subjects open to international agreement, any obstacle or provision to hinder a State from making a commitment of this kind. A State, which is free to decide upon the principle and methods of popular consultation within its domestic order, is sovereign for the purpose of accepting limitation of its sovereignty in this field.[41]

---

[37] Peter J. Formuth, 'The Making of a Security Community: The United Nations After the Cold War', *Journal of International Affairs* 46(2), Winter 1993, p.346.

[38] *Ibid.*, p.347.

[39] Christopher Greenwood, 'Is there a right of humanitarian intervention?', *The World Today* 49(2), February 1993: 34-40, p.35.

[40] Ernest B. Haas, 'Beware the Slippery Slope: Notes toward the Definition of Justifiable Intervention', in Laura W. Reed and Carl Kaysen, eds., *Emerging Norms of Justified Intervention*, American Academy of Arts and Sciences, 1993, p.65. Note that this is not the author's own view.

[41] *ICJ Report 1986*, para.259.

By this analogy, the domain of sovereignty diminishes along with the development of international human rights norms as well as other treaties. However, this argument does not justify military intervention circumventing the forum of the Security Council.

1.2.1 Safe Havens in Iraq

In the aftermath of the Gulf crisis, American, British and French forces established 'safe havens' in northern Iraq for Kurdish refugees. This operation was carried out by Member States acting on their own initiative and not by UN forces or pursuant to an explicit UN decision. The action was claimed by participating States to be consistent with the objectives of Security Council resolution 688 of 5 April 1991.[42] Some commentators affirmed that Security Council resolution 688 was the turning point by which the human rights abuses in a State became subject to the direct scrutiny of the Security Council.[43] However, this resolution shows an interesting effort to strike a balance between the sovereignty of Iraq and the Security Council's concerns on human rights. The preamble first 'recalls' Article 2(7) of the Charter and continues:

> *Gravely concerned* by the repression of the Iraqi civilian population in many parts of Iraq, including most recently in Kurdish-populated areas, which led to a massive flow of refugees towards and across international frontiers and to cross-border incursions, which threaten international peace and security in the region ...

Despite the fact that the central issue of concern here is a domestic situation, this paragraph highlights the international element of the case, namely, a massive flow of refugees beyond the national border. The Security Council is cautious enough to have further inserted the paragraph below:

---

[42]   S/RES/688(1991), SCOR 46 RES. Adopted by 10 in favour, 3 against (Cuba, Yemen and Zimbabwe), and 2 abstentions (China and India). 'United Kingdom Materials on International Law', *BYIL* 1992, p.827.

[43]   See, e.g., Kelly Kate Pease and David P. Forsythe, 'Human Rights, Humanitarian Intervention, and World Politics', *Human Rights Quarterly* 15, 1993: 290-314, p.303; and Yassini El-Ayouty, 'International Action on the Doctrine of Humanitarian Intervention: The Case of Southern Iraq (1991-1992)', *New York State Bar Journal*, July/August 1996: 12-21, p.19.

> *Reaffirming* the commitment of all Member States to respect the sovereignty, territorial integrity and political independence of Iraq and of all States in the area ...

Reference to 'international peace and security' is repeated in the operative paragraphs as well:

> 1. *Condemns* the repression of the Iraqi civilian population in many parts of Iraq, including most recently in Kurdish-populated areas, the consequences of which threaten international peace and security in the region,
>
> 2. *Demands* that Iraq, as contribution to removing the threat to international peace and security in the region, immediately end this repression and, in the same context, expresses the hope that an open dialogue will take place to ensure that the human and political rights of all Iraqi citizens are respected.

Careful reading of Resolution 688, therefore, proves that it does not purport to drastically change the principle of non-intervention in regard to matters which are essentially within the domestic jurisdiction of any state. What the Security Council did through this resolution was to recognise that a major human rights violation by a state authority, namely "the repression of the Iraqi civilian population" which caused "a massive flow of refugees", was a threat to international peace and security.[44]

Mr. A. Aust, Legal Counsellor, Foreign and Commonwealth Office, UK, explained the action in Iraq as follows to the HC Foreign Affairs Committee on 2 December 1992:

> Resolution 688, which applies not only to northern Iraq but to the whole of Iraq, was not made under chapter VII. Resolution 688 recognised that there was a severe human rights and humanitarian situation in Iraq and, in particular, northern Iraq; but the intervention in northern Iraq 'Provide Comfort' was in fact, not specifically mandated by the United Nations, but the states taking action in northern Iraq did so in exercise of the

---

[44] But see Fernado R. Teson, 'Changing Perceptions of Domestic Jurisdiction and Intervention', in Tom Farer, ed., *Beyond Sovereignty: Collectively Defending Democracy in the Americas*, The Johns Hopkins University Press, p.41. Teson may call this kind of view "excessively formalistic". He states: "A reasonable interpretation of Resolution 688 is that the Security Council was centrally concerned with the human rights violations themselves and that the reference to the threat to peace and security was added for good measure."

customary international law principle of humanitarian intervention.[45]

This operation, therefore, is arguably an example of humanitarian intervention. The Allies' determination to protect human rights, however, was not manifest, because they did not react to Turkish raids on villages within the allied security zone in Iraq. The Turkish government contended that its attack was against Turkish Kurds, but Iraqi Kurds who returned from Turkey to the safe haven had to flee again. The Allies' explanation was that they were there to protect the Kurds from Iraq but not those from Turkey.[46] It is such inconsistency in action that causes mistrust in the genuineness of the purpose of asserted humanitarian intervention.

1.2.2 Kosovo

The Operation Allied Force, air strikes by the North Atlantic Treaty Organisation (NATO) against the Federal Republic of Yugoslavia (FRY) in 1999, was another example of multilateral intervention without authorisation from the UN Security Council. The justification used by NATO member states for Operation Allied Force was quite similar to that used concerning the establishment of safe havens for Iraq Kurds. The main argument relied upon by member states of NATO was the doctrine of humanitarian intervention.

The significant majority of the population in Kosovo, a region of the FRY, is ethnic Albanians. The Federal government had taken repressive measures against the Albanians' claims for more autonomy or ultimate independence of Kosovo. In resolution 1199 of 23 September 1998, the UN Security Council expressed grave concern regarding "the recent intense fighting in Kosovo and in particular the excessive and indiscriminate use of force by Serbian security forces and the Yugoslav Army which have resulted in numerous civilian casualties and ... the displacement of over 230,000 persons from their homes".[47] The Council was also concerned by the influx of refugees into the neighbouring countries and the increasing number of displaced persons. The Council, acting under Chapter VII, in principal, demanded the cessation of hostilities and called for a dialogue. In this

---

[45] 'UK Materials on International Law 1992', *BYIL* 1992, P.827.

[46] Lawrence Freedman and David Boren, "Safe havens' for Kurds in post-war Iraq' in Rodley, ed., *supra* note 21, 1992, pp.78-79. Also it should be noted that on several occasions the United Nations failed to act against human rights violations by the Iraqi government against the Kurds, including the use of chemical weapons in 1987 and 1988. See Alston, *supra* note 36, pp.117-124.

[47] SC res. 1199, 23 September 1998, SCOR, 3930th mtg., UN Doc. S/RES/1199(1998).

resolution, the Council did not fail to mention the sovereignty and territorial integrity of the FRY. The Council however decided that if the need arose it would consider further action and additional measures to maintain or restore peace and stability in the region.

The massacre of 45 Kosovars in the village of Racak, discovered on 15 January 1999, triggered the military action by the NATO that commenced on 24 March 1999. The refusal by the FRY government to accept the interim political settlement negotiated at Rambouillet and to observe the limits on security force levels agreed on 25 October 1998 led NATO to decide that there was no option other than the use of force.[48] The NATO Secretary-General, Javier Solana, in a press conference on 23 March, explained the objectives of the action as follows:[49]

> This military action is intended to support the political aims of the international community. It will be directed towards disrupting the violent attacks being committed by the Serb Army and Special Police Forces and weakening their ability to cause further humanitarian catastrophe.

The Secretary-General emphasised that the NATO was not waging war against Yugoslavia.

> Our objective is to prevent more human suffering and more repression and violence against the civilian population of Kosovo.[50]

In addition to this humanitarian objective, there was a security reason as well as NATO member states' disagreement with the policy of the government of the Federal Republic of Yugoslavia:

> We must also act to prevent instability spreading in the region.
> ... We must stop an authoritarian regime from repressing its

---

[48] It is questionable if every means of peaceful settlement had been exhausted, since the settlement after the NATO operation could have been achieved before the operation. It could be argued that the conditions insisted on by NATO in the Rambouillet negotiations were unfair to the FRY, or at least not well considered. Richard B. Bilder, 'Kosovo and the "New Interventionism": Promise or Peril?', *Journal of Transnational Law and Policy*, 1999: 153-182, p.180.

[49] NATO Press Release (1999)040 on 23 March 1999. Available at http://www.nato.int/docu/pr/1999/p99-040e.htm (visited on 4 November 2001).

[50] *Ibid.*

people in Europe at the end of the 20th century. We have a moral duty to do so.[51]

U.S. Secretary of State Madeleine K. Albright was of the opinion that the already existing UN Security Council resolutions were sufficient for NATO to take military action and that no additional resolution was required.[52] The views of the UK Government expressed in the Security Council meeting on 24 March also affirmed the humanitarian purpose of the NATO action:

> Every means short of force has been tried to avert this situation. In these circumstances, and as an exceptional measure on grounds of overwhelming humanitarian necessity, military intervention is legally justifiable. The force now proposed is directed exclusively to averting a humanitarian catastrophe, and is the minimum judged necessary for that purpose.[53]

Although there has been speculation as to other motivations behind this intervention, the official cause of intervention was the human rights violations and humanitarian catastrophe caused by the repressive policy of the FRY government.[54] The military action, which was taken without UN authorisation, arguably is another humanitarian intervention following the example of the operation that established the safe havens in Iraq. The serious problem in the doctrine of humanitarian intervention is, notwithstanding the arguments for and against the existence of such customary international law, that the intervening state authorises itself to use force against another state based on its own value judgment.

In the 1950s, while discussing the concept of self-defence, Professor Bowett warned of the danger of interpreting this concept broadly to the extent of undermining the authority of the Security Council. Bowett emphasised that to allow States which are not individually in a state of self-defence to take action or join in collective action would "completely nullify the whole system of collective security and signal a return to the very

---

[51] *Ibid.*

[52] Statement at a press conference on Kosovo, Brussels, Belgium, October 8, 1998, as released by the Office of the Spokesman, U.S. Department of State. Available at http://secretary.state.gov/www/statements/1998/981008.html (visited on 4 November 2001).

[53] Statement in the United Nations Security Council by Sir Jeremy Greenstock, Permanent Representative of the United Kingdom, 24 March 1999. Available at: http://www.fco.gov.uk/news/newstext.asp?2157 (visited on 4 November 2001).

[54] For other motivations of the intervention, see Adam Roberts, 'NATO's 'Humanitarian War' over Kosovo', *Survival* 41(3), Autumn 1999:102-23; and Bilder, *supra* note 48, p.156.

anarchy which the system of collective security is designed to prevent".[55] He continued:

> The right of States which are not acting in self-defence to inter-
> vene must await the authorisation of the competent organ of the
> centralised machinery, and this obligation cannot be avoided by
> a perversion of the concept of collective self-defence.[56]

Use of force by individual states based on the doctrine of the humanitarian intervention is subject to the analogous warning as referred to by Professor Bowett. To allow the humanitarian intervention would nullify the system of collective security envisaged in the UN Charter. Therefore the states which intend to prevent serious human rights abuses in another State must await the authorisation of the Security Council.

1.3   Legal and Political Evaluation of the Use of Force to Protect Human Rights

The Operation Allied Force has been subject to criticism despite NATO's claim of the high morality of its purpose. Prominent legal scholars assert that NATO violated international law by using force without the authorisation of the UN Security Council.[57] Also, NATO has arguably violated the principles of international humanitarian law, necessity and proportionality. The method used in the operation is questioned, since the air strikes caused massive flow of refugees and also caused so-called "collateral damage".[58] Further, there are some who doubt the real purpose and motivation behind this operation.[59]

---

[55]   Bowett, 'Collective Self-Defence under the Charter of the United Nations', *supra* FN3 of Chapter 1, pp.159-160.

[56]   *Ibid.*

[57]   Bruno Simma, 'NATO, the UN and the Use of Force: Legal Aspects', 10 *EJIL*, 1999: 1-22; Cassese, *supra* note 23; Bilder, *supra* note 48, and Jonathan I. Charney, 'Anticipatory Humanitarian Intervention in Kosovo', *Vanderbilt Journal of Transnational Law*, November 1999: 1231-1248.

[58]   Amnesty International publicly condemns the NATO for violations of the laws of war during Operation Allied Force. Amnesty International, *"Collateral Damage" or Unlawful Killings?: Violations of the laws of war by NATO during Operation Allied Force*, June 2000. Available at: http://www.amnesty.org/ailib/intcam/kosovo/ (visited on 13 December 2001). On 2 June 2000, the Chief Prosecutor of the UN war crimes tribunals stated in the Security Council that there was no basis for opening an investigation into allegations that war crimes had been committed by NATO personnel and leaders. News report available at: http://www.un.org/peace/kosovo/news/kosovo2.htm#Anchor56 (visited on 3 June 2000).

[59]   *Supra* note 54 and accompanying text.

It would have been less ambiguous if NATO had sent in ground troops to stop the repression of ethnic Albanians by the FRY government.[60] Furthermore, the Operation did not solve the root cause of the conflict in Kosovo. In fact, it is obvious that air strikes cannot achieve the resolution of ethnic conflicts.[61] The Operation only succeeded in coercing the FRY government to agree to the deployment of multinational troops in Kosovo. Nevertheless, harassment and violence between Albanians and Serbs continue.

To stop human rights abuses by the use of force is not a simple technique. One may succeed temporarily by risking one's own life or by using massive force, but this does not lead to a stable solution. States which send their troops are usually very sensitive about the number of deaths among their own troops. In Srebrenica, the Netherlands wanted to withdraw their troops for their own safety rather than to protect local civilians. In Kosovo, NATO used high-altitude air strikes in order to protect their own safety, even though this caused "collateral damage". If States are not ready to physically confront the perpetrators of human rights violations, we need to find ways of stopping human rights violations other than the inappropriate use of force. Particularly if expensive military operations stop abuses only temporarily, a more cost-effective way would be to address the root causes without resorting to force.

2. UNITED NATIONS PEACEKEEPING FORCE AS PROTECTING POWERS

Through operations under Chapter VII, the Organisation experienced increasing casualties among its peacekeepers. In December 1994, the UN put forward for signature a new Convention on the Safety of United Nations and Associated Personnel, pursuant to which attacks against peacekeepers

---

[60]   One commentator warns regarding humanitarian intervention in general:

Campaigning and lobbying for the use of military force to protect human rights unavoidably entails that those who call for military action will be considered responsible for the way in which the operation is carried out.

R. Marx, *supra* note 8, p.138

[61]   Professor Bilder rightly asks:

...wasn't it completely predictable that the bombing, against which the Serb soldiers and civilians were virtually helpless, would not only fail to protect the Kosovars, but would also further enrage and increase atrocities by the Serbs against the Kosovars, whom they would certainly blame for encouraging and being the intended beneficiaries of the bombing?

Bilder, *supra* note 48, p.170.

constitute crimes.[62] Whereas the safety of peacekeepers is sought, there is also a discussion as to whether peacekeeping forces are subject to international humanitarian law. Since the Geneva Conventions and the additional Protocols have no provisions regarding accession by the United Nations or any other international organisations, the Organisation is not formally bound by these treaties.[63] However, the Organisation is bound by humanitarian law requirements under customary international law. One commentator argues:

> To the extent that humanitarian law applies intrinsically to adversaries and effectively confers a belligerent status on their armed forces, its application to U.N. peacekeeping forces is inconsistent with the neutrality and impartiality attributed to peacekeeping functions.[64]

On 12 August 1999, the *Secretary-General's Bulletin: Observance by United Nations forces of international humanitarian law* entered into force. This Bulletin sets forth that the UN undertakes to ensure, in the status-of-force agreement, that the force shall conduct its operations with full respect for the principles and the rules of the general conventions applicable to the conduct of military personnel.[65] The Bulletin applies both to enforcement actions and peacekeeping operations.

Regarding the role of peacekeepers to protect human rights of civilians, some commentators suggested comparing it with that of a "Protecting Power" envisioned in the Geneva Conventions.[66] The Protecting Power has duty "to safeguard the interests of the Parties to the conflict".[67] According to this analogy, the peacekeepers would have the obligation of preventing human rights violations through the means at their disposal. This role seems to have already been carried out in practice to a certain extent when we consult the explanation of this mechanism by Yves Sandoz:

---

[62]   GA res. 49/59, 9 December 1994. UN GAOR, 49th Sess., Agenda Item 141, UN Doc. A/RES/49/59(1994). This Convention does not apply to an enforcement action under Chapter VII. It is explicitly set forth that in such an operation, the law of international armed conflict applies (Article 2).

[63]   Tittemore, 'Belligerents in Blue Helmets', *supra* FN220 of Chapter 6, pp.96-97.

[64]   *Ibid.*, p.106.

[65]   UN Doc. ST/SGB/1999/13, 6 August 1999.

[66]   Robert O. Wein Er and Fionnuala Ni Aolain, 'Beyond the Laws of War: Peacekeeping in Search of a Legal Framework', *Columbia Human Rights Law Review*, Winter 1996: 293-354, p.304.

[67]   Articles 8, 8, 8, and 9 of the Geneva Conventions I-IV. Also Article 5 of the Protocol I.

C'est le rôle de contrôle confié à ces Puissances qui est essentiel. La protection est donc indirecte. ... Certes, la Puissance protectrice est incapable de retenir la main du tortionnaire, elle ne dispose pas de la force. Mais elle peut faire écarter ce tortionnaire en le dénonçant aux autorités ou, si celles-ci sont complices et ne veulent pas changer de politique, dire son impuissance à la Partie au conflict dont elle cherche à défendre les intérêts humanitaires, voire alerter la communauté internationale.[68]

Taking into account that peacekeepers do perform such a role in practice, and given the fact that this mechanism has never been utilised in a significant way,[69] to explicitly recognise peacekeepers' duties in this respect may not remarkably enhance the observance of international humanitarian law. If the duties required go beyond those set forth for the Protecting Power and include the physical protection of civilians, such a task would not be politically feasible for a peacekeeping force, because States will then be reluctant to send their troops to carry out peacekeeping operations. We also have to bear in mind that peacekeeping operations ought to be distinguished from enforcement action, since in the former the use of force is limited to self-defence, they are impartial and they are deployed with the consent of the conflicting parties. However, it would be meaningful to codify the principle that peacekeepers should do their best to protect human rights without risking their own lives. Peacekeepers are sometimes prevented from acting for prevention of human rights violations in fear of exceeding their mandate. The principle cannot be codified in detail since the decision as to how to carry out such a responsibility should be made in the field, on a case-by-case basis, measuring the security risks the peacekeepers would face. For instance, it is difficult to argue that the Dutch battalion in Srebrenica should have fought against the Bosnian Serb troops. They were not combat troops and they did not have either the means or the mandate to do so. However, they could have insisted strongly that no civilians under their protection could be handed over to the Bosnian Serbs.

---

[68] Yves Sandoz, 'La notion de protection dans le droit international humanitaire et au sein du Mouvement de la Croix Rouge', in Christophe Swinarski, ed., *Etudes et essais sur le droit international humanitaire et sur les principes de la Croix-Rouge*, Geneva & The Hague: Martinus Nijhoff Publishers, 1984: 976-987, p.982.

[69] A.H. Robertson, 'Humanitarian law and human rights' in Swinarski, ed., *supra* note 68: 793-802, p.799. Also Yves Sandoz, 'Implementing International Humanitarian Law', in Henry Dunant Institute, *International Dimension of Humanitarian Law*, UNESCO, 1988: 259-282, p.271.

3.   PROTECTION OF HUMAN RIGHTS THROUGH NON-MILITARY MEASURES

As discussed in previous chapters, recent peacekeeping operations played a significant role in protecting and promoting human rights through non-military measures. Such human rights functions are imperative in order to maintain or restore peace in post-conflict areas. The limit of what "humanitarian intervention" could achieve was manifest in the case of NATO's operation in Kosovo. The real human rights functions were not carried out by the air strikes but they are under way by current multi-polar operation in Kosovo.

The United Nations Interim Administration Mission in Kosovo (UNMIK) was established in accordance with Security Council resolution 1244 of 10 June 1999, which authorised an interim international civilian administration "under which the people of Kosovo can enjoy substantial autonomy within the Federal Republic of Yugoslavia".[70] The Mission consists of "four pillars" which various organisations and one agency are in charge of: civil administration by the UN, humanitarian assistance by the UNHCR, democratisation and institution-building by the OSCE, and economic reconstruction by the European Union.[71] The four sectors are all presided over by the Special Representative of the Secretary General. The power of the UNMIK is much broader than that of UNTAC or UNTAES:

> All legislative and executive powers, including the administration of the judiciary, will ... be vested in UNMIK.[72]

In UNMIK, the OSCE is in charge of human rights monitoring. However, the Secretary-General underlines the application of human rights concept through its operation:

> In assuming its responsibilities, UNMIK will be guided by internationally recognised standards of human rights as the basis for the exercise of its authority in Kosovo. UNMIK will embed a culture of human rights in all areas of activity, and will

---

[70]   SC res. 1244, 10 June 1999. SCOR, 4011th mtg., UN Doc. S/RES/1244(1999).

[71]   For details, see *Report of the Secretary-General pursuant to Paragraph 10 of the Security Council resolution 1244 (1999)*, UN Doc. S/1999/672, 12 June 1999; and *Report of the Secretary-General on the United Nations Interim Administration Mission in Kosovo*, UN Doc. S/1999/779, 12 July 1999. Also *Rambouillet Accords: Interim Agreement for Peace and Self-Government in Kosovo*, UN Doc. S/1999/648, 7 June 1999.

[72]   *Report of the Secretary-General on the United Nations Interim Administration Mission in Kosovo*, UN Doc. S/1999/779, 12 July 1999, para.35.

adopt human rights policies in respect of its administrative functions.[73]

UNMIK is a politically and legally highly sensitive operation, since the future status of Kosovo is not determined. Although UNTAES operated in a similar situation, the local institution was functioning in the Region far better than that in Kosovo, and thus UNTAES played an advisory and supervisory role in local administration rather than undertaking it by itself. In contrast, UNMIK is an ambitious operation to run the civil administration in every respect, including the institution-building. It is surely a challenge for the Organisation to design a system which would provide protection for a high standard of human rights.

A big advantage of a field presence in terms of human rights protection is that human rights officers are able to detect warning signs. Such information can be used for preventive measures. For example, under the transitional administration of UNTAES, there were a large number of reports regarding hate calls. Most of the calls carried the same message: the Serbs should leave Croatia. Such calls were from a Croat house owner to an internally displaced Serb family who temporarily occupy his/her house, or calls to the Serbs remaining in the same village from ex-neighbours who had been displaced.[74] The message had patterns such as "what are you waiting for?" in the most moderate case, and "when I come back I will slaughter you and I will rape your wife and daughter" in the worst case. The reaction of UNTAES was very reserved. The major view of international officers was that hate calls exist in "my" country as well. However, such a sign should have been considered in the context of the society in question. The message was sent from one person to another, both of them had possibly actually witnessed instances of slaughter and rape. The receivers of such messages were in fear and anxiety even without such calls about their future after reintegration. Close to the end of UNTAES's mandate, border monitors' statistics showed that a high percentage of people leaving the UNTAES administered area had given such hate calls as being their reason for leaving. The first lesson to be learned from this experience is that we are not able to apply the yardstick applicable to our own society, but that we need to examine the background and circumstances of the signs we detect on the ground. The second lesson is

---

[73] *Ibid.*, para.42.

[74] The relationship between house owners and the occupants was not always bad. Some house owners appreciated that the occupants were keeping the house in good condition and even asked them to stay until the time they themselves were able to return. On the other hand, there were cases in which the occupants left, having looted all the furniture and destroyed the house.

that human rights field activities cannot always stay within the text of law. To seek accountability, it is the existing law which should be consulted according to the principle of *nullum crimen sine lege*. When we fail to prevent widespread and systematic killings, torture, rape, or any other human rights abuses, we must at least seek accountability of perpetrators pursuant to the existing law. However, it would be absurd for field officers to wait for widespread or systematic human rights abuses before taking any action. In this sense, human rights field activities are not limited to the sphere of black letter human rights law.[75] Institution-building is essentially a preventive measure. Also, an increase of patrols in an area where certain signs of risk are detected may prevent incidents. Such sensitive functions are exactly what a peacekeeping operation can manage if human rights expertise merges with a peacekeeping force.

---

[75] William Clarance states: "the most appropriately imaginative and effective ideas on how to respond to specific challenges and needs come from field workers whose thinking is forged from interaction with the principal actors and inductive observation of dynamics and needs on the ground." Clarance, 'The Human Rights Field Operation in Rwanda', *supra* FN135 of Chapter 5, p.306.

Conclusion

DEVELOPMENT OF INTERNATIONAL LAW AND PEACEKEEPING

The Security Council has treated a wide range of situations as threats to international peace and security, especially since the end of the Cold War.[1] Humanitarian crisis or serious human rights violations within a state border are tolerated less by other states in the world today.[2] Legal concepts relevant to peacekeeping are under transformation in conjunction with political realities where the international community is increasingly reactive to serious human rights violations. Peacekeeping operations have been carried out in many internal conflict situations since the early 1990s. Peace agreements have been concluded with or by non-state parties, such as the agreements between El Salvador government and FMLN,[3] and between Bosnian Muslims and Bosnian Croats.[4] The implementation of such agreements is often supervised by UN peacekeeping operations, as is clear from the mandates analysed in the four case-studies examined in previous chapters of this book.

David Wippman of Cornell Law School discusses the issue of consent to military intervention when no single faction can credibly claim to speak for the state in question:

> To the extent that international law treats control of the state as a sufficient basis for expressing the state's consent to external military intervention, it seems reasonable to conclude that the collective consent of the various warring factions, which together control the state as a whole, constitutes the best available alternative to consent by a recognized, effective government.[5]

Although peacekeeping is distinct from military intervention, consent to a peacekeeping operation by the host state in cases of internal conflicts can be

---

[1] See Chapter 2, FN112 & 113 and accompanying text.
[2] See Chapter 7, FN35-41 and accompanying text.
[3] See Chapter 3, FN13-19 and accompanying text.
[4] See Chapter 6, FN58 and accompanying text.
[5] David Wippman, 'Military Intervention, Regional Organizations, and Host-State Consent', *Duke Journal of Comparative and International Law*, Fall 1996: 209-239, p.230.

treated in an analogous way. The question of representing a State then would be more concerned with the effective control of the territory of the State than with the recognition of the State in the international community, in other words, the empirical or internal sovereignty rather than the juridical or external sovereignty weighs more.[6] A group of people inside internationally recognised state boundaries may partly represent state sovereignty and participate in a peace process supported by the international community. This is, however, not yet a general view. For instance, Christine Gray of Oxford University gives a more reserved view while recognising the practical importance of the consent of parties involved in a conflict:

> It would ... be going too far to assert that existing international law already looks beyond the government to groups within the state for consent to U.N. intervention, even if the government no longer has control over the whole territory.[7]

Regarding the participation of non-state parties in peace accords, Steven R. Ratner emphasises the obligation pertaining to non-state signatories:

> When nonstate actors sign these agreements, the presumption is that *pacta sunt servanda* applies to them as well: a nonstate party that acts in contravention of an agreement it has signed is considered to be violating international law.[8]

It is therefore clear that non-state parties in a peace process bear legal obligations pursuant to the accords they have signed, and also that they would have certain rights pursuant to the same, if not to speak of the right to the partial representation of state sovereignty.

In conjunction with the expansion of the concept of peace and security, peacekeeping has broadened its area of activities. Multifunctional peacekeeping is an endeavour to maintain or restore peace and security by tackling problems in a number of areas, including human rights. Respect for human

---

[6]   *Ibid.*, p.223. See also discussion in *supra* FN116-120 of Chapter 2. For views on the change in the concept of sovereignty, see also Rosenau, 'Normative Challenges in a Turbulent World', and Chopra and Weiss, 'Sovereignty Is No Longer Sacrosanct', both *supra* FN35 of Chapter 7; as well as Samuel M. Makinda, 'Sovereignty and International Security: Challenges for the United Nations', *Global Governance* 2, 1996: 149-168.

[7]   Christine Gray, 'Host-State Consent and United Nations Peacekeeping in Yugoslavia', *Duke Journal of Comparative and International Law*, Fall 1996: 241-269, p.245. Dr. White also seems to take the position that in practice, it is preferable to acquire the consent of the conflicting factions. White, *Keeping the Peace*, *supra* FN4 of Chapter 1, pp.232-235.

[8]   Ratner, *supra* FN83 of Chapter 1, p.26.

rights is an essential condition for the peace and security of a community. The investigation and reporting of human rights violations has two main purposes: to establish the accountability of the perpetrators of human rights violations; and to identify the system that has allowed such perpetrators to violate human rights. Finding out problems and subsequently reporting them are not the ultimate goal of human rights work. In order to help restore the peace and security in the society where peacekeeping operations are deployed, peacekeepers have much to contribute *vis-à-vis* institution-building which will help to protect human rights. Experience tells us that it is easier to establish a co-operative relationship between peacekeepers and the host state by combining two types of functions: investigation, supervision and reporting on the one hand, and institution-building on the other.[9]

HUMAN RIGHTS FUNCTIONS OF UN PEACE-KEEPING OPERATIONS

Composition and Mandate of UN Peacekeeping Operations

Human rights functions have been undertaken in various forms depending on the composition of the respective peacekeeping operations. ONUSAL in El Salvador was established as a human rights observation mission and UNTAC in Cambodia had a human rights component, albeit with a small number of staff.[10] UNAMIR in Rwanda had only one human rights officer in 1993.[11] Since UNAMIR did not have a unit specialised in human rights issues, civilian police undertook certain investigation work.[12] The Human Rights Field Operation for Rwanda under the auspices of the High Commissioner for Human Rights was deployed after the genocide, and operated independently from the ongoing peacekeeping operation of UNAMIR. Neither UNAMIR nor UNPROFOR in the former Yugoslavia had a unit specialised in human rights, although both Rwanda and the former Yugoslavia saw massive human rights violations, and international tribunals were established for the two conflict areas. There is a lack of attention to human rights issues at the phase of mission planning, and this needs to be addressed seriously. UNMIBH in Bosnia and Herzegovina presents a new type of composition as

---

[9] For instance, see Chapter 5, FN 155 and accompanying text.

[10] FN21 and accompanying text of Chapter 3, and FN29 and accompanying text of Chapter 4.

[11] FN13 and accompanying text of Chapter 5.

[12] FN18 & 19, and accompanying text of Chapter 5.

a peacekeeping operation. It does not include a military component in itself, and a NATO-led multinational force is undertaking the security role. The main part of the operation is conducted by UN civilian police, the International Police Task Force (IPTF), and other civilians are supporting the police force through good office, political assessment and liaison with other international organisations.[13] Since the end of 1996, the IPTF has been responsible for the investigation of human rights abuses by local police forces. UNMIBH increased its involvement in human rights activities by the establishment of the human rights office in the summer of 1997. More than 90% of this office consists of police officers.[14]

For human rights functions in a peacekeeping operation to be effective, there should be a clear mandate. The mandate of ONUSAL explicitly set forth their rights of access to people and places for the purpose of human rights investigation.[15] The mandate of UNTAC was less explicit in that respect, but a remarkable novelty was the specific reference to corrective action.[16] The mandate of UNTAES in Croatia included monitoring of "the parties' compliance with their commitments to respect the highest standards of human rights and fundamental freedoms".[17] However, unlike in the case of ONUSAL and UNTAC, no means for such function were explicitly set forth in any legal documents. The mandate should not be limited to "monitoring" or to "observing" human rights situations. If the mandate is provided for in these terms, the basis for human rights work will be very weak.

Recruitment and Training

In all four of the cases studied, problems in recruitment were experienced by the UN operations. Human rights officers sent to missions often lacked expertise either in human rights or law, or even both. The recruitment of personnel for peacekeeping operations is, in general, difficult because of the shortage of time for preparation and the limitations to funding. In addition, initial mission planning is not always fully carried out. The situation on the ground changes from day to day and the planning can be changed in accordance with the needs on the ground. Particularly within the civilian component, it was not unusual for personnel to be transferred from one unit to

---

[13] FN72 and accompanying text of Chapter 6.

[14] FN73 & 74,, and accompanying text of Chapter 6.

[15] FN26 and accompanying text of Chapter 3.

[16] See 2. 'Composition and Mandate of UNTAC' of Chapter 4.

[17] FN46 and accompanying text of Chapter 6.

another. This may occasionally cause failure in utilising the expertise of the personnel deployed. Furthermore, peacekeeping missions are usually established for a limited period that is subject to review, after which there may possibly be an extension. These unstable conditions of employment may cause difficulty in recruiting highly qualified personnel.[18]

The training of human rights officers is another common problem. Even if the officers have sufficient knowledge of international human rights law and humanitarian law, country-specific information, including its history, political situation, domestic legal and administrative system, and customs, is essential for their work. Also for those who are not familiar with UN peace-keeping operations, they need to know the concept, mechanism and rules of peacekeeping before they commence with their work. Furthermore, human rights training is necessary for all the staff of peacekeeping operations, particularly taking into account the frequent involvement of civilian police in human rights functions. It is unrealistic to expect a familiarity with international human rights law in most of the UN civilian police collected from all over the world, at least for the time being. In this regard, the training of IPTF officers in Bosnia-Herzegovina by the UN Centre for Human Rights can set a good example.[19] The qualification of police personnel should be examined with specific reference to the job description. It is essential that the civilian police officers are also trained adequately as regards international human rights standards and proper rules of conduct. During interviews carried out by this writer with several IPTF officers, a Chief of Human Rights Investigation from a Western European country mentioned that he had never read the Universal Declaration of Human Rights until he was posted in Bosnia-Herzegovina. However, he was highly motivated and, despite this statement, the present writer did not have any concern as to whether he was able to perform his task. The thought that did arise at that moment was that the relevant authorities in his country had the responsibility of disseminating human rights norms. Codification of human rights law is important both at the national and international level; further, both the individual countries and the UN need to undertake the responsibilities of implementing, disseminating and making public the norms contained within the codified laws.

---

18 The problem of recruiting qualified personnel for UN peacekeeping is not only limited to human rights officers. Problems regarding UN civilian police were already mentioned in previous chapters. As to Military Observers, see a case study of UNOGIL in Lebanon: Istvan Pogany, 'The Evaluation of United Nations Peace-keeping Operations', *BYIL*, 1986: 357-369.

19 FN97 & 98, and accompanying text of Chapter 6.

Relationship with the Host State

It is important that not only the consent to the presence of a UN peace-keeping operation, but also the activities of a peacekeeping operation are explicit in the documents setting forth the operation's mandate so that the host-state government as well as the conflicting parties clearly understand them. Such documents can be peace agreements, Security Council resolutions, Status-of-Force agreements and other such agreements. These documents give the legal basis for the activities of the operations. In practice, genuine co-operation between peacekeepers and the host state agents may be difficult to achieve even if such documents have precise provisions regarding the peacekeepers' mandate. The co-operation sometimes varies on an individual basis. The best possible way is, nevertheless, to secure the legal basis of activities and to try to establish good personal contacts.

In case of a transitional administration effected by a peacekeeping operation, the administrator is required to exercise particular caution regarding jurisdictional matters. For instance, the Special Representative of the Secretary-General for Cambodia had the power to issue directives. One directive established procedures for the prosecution of persons responsible for human rights violations. The directive also vested UNTAC with powers to arrest, detain and prosecute suspects.[20] However, the local municipal court refused to initiate proceedings against persons arrested by UNTAC, claiming that the cases were outside the Court's jurisdiction.[21] Another directive was also problematic. Since the UNTAC prosecutor considered that a suspect who was a Khmer Rouge soldier would not enjoy a fair trial under the courts controlled by the State of Cambodia, the directive allowed the detention of the suspect until such time as independent courts could conduct fair trials.[22] Consequently UNTAC undermined the right to due process of law by maintaining detention without judicial review. This embarrassing situation for the UN was prompted by the lack of co-operation from the Cambodian side on this matter. Although the Agreement setting forth the Transitional Authority's power was signed by the Cambodian parties, they still felt that the Directive in question encroached upon their sovereignty. In the case of the UN transitional administration, the principle regarding the degree of UN's involvement needs to be clear and consistent.[23]

---

[20] FN79 & 80, and accompanying text of Chapter 4.

[21] FN84 & 85, and accompanying text of Chapter 4.

[22] FN86 and accompanying text of Chapter 4.

[23] See the interesting study on the current situation of UNMIK and UNTAET by James Traub, 'Inventing East Timor', *Foreign Affairs*, July/August, 2000: 74-89.

Investigation

Investigation activities are important not only for solving the relevant case but to identify the problem of justice system. Through follow-up of cases, one can closely examine the local justice system and further the investigators will have opportunities to hear voices of the local population.

Both in ONUSAL and UNTAC, human rights investigations were conducted by human rights officers and civilian police officers. The ideal way is for the expertise of both groups of officers to be used in tandem.

An experienced UN officer commented that UN human rights officers should not deal with individual cases and must concentrate on institution-building.[24] For instance, in a situation where a large number of harassment cases against an ethnic minority occur, it would in fact be impossible to investigate each case owing to the limited availability of human resources. Priority should then be given to grasping the general situation and to taking such measures as increasing the presence of UN troops or civilian police in the area. The human rights investigation required in this kind of situation is different from a criminal investigation which should, theoretically, be conducted separately by the competent agency. The expertise of human rights officers can be used for the policy-making aspect of the peacekeeping operation in co-operation with the UN troops, military observers and civilian police.

Reporting

A unified human rights reporting form is quite rare in peacekeeping operations. ONUSAL in El Salvador established certain reporting criteria after more than one year following its deployment. There is a view that a unified form may unnecessarily restrict the reporting style of human rights officers.[25]

Reporting can be classified according to the addressees. Most of human rights reports in UN peacekeeping operations have been internal reports of a confidential nature. Incident reports may have to be confidential for the purpose of protecting victims and witnesses. Some reports are published as a press release, or as a report to the Security Council through the Secretary-General.

One issue which to date has not been studied sufficiently is how to make human rights activities known to the public of the host state. Because of the need to protect victims and witnesses, or of the political sensitivity, the

---

[24]   Interview with Mr. Graham Day, Sarajevo, 25 June 1999.
[25]   FN97 and accompanying text of Chapter 4.

measures taken against alleged perpetrators remain mostly unknown. The problem is that the local population may then wrongly believe that the peacekeepers are in fact taking no measures to protect human rights. If this does not concern specific cases, peacekeeping operations can use the media more effectively for human rights functions. For example, media information countering the propaganda of Hutu extremists in Rwanda could have been an effective preventive measure against the reported mass killings.[26]

Institution-building

The human rights situation to be dealt with by peacekeepers differs from one operation to another. However, there are some elements common to many operations. Quite often, the limited scale of armed conflict continues even after the deployment of peacekeeping troops. In such situations, killings, torture and arbitrary detention are the important and urgent issues to be focused on. Once a certain level of security is restored, the return of refugees and displaced persons are organised. In addition to their security, their identification documents, which are the legal basis of their various rights, become an issue. In the case of internal conflict, the security of the minority is often one of the major concerns. When the armed conflict ceases and a new administration takes control, care should be taken to ensure that the minority would not be subjected to administrative discrimination.

If the human rights functions of a peacekeeping operation involve merely investigating alleged violations and reporting on them, it is highly likely that, once the peacekeepers leave, the perpetrators will feel free to behave as they wish. As mentioned above, it is important to establish local institutions that will continue the protection and promotion of human rights. ONUSAL in El Salvador was a good example of the institution-building function of the Organisation. In particular the co-location of its staff with the human rights ombudsman's office had very positive result.[27] IPTF in Bosnia and Herzegovina is also co-locating its police monitors with local chiefs of police or senior police officers.[28] However physical co-location does not necessarily mean that meaningful interaction exists, and much depends on the personnel of both sides.

---

[26] Note that HRFOR did not exist at this point and UNAMIR did not have a component specialised in human rights.

[27] FN129-132, and accompanying text of Chapter 3.

[28] FN210 and accompanying text of Chapter 6.

The institutions that are created by the Organisation should incorporate within themselves the principles of the rule of law.[29] One commentator classified reforms to preserve rule of law in three types.[30] Type one is to revise laws or whole codes. Type two is strengthening of law-related institutions such as the police, prosecutors, public defenders, and prisons. Type three has the goal of increasing government's compliance with law. Peacekeeping operations have already been involved in these kinds of activities through the provision of education and technical assistance.

The amendment or codification of laws is a very sensitive area. One commentator points out:

> Transitional countries are bombarded with fervent but contra-dictory advice on judicial and legal reform.[31]

The required reform cannot be determined without thorough study of the existing legal system and the defects of that system. The *ad hoc* international tribunals, the ICTY and the ICTR, show the difficulty and importance of combining two different legal systems, the common law system and the civil law system.[32] Also there is a risk that a legal model is applied as a tool for exerting the influence of a powerful country, disregarding the specific conditions in the target country.[33] It should be the people of that state who ultimately choose the legal system to be applied.

---

[29] Some NGOs may be going ahead of the United Nations in seeking a systematic approach of legal assistance in post-conflict areas. See as an example, Mark S. Ellis, 'The Facilitation of National and International Accountability Mechanisms: The Creation of the International Legal Assistance Consortium (ILAC)', 4 *ILSA Journal of International and Comparative Law*, 1998: 407-414. It should also be noted that the concept of the rule of law itself is complex, and that there are varied interpretations. See, as a discussion in the US context, Richard H. Fallon, Jr., '"The Rule of Law" as a Concept in Constitutional Discourse', *Columbia Law Review*, January 1997: 1-56.

[30] Thomas Carothers, 'The Rule of Law Revival', *Foreign Affairs* 77(2), March/April 1998: 95-106, pp.99-100. See also Mark Plunkett, 'Reestablishing Law and Order in Peace-Maintenance', *Global Governance* 4, 1998: 61-79, pp. 68-69 [listing core objectives of a justice package for peace-maintenance].

[31] Carothers, *op. cit.*

[32] See, for example, Christopher L. Blakesley, 'Jurisdiction, Definition of Crimes, and Trig-gering Mechanisms', 25 *Denver Journal of International Law and Policy*, Winter 1997: FN138 and accompanying text; and Richard May and Marieke Wierda, 'Trends in International Criminal Evidence: Nuremberg, Tokyo, The Hague, and Arusha', *Columbia Journal of Transnational Law*, 1999: 725-764.

[33] A commentator gives an example of Cambodia: "legal experts from the United States and France fought bitterly over which legal system, common law or civil law, should be introduced, although apparently neither side could articulate clearly the differences between the two or their comparative advantages for Cambodia." Rama Mani, 'Conflict

A similar question arises concerning the establishment of a democratic police force. It is important to clarify which kind of police model the Organisation tries to promote. The UN Civilian Police force itself, which consists of police from diverse countries, encounters difficulties in co-ordinating and clarifying the standards according to which they operate.[34] The qualification of police to serve in the UN police force requires more careful consideration. In practice, members of UN Civilian Police are not always civilian police; some are military police or even prison warders.[35] In the event that the mandate of the police component in a peacekeeping operation includes the training of a local civilian police force, the conditions for recruitment should also contain a requirement for the same qualifications as those for a civilian police officer.

Human Rights Education

Education is a part of institution-building. In addition to the human rights education of the professionals referred to above, public education is also important. It will be the local population who will monitor the behaviour of state agents in the long term. The public's knowledge of their rights under international human rights law and domestic law also deters the state agents from abusing their powers. Field officers have used diverse methods for the dissemination of human rights concepts such as using puzzles and videos, and theatrical performances.[36] The use of the media in human rights

---

Resolution, Justice and the Law: Rebuilding the Rule of Law in the Aftermath of Complex Political Emergencies', *International Peacekeeping* 5(3), 1998: 1-25, pp.7-8.

[34] This author interviewed some police monitors working in the IPTF and OSCE missions in Croatia and Bosnia-Herzegovina. Some of them suggested that it would be better if an operation in Europe consisted of European monitors. One reason for this related to motivation. For monitors from a developing country, the salaries they receive for participating in a UN peacekeeping operation may amount to ten times, or more, than their normal salaries at home. It was suggested by interviewees that, when the motivation to work is only the salary, those monitors tended to do a minimum amount of work. Another reason was the standard of police work. Some European monitors found even American monitors' standard quite different.

[35] Anonymous interview with a Deputy Regional Commander Operation, IPTF, November 1998. In contrast, the employment of military police or national guard personnel could be considered for a different type of operation. See Henry H. Perritt, Jr., 'Policing International Peace and Security: International Police Forces', *Wisconsin International Law Journal*, Summer 1999: 281-324, pp.296-298; and Alice Hills, 'International Peace Support Operations and CIVPOL: Should there be a Permanent Global Gendarmerie?', *International Peacekeeping* 5(3), Autumn 1998: 26-41.

[36] FN141 and accompanying text of Chapter 3, and FN128 and accompanying text of Chapter 4.

education can be enhanced as a part of peacekeeping operations. Furthermore, in a country where an armed conflict has caused immense material destruction, the provision of human rights law texts or human rights law courses can make a significant difference to human rights education, as in the case of Cambodia and Rwanda.[37]

Co-operation between the UN Agencies

The case studies showed the rivalry between the components of a peace-keeping operation as well as between a given peacekeeping operation and other UN agencies. For example, ONUSAL and HRFOR both had difficulty in relating to the UNDP.[38] Different UN agencies compete with each other in order to secure their areas of responsibility. The Special Rapporteur of the Commission on Human Rights on the human rights situation in Rwanda had problems in working with HRFOR. HRFOR was theoretically supposed to support the work of the Special Rapporteur, but the co-operation was practically blocked by the bureaucracy of the Centre for Human Rights.[39] This is particularly disturbing since the Special Rapporteur, the Centre for Human Rights and HRFOR were all responsible for working for human rights. The primary consideration should always be the benefit of people for whom those operations were established, not the individual achievements or the celebrity of the organisation.

Co-operation with Local NGOs

Co-operation with local NGOs varies from one operation to another, depending on how active those NGOs are at the time a peacekeeping operation is deployed. For instance, UNTAC made a significant contribution to the development of human rights activities in Cambodia. While no human rights NGOs existed at the time of the deployment of UNTAC in Cambodia, the membership of Cambodian human rights NGOs grew to 150,000 by the time of the elections in 1993.[40] In any situation, co-operation and com-munication with local NGOs are desirable for two reasons. Firstly, the local NGOs can be an important source of information. Secondly, such NGOs can develop the human rights work initiated or supported by a peacekeeping

---

[37] FN132 and accompanying text of Chapter 4. Also FN205 of Chapter 5.
[38] FN153 and accompanying text of Chapter 3, and FN167 and accompanying text of Chapter 5.
[39] FN168-172, and accompanying text of Chapter 5.
[40] FN143 & 144, and accompanying text of Chapter 4.

operation even after its departure. The involvement of the local population in human rights work will help to foster the concept of human rights deep into the local society.

PEACE AND HUMAN RIGHTS

It is important to include a human rights mandate in every United Nations peacekeeping operation, since it is one of the essential factors for the peace and security of the society and also because that is one of the principal purposes of the Organisation. The fact that the Security Council recognises an increasingly broad range of circumstances as being relevant to international peace and security is a welcome development, if that leads peace-keeping operations to tackle the root causes of the conflicts. To have a human rights component is an integral and vital function of a peacekeeping operation and not just an exercise in public relations. The protection and promotion of human rights needs to be considered in the diverse aspects of the given society, such as police work, the justice system, education, the return of refugees and displaced persons, and the minority groups. We therefore do not need to decide on one specific type of composition. However, the case study of HRFOR in Rwanda casts doubt on the creation of an independent operation for human rights. The involvement of different agencies inevitably adds bureaucratic obstacles. A specialised component on human rights should be established in a peacekeeping operation, as in the case of ONUSAL or UNTAC; alternatively, human rights specialists can work in different components within the peacekeeping operation. For instance, each component, such as the civil administration unit, the legal unit and the public information unit, can include some human rights experts.

Unlike enforcement action, most peacekeeping operations are not designed to confront massive human rights violations with the use of force.[41] Their merit in the field is rather to find warning signs before the situation gets out of hand. The presence of peacekeepers also has a deterrent effect. If the armed conflict resumes despite their presence, peacekeepers can play the role of a Protecting Power.[42] In accordance with the development of both international humanitarian law and international criminal law, the accountability of individual perpetrators of serious human rights violations may be

---

[41] As discussed thoroughly in Chapter 2, this author takes the view that enforcement and peacekeeping should be clearly distinguished. For different views that accept a certain level of the use of force in peacekeeping, see 2.2 'Second-Generation Peacekeeping' and 2.3 'Third-Generation Peacekeeping' of Chapter 2.

[42] See 2. 'United Nations Peacekeeping Force as Protecting Powers' in Chapter 7.

sought before an international court. The ICTY and the ICTR are developing the jurisprudence governing international crimes. With the eventual establishment of the permanent International Criminal Court, peacekeeping operations may contribute to such international justice by providing evidence.[43]

Peace and security hardly exist where human rights are threatened. Building a system that protects and promotes human rights helps in transforming a society where people have been subjected to coercion and violence into one that is governed by the rule of law. The peacekeeping operations may contribute in this process through human rights functions which bridge the international human rights law and humanitarian law and the lawless reality on the ground.

---

[43] Regarding the International Criminal Court, see references in FN92 of Chapter 6.

Index

Bibliography

BOOKS

African Rights, *Rwanda: Death, Despair and Defiance,* 2nd ed., 1995.

Aikyo, Masanori; and Yotsumoto, Kenji, *Gendai Cambodia no hou to jinken ni tsuite (Law and Human Rights in Cambodia Today)*, Nagoya daigaku houseironshu Vol. 157, 1994.

Arend, Anthony Clark and Beck, Robert J., *International Law and the Use of Force: Beyond the UN Charter Paradigm*, Routledge, 1993.

Bideleux, Robert, and Jeffries, Ian, *A History of Eastern Europe: Crisis and Change*, Routledge, 1998.

Boutros-Ghali, Boutros, *An Agenda for Peace: Preventive Diplomacy, Peacemaking and Peace-keeping*, New York: United Nations, 1992.

Bowett, D. W., *United Nations Forces: A Legal Study of United Nations Practice*, Stevens & Sons, 1964.

Brown, Frederick Z. ed., *Rebuilding Cambodia: Human Resources, Human Rights, and Law*, Arlington: Public Interest Publications, 1993.

Brownlie, Ian, *International Law and the Use of Force by States*, Oxford University Press, 1963.

Brownlie, Ian, *Principles of Public International Law*, 4th ed., Clarendon Press, 1990.

Burg, Steven L.; and Shoup, Paul S., *The War in Bosnia-Herzegovina: Ethnic Conflict and International Intervention*, M. E. Sharpe, 1999.

Campbell, David, *National Deconstruction: Violence, Identity, and Justice in Bosnia,* Minneapolis & London: University of Minnesota Press, 1998.

Chandler, David P., *The Tragedy of Cambodian History: Politics, War, and Revolution since 1945*, New Haven & London: Yale University Press, 1991.

Cohen, Leonard J., *Broken Bonds: Yugoslavia's Disintegration and Balkan Politics in Transition*, 2nd ed., Westview Press, 1995.

Daillier, Patrick, and Pellet, Alain, *Droit International Public*, Paris: Librairie Générale de Droit et de Jurisprudence, 6th ed., 1999.

Damrosch, Lori Fisler, ed., *Enforcing Restraint: Collective Intervention in Internal Conflicts*, Council on Foreign Relations, Inc., 1993.

de Rossanet, Bertrand., *War and Peace in the Former Yugoslavia*, Kluwer Law International, 1997.

Doyle, Michael W., *UN Peacekeeping in Cambodia: UNTAC's Civil Mandate*, Lynne Rienner Publishers, 1995.

Doyle, Michael W., Johnstone, Ian, and Orr, Robert C. eds., *Keeping the Peace: Multidimensional UN Operations in Cambodia and El Salvador*, Cambridge University Press, 1997.

Durch, William J., *The Evolution of UN Peace-keeping*, New York: St. Martin's Press, 1993.

Durch, William J., ed., *UN Peace-keeping, American Politics, and the Uncivil Wars of the 1990s*, Macmillan, 1997.

Farer, Tom, ed., *Beyond Sovereignty: Collectively Defending Democracy in the Americas*, The Johns Hopkins University Press, 1996.

Fernando, J. Basil, *The Inability to Prosecute: Courts and Human Rights in Cambodia and Sri Lanka*, Hong Kong: Future Asia Link, 1993.

Fetherston, A. B., *Towards a Theory of United Nations Peace-keeping*, Macmillan, 1994.

Fitzpatrik, Joan, *Human Rights in Crisis: The International System for Protecting Rights During States of Emergency*, Vol. 19, Procedural Aspects of International Law Series, University of Pennsylvania Press, 1994.

Franz, Gisbert H. ed., *Constitutions of the Countries of the World: Republic of El Salvador*, Booklet 1, Translated by Reka Koerner, Dobbs Ferry, New York: Oceana Publications, Inc., 1998.

Goodrich, Leland M., Hambro, Edvard, and Simons, Anne Patricia, *Charter of the United Nations: Commentary and Documents*, Third and Revised Ed., New York and London: Columbia University Press, 1969.

Gourevitch, Philip, *We wish to inform you that tomorrow we will be killed with our families*, London & Basingstoke: PICADOR, 1998.

Hannum, Hurst, ed., *Guide to International Human Rights Practice*, 2nd ed., University of Pennsylvania Press, 1992.

Henkin, Alice H., ed., *Honoring Human Rights: From Peace to Justice*, Washington: The Aspen Institute, 1998.

Higgins, Rosalyn, *United Nations Peace-keeping 1946-1967: Documents and Commentary*, Vol. I. The Middle East, Oxford University Press, 1969.

Higgins, Rosalyn, *United Nations Peace-keeping 1946-1967: Documents and Commentary*, Vol. III, Africa, Oxford University Press, 1980.

Higgins, Rosalyn, *United Nations Peace-keeping: 1946-1979 Documents and Commentary*, Vol. IV Europe, Oxford University Press, 1981.

Honig, Jan Willem, and Both, Norbert, *Srebrenica: Record of a War Crime*, Penguin Books, 1996.

Hughes, Catherine, *UNTAC in Cambodia: The impact on human rights*, Singapore: Institute of Southeast Asian Studies, 1996.

Human Rights Watch, *The Lost Agenda: Human Rights and U.N. Field Operations*, 1993.

James, Alan, *Peace-keeping in International Politics*, Houndmills and London: Macmillan, 1990: 87-92.

Jennings, Robert (Sir), and Watts, Arthur (Sir), eds., *Oppenheim's International Law*, 9th ed., Vol. I Peace.

Johnstone, Ian, *Rights and Reconciliation: UN Strategies in El Salvador*, Lynne Reinner Publishers, 1995.

Joint Evaluation of Emergency Assistance to Rwanda, *The International Response to Conflict and Genocide: Lessons from the Rwanda Experience*, Study 4, Rebuilding Post-War Rwanda.

Jongman, Albert J. ed., *Comtemporary Genocides: Causes, Cases, Consequences*, PIOOM, 1996.

Judah, Tim, *The Serbs: History, Myth and the Destruction of Yugoslavia*, Yale University Press, 1997.

Kiernan, Ben, ed., *Genocide and Democracy in Cambodia: The Khmer Rouge, the United Nations and the International Community*, Yale University of Southeast Asia Studies, 1993.

Lawyers Committee for Human Rights, *Imposing History: A Critical Evaluation of the United Nations Observer Mission in El Salvador*, December 1995.

Lutz, Ellen L., Hannum, Hurst, and Burke, Kathryn J. eds., *New Directions in Human Rights*, University of Pennsylvania Press, 1989.

Müllerson, Rein, Fitzmaurice, Malgosia, and Andenas, Mads, eds., *Constitutional Reform and International Law in Central and Eastern Europe*, Kluwer Law International, 1998.

Malanczuk, Peter, *Akehurst's Modern Introduction to International Law*, 7th revised ed., Routledge, 1997.

Malcolm, Noel, *Bosnia: A Short History*, Papermac, 1996.

Montgomery, Tommie Sue, *Revolution in El Salvador: From Civil Strife to Civil Peace*, Westview Press, 2nd ed., 1995.

Moore, John Norton, ed., *Law and Civil War in the Modern World*, Baltimore: Johns Hopkins Press, 1974.

Neier, Aryeh, *War Crimes: Brutality, Genocide, Terror, and the Struggle for Justice*, Times Books, 1998.

Oakley, Robert B., Dziedzic, Michael J., and Goldberg, Eliot M., eds., *Policing the New World Disorder: Peace Operations and Public Security*, Institute for National Strategic Studies, text available at: http://www.ndu.edu/inss/books/policing/chapter4.html.

Oràà, Jaime, *Human Rights in States of Emergency in International Law*, Clarendon Press, 1992.

Pearson, Raymond, *National Minorities in Eastern Europe 1848-1945*, Macmillan, 1983.

Pogany, Istvan, *The Security Council and the Arab-Israeli Conflict*, Aldershot: Gower, 1984.

Ponchaud, François, *Cambodia Year Zero*, Penguin Books, 1977

Prunier, Gérard, *The Rwanda Crisis 1959-1994: History of Genocide*, London: Hurst & Company, 1995.

Ratner, Steven R., *The New UN Peacekeeping: Building Peace in Lands of Conflict after the Cold War*, London: Macmillan, 1997.

Reed, Laura W., and Kaysen, Carl, eds., *Emerging Norms of Justified Intervention*, American Academy of Arts and Sciences, 1993.

Ricci, Roberto, *One Year of Human Rights Monitoring with the UN High Commissioner for Human Rights in Rwanda: Afterthoughts*, Human Rights Centre, University of Essex, 1998.

Robertson, Geoffrey, *Crimes Against Humanity: The Struggle for Global Justice*, Allen Lane The Penguin Press, 1999.

Rodley, Nigel, ed., *To Loose the Bands of Wickedness: International Intervention in Defence of Human Rights*, Brassey's (UK), 1992.

Ronzitti, Natalino, *Rescuing Nationals Abroad and Intervention on Grounds of Humanity*, Martinus Nijhoff, 1985.

Rose (General Sir), Michael, *Fighting for Peace: Bosnia 1994*, London: The Harvill Press, 1998.

Rothschild, Joseph, *Return to Diversity: A Political History of East Central Europe Since World War II*, 2nd ed., Oxford University Press, 1993.

Sarooshi, Danesh, *The United Nations and the Development of Collective Security: The Delegation by the UN Security Council of its Chapter VII Powers*, Clarendon Press: Oxford, 1999.

Seyersted, F., *United Nations Forces*, 1966.

Shaw, Malcolm N., *International Law*, 4th ed., Cambridge University Press, 1997.

Shawcross, William, *The Quality of Mercy: Cambodia, Holocaust and Modern Conscience*, London: Andre Deutsch, 1984.

Shawcross, William, *Cambodia's New Deal*, Contemporary Issues Paper #1, Washington D.C.: Carnegie Endowment for International Peace, 1994.

Sieghart, Paul, *The International Law of Human Rights*, Clarendon Press, 1983.

Silber, Laura, and Little, Allan, *The Death of Yugoslavia*, Penguin Books, 1995.

Simma, Bruno, ed., *The Charter of the United Nations: A Commentary*, Oxford University Press, 1995.

Stiglmayer, Alexandra, ed., *Mass Rape: The War against Women in Bosnia-Herzegovina*, Lincoln & London: University of Nebraska Press, 1994.

Swinarski, Christophe, ed., *Etudes et essais sur le droit international humanitaire et sur les principes de la Croix-Rouge*, Geneva & The Hague: Martinus Nijhoff Publishers, 1984.

Tabata, Shigejiro, Kokusaihoukougi (International Law Lectures), Vol.2, Yushindo, 1984.

Tanner, Marcus, *Croatia: A Nation Forged in War*, New Haven & London: Yale University Press, 1997.

Teson, R., *Humanitarian Intervention: An Inquiry into Law and Morality*, Transnational Publishers, Dobbs Ferry, 1988.

Tulchin, Joseph S. with Bland, Gary, eds., *Is There a Transition to Democracy in El Salvador?*, Lynne Reinner Publishers, 1992.

United Nations, *The Blue Helmets: A Review of United Nations Peacekeeping*, The United Nations Department of Public Information, 3rd ed., 1996.

United Nations, *United Nations Year Book 1993*.

United Nations, *United Nations Year Book 1994*.

United Nations, *The United Nations and Rwanda 1993-1996*, The UN Blue Book Series, Volume X, 1996.

United Nations, *The United Nations and Cambodia 1991-1995*, The United Nations Blue Book Series, Volume II, 1995.

United Nations, *The United Nations and El Salvador 1990-1995*, The United Nations Blue Books Series, Volume IV, United Nations Department of Public Information, 1995.

Urquhart, Brian, *A Life in Peace and War*, W.W. Norton & Company, 1987.

Vickery, Michael, *Cambodia: 1975-1982*, South End Press: Boston, 1984.

Warner, Daniel, ed., *Human Rights and Humanitarian Law: The Quest for Universality*, Martinus Nijhoff Publishers, 1997.

Weiss, Thomas G., Forsythe, David P., and Coate, Roger A., *The United Nations and Changing World Politics*, Boulder, Westview Press, 1994.

White, N.D., *Keeping the Peace: The United Nations and the Maintenance of International Peace and Security*, Manchester University Press, 2nd ed., 1997.

Whitman, Jim; and Pocock, David eds., *After Rwanda: The Coordination of United Nations Humanitarian Assistance*, Macmillan, 1996.

ARTICLES

Abi-Saab, Rosemary, 'Human rights and Humanitarian Law in Internal Conflicts', in Warner, ed., (1997): 107-123.

Abrams, Jason S. and Ratner, Steven R., 'The Attempt to bring the Perpetrators of the Cambodian Genocide to Trial', in Jongman, ed. (1996): 77-78.

Adams, Brad, 'UN Human Rights Work in Cambodia: Efforts to Preserve the Jewel in the Peacekeeping Crown', in Henkin, ed. (1998): 189-226.

Aikyo, Masanori, 'The 1993 Constitution of Cambodia', in Aikyo and Yotsumoto (1994): 159-179.

Akashi, Yasushi, 'The Challenge of Peacekeeping in Cambodia', *International Peacekeeping* 1(2), Summer 1994: 204-215.

Akhavan, Payam, 'Justice and Reconciliation in the Great Lakes Region of Africa: The Contribution of the International Criminal Tribunal for Rwanda', *Duke Journal of Comparative and International Law*, Spring 1997: 325-348.

Akhavan, Payam, 'The International Criminal Tribunal for Rwanda: The Politics and Pragmatics of Punishment', *AJIL* 90, 1996: 501-510.

Alston, Philip, 'The Security Council and Human Rights: Lessons to be Learned from the Iraq-Kuwait Crisis and its Aftermath', 13 *Australian Year Book of International Law*, 1992: 107-176.

Alvarez, Jose E., 'Crimes of States/Crimes of Hate: Lessons from Rwanda', *Yale Journal of International Law*, Summer 1999: 365-483.

Amann, Diane Marie, 'Prosecutor v. Akayesu', *AJIL* 93, 1999: 195-199.

Andrassy, Juraj, 'Uniting for Peace', *AJIL* 50, 1956: 563-582.

Aolain, Fionnuala Ni, 'The Emergence of Diversity: Differences in Human Rights Jurisprudence', *Fordham International Law Journal*, October 1995: 101-142.

Aolain, Fionnuala Ni, 'The Fractured Soul of the Dayton Peace Agreement: A Legal Analysis', *Michigan Journal of International Law*, Summer 1998: 957-1004.

Arsanjani, Mahnoush H., 'The Rome Statute of the International Criminal Court', *AJIL* 93, 1999: 22-43.

Ashkin, Kelly D., 'Sexual Violence in Decisions and Indictments of the Yugoslav and Rwandan Tribunals: Current Status', *AJIL* 93, 1999: 97-123.

Ashkin, Kelly D., 'The International War Crimes Trial of Anto Furundžija: Major Progress Toward Ending the Cycle of Impunity for Rape Crimes', *Leiden Journal of International Law* 12(4), 1999: 935-955.

Barnett, Michael, 'The New United Nations Politics of Peace: From Juridical Sovereignty to Empirical Sovereignty', *Global Governance* 1, 1995:79-97.

Barnett, Michael N., 'The Security Council, Indifference, and Genocide in Rwanda', *Cultural Anthropology* 12(4), 1997: 551-578.

Bassiouni, M. Cherif, 'Searching for Peace and Achieving Justice: The Need for Accountability', *Law and Contemporary Problems*, 1996: 9-28.

Biermann, Wolfgang, and Frederik, Ole Ugland, 'Lessons Learned in the Field: A Survey of UNPORFOR Officers', in Biermann, Wolfgang, and Vadset, Martin, eds., *UN Peacekeeping in Trouble: Lessons Learned from the Former Yugoslavia: Peacekeepers' Views on the Limits and Possibilities of the United Nations in a Civil War-like Conflict*, Ashgate, 1999: 81-122.

Bilder, Richard B., 'Kosovo and the "New Interventionism": Promise or Peril?', *Journal of Transnational Law and Policy*, 1999: 153-182.

Birgisson, Karl Th., 'United Nations Special Committee on the Balkans,' in Durch, ed. (1993), Chapter 5: 77-83.

Blakesley, Christopher L., 'Jurisdiction, Definition of Crimes, and Triggering Mechanisms', 25 *Denver Journal of International Law and Policy*, Winter 1997.

Bowett, D. W., 'Collective Self-Defence Under the Charter of the United Nations', *BYIL* 32, 1955-56: 130-161.

Brody, Reed, 'The United Nations and Human Rights in El Salvador's "Negotiated Revolution"', *Harvard Human Rights Journal*, Spring, 1995: 153-178.

Brownlie, Ian, 'Humanitarian Intervention', in Moore, John Norton, ed., *Law and Civil War in the Modern World*, Johns Hopkins Press, 1974.

Buergenthal, Thomas, 'The United Nations Truth Commission for El Salvador', *Vanderbit Journal of Transnational Law*, October 1994: 497-544.

Burgler, Roel A., 'The Case of Cambodia: the Khmer Rouge's Reign of Terror', in Jongman, ed. (1996): 59-76.

Caron, David D., 'The Legitimacy of the Collective Authority of the Security Council', *AJIL* 1993: 552-588.

Carothers, Thomas, 'The Rule of Law Revival', *Foreign Affairs* 77(2), March/April 1998: 95-106.

Cassese, Antonio, '*Ex iniuria ius oritur*: Are We Moving towards International Legitimation of Forcible Humanitarian Countermeasures in the World Community?', 10 *EJIL* 1999: 23-30.

Cassese, Antonio, 'Modern Constitutions and International Law', *Recueil des cours*, 1985 III: 335-473.

Cassese, Antonio, 'On the Current Trends towards Criminal Prosecution and Punishment of Breaches of International Humanitarian Law', 9 *EJIL*, 1998: 2-17.

Charney, Jonathan I., 'Anticipatory Humanitarian Intervention in Kosovo', *Vanderbilt Journal of Transnational Law*, November 1999: 1231-1248.

Chinkin, Christine, 'Rape and Sexual Abuse of Women in International Law', 5 *EJIL*, 1994, 326-341.

Chopra, Jarat; and Weiss, Thomas G., 'Sovereignty Is No Longer Sacrosanct: Codifying Humanitarian Intervention', *Ethics & International Affairs* 6, 1992: 95-117.

Cisse, Catherine, 'The International Tribunal for the Former Yugoslavia and Rwanda: Some Elements of Comparison', *The Transnational Law and Contemporary Problems*, 1997:104-118.

Clarance, William, 'Field Strategy for the Protection of Human Rights', *International Journal of Refugee Law* 9(2), 1997: 229-254.

Clarance, William, 'The Human Rights Field Operation in Rwanda: Protective Practice Evolves on the Ground', *International Peacekeeping* 2(3), Autumn 1995:291-308.

Costa, Gino, 'The United Nations and Reform of the Police in El Salvador', *International Peacekeeping* 2(3), Autumn 1995: 365-90.

Cousens, Elizabeth M., 'Making Peace in Bosnia Work', *Cornell International Law Journal, 1997*: 789-818.

Crawford, Neta C., 'Decolonization as an International Norm: The Evolution of Practices, Arguments and Beliefs', in Reed and Kaysen eds. (1993).

Cunningham, J., 'The European Convention on Human Rights, Customary International Law and the Constitution', *ICLQ* 43, 1994: 537-567 .

Daniel, Donald C. F., and Hayes, Bradd C., 'Securing Observance of UN Mandates Through the Employment of Military Force', *International Peace-keeping* 3(4), Winter 1996: 105-125.

de Lapresle, Bertrand, 'Principles to be Observed: for the Use of Military Forces Aimed at De-escalation and Resolution of Conflict', in Biermann and Vadset, eds. (1999): 137-152.

del Castillo, Graciana, 'The arms-for-land deal in El Salvador', in Doyle *et al.*, eds. (1997) : 342-365.

Dobbie, Charles, 'A Concept for Post-Cold War Peace-keeping', *Survival* 36(3), Autumn 1994: 121-48.

Dommen, Caroline, 'The UN Human Rights Regime: Is it Effective?', *American Society of International Law Proceedings*, 1997: 460-484.

Donovan, Dolores A., 'The Cambodian Legal System: An Overview', in Brown, ed., (1993): 69-107.

Doyle, Michael W., and Suntharalingam, Nishkala, 'The UN in Cambodia: Lessons for Complex Peacekeeping', *International Peacekeeping* 1(2), Summer 1994: 117-147.

Drumbl, Mark A., 'Rule of Law and Lawlessness: Counselling the Accused in Rwanda's Domestic Genocide Trials', *Columbia Human Rights Law Review*, Summer 1998: 545-639.

Durch, William J., 'Structural Issues and the Future of UN Peace Operations' in Donald C. F. Daniel and Bradd C. Hayes, eds., *Beyond Traditional Peace-keeping*, Macmillan, 1995.

Durch, William, ed., 'The UN Operation in Congo', in Durch, ed. (1997), Chapter 19: 315-352.

El-Ayouty, Yassini, 'International Action on the Doctrine of Humanitarian Intervention: The Case of Southern Iraq (1991-1992)', *New York State Bar Journal*, July/August 1996: 12-21.

Ellis, Mark S., 'The Facilitation of National and International Accountability Mechanisms: The Creation of the International Legal Assistance Consortium (ILAC)', 4 *ILSA Journal of International and Comparative Law*, 1998: 407-414

Ensalaco, Mark, 'Truth Commission for Chile and El Salvador: A Report and Assessment', *Human Rights Quarterly* 16, 1994: 656-675.

Er, Robert O. Wein, and Aolain, Fionnuala Ni, 'Beyond the Laws of War: Peacekeeping in Search of a Legal Framework', *Columbia Human Rights Law Review*, Winter 1996: 293-354.

Fallon, Jr., Richard H., '"The Rule of Law" as a Concept in Constitutional Discourse', *Columbia Law Review*, January 1997: 1-56.

Fernando, Basil, 'Shinsei Cambodia ni okeru hou to jinken (Law and Human Rights in New Cambodia)' (a lecture given on 7 March 1994 at Nagoya University. Translated into Japanese by Kenji Yotsumoto), in Aikyo and Yotsumoto (1994).

Fetherston, A. B., Ramsbotham, O., and Woodhouse, T., 'UNPROFOR: Some Observations from a Conflict Resolution Perspective', *International Peacekeeping* 1(2), Summer 1994: 179-203.

Formuth, Peter J., 'The Making of a Security Community: The United Nations After the Cold War', *Journal of International Affairs* 46(2), Winter 1993: 341-66.

Franck, Thomas M., 'Who Killed Article 2(4)?', *AJIL* 64, 1970: 809-837.

Franck, Thomas M., and Rodley, Nigel S., 'After Bangladesh: The Law of Humanitarian Intervention by Military Force', *AJIL* 67, 1973: 275-300.

Frank, Thomas M., and Patel, Faiza, 'UN Police Action in Lieu of War', *AJIL* 85, 1991: 63-74.

Freedman, Lawrence; and Boren, David, '"Safe havens' for Kurds in post-war Iraq' in Rodley, ed. (1992): 43-92.

García-Sayán, Diego, 'Human Rights and Peace-keeping Operations', *University of Richmond Law Review*, 1994: 41-65.

Ghali, Mona, 'United Nations Emergency Force I', in Durch, ed. (1997), Chapter 7: 104-130.

Ghali, Mona, 'United Nations Truce Supervision Organisation: 1948-Present', in Durch, ed. (1997), Chapter 6: 84-103.

Goldstone, Richard J., 'Justice as a Tool for Peace-Making: Truth Commissions and International Criminal Tribunals', *New York University Journal of International Law and Politics*, 1996: 485-503.

Goulding, Marrack, 'The Evolution of United Nations Peace-keeping', *International Affairs* 69(3), 1993: 451-64.

Goulding, Marrack, 'The Use of Force by the United Nations', *International Peace-keeping* 3(1), Spring 1996:1-18.

Gray, Christine, 'Host-State Consent and United Nations Peacekeeping in Yugoslavia', *Duke Journal of Comparative and International Law*, Fall 1996: 241-269, p.245.

Greenwood, Christopher, 'International Humanitarian Law and the *Tadic Case*', 7 *EJIL*, 1996: 265-283.

Greenwood, Christopher, 'Is there a right of humanitarian intervention?', *The World Today* 49(2), February 1993: 34-40.

Greig, D.W., 'Self-Defence and the Security Council: What Does Article 51 Require?', *ICLQ* 40, 1991: 366-402.

Gross, Oren, 'The Grave Breaches System and the Armed Conflict in the Former Yugoslavia', *Michigan Journal of International Law*, Spring, 1995: 783-829.

Haas, Ernest B., 'Beware the Slippery Slope: Notes toward the Definition of Justifiable Intervention', in Reed and Kaysen, eds. (1993): 63-87.

Han, Sonia K., 'Building a Peace that Lasts: The United Nations and Post-Civil War Peace-Building', *New York University Journal of International Law and Politics*, Summer 1994: 837-892.

Hannum, Hurst, 'International Law and Cambodian Genocide: The Sounds of Silence', *Human Rights Quarterly* 11, 1989: 82-138.

Hayner, Priscilla B., 'Commissioning the truth: further research questions', *Third World Quarterly* 17(1), 1996: 19-29.

Hayner, Priscilla B., 'Fifteen Truth Commissions – 1974 to 1994: A Comparative Study', *Human Rights Quarterly* 16, 1994: 597-655.

Higgins, Rosalyn, 'Derogations under Human Rights Treaties', *BYIL* 48, 1976-7: 281-320.

Higgins, Rosalyn, 'Second-Generation Peacekeeping', *ASIL Proceedings*, 1995.

Higgins, Rosalyn, 'The Legal Limits to the Use of Force by Sovereign States: United Nations Practice', *BYIL* 37, 1961: 269-319.

Hille, Saskia, 'Mutual Recognition of Croatia and Serbia (+Montenegro)', 6 *EJIL*, 1995: 598-611.

Hills, Alice, 'International Peace Support Operations and CIVPOL: Should there be a Permanent Global Gendarmerie?', *International Peacekeeping* 5(3), Autumn 1998: 26-41.

Howland, Todd, 'Refoulement of Rwandan Refugees: The UNHCR's Lost Opportunity to Ground Temporary Refuge in Human Rights Law', *U.C. Davis Journal of International Law and Policy*, Winter 1998:73-101.

Howland, Todd, and Calathes, William, 'The U.N.'s International Criminal Tribunal, Is it Justice or Jingoism for Rwanda? A Call for Transformation', *Virginia Journal of International Law*, Fall 1998: 135-167.

Iwasawa, Yuji, 'The Relationship between International Law and National Law: Japanese Experiences', *BYIL* 64, 1993: 333-390.

James, Alan, 'Peace-keeping in the post-Cold War era', *International Journal*, vol.L, no.2, Spring 1995:241-265.

Jernow, Allison L., 'Ad Hoc and Extra-Conventional Means for Human Rights Monitoring', *New York University Journal of International Law and Politics*, 1996: 785-836.

Johnstone, Ian, 'Rights and reconciliation in El Salvador', in Doyle *et al.*, eds. (1997): 312-341.

Jones, Sydney and PoKempner, Dinah, 'Human Rights in Cambodia: Past, Present, and Future', in Z. Brown, ed. (1993): 43-68.

Kaikobad, Kaiyan Homi, 'Self-Defence, Enforcement Action and the Gulf Wars, 1980-88 and 1990-1991', *BYIL* 63, 1992: 299-366.

Karhilo, Jaana, 'The Establishment of the International Tribunal for Rwanda', *Nordic Journal of International Law* 64, 1995: 683-713.

Kelsen, Hans, 'Collective Security and Collective Self-Defense under the Charter of the United Nations', *AJIL* 42, 1948: 783-796.

Kenny, Karen, 'Introducing the Sustainability Principle to Human Rights Operations', *International Peacekeeping* 4(4), Winter 1997: 61-78.

King, Faiza Patel; and La Rosa, Anne-Marie, 'International Criminal Tribunal for the Former Yugoslavia', 9 *EJIL*, 1998: 757-760.

Kirsch, Philippe, and Holmes, John T., 'The Rome Conference on an International Criminal Court: The Negotiating Process', *AJIL* 93, 1999: 2-12.

Knudsen, Tonny Brems, 'Humanitarian Intervention Revisited: Post-Cold War Responses to Classical Problems', *International Peacekeeping* 3(4), Winter 1996 :146- 165.

Lee, Roy S., 'United Nations Peacekeeping: Development and Prospects', *Cornell International Law Journal*, 1995: 619-627.

LeVine, Mark, 'Peacemaking in El Salvador', in Doyle *et al.*, eds., (1997): 227-254.

Lewis-Anthony, Siân, 'Treaty-based Procedures for Making Human Rights Complaints Within the UN System', in Hannum, ed. (1992): 41-59.

Lillich, Richard B., 'Humanitarian Intervention: A Reply to Ian Brownlie and a Plea for Constructive Alternatives', in Moore, ed. (1974).

Mackinlay, J. and Chopra, J., 'Second Generation Multinational Operations', *The Washington Quarterly* 15, Summer 1992.

Mackinlay, John, 'Improving Multifunctional Forces', *Survival* 36(3), Autumn 1994: 149-73.

Mackintosh, Anne, 'Rwanda: beyond 'ethnic conflict'', *Development in Practice* 7(4), November 1997: 464-474.

Makinda, Samuel M., 'Sovereignty and International Security: Challenges for the United Nations', *Global Governance* 2, 1996: 149-168.

Malanczuk, Peter, 'The Kurdish Crisis and Allied Intervention in the Aftermath of the Second Gulf War', *EJIL* 2, 1991: 114-32.

Maloney, Sean M., 'Operation Bolster: Canada and the European Community Monitor Mission in Former Yugoslavia, 1991-1992', *International Peacekeeping* 4(1), Spring 1997: 26-50.

Mani, Rama, 'Conflict Resolution, Justice and the Law: Rebuilding the Rule of Law in the Aftermath of Complex Political Emergencies', *International Peacekeeping* 5(3), Autumn 1998: 1-25.

Marks, Stephen P., 'Forgetting "the Policies and Practices of the Past": Impunity in Cambodia', *Fletcher Forum of World Affairs*, Summer/Fall 1994: 17-43.

Marks, Stephen P. 'The New Cambodian Constitution: From Civil Law to a Fragile Democracy', *Columbia Human Rights Law Review*, Fall 1994: 45-110.

Marlowe, Lara, '"Cleansed" Wound', *TIME*, 14 September 1992: 34-35.

Martin, Ian, 'After Genocide: The UN Human Rights Field Operation in Rwanda', in Henkin, ed. (1998): 97-132.

Marx, Reinhard, 'A Non-Governmental Human Rights Strategy for Peacekeeping?', *Netherlands Quarterly of Human Rights* 14(2), 1996: 127-145.

May, Richard, and Wierda, Marieke, 'Trends in International Criminal Evidence: Nuremberg, Tokyo, The Hague, and Arusha', *Columbia Journal of Transnational Law*, 1999: 725-764.

Mcallister, J. F. O., 'Atrocity and Outrage', *TIME*, 17 August, 1992: 21-24.

Melvern, Linda, 'Genocide behind the Thin Blue Line', *Security Dialogue* 28(3): 333-346.

Meron, Theodor, 'International Criminalization of Internal Atrocities'; *AJIL* 89, 1995: 554-577.

Meron, Theodor, 'International Humanitarian Law and Human Rights Law', in Warner, ed. (1997): 97-195.

Meron, Theodor, 'Rape as a Crime Under International Humanitarian Law', *AJIL* 87, 1993: 424-428.

Meron, Theodor, 'War Crimes in Yugoslavia and the Development of International Law', *AJIL* 88, 1994: 78-87.

Metzl, Jamie Frederic, 'The U.N. Commission on Human Rights and Cambodia, 1975-1980', *Buffalo Journal of International Law*, 1996: 67-98.

Metzl, Jamie Frederic, 'The Vietnamese of Cambodia', *Harvard Human Rights Journal*, Spring 1995: 269-275.

Mubiala, Mutoy, 'L'opération des Nations Unies pour les droits de l'homme au Rwanda', *Hague Yearbook of International Law*, 1995:11-16

Mullerson, Rein, 'The Continuity and Succession of States, by Reference to the Former USSR and Yugoslavia', *ICLQ* 42, July 1993: 473-493.

Murase, Shinya, 'Kokusaihou no doutai (Dynamism of Contemporary International Law)' in Murase *et al.*, *Gendai kokusaihou no shihyou (Characteristics of Contemporary International Law)*, Tokyo: Yuhikaku, 1994: 1-61.

Murphy, Sean, 'The Security Council, Legitimacy, and the Concept of Collective Security After the Cold War', *Columbia Journal of Transnational Law*, 1994: 201-288.

Murphy, Sean D., 'Progress and Jurisprudence of the International Criminal Tribunal for the Former Yugoslavia', *AJIL* 93, 1999: 57-97.

O'Brien, James C., 'Current Developments: The International Tribunal for Violations of International Humanitarian Law in the Former Yugoslavia', *AJIL* 87, 1993: 639-659.

O'Flaherty, Michael, 'International Human Rights Operation in Bosnia and Herzegovina', in Henkin, ed. (1998): 71-95.

Ocran, T. Modibo, 'How Blessed Were the UN Peacekeepers in Former Yugoslavia? The Involvement of UNPROFOR and Human Rights Issues in Croatia, 1992-1996', *Wisconsin International Law Journal*, Winter 2000: 193-255.

Ofuatey-Kodjoe, W., 'Regional Organizations and the Resolution of Internal Conflict: The ECOWAS Intervention in Liberia', *International Peace-keeping* 1(3), Autumn 1994: 261-302.

Olonisakin, Funmi, 'UN Co-operation with Regional Organizations in Peace-keeping: The Experience of ECOMOG and UNOMIL in Liberia', *International Peace-keeping* 3(3), Autumn 1996: 33-51.

Pajić, Zoran, 'The Dayton Constitution of Bosnia and Herzegovina – A Critical Appraisal of its Human Rights Provisions', in Müllerson *et al.*, eds. (1998).

Pease, Kelly Kate, and Forsythe, David P., 'Human Rights, Humanitarian Intervention, and World Politics', *Human Rights Quarterly* 15, 1993: 290-314.

Perritt, Jr., Henry H., 'Policing International Peace and Security: International Police Forces', *Wisconsin International Law Journal*, Summer 1999: 281-324.

Petersen, Keith S., 'The Uses of the Unitig for Peace Resolution since 1950', 8 *International Organisation*, 1959: 219-232.

Petrasek, David, 'Moving Forward on the Development of Minimum Humanitarian Standards', *AJIL* 92, 1998: 557-563.

Petrovic, Drazen, 'Ethnic Cleansing – An Attempt at Methodology', 5 *EJIL*, 1994: 342-359.

Plunkett, Mark, 'Reestablishing Law and Order in Peace-Maintenance', *Global Governance* 4, 1998: 61-79.

Pogany, Istvan, 'The Evaluation of United Nations Peace-keeping Operations', *BYIL*, 1986: 357-369.

Quigley, John, 'State Responsibility for Ethnic Cleansing', *U.C. Davis Law Review*, Winter 1999: 341-387.

Quigley, John, 'The "Privatization" of Security Council Enforcement Action: A Threat to Multilateralism', *Michigan Journal of International Law*, Winter 1996: 249-283.

Ratner, Steven, 'The Cambodia Settlement Agreements', *AJIL* 87, 1993: 1-41.

Ratner, Steven R., 'The Schizophrenias of International Criminal Law', *Texas International Law Journal*, 1998: 237-256.

Reisman, W. Michael, 'Sovereignty and Human Rights in Contemporary International Law', *AJIL* 84, 1990, 866-876.

Rich, Roland, 'Recognition of States: The Collapse of Yugoslavia and the Soviet Union', 4 *EJIL* 1993: 36-65.

Roberts, Adam, 'From San Francisco to Sarajevo: The UN and the use of force,' *Survival* 37(4), Winter 95-96: 7-28.

Roberts, Adam, 'NATO's 'Humanitarian War' over Kosovo', *Survival* 41(3), Autumn 1999: 102-23.

Roberts, Adam, 'The Crisis in UN Peace-keeping', *Survival* 36(3), Autumn 1994: 93-120.

Robertson, A. H., 'Humanitarian law and human rights' in Swinarski, ed. (1984): 793-802.

Robinson, Darryl, 'Defining "Crimes Against Humanity" at the Rome Conference', *AJIL* 93, 1999: 43-57.

Rodley, Nigel, 'Collective intervention to protect human rights and civilian populations: the legal framework', in Rodley, ed. (1992).

Rodley, Nigel S., 'United Nations Non-Treaty Procedures for Dealing with Human Rights Violations', in Hannum, ed. (1992): 60-85.

Rose, Michael (Sir), 'Field Coordination of UN Humanitarian Assistance, Bosnia, 1994', in Whitman and Pocock, eds. (1996): 149-160.

Rosenau, James N., 'Normative Challenges in a Turbulent World', *Ethics & International Affairs* 6, 1992: 1-19.

Ruggie, John Gerard, 'The UN and the Collective Use of Force: Whither or Whether?', *International Peace-keeping* 3(4), Winter 1996: 1-20.

Ruggie, John Gerard, 'Wandering in the Void: Charting the U.N.'s New Strategic Role', *Foreign Affairs* 72(5), Nov/Dec 1993: 26-31.

Ryan, Samantha I.,'From the Furies of Nanking to the Eumenides of the International Criminal Court: The Evolution of Sexual Assaults as International Crimes', *Pace International Law Review*, Fall 1999: 447-485.

Sakai, 'Cambodia no shihou, hougaku kyouiku no genjou – kirihirakitai houchikokka he no michi (The current situation of Cambodian judicial system and legal education – a desired way toward a state with rule of law)', *Hou to minshushugi (Law and Democracy)* No. 278, June 1996: 22-30.

Sandoz, Yves, 'Implementing International Humanitarian Law', in Henry Dunant Institute, *International Dimension of Humanitarian Law*, UNESCO, 1988: 259-282.

Sandoz, Yves, 'La notion de protection dans le droit international humani-taire et au sein du Mouvement de la Croix Rouge', in Swinarski, ed. (1984): 976-987.

Sarooshi, Danesh, 'The Powers of the United Nations International Criminal Tribunals', *Max Planck Yearbook of United Nations Law*, 2, 1998: 141-167.

Sarooshi, Danesh, 'The Statute of the International Criminal Court', *ICLQ* 48, 1999: 387-404.

Sato, Yasunobu, 'Cambodia dayori: Pandora no hako wo aketa UNTAC (Letters from Cambodia: UNTAC opened the Pandora's box)', *Hogaku Seminar* (Seminar of Legal Studies), No.460, April 1993: 18-19.

Sato, Yasunobu, 'Cambodia dayori: Risou to genjitsu no hazama de (Letters from Cambodia: Between the ideals and the reality)', *Hogaku Seminar* (Seminar of Legal Studies), No.461, May 1993: 16-17.

Sato, Yasunobu, 'Lessons from UNTAC Human Rights Operation: Human Rights for Peace and Development', *Technology and Development*, No.10, January 1997:45-53.

Schabas, William A., 'Justice, Democracy, and Impunity in Post-genocide Rwanda: Searching for Solutions to Impossible Problems', *Criminal Law Forum* 7(3), 1996: 523-560.

Schachter, Oscar, 'Self-Defense and the Rule of Law', *AJIL* 83, 1989: 259-277.

Schachter, Oscar, 'United Nations Law in the Gulf Conflict', *AJIL* 85, 1991: 452-473.

Schear, James A., 'Riding the Tiger: The United Nations and Cambodia's Struggle for Peace', in Durch, ed. (1997): Chapter 5, 135-191.

Scheffer, David J., 'The United States and the International Criminal Court', *AJIL* 93, 1999: 12-22.

Scheffer, David J., 'Towards a Modern Doctrine of Humanitarian Intervention', *University of Toledo Law Review*, Winter 1992:253-293.

Schmidt, Markus G., 'Does the United Nations Human Rights Program Make a Difference?', in Dommen (1997): 461-466.

Shraga, Daphna, and Zacklin, Ralph, 'The International Criminal Tribunal for the Former Yugoslavia', 5 *EJIL*, 1994: 360-380.

Simma, Bruno, 'NATO, the UN and the Use of Force: Legal Aspects', 10 *EJIL*, 1999: 1-22.

Sloan, James, 'The Dayton Peace Agreement: Human Rights Guarantees and their Implementation', 7 *EJIL*, 1996:207-225.

Smith, Brian D., and Durch, William J., 'UN Observer Group in Central America', in Durch, ed. (1993): 436-362.

Sommaruga, Cornelio, 'Humanitarian Law and Human Rights in the Legal Arsenal of the ICRC', in Warner, ed. (1997): 125-133.

Stanley, William, and Loosle, Robert, 'El Salvador: The Civilian Police Component of Peace Operations', in Oakley *et al.*, eds.

Stanley, William, and Holiday, David, 'Peace Mission Strategy and Domestic Actors: UN Mediation, Verification and Institution-building in El Salvador', *International Peacekeeping* 4(2), Summer 1997: 22-49.

Stanton, Gregory H., 'The Cambodian Genocide and International Law', in Kiernan, ed. (1993): 141-161.

Stapleton, Sara, 'Ensuring a Fair Trial in the International Criminal Court: Statutory Interpretation and the Impermissibility of Derogation', *New York University Journal of International Law and Politics*, 1999: 535-609.

Steele, David B., "Securing Peace for 'Humanitarian Aid?'", *International Peacekeeping* 5(1), Spring 1998: 66-88.

Stein, Eric, 'International Law in Internal Law: Toward Internationalization of Central-Eastern Constitutions?', *AJIL* 88, 1994: 427-450 .

Terriff, Terry, and Keeley, James F., 'The United Nations, Conflict Management and Spheres of Interest', *International Peacekeeping* 2(4), Winter 1995: 510-35.

Teson, Fernando R., 'Changing Perceptions of Domestic Jurisdiction and Intervention', in Farer, ed. (1996).

Tierney, Stephen, 'In a State of Flux: Self-Determination and the Collapse of Yugoslavia', *International Journal on Minority and Group Rights* 6(1/2), 1999: 197-233.

Tittemore, Brian D., 'Belligerents in Blue Helmets: Applying International Humanitarian Law to United Nations Peace Operations', *Stanford Journal of International Law*, Winter 1997: 61-117.

Torres-Rivas, Edelberto, 'Insurrection and civil war in El Salvador', in Doyle *et al.*, eds.: 209-226.

Traub, James, 'Inventing East Timor', *Foreign Affairs*, July/August, 2000: 74-89.

Turns, David, 'The International Criminal Tribunal for the Former Yugoslavia: The Erdemovic Case', *ICLQ* 47, 1998: 461-474.

Vallat, F. A., 'The General Assembly and the Security Council of the United Nations', 29 *BYIL*: 63-104.

van Boven, Theo, 'Creative and Dynamic Strategies for Using United Nations Institutions and Procedures: The Frank Newman File', in Lutz *et al.*, eds. (1989): 215-230.

van der Vyver, Johan D., 'Prosecution and Punishment of the Crime of Genocide', *Fordham International Law Journal*, December 1999: 286-356.

van Schaack, Beth, 'The Definition of Crimes against Humanity: Resolving the Incoherence', *Columbia Journal of Transnational Law*, 1999: 787-850.

Vereshchetin, Andrew Valden S., 'New Constitutions and the Old Problem of the Relationship between International Law and National Law', *EJIL* 7(1): 1996: 29-41.

Vereshchetin, V.S., 'Some Reflections on the Relationship between International Law and National Law in the Light of New Constitutions', in Müllerson *et al.*, eds. (1998): 5-13.

Vickers, George R., 'The Political Reality After Eleven Years of War', in Tulchin, ed. (1992): 25-57.

Warbrick, Colin, and Rowe, Peter, 'The International Criminal Tribunal for Yugoslavia: The Decision of the Appeals Chamber on the Interlocutory Appeal on Jurisdiction in the Tadić Case', *ICLQ* 45, 1996: 691-701.

Watson, Russell *et al.*, 'Ethnic Cleansing', *Newsweek*, 17 August 1992: 13-14.

Weissbrodt, David, 'Ways International Organizations Can Improve Their Implementation of Human Rights and Humanitarian Law in Situations of Armed Conflict', in Lutz *et al.*, eds., (1989): 63-90.

Weston, Burns H., 'Security Council Resolution 678 and Persian Gulf Decision Making: Precarious Legitimacy', *AJIL* 85, 1991: 516-535.

Whitfield, Teresa, 'Staying the Course in El Salvador', in Henkin, ed. (1998): 163-188.

Wiebe, Virgil, 'The Prevention of Civil War through the Use of the Human Rights System', *New York University Journal of International Law and Politics*, Winter 1995: 409-468.

Wilkins, Timothy A., 'The El Salvador Peace Accords: using international and domestic law norms to build peace', in Doyle *et al.*, eds. (1997): 255-281.

Wippman, David, 'Enforcing the Peace: ECOWAS and the Liberian Civil War', in Damrosch, ed. (1993), Chapter 4: 157-203.

Wippman, David, 'Military Intervention, Regional Organizations, and Host-State Consent', *Duke Journal of Comparative and International Law*, Fall 1996: 209-239.

Wippman, David, 'Treaty-Based Intervention: Who Can Say No?', *University of Chicago Law Review*, Spring 1995: 607-687.

Woodward, Susan L., 'Bosnia After Dayton: Year Two', *Current History* 96(608): 97-103.

Woolsey, L. H., 'The "Uniting for Peace" Resolution of the United Nations', *AJIL* 45, 1951: 129-137.

Zhang, Saijin, 'Victim Assistance in Peace-keeping Operations', a paper presented at Expert Group Meeting on Victims of Crime and Abuse of Power in the International Setting held at Vienna, 18-22 November 1995.

REPORTS

African Rights, *Rwanda: the Insurgency in the Northwest*, available at: http://www. unimondo.org/African Rights/insurgency.html_(visited on 14 May 2000).

Americas Watch, *El Salvador - Peace and Human Rights: Successes and Shortcomings of the United Nations Observer Mission in El Salvador (ONUSAL)*, 2 September, 1992.

Amnesty International, *"Collateral Damage" or Unlawful Killings?: Violations of the laws of war by NATO during Operation Allied Force*, June 2000. Available at: http://www.amnesty.org/ailib/intcam/kosovo/.

Amnesty International, *Croatia: Shortchanging Justice – the "Sodolovci" Group*, Amenesty International Report, EUR 64/06/99, December 1999, available at: http://web.amnesty.org/ai.nsf/Index/EUR640061999?OpenDocument&of = COUNTRIES¥CROATIA.

Human Rights Watch, *Cambodia: Fair Elections not Possible*, Human Rights Watch Report, Vol. 10, No.4, June 1998.

Human Rights Watch/Helsinki, *Croatia: Human Rights in Eastern Slavonia during and after the Transition of Authority*, A Human Rights Watch/ Helsinki Report, Vol.9, No.6(D), April 1997.

OSCE, *Report of the OSCE Mission to the Republic of Croatia on Croatia's progress in meeting international commitments since May 1999*, 28 September 1999.

UN DOCUMENTS

Security Council Resolutions

SC res. 48, UN Doc. S/727

SC res. 49, UN Doc. S/773

SC res. 50, UN Doc. S/801

SC res. 83, UN Doc. S/1511

SC res. 143, UN Doc. S/4387

SC res. 161, UN Doc. S/4741

SC res. 169, UN Doc. S/5002

SC res. 276, UN Doc. S/RES/276

SC Res. 339, UN Doc. S/RES/339

SC Res. 555, UN Doc. S/RES/555

SC res. 622, UN Doc. S/RES/622 (1988)

SC res. 644, UN Doc. S/RES/644 (1989)

SC res. 661, UN Doc. S/RES/661 (1990)

SC res. 678, UN Doc. S/RES/678 (1990)

SC res. 688, UN Doc. S/RES/688 (1991)

SC res. 713, UN Doc. S/RES/713 (1991)

SC res. 715, UN Doc. S/RES/715 (1992)

SC res. 717, UN Doc. S/RES/717 (1991)

SC res. 729, UN Doc. S/RES/729 (1992)

SC res. 743, UN Doc. S/RES/743 (1992)

SC res. 745, UN Doc. S/RES 745 (1992)

SC res. 758, UN Doc. S/RES/758 (1992)

SC res. 762, UN Doc. S/RES/762 (1992)

SC res. 767, UN Doc. S/RES/767 (1992)

SC res. 769, UN Doc. S/RES/769 (1992)

SC res. 770, UN Doc. S/RES/770 (1992)

SC res. 779, UN Doc. S/RES/779 (1992)

SC res. 780, UN Doc. S/RES/780 (1992)

SC res. 781, UN Doc. S/RES/781 (1992)

SC res. 788, UN Doc. S/RES/788 (1992)

SC res. 794, UN Doc. S/RES/794 (1992)

SC res. 795, UN Doc. S/RES/795 (1992)

SC res. 798, UN Doc. S/RES/798 (1992)

SC res. 808, UN Doc. S/RES/808 (1993)

SC res. 810, UN Doc. S/RES/810(1993)

SC res. 815, UN Doc. S/RES/815 (1993)

SC res. 819, UN Doc. S/RES/819 (1993)

SC res. 824, UN Doc. S/RES/824 (1993)

SC res. 827, UN Doc. S/RES/827 (1993)

SC res. 832, UN Doc. S/RES/832 (1993)

SC res. 836, UN Doc. S/RES/836 (1993)

SC res. 846, UN Doc. S/RES/846 (1993)

SC res. 866, UN Doc. S/RES/866 (1993)

SC res. 871, UN Doc. S/RES/871 (1993)

SC res. 872, UN Doc. S/RES/872 (1993)

SC res. 897, UN Doc. S/RES/897 (1994)

SC res. 909, UN Doc. S/RES/909 (1994)

SC res. 912, UN Doc. S/RES/912 (1994)

SC res. 918, UN Doc. S/RES/918 (1994)

SC res. 929, UN Doc. S/RES/929 (1994)

SC res. 935, UN Doc. S/RES/935 (1994)

SC res. 940 UN Doc. S/RES/940 (1994)

SC res. 955, UN Doc. S/RES/955 (1994)

SC res. 965, UN Doc. S/RES/965 (1994)

SC res. 981, UN Doc. S/RES/981 (1995)

SC res. 982, UN Doc. S/RES/982 (1995)

SC res. 983, UN Doc. S/RES/983 (1995)

SC res. 997, UN Doc. S/RES/997 (1995)

SC res.1023, UN Doc. S/RES/ 1023 (1995)

SC res.1029, UN Doc. S/RES/ 1029(1995)

SC res. 1037, UN Doc. S/RES/ 1037(1996)

SC res. 1088, UN Doc. S/RES/ 1088(1996)

SC res. 1145, UN Doc. S/RES/ 1145(1997)

SC res. 1199, UN Doc. S/RES/ 1199(1998)

SC res. 1244, UN Doc. S/RES/ 1244(1999)

SC res. 1272, UN Doc. S/RES/ 1272(1999)

SC res. 1305, UN Doc. S/RES/ 1305(2000)

Secretary-General's Reports

1973

Report of the Secretary-General on the implementation of Security Council resolution 340 (1973), UN Doc. S/11052/Rev.1 of 27 October 1973.

1992

Report of the Secretary-General on Cambodia containing his proposed implementation plan for UNTAC, including administrative and financial aspects, UN Doc. S/23613, 19 February 1992.

Report of the Secretary-General on ONUSAL, UN Doc. S/23632, 25 February 1992.

First progress report of the Secretary-General on UNTAC, UN Doc. S/23870, 1 May 1992.

Report of the Secretary-General on the activities of ONUSAL since the cease-fire (1 February 1992) between the Government of El Salvador and the FMLN, UN Doc. S/23999, 26 May 1992.

Report of the Secretary-General, 26 June 1992, S/24188 & Add.1.

Second special report of the Secretary-General on UNTAC and phase II of the cease-fire, UN Doc. S/24286, 14 July 1992.

Report of the Secretary-General, 27 July 1992, S/24353 & Add.1.

Second progress report of the Secretary-General on UNTAC, UN Doc. S/24578, 21 September 1992.

Report of the Secretary-General on the implementation of Security Council resolution 783 (1992) on the Cambodia peace process, UN Doc. S/24800, 15 November 1992.

Report of the Secretary-General on the activities of ONUSAL, UN Doc. S/24833, 23 November 1992.

1993

Third progress report of the Secretary-General on UNTAC, UN doc. S/25154, 25 January 1993.

Report of the Secretary-General on the implementation of Security Council resolution 792 (1992), UN Doc. S/25289, 13 February 1993.

Report of the Secretary-General, 3 March 1993, UN Doc. S/25354, SCOR 48 Supp. January-March 1993.

Fourth progress report of the Secretary-General on UNTAC, UN Doc. S/25179, 3 May 1993.

Report of the Secretary-General on all aspects of ONUSAL's operations, UN Doc. S/25812, 21 May 1993.

Report of the Secretary-General on the conduct and results of the election in Cambodia, UN Doc. S/25913, 10 June 1993.

Further report of the Secretary-General pursuant to paragraph 7 of resolution 840 (1993), UN Doc. S/26360, 26 August 1993.

Report of the Secretary-General on Rwanda, requesting establishment of a United Nations Assistance Mission for Rwanda (UNAMIR) and the integration of UNOMUR into UNAMIR, UN Doc., S/26488, 24 September 1993.

Report of the Secretary-General on UNAMIR, UN Doc. S/26927, 30 December 1993

Further report of the Secretary-General on the implementation of Security Council resolution 745 (1992), UN Doc. S/26259, 5 October 1993.

1994

Report of the Secretary-General, 11 March 1994, UN Doc. S/1994/291 & Corr.1.

Report of the Secretary-General, 16 March 1994, UN Doc. S/1994/300.

Report of the Secretary-General on the activities of the ONUSAL Electoral Division, UN Doc. S/1994/304, 16 March, 1994.

Second progress report of the Secretary-General on UNAMIR for the period from 30 December 1993 to 30 March 1994, UN Doc. S/1994/360, 30 March 1994.

Special report of the Secretary-General on UNAMIR, containing a summary of the developing crisis in Rwanda and proposing three options for the role of the United Nations in Rwanda, UN Doc. S/1994/470, 20 April 1994.

Report to the Secretary-General on the investigation of serious violations of international humanitarian law committed in Rwanda during the conflict, UN Doc. S/1994/867, 25 July 1994.

Report of the Secretary-General on the situation in Rwanda, UN Doc. S/1994/924, 3 August 1994.

Report of the Secretary-General, UN Doc. S/1994/1067, 17 September 1994.

Progress report of the Secretary-General on UNAMIR for the period from 3 August to 6 October 1994, UN Doc. S/1994/1133, 6 October 1994.

Report of the Secretary-General to the General Assembly on emergency assistance for the socio-economic rehabilitation of Rwanda, UN Doc. A/49/516, 14 October 1994.

Progress report of the Secretary-General on UNAMIR for the period from 7 October to 25 November 1994, UN Doc. S/1994/1344, 25 November 1994.

Report of the Secretary-General, 1 December 1994, UN Doc. S/1994/1389.

1995

Supplement to an Agenda for Peace: Position paper of the Secretary-General on the occasion of the fiftieth anniversary of the United Nations, UN Doc. A/50/60 (S/1995/1), 3 January 1995.

Report of the Secretary-General submitted pursuant to Paragraph 4 of Security Council resolution 947(1994), UN Doc. S/1995/38, 14 January 1995.

Progress report of the Secretary-General on UNAMIR for the period from 25 November to 6 February 1995, UN Doc. S/1995/107, 6 February 1995.

Report of the Secretary-General pursuant to Security Council resolution 947 (1994), UN Doc. S/1995/222, 22 March 1995.

Progress report of the Secretary-General on UNAMIR for the period from 7 February to 9 April 1995, UN Doc. S/1995/297, 9 April 1995.

Report of the Secretary-General pursuant to Security Council resolutions 982(1995) and 987(1995), UN Doc. S/1995/444, 30 May 1995.

Report of the Secretary-General on UNAMIR for the period from 10 April to 4 June 1995, UN Doc. S/1995/457, 4 June 1995.

Report of the Secretary-General submitted pursuant to Security Council resolution 994(1995), UN Doc. S/1995/467, 9 June 1995.

Report of the Secretary-General submitted pursuant to Security Council resolution 981(1995), UN Doc. S/1995/650, 3 August 1995.

Report of the Secretary-General submitted pursuant to Security Council resolution 1009 (1995), UN Doc. S/1995/730.

Report of the Secretary-General pursuant to Security Council resolution 1009 (1995), UN Doc. S/1995/835, 29 September 1995.

Progress report of the Secretary-General on UNAMIR, UN Doc. S/1995/848, 7 October 1995.

Report of the Secretary-General pursuant to Security Council resolutions 981(1995), 982(1995) and 983(1995), UN Doc. S/1995/987, 23 November 1995.

Report of the Secretary-General pursuant to Security Council resolution 1019 (1995) on violation of international humanitarian law in the areas of Srebrenica, Zepa, Banja Luka and Sanski Most, UN Doc. S/1995/988, 27 November 1995.

Report of the Secretary-General on UNAMIR for the period from 8 October to 1 December 1995, UN Doc. S/1995/1002, 1 December 1995.

Report of the Secretary-General pursuant to Security Council resolution 1025 (1995), UN Doc. S/1995/1028, 13 December 1995.

Report of the Secretary-General pursuant to Security Council resolution 1026 (1995), UN Doc. S/1995/1031, 13 December 1995.

1996

Report of the Secretary-General outlining possible options for a United Nations role in Rwanda after the completion of UNAMIR's withdrawal, UN Doc. S/1996/149, 29 February 1996.

Report of the Secretary-General pursuant to Security Council resolution 1035 (1995), UN Doc. S/1996/210, 29 March 1996.

Report of the Secretary-General pursuant to Security Council resolution 1019 (1995), UN Doc. S/1996/456, 21 June 1996.

Report of the Secretary-General pursuant to resolution 1035 (1995), UN Doc. S/1996/460, 21 June 1996.

Report of the Secretary-General on the United Nations Transitional Administration for Eastern Slavonia, Baranja and Western Sirmium, UN Doc. S/1996/622, 5 August 1996.

Report of the Secretary-General on the United Nations Transitional Administration for Eastern Slavonia, Baranja and Western Sirmium, 28 August, 1996, UN Doc. S/1996/705.

Report of the Secretary-General pursuant Security Council resolution 1035 (1995), UN Doc. S/1996/820, 1 October 1996.

Report of the Secretary-General on the United Nations Transitional Administration for Eastern Slavonia, Baranja and Western Sirmium, UN Doc. S/1996/883, 26 October 1996.

1997

Report of the Secretary-General pursuant to Security Council resolution 1088 (1996), UN Doc. S/1997/224, 14 March 1997.

Report of the Secretary-General on the United Nations Mission in Bosnia-Herzegovina, UN Doc. S/1997/468, 19 June 1997.

Report of the Secretary-General on the United Nations Mission in Bosnia and Herzegovina, UN Doc. S/1997/694, 8 September 1997.

Report of the Secretary-General on the United Nations Mission in Bosnia and Herzegovina, UN Doc. S/1997/966, 10 December 1997.

1998

Report of the Secretary-General on the United Nations Mission in Bosnia and Herzegovina, UN Doc. S/1998/227, 12 March 1998.

Report of the Secretary-General on the United Nations Mission in Bosnia and Herzegovina, UN Doc. S/1998/491, 10 June 1998.

Report of the Secretary-General on the United Nations Mission in Bosnia and Herzegovina, UN Doc. S/1998/862, 16 September 1998.

Final Report of the Secretary-General on the United Nations Police Support Group, UN Doc. S/1998/1004, 27 October 1998.

1999

Report of the Secretary-General on the United Nations Mission in Bosnia and Herzegovina, UN Doc. S/1999/670, 11 June 1999. *Report of the Secretary-General pursuant to Paragraph 10 of the Security Council resolution 1244 (1999)*, UN Doc. S/1999/672, 12 June 1999.

Report of the Secretary-General on the United Nations Interim Administration Mission in Kosovo, UN Doc. S/1999/779, 12 July 1999.

Report of the Secretary-General pursuant to General Assembly resolution 53/35: The Fall of Srebrenica, UN Doc. A/54/549, 15 November 1999.

Other Selected UN Documents

Instructions given by UN Mediator to UN observers engaged in supervision of the Truce in Palestine, UN Doc. S/928, 28 July 1948.

Introduction to the Regulations for the United Nations Emergency Force, UN Doc. A/3552.

Agreement between the United Nations and Egypt, 8 February 1957, UN Doc. A/3527.

Protocol to the Agreement on Disengagement between Israeli and Syrian Forces concerning the United Nations Disengagement Observer Force, UN Doc. S/11302/Add.1 Annex II of 30 May 1974.

Rome Statute of the International Criminal Court, UN Doc. A/CONF.183/9, 17 July 1998.

Report of Panel on United Nations Peace Operations, UN Doc. A/55/305 – S/2000/809, 17 August 2000. Available at: www.un.org/peace/reports/peace-operations/

(El Salvador)

Note verbale dated 14 August 1990 from El Salvador transmitting text of the Agreement on human rights signed at San José, Costa Rica, on 26 July 1990 between the Government of El Salvador and the FMLN, UN Doc. A/44/971-S/21541, 16 August 1990.

Letter dated 8 October 1991 from El Salvador transmitting the text of the Mexico Agreement and annexes signed on 27 April 1991 by the government of El Salvador and the FMLN, UN Doc. A/46/553-S/23130, 9 October 1991.

Letter dated 26 September 1991 and 4 October 1991 from El Salvador transmitting texts of the New York Agreement and the Compressed Negotiations, signed on 25 September 1991 by the Government of El Salvador and the FMLN, UN Doc. A/46/502-S/23082.

UN Doc. A/46/864-S/23501, 30 January 1992.

First report of the United Nations Observer Mission in El Salvador, Annex to *Report of the Secretary-General on ONUSAL and first report of the ONUSAL Human Rights Division*, UN Doc. A/45/1055-S23037, 16 September 1991.

Second Report of the United Nations Observer Mission in El Salvador, UN Doc. A/46/658-S/23222, 15 November 1991.

Report of the ONUSAL Human Rights Division

UN Doc. A/46/935-S/24066, 5 June 1992.

UN Doc. A/46/955-S/24375, 12 August 1992.

UN Doc. A/47/912-S/25521, 5 April 1993.

UN Doc. A/47/968-S/26033, 2 July 1993.

UN Doc. A/47/1012-S/26416, 15 September 1993.

UN Doc. A/49/281-S/1994/886, 28 July 1994.

UN Doc. A/49/585-S/1994/1220, 31 October 1994.

Principles for the establishment of a joint group for the investigation of politically motivated illegal armed groups, Annex to *Letter dated 7 December 1993 from the Secretary-General to the President of the Security Council concerning implementation of the recommendations of the Commission on the Truth regarding the investigation of illegal groups*, UN Doc. S/26865, 11 December 1993.

The Commission on the Truth for El Salvador, *From Madness to Hope: The 12-year War in El Salvador* (hereinafter, *Truth Commission Report*), UN Doc. S/25500, 1 April 1993.

(Cambodia)

Framework for a Comprehensive Political Settlement of the Cambodia Conflict, UN Doc. A/45/472-S/21689, 31 August 1990.

Final communiqué of the Supreme National Council of Cambodia, I.1; Annex to *Letter dated 23 September 1991 from the President of the Supreme National Council transmitting final communiqué of the Council's meeting in Pattaya, 26-29 August 1991*, UN Doc. A/46/494-S/23066, 24 September 1991.

Declaration on the rehabilitation and reconstruction of Cambodia, UN Doc. A/46/608-S23/77, 30 October 1991.

Report of the Special Representative of the Secretary-General, Mr. Michael Kirby, on the situation of human rights in Cambodia submitted pursuant to Commission on Human Rights Resolution 1993/6, Commission on Human Rights, 50th Sess., Agenda Item 19, at 35. UN Doc. E/CN.4/1994/73, E/CN.4/1994/73/Add.1 (1994).

(Rwanda)

Statute of the International Tribunal for Rwanda, Annex to SC res. 955, 8 November 1994, SCOR, 3453rd mtg., UN Doc. S/RES/955(1994).

Annex to *Letter from the Permanent Representative of Rwanda to the United Nations addressed to the President of the Security Council, transmitting the Declaration of the Conference on the Great Lakes Region, signed in Cairo on 29 November 1995*, UN Doc. S/1995/1001, 30 November 1995.

Report by the Special Rapporteur on extrajudicial, summary or arbitrary executions on his mission to Rwanda, 8-17 April 1993, E/CN.4/1994/7/Add.1, 11 August 1993.

Report of the United Nations High Commissioner for Human Rights on his mission to Rwanda of 11-12 May 1994, UN Doc. E/CN.4/S-3/3, 19 May 1994.

Preliminary report of the Independent Commission of Experts established in accordance with Security Council resolution 935 (1994), S/1994/1125, 4 October 1994.

Final report of the Commission of Experts established pursuant to Security Council resolution 935 (1994), UN Doc. S/1994/1405, 9 December 1994.

Report of the Independent International Commission of Inquiry into the events at Kibeho in April 1995, UN Doc. S/1995/411, 23 May 1995.

Statement delivered 13 July 1995 by the Secretary-General to the Rwandan Parliament, inviting it and the Government to promote national reconciliation to help encourage the return of refugees, UN Press Release SG/SM/5687, 20 July 1995.

Report of the Special Rapporteur of the Commission on Human Rights on the situation of human rights in Rwanda, A/50/709-S/1995/915, 2 November 1995.

Report of the Special Rapporteur on the situation of human rights in Rwanda, E/CN.4/1996/68, 29 January 1996.

Report of the United Nations High Commissioner for Human Rights on the activities of the Human Rights Field Operation in Rwanda (HRFOR), UN Doc. E/CN.4/1996/111, 2 April 1996.

Report of the United Nations High Commissioner for Human rights on the Human Rights Field Operation in Rwanda (HRFOR), UN Doc. A/50/743, 13 November 1995.

Report of the High Commissioner for Human Rights on the activities of Human Rights Field Operation for Rwanda (HRFOR), UN Doc. E/CN.4/1997/52, 17 March 1997.

Report of the High Commissioner for Human Rights on the activities of HRFOR, UN Doc. E/CN.4/1997/52, 17 March 1997.

"First genocide proceedings in Kibungo, Kigali, and Byumba on 27, 30, and 31 December 1996 and 3 January 1997, *Status reports as at 6 January 1997*

"Genocide proceedings in Byumba, Butare, Gisenyi, and Kigali ville prefectures 8-20 January 1997", *Status report as at 24 January 1997*.

"Killings and other attacks against genocide survivors and persons associated with them January to December 1996", *Status report as at 24 January 1997*.

"Killings and other attacks against genocide survivors and persons associated with them from the beginning of January to mid February 1997", *Status report as at 27 February 1997*.

"Seminar for the high command of the Rwandese Patriotic Army, 3-7 February 1997", *Status report as at 27 February 1997*.

"Five members of HRFOR killed in Karengera commune, Cyangugu prefecture, on 4 February 997", *Status report as at 27 February 1997*.

"Genocide Trials to 30 June 1997", *Status report as of 15 July 1997*.

"Deterioration of the security and human rights situation in Ruhengeri prefecture, including killings of civilians during military operations, May-June 1997", *Status report as of 7 August 1997*.

Report of the Independent Inquiry into the actions of the United Nations during the 1994 genocide in Rwanda, 15 December 1999. Available at: http://www.un.org/News/rwanda_report.htm.

(The Former Yugoslavia)

Further report on the situation of human rights in Croatia pursuant to Security Council resolution 1019 (1995), UN Doc. S/1996/109, 14 February 1996.

Dayton Agreement, UN Doc. S/1995/999.

First interim report of the Commission of Experts, UN Doc. S/25274.

Report on the situation on human rights in the territory of the former Yugoslavia, 10 February 1993, UN Doc. E/CN.4/1993/50.

Further report on the situation of human rights in Croatia pursuant to Security Council resolution 1019 (1995), UN Doc. S/1996/101.

United Nations Task Force to Establish the Transitional Administration in Sector East, *Approaches to monitor and influence human rights observance in Sector East*, Annex Q to *Background Report on the Region of Eastern Slavonia, Baranja and Western Sirmium*, Zagreb, December 1995.

Rambouillet Accords: Interim Agreement for Peace and Self-Government in Kosovo, UN Doc. S/1999/648, 7 June 1999.

OTHER DOCUMENTS

'UN operations: Not only expanding, but breaking new ground', *UN Chronicle*, Vol.30, No.3, September 1993, p.44.

'United Kingdom Materials on International Law 1990', *BYIL* 1990.

'United Kingdom Materials on International Law', *BYIL* 1992.

Final Communiqué of the First Session of the Community Standing Mediation Committee, ECOWAS, Banjul, Republic of the Gambia, August 6-7, 1990.

NATO Press Release (1999)040 on 23 March 1999. Available at: http://www.nato.int/docu/pr/1999/p99-040e.htm

Statement at a press conference on Kosovo, Brussels, Belgium, October 8, 1998, as released by the Office of the Spokesman, U.S. Department of State. Available at http://secretary.state.gov/www/statements/1998/981008.html

Statement by the Presidency on the Recognition of Yugoslav Republics, Brussels, 15 January 1992, EPC Press Release 9/92.

Statement in the United Nations Security Council by Sir Jeremy Greenstock, Permanent Representative of the United Kingdom, 24 March 1999. Available at: http://www.fco.gov.uk/news/newstext.asp?2157

The EPC Declaration on Yugoslavia, Brussels, 6 April 1992, EPC Press Release 40/92.

Wider Peacekeeping, HMSO, 1995.

Newspaper and Magazine Articles

'Price of Justice', *Far Eastern Economic Review*, 17 February 2000, p.27.

'Man in a Minefield', *Far Eastern Economic Review*, 24 February 2000, p.25.

Die Presse, translated and reported in *Glas Slavonije*, 17 November 1999.

The Guardian, 19 February 1994, p.12.

INTERNET SOURCES

http://secretary.state.gov/www/statements/1998/981008.html

http://www.batin.com.vn/vninfo/constitution/chaptr5c.htm

http://www.fco.gov.uk/news/newstext.asp?2157

http://www.ictr.org/

http://www.nato.int/docu/pr/1999/p99-040e.htm

http://www.un.org/Depts/dpko

http://www.un.org/Depts/DPKO/Missions/undof/undofF.htm

http://www.un.org/Depts/DPKO/Missions/unficyp/unficypF.htm

http://www.un.org/Depts/DPKO/Missions/unifil/unifilF.htm

http://www.un.org/Depts/DPKO/Missions/unikom/unikomF.htm

http://www.un.org/Depts/DPKO/Missions/unmogip/unmogipF.htm

http://www.un.org/Depts/DPKO/Missions/unikom/unikomF.htm

http://www.un.org/icty/glance/indictlist-e.htm

http://www.un.org/News/rwanda_report.htm

http://www.un.org/peace/kosovo/news/kosovo2.htm#Anchor56

http://www.uni-wuerzburg.de/law/ez00000_.html

Appendix

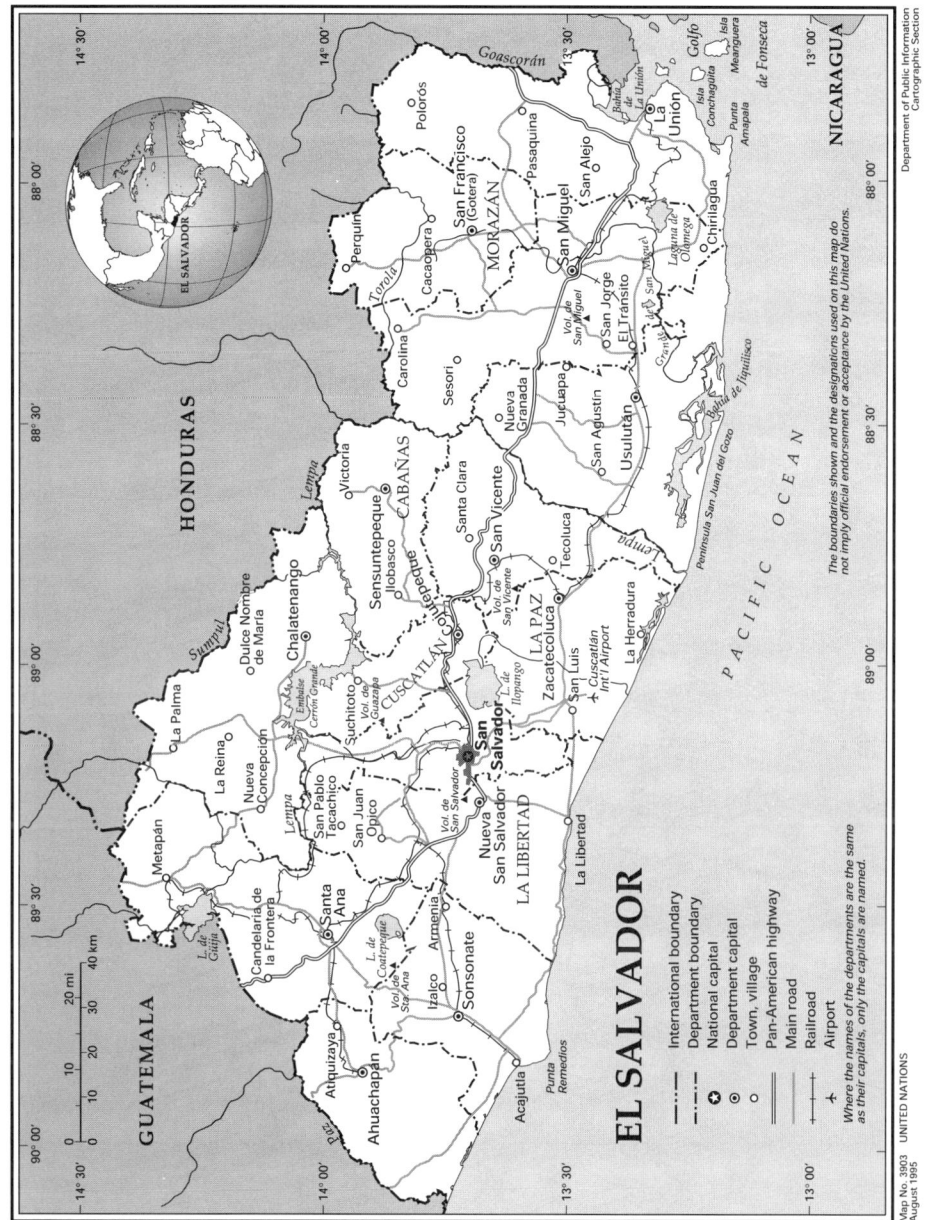

EL SALVADOR

- ⊗ International boundary
- Department boundary
- ⊗ National capital
- ⊙ Department capital
- ○ Town, village
- Pan-American highway
- Main road
- Railroad
- ✈ Airport

Where the names of the departments are the same as their capitals, only the capitals are named.

Map No. 3903   UNITED NATIONS
August 1995

Department of Public Information
Cartographic Section

The boundaries shown and the designations used on this map do not imply official endorsement or acceptance by the United Nations.

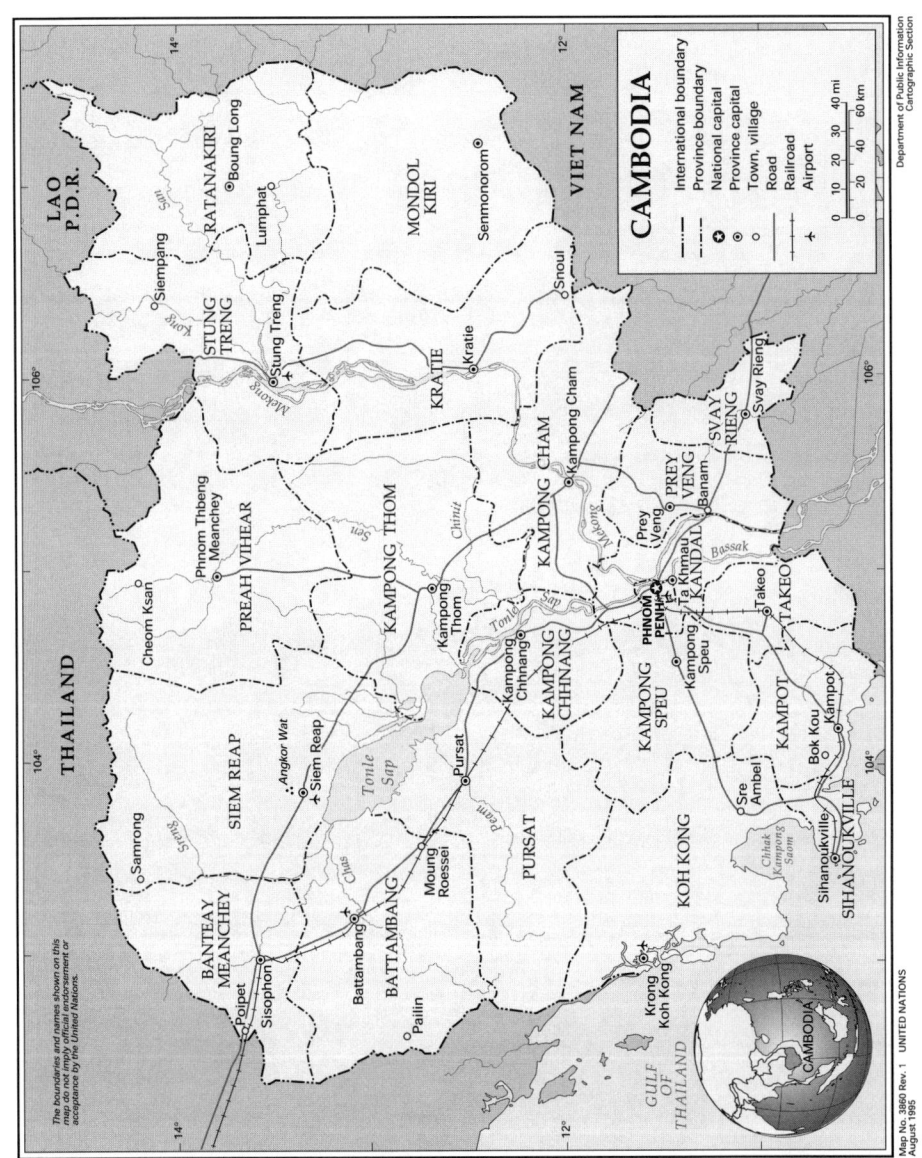

CAMBODIA

- International boundary
- Province boundary
- ⊕ National capital
- ◉ Province capital
- ○ Town, village
- Road
- Railroad
- + Airport

0 10 20 30 40 mi
0 20 40 60 km

Department of Public Information
Cartographic Section

The boundaries and names shown on this map do not imply official endorsement or acceptance by the United Nations.

Map No. 3860 Rev. 1   UNITED NATIONS
August 1995

LAO P.D.R.

THAILAND

VIET NAM

RATANAKIRI
Boung Long
Lumphat

MONDOL KIRI
Senmonorom

STUNG TRENG
Siempang
Stung Treng

KRATIE
Kratie
Snoul

KAMPONG CHAM
Kampong Cham

PREAH VIHEAR
Phnom Thbeng Meanchey
Cheom Ksan

KAMPONG THOM
Kampong Thom

PREY VENG
Prey Veng
Banam

SVAY RIENG
Svay Rieng

SIEM REAP
Samrong
Angkor Wat
Siem Reap

KANDAL
Ta Khmau

PHNOM PENH

KAMPONG CHHNANG
Kampong Chhnang

KAMPONG SPEU
Kampong Speu

TAKEO
Takeo

KAMPOT
Bok Kou
Kâmpot

BANTEAY MEANCHEY
Poipet
Sisophon

BATTAMBANG
Battambang
Moung Roessei
Pailin

PURSAT
Pursat

KOH KONG
Sre Ambel
Krong Koh Kong

SIHANOUKVILLE
Sihanoukville

Tonle Sap

GULF OF THAILAND

Mekong
Kong
Sen
Chinit
Sap
Bassak
Sreng
Chas
Pursat
Pedm
Chhak Kompong Saom

CAMBODIA

104°   106°
14°   12°

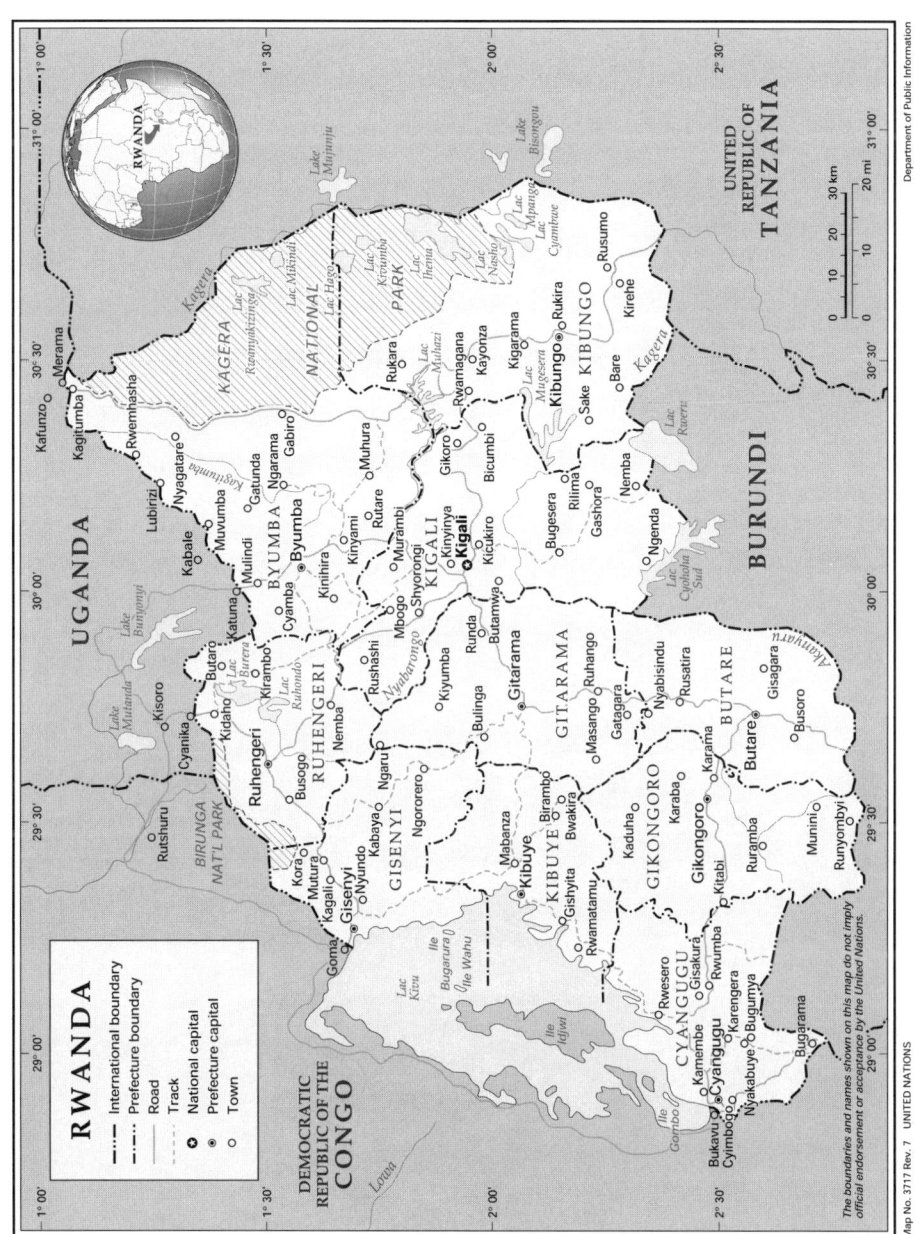

RWANDA

- ─ ∙ ─ International boundary
- ─ ∙ ∙ ─ Prefecture boundary
- ─── Road
- Track
- ✪ National capital
- ◉ Prefecture capital
- ○ Town

Map No. 3717 Rev. 7   UNITED NATIONS
December 1997   (Colour)

The boundaries and names shown on this map do not imply official endorsement or acceptance by the United Nations.

Department of Public Information
Cartographic Section

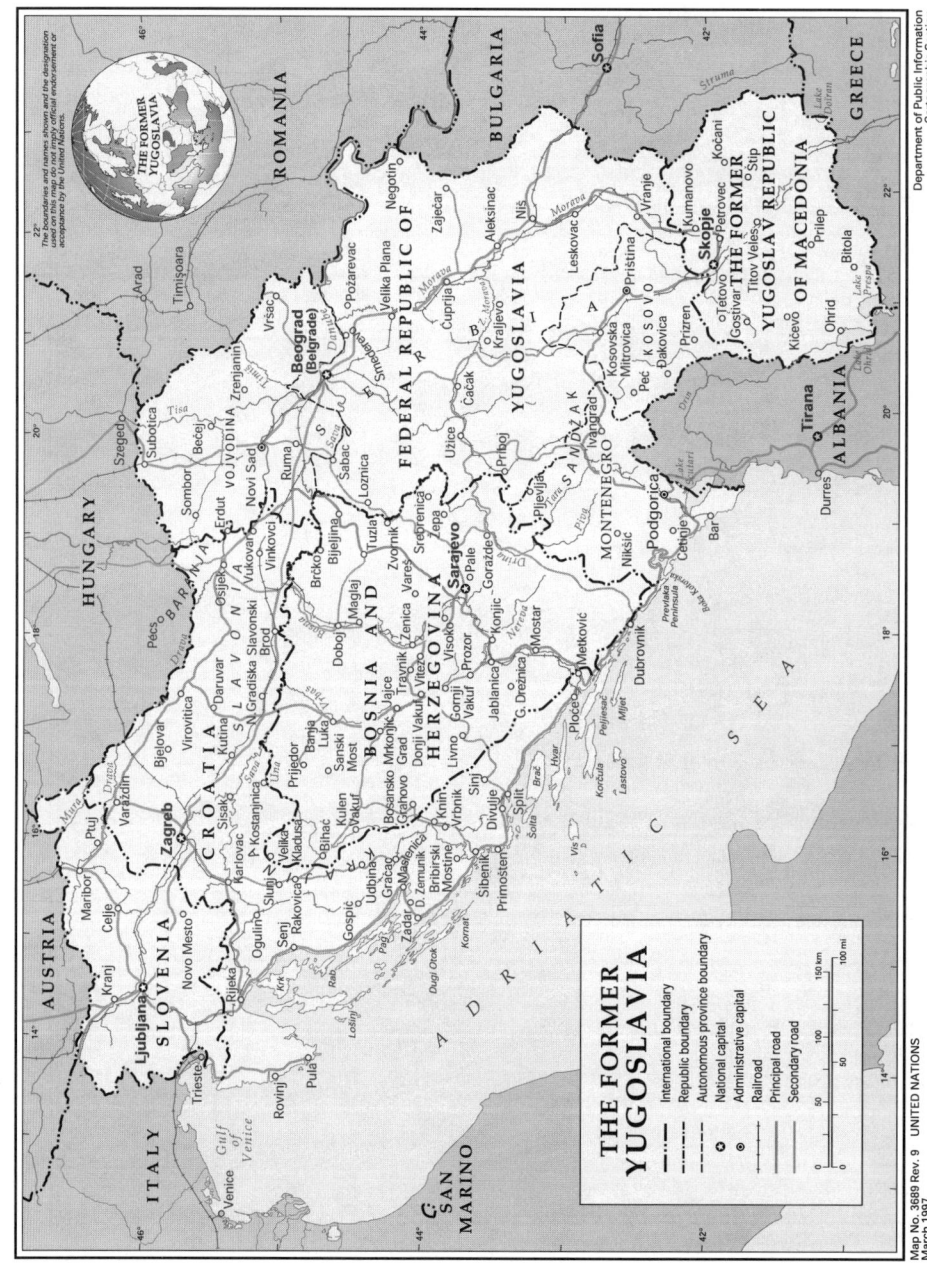

THE FORMER YUGOSLAVIA

	International boundary
	Republic boundary
	Autonomous province boundary
⊛	National capital
⊚	Administrative capital
	Railroad
	Principal road
	Secondary road

Map No. 3689 Rev. 9   UNITED NATIONS
March 1997

Department of Public Information
Cartographic Section

International Studies in Human Rights

1. B. G. Ramcharan (ed.): *International Law and Fact-finding in the Field of Human Rights.* 1982   ISBN 90-247-3042-2

2. B. G. Ramcharan: *Humanitarian Good Offices in International Law.* The Good Offices of the United Nations Secretary-General in the Field of Human Rights. 1983
                                                                    ISBN 90-247-2805-3

3. B. G. Ramcharan (ed.): *The Right to Life in International Law.* 1985
                                                                    ISBN 90-247-3074-0

4. P. Alston and K. Tomaševski (eds.): *The Right to Food.* 1984   ISBN 90-247-3087-2

5. A. Bloed and P. van Dijk (eds.): *Essays on Human Rights in the Helsinki Process.* 1985
                                                                    ISBN 90-247-3211-5

6. K. Törnudd: *Finland and the International Norms of Human Rights.* 1986
                                                                    ISBN 90-247-3257-3

7. H. Thoolen and B. Verstappen: *Human Rights Missions.* A Study of the Fact-finding Practice of Non-governmental Organizations. 1986   ISBN 90-247-3364-2

8. H. Hannum: *The Right to Leave and Return in International Law and Practice.* 1987
                                                                    ISBN 90-247-3445-2

9. J. H. Burgers and H. Danelius: *The United Nations Convention against Torture.* A Handbook on the Convention against Torture and Other Cruel, Inhuman or Degrading Treatment or Punishment. 1988   ISBN 90-247-3609-9

10. D. A. Martin (ed.): *The New Asylum Seekers: Refugee Law in the 1980s.* The Ninth Sokol Colloquium on International Law. 1988   ISBN 90-247-3730-3

11. C. M. Quiroga: *The Battle of Human Rights.* Gross, Systematic Violations and the Inter-American System. 1988   ISBN 90-247-3687-0

12. L. A. Rehof and C. Gulmann (eds.): *Human Rights in Domestic Law and Development Assistance Policies of the Nordic Countries.* 1989   ISBN 90-247-3743-5

13. B. G. Ramcharan: *The Concept and Present Status of International Protection of Human Rights.* Forty Years After the Universal Declaration. 1989   ISBN 90-247-3759-1

14. A. D. Byre and B. Y. Byfield (eds.): *International Human Rights Law in the Common-wealth Caribbean.* 1991   ISBN 90-247-3785-0

15. N. Lerner: *Groups Rights and Discrimination in International Law.* 1991
                                                                    ISBN 0-7923-0853-0

16. S. Shetreet (ed.): *Free Speech and National Security.* 1991   ISBN 0-7923-1030-6

17. G. Gilbert: *Aspects of Extradition Law.* 1991   ISBN 0-7923-1162-0

18. P.E. Veerman: *The Rights of the Child and the Changing Image of Childhood.* 1991
                                                                    ISBN 0-7923-1250-3

19. M. Delmas-Marty (ed.): *The European Convention for the Protection of Human Rights.* International Protection versus National Restrictions. 1991   ISBN 0-7923-1283-X

International Studies in Human Rights

20. A. Bloed and P. van Dijk (eds.): *The Human Dimension of the Helsinki Process*. The Vienna Follow-up Meeting and its Aftermath. 1991   ISBN 0-7923-1337-2

21. L.S. Sunga: *Individual Responsibility in International Law for Serious Human Rights Violations*. 1992   ISBN 0-7923-1453-0

22. S. Frankowski and D. Shelton (eds.): *Preventive Detention*. A Comparative and International Law Perspective. 1992   ISBN 0-7923-1465-4

23. M. Freeman and P. Veerman (eds.): *The Ideologies of Children's Rights*. 1992
          ISBN 0-7923-1800-5

24. S. Stavros: *The Guarantees for Accused Persons Under Article 6 of the European Convention on Human Rights*. An Analysis of the Application of the Convention and a Comparison with Other Instruments. 1993   ISBN 0-7923-1897-8

25. A. Rosas and J. Helgesen (eds.): *The Strength of Diversity*. Human Rights and Pluralist Democracy. 1992   ISBN 0-7923-1987-7

26. K. Waaldijk and A. Clapham (eds.): *Homosexuality: A European Community Issue*. Essays on Lesbian and Gay Rights in European Law and Policy. 1993
          ISBN 0-7923-2038-7; Pb: 0-7923-2240-1

27. Y.K. Tyagi: *The Law and Practice of the UN Human Rights Committee*. 1993
          ISBN 0-7923-2040-9

28. H.Ch. Yourow: *The Margin of Appreciation Doctrine in the Dynamics of European Human Rights Jurisprudence*. 1996   ISBN 0-7923-3338-1

29. L.A. Rehof: *Guide to the* Travaux Préparatoires *of the United Nations Convention on the Elimination of All Forms of Discrimination against Women*. 1993 ISBN 0-7923-2222-3

30. A. Bloed, L. Leicht, M. Novak and A. Rosas (eds.): *Monitoring Human Rights in Europe*. Comparing International Procedures and Mechanisms. 1993   ISBN 0-7923-2383-1

31. A. Harding and J. Hatchard (eds.): *Preventive Detention and Security Law*. A Comparative Survey. 1993   ISBN 0-7923-2432-3

32. Y. Beigbeder: *International Monitoring of Plebiscites, Referenda and National Elections*. Self-determination and Transition to Democracy. 1994   ISBN 0-7923-2563-X

33. T.D. Jones: *Human Rights: Group Defamation, Freedom of Expression and the Law of Nations*. 1997   ISBN 90-411-0265-5

34. D.M. Beatty (ed.): *Human Rights and Judicial Review*. A Comparative Perspective. 1994   ISBN 0-7923-2968-6

35. G. Van Bueren, *The International Law on the Rights of the Child*. 1995
          ISBN 0-7923-2687-3

36. T. Zwart: *The Admissibility of Human Rights Petitions*. The Case Law of the European Commission of Human Rights and the Human Rights Committee. 1994
          ISBN 0-7923-3146-X; Pb: 0-7923-3147-8

37. H. Lambert: *Seeking Asylum*. Comparative Law and Practice in Selected European Countries. 1995   ISBN 0-7923-3152-4

International Studies in Human Rights

38.   E. Lijnzaad: *Reservations to UN-Human Rights Treaties*. Ratify and Ruin? 1994
ISBN 0-7923-3256-3

39.   L.G. Loucaides: *Essays on the Developing Law of Human Rights*. 1995
ISBN 0-7923-3276-8

40.   T. Degener and Y. Koster-Dreese (eds.): *Human Rights and Disabled Persons*. Essays
and Relevant Human Rights Instruments. 1995   ISBN 0-7923-3298-9

41.   J.-M. Henckaerts: *Mass Expulsion in Modern International Law and Practice*. 1995
ISBN 90-411-0072-5

42.   N.A. Neuwahl and A. Rosas (eds.): *The European Union and Human Rights*. 1995
ISBN 90-411-0124-1

43.   H. Hey: *Gross Human Rights Violations: A Search for Causes*. A Study of Guatemala
and Costa Rica. 1995   ISBN 90-411-0146-2

44.   B.G. Tahzib: *Freedom of Religion or Belief*. Ensuring Effective International Legal
Protection. 1996   ISBN 90-411-0159-4

45.   F. de Varennes: *Language, Minorities and Human Rights*. 1996   ISBN 90-411-0206-X

46.   J. Räikkä (ed.): *Do We Need Minority Rights?* Conceptual Issues. 1996
ISBN 90-411-0309-0

47.   J. Bröhmer: *State Immunity and the Violation of Human Rights*. 1997
ISBN 90-411-0322-8

48.   C.A. Gearty (ed.): *European Civil Liberties and the European Convention on Human
Rights*. A Comparative Study. 1997   ISBN 90-411-0253-1

49.   B. Conforti and F. Francioni (eds.): *Enforcing International Human Rights in Domestic
Courts*. 1997   ISBN 90-411-0393-7

50.   A. Spiliopoulou Åkermark: *Justifications of Minority Protection in International Law*.
1997   ISBN 90-411-0424-0

51.   A. Boulesbaa: *The U.N. Convention on Torture and the Prospects for Enforcement*. 1997
ISBN 90-411-0457-7

52.   S. Bowen (ed.): *Human Rights, Self-Determination and Political Change in the Occupied
Palestinian Territories*. 1997   ISBN 90-411-0502-6

53.   M. O'Flaherty and G. Gisvold (eds.): *Post-War Protection of Human Rights in Bosnia
and Herzegovina*. 1998   ISBN 90-411-1020-8

54.   A.-L. Svensson-McCarthy: *The International Law of Human Rights and States of Exception*. With Special Reference to the *Travaux Préparatoires* and Case-Law of the International Monitoring Organs. 1998   ISBN 90-411-1021-6

55.   G. Gilbert: *Transnational Fugitive Offenders in International Law*. Extradition and
Other Mechanisms. 1998   ISBN 90-411-1040-2

56.   M. Jones and L.A. Basser Marks (eds.): *Disability, Divers-ability and Legal Change*.
1998   ISBN 90-411-1086-0

International Studies in Human Rights

International Studies in Human Rights

75.   B.G. Ramcharan: *The Security Council and the Protection of Human Rights*. 2002
ISBN 90-411-1878-0

This series is designed to shed light on current legal and political aspects of process and organization in the field of human rights.

MARTINUS NIJHOFF PUBLISHERS – THE HAGUE / BOSTON / LONDON